The Outbreak of the Peloponnesian War

The Outbreak of the Peloponnesian War

DONALD KAGAN

Cornell University Press

ITHACA AND LONDON

First published 1969

THIS BOOK HAS BEEN PUBLISHED WITH THE AID OF A GRANT FROM THE HULL MEMORIAL PUBLICATION FUND OF CORNELL UNIVERSITY.

Standard Book Number 8014–0501–7
Library of Congress Catalog Card Number 69-18212

PRINTED IN THE UNITED STATES OF AMERICA
BY AMERICAN BOOK–STRATFORD PRESS, INC.

For my son, Bobby

Preface

The attempt to write another book on a subject so old and so often treated requires an explanation, perhaps even a defense. Thucydides, after all, dealt with it authoritatively, and most of our evidence comes from his history. Yet it is rewarding to take up the matter once again. In the nineteenth century and in the early years of the twentieth, to be sure, such titanic figures as Grote, Beloch, Busolt, and Meyer undertook encyclopaedic histories of Greece in which they dealt with the origins of the Peloponnesian War in detail and with great intelligence and learning. In my judgment there is, even today, no better study of the problem than the sober and magisterial account of Busolt. Therein lies one of the reasons for writing this book, for in the years since Busolt wrote, a great deal of new material has been given to us, chiefly in the form of Athenian inscriptions. In addition, more than half a century of important scholarship has illuminated Greek history. No one can write about Thucydides and the Peloponnesian War in quite the same way after the publication of the *Athenian Tribute Lists,* Gomme's *Historical Commentary on Thucydides,* or Mme de Romilly's *Thucydide et l'impérialisme athénien,* not to mention many other important monographs and articles. It therefore seems desirable to treat the question once again in a thorough and detailed manner, taking account of the new epigraphical evidence and the great mass of modern scholarship.

Each generation needs to write its history for itself. Our questions are likely to differ from our fathers' and grandfathers'. Constant reappraisal can only be beneficial for the discovery of the past and its meaning, for over the years only the permanently illuminating questions will remain vital. I should be less than candid if I did not admit yet another purpose in writing this history. I agree with Thucydides that useful truths about human behavior in political situations can be learned from a careful and accurate study of the past. I believe some truths of great relevance to our modern predicament may arise from an investigation of how the Greek states came to fight a terrible war that destroyed the vitality of a great civilization.

The origin of the Peloponnesian War is a problem in diplomatic history, and I am convinced that diplomacy cannot, without serious distortion, be treated in isolation from the internal history of the states involved. As a result, I have tried, where the evidence permits, to trace the connection between domestic politics, constitutional organization, and foreign affairs. It is clear, of course, that questions of a social and economic nature may also have a great effect on foreign affairs, though a rather smaller one in antiquity than they seem to have now. Our evidence, however, does not allow us to see any certain or even probable influence, except in the most indirect way. Our ancient sources view the problem chiefly in political terms. My own conviction is that they do not seriously mislead us.

Some remarks about method are in order. It seems to me that anyone who works with Thucydides must make patent his judgment on two basic questions: the history of the composition of the work, and the authenticity of the speeches in it. I shall discuss these questions in greater detail in connection with my interpretation of particular events, but the reader deserves to know in advance my general opinion. On the question of composition it is essentially unitarian, and very close to that of John Finley, who assumes that the work as we have it is not too far from what Thucydides ultimately intended:

> That is not to say that early passages may not exist in the *History;* it is inconceivable that Thucydides did not take notes or that he failed to use them when he wrote his final work. It is merely to say that the work which we have should not be regarded as an agglomeration of passages written at widely different times and imperfectly blended together by reason of the author's premature death, but rather as composed primarily at one time with the help of earlier notes and, if broken at the end, incomplete perhaps in several places, yet possessing after all the unity which might be expected to result from a period of more or less sustained composition.[1]

[1] John H. Finley, Jr., *HSCP,* Suppl. I (1940), 257.

Assuming the essential unity of composition, I have avoided using the excuse that Thucydides had no time to fill in the gaps or to reconcile his later opinions with earlier ones as a means of explaining difficult passages.

The problem of the speeches is old and persistent. Opinions range from one extreme, that they are fictions completely invented by Thucydides, to the other, that they are close to verbatim reports of what the speakers said. The truth is clearly in between, but I am persuaded that it is far closer to the latter view. A great deal of the debate has surrounded the admitted ambiguity of the words ὡς δ' ἄν ἐδόκουν μοι ἕκαστοι περὶ τῶν ἀεὶ παρόντων τὰ δέοντα μάλιστ' εἰπεῖν, which Richard Crawley translates, "what was in my opinion demanded of them by the various occasions." Far too little attention has been given to the unequivocal force of the words that follow: ἐχομένῳ ὅτι ἐγγύτατα τῆς ξυμπάσης γνώμης τῶν ἀληθῶς λεχθέντων, οὕτως εἴρηται,[2] which Crawley translates, "of course adhering as closely as possible to what they really said." My own judgment is the same as that of F. E. Adcock:

> We are told, indeed, that, in composing his speeches, the historian kept as closely as possible to "the overall purport or purpose of what was actually said," written in such a way as to coincide with his opinion of what the several speakers would most likely have presented to their hearers as being "what the situation required." The reference to his own opinion represents a limiting factor in one way, as his reference to the "overall purport or purpose of what was actually said" is a limiting factor in another way. Thus when the procedure has been applied, the reader will know something at least of what was actually said. Thucydides limits his knowledge in terms of the difficulty (or even impossibility) of remembering precisely what was said.[3]

Thucydides' statement, of course, precludes the possibility that he invented any of the speeches he reports. As long ago as 1889, Nissen dismissed Grote's treatment of the Peloponnesian War, expressing astonishment that "he even treats the speeches as contemporary documents." [4] The reader will find me guilty of the same naïveté.

A word is necessary, too, about the use of ancient literary sources

[2] 1. 22. 1. References are to Thucydides unless otherwise attributed.
[3] F. E. Adcock, *Thucydides and his History* (Cambridge, 1963), 27–42.
[4] H. Nissen, *Historische Zeitschrift,* N. F., XXVII (1889), 386.

other than Thucydides, chiefly Plutarch and Diodorus Siculus. The *Lives* of Plutarch are based on a wide variety of sources, some good and some bad, some going back to the fifth century and some much later. For the period with which we are concerned, Diodorus depended chiefly on Ephorus when he was not following Herodotus or Thucydides. Ephorus wrote in the fourth century and is not to be compared with Thucydides either as a source or as a historian, but he did include some material omitted by Thucydides, as did Plutarch. As far as I have discovered, there is rarely any reason to prefer either Plutarch or Diodorus to Thucydides where they contradict him. The problem is what to do when they merely supply additional material. The recent tendency has been to be rather severe in judging the value of their data. We may all agree that their chronology is usually untrustworthy and that they do not deserve the authority of Thucydides' reports, but it seems to me that criticism has gone too far. My own approach is somewhat more trusting. Plutarch is like Herodotus, for he compares the various reports he has (written, to be sure, unlike the oral accounts received by Herodotus); he often cites his authorities; and he is prepared to reject lies and absurdities. Whatever the merits of his own judgment, there is no doubt that he preserves much that is valuable. Ephorus is less useful, but does not deserve to be ignored. I have applied the same criteria to the information supplied by Plutarch and Diodorus as I have to other ancient sources. I believe it to be true unless it is demonstrably self-contradictory, absurd, or false. Employing these canons, I have made more than a little use of their work.

It remains to speak of a device that the reader will from time to time encounter. I have often drawn historical analogies between situations in the fifth century B.C. and modern events. I am fully conscious of the danger in such analogies. I hope that I have used them appropriately and with due caution, but in any case, I think it better to show openly what was in my mind when I arrived at my conclusions and generalizations. As a historian, I naturally think of events and situations that seem similar to the ones I am studying. My judgments about historical events are based on my own experience, what I have learned of the events of my own time, extended by what I have learned of previous ages. As M. I. Finley has put it, "historians generalize all the time at the beginning and in the course of every study they make, and the more conscious they are of this, the more control they will have over their generalizations."[5] I have tried to make the sources of my own generalizations more explicit by means of the analogies I have drawn. The reader will find that a large number of them come from the period preceding the First World War. This is not accidental, for I have been much impressed by the illumination a close study of the origins of that war, so copiously documented, can provide for an understanding of the outbreak of the Peloponnesian War. The reader can judge for himself whether that impression is justified.

I should like to thank Bernard Knox, B. D. Meritt, and my colleague Walter LaFeber, who read this book in typescript and helped me to avoid many errors. I am grateful to the Cornell Research Grants Committee and to the Humanities Faculty Research Grants Committee of Cornell University for supporting my work and helping me with the preparation of the typescript. Special thanks are due to the Senior Fellows of the Center for Hellenic Studies in Washington, D.C., for providing me with a splendid and uninterrupted year of scholarship at the Center. I am most grateful to my colleagues who held junior fellowships that year for making it a pleasant and enlightening experience. My greatest debt is to Mr. Knox, whose skill in directing the Center for Hellenic Studies is matched by his keen wit, broad knowledge, and deep devotion to Classical studies. Finally, I should like to declare how much I owe my wife, who has made my home a place of refreshment and recreation from which I can return to my studies with renewed vigor.

D. K.

Ithaca, New York
October 1968

[5] M. I. Finley in *Generalization in the Writing of History,* Louis Gottschalk, ed. (Chicago, 1963), 27.

Contents

Abbreviations and Short Titles

AC	*L'Antiquité Classique*
AHR	*American Historical Review*
AJA	*American Journal of Archaeology*
AJP	*American Journal of Philology*
ASI	E. Badian, ed., *Ancient Societies and Institutions*
ATL	B. D. Meritt, H. T. Wade-Gery, and F. M. McGregor, *The Athenian Tribute Lists*
BSA	*Proceedings of the British School at Athens*
Beloch, *GG* [2]	K. J. Beloch, *Griechische Geschichte,* 2nd ed.
Bengtson, *GG*	H. Bengtson, *Griechische Geschichte,* 2nd ed.
Busolt, *GG*	Georg Busolt, *Griechische Geschichte*
Busolt and Swoboda, *GS*	Georg Busolt and Heinrich Swoboda, *Griechische Staatskunde*
CAH	*Cambridge Ancient History*
CP	*Classical Philology*
CQ	*Classical Quarterly*
CR	*Classical Review*
CW	*Classical World*
De Sanctis, *SdG.*	Gaetano De Sanctis, *Storia dei Greci*
FGrH	F. Jacoby, *Die Fragmente der griechischen Historiker*
Glotz and Cohen, *HG*	Gustave Glotz and Robert Cohen, *Histoire Grecque,* II
Gomme, *Hist. Comm.*	A. W. Gomme, *A Historical Commentary on Thucydides*
Grote	George Grote, *A History of Greece*
HSCP	*Harvard Studies in Classical Philology*
IG	*Inscriptiones Graecae*

JHS	*Journal of Hellenic Studies*
LCL	*Loeb Classical Library*
Meyer, *Forschungen*	Eduard Meyer, *Forschungen zur alten Geschichte,* II
Meyer, *GdA*	Eduard Meyer, *Geschichte des Altertums*
PACA	*Proceedings of the African Classical Association*
PW	Pauly-Wissowa and others, *Realenzyklopädie der klassischen Altertumswissenschaft*
Riv. di fil.	*Rivista di filologia e di istruzione classica*
SEG	*Supplementum Epigraphicum Graecum*
SIG	W. Dittenberger, *Sylloge Inscriptionum Graecarum*
TAPA	*Transactions of the American Phililogical Association*
Tod	M. N. Tod, *A Selection of Greek Historical Inscriptions to the End of the Fifth Century*

The Outbreak of the Peloponnesian War

Le cose passate fanno luce alle future, perché el mondo fu sempre di una medesima sorte, e tutto quello che è e sarà è stato in altro tempo, e le cose medesime ritornano, ma sotto diversi nomi e colori; però ognuno non le ricognosce, ma solo chi e savio è le osserva e considera diligentemente.

FRANCESCO GUICCIARDINI
Ricordi, Serie Prima, 114

Introduction

Thucydides began to write a history of the war between the Athenians and the Peloponnesians because he expected that it would be "great and most worthy of the telling." [1] He was not disappointed, for in duration, extent, fierceness, and significance it surpassed all previous Greek wars. It was the "greatest upheaval that had come to the Greeks, to some portion of the barbarians, one might even say to the greater part of mankind." [2] From our viewpoint it was something even more; it was the crucible in which the life of the polis was tested.

Even by ancient standards, the city-states that emerged from the chaos of the Greek dark ages were weak and insubstantial creatures. Their economic well-being depended upon social and political stability and on freedom from external attack. Good fortune freed them from the danger of predatory neighbors during their most vulnerable period. No great aggressive empire held sway in the eastern Mediterranean in the vital years between the Dorian invasion and the Battle of Marathon. In the west, the Roman giant was still only an embryo. Colonization, which siphoned off excess population, and transient popular tyrannies, which broadened the political and social base of the city-state, allowed it to survive and flourish in the seventh and sixth centuries. By the time the Persian Empire could mount a serious external threat, the Greek cities were strong enough to combine and to offer a successful resistance.

[1] All translations are my own unless otherwise attributed. In translating Thucydides I have made frequent use of the Loeb translation of C. Forster Smith and the Budé edition by Mme de Romilly. I have not hesitated to borrow their phrasing when I could not improve upon it.

[2] 1. 1. 2.

The Persian Wars, however, made dramatically clear the inherent contradiction in the life of the polis. Freedom, independence, autonomy, even self-sufficiency were its ideals. In practice, of course, they had always been limited, but the essence of the Greek political system was a number of independent states, each observing its own constitution and each conducting its own foreign affairs. To be sure, the Peloponnesian League and other local organizations had come into being, but the members maintained much of their freedom and autonomy. The war with Persia showed that survival might depend on the ability of the Greeks to unite against a common danger on a long-range basis. The problem how to reconcile freedom and autonomy with the necessary subordination of sovereignty was now thrust upon the Greeks.

Plataea and Mycale did not end the Persian threat, so the Delian League under Athenian leadership was invented to meet it. The league became the Athenian Empire, an organization different from, but not completely dissimilar to, the Peloponnesian League. Greece was now divided into two great power blocs that came into conflict in the fifth and sixth decades of the fifth century. The mid-century battles did not immediately resolve the issue of hegemony. Each side emerged with its organization intact, but worn out by the effort of competition and sobered by the knowledge of its rival's strength. The Thirty Years' Peace presented an opportunity for the Greek states to adapt themselves to the new realities. Two great states now led the Greeks. They differed in character, in ideology, and in the nature of their power. If they could limit their desires, avoid conflict, and refuse to be dragged into wars by lesser states, they might hope to live in harmony with one another and so bring a general peace to the Hellenic world. Had they done so, no foreign enemy could have prevailed against their combined power, and in peace and prosperity, the polis could have further developed its genius. In the event, Sparta and Athens were unable to live in peace; the Peloponnesian War came, bringing death, poverty, civil strife, and foreign domination. It permanently damaged the economic well-being, the social stability, the military power, and, finally, the self-confidence of the Greek city-states.

Thucydides thought that the war was inevitable. "I think," he said, "that the truest cause, but the least spoken of, was the growth of Athenian power, which presented an object of fear to the Spartans and forced them to go to war."[3] Modern historians have argued about the causes of the war, but few have doubted its inevitability, and small wonder. Thucydides' account of the events leading to war is powerful and compelling, while rival explanations, both ancient and modern, have been infinitely less persuasive. His terse, carefully arranged description of the growth of the Athenian Empire and the Spartan response seems to leave no alternative to war.

It is precisely the question of inevitability which most engages the interest of the modern reader, and probably Thucydides would have wished it so. He saw his work as a "possession for eternity," useful to "such men as might wish to see clearly what has happened and what will happen again, in all human probability, in the same or a similar way."[4] He would expect us to seek insights into modern problems in his account of the great war between Athens and Sparta, and not the least of such insights would be the inevitability of a war arising from the conditions he describes. Must a rivalry between two powers leading rival blocs come to blows? So general a question cannot be answered by the historian; indeed, in his professional capacity he cannot even ask it. But there are other questions that he can and must ask; though they cannot be answered with certainty, the questions are legitimate, and the attempt to answer them may teach us something about that "human probability" of which Thucydides wrote.

We must ask whether the *détente* achieved by the Thirty Years' Peace could have endured, whether there were real alternatives to the policies that led to war. Did Spartan or Athenian interests demand a final resort to war? Or did war come in spite of those interests? In attempting to answer these questions, we must resist the temptation to follow blindly the greatest of ancient historians. His account was begun during the war, and he did not survive it by many years. The persuasive force of a brilliant contemporary account by a historian who was a participant in some of the events and an

[3] 1. 23. 6. *τὴν μὲν γὰρ ἀληθεστάτην πρόφασιν, ἀφανεστάτην δὲ λόγῳ, τοὺς Ἀθηναίους ἡγοῦμαι μεγάλους γιγνομένους καὶ φόβον παρέχοντας τοῦ Λακεδαιμονίοις ἀναγκάσαι ἐς τὸ πολεμεῖν.*

[4] 1. 22. 4. *ὅσοι δὲ βουλήσονται τῶν τε γενομένων τὸ σαφὲς σκοπεῖν καὶ τῶν μελλόντων ποτὲ αὖθις κατὰ τὸ ἀνθρώπινον τοιούτων καὶ παραπλησίων ἔσεσθαι.*

eyewitness to many others, who questioned and cross-questioned witnesses to events he did not see himself, must be enormous. But the viewpoint of a contemporary has its shortcomings. The force of the *fait accompli,* the feeling that what happened had to happen, is compelling even for those with the perspective of many centuries. How much more so it must have been for Thucydides. We must resist the powerful attraction of his interpretation, at least provisionally, in order to test its validity.

The very concept of inevitability presents some problems. What does inevitability mean in the realm of human affairs? Leaving aside the metaphysical question of free will versus determinism, we may still raise legitimate questions as to the extent of man's freedom to make political decisions. There can be no doubt that some apparent choices in the realm of human affairs are in fact precluded by previous events, while others are made more likely. But men can make decisions that alter the course of events. It is the difficult but necessary task of the historian to distinguish between relatively open choices and those that are only apparent. When Thucydides suggests that the Peloponnesian War was inevitable, he is, of course, correct. That is, at some point in time before the clash of arms, there was no way to alter the course leading to war. What makes the assertion of inevitability challenging and important is the selection of that point in time. To say that the war became inevitable once the Spartan army crossed the Athenian frontier is obvious and trivial. That the war was fated from the beginning of time is a philosophical or metaphysical proposition not subject to historical analysis. It is on the ground between these extreme positions that historical discussion must take place.

The Thucydidean view is neither trivial nor metaphysical. It is clear that Thucydides believed that the rise of the Athenian Empire after the Persian Wars, in a world where another great power already existed, made a clash between them unavoidable. His famous excursus which begins in 479 with the retreat of the Persians and describes the rise of Athenian power is intended to support that interpretation. We may believe that Thucydides was right about the causes of the First Peloponnesian War (461–445), but we must remember that it was ended by a peace whose transitory nature, obvious to us, may not have been so to contemporaries. The question before us is whether that peace might have been maintained, whether Athens and Sparta were destined to go to war *after* 445.

Our best source of information for the years 445–431 is the history of Thucydides. Let us examine it, along with our other evidence, to see what events took place and what decisions were made that led to war, but let us ask at every opportunity whether another decision was humanly possible. Freely admitting that at some particular moment circumstances may offer men only one practicable course of action, let us not forget that at other times they are free to choose among several possibilities and so influence their destinies for good or ill; the fault is often not in our stars, but in our selves.

Part One

The Alliance System and the Division of the Greek World

1. The Spartan Alliance

The Peloponnesian War was not fought by individual Greek states but by two great coalitions, the Peloponnesian League and the Athenian Empire. In some important ways the two were similar, each providing an example of what has been called an "Alliance Under a Hegemon." [1] Each was "an alliance of a leading state with a number of others, not limited in time or by any specific aim, implying a leading position of the one state in war, and soon also in politics, loosely organized at first, but clearly an attempt at a unit transcending the single state." [2] But in many crucial ways they were different, and the differences affected their capacities both to wage war and to keep the peace. The two alliances, moreover, were historically related and not always at odds. If we are to understand the coming of the great war, we must have a clear picture of the nature of the two leagues and of how they came into conflict.

Historians with a taste for paradox are accustomed, with Voltaire, to say of the Holy Roman Empire that it was not holy, neither was it Roman, nor was it an empire. Similarly, it is tempting to say of the Peloponnesian League that it was not really a league, nor, strictly speaking, was it altogether Peloponnesian. It included states to the north of the Isthmus of Corinth, and relationships among its members were loose enough to make such terms as *league* or *confederation*

[1] The designation was invented by Victor Ehrenberg (*The Greek State* [Oxford, 1960], 112) and comprehends the Peloponnesian League, the first and second Athenian leagues, and the League of Corinth.

[2] *Idem.*

inappropriate. The term most frequently used in antiquity was *symmachia,* which we may translate as "alliance," a term as ambiguous in English as it is in Greek. The ancients usually called the group the "Lacedaemonians and their Allies," [3] a term that modern historians would do well to adopt, had not the title Peloponnesian League already gained universal currency.

The evidence for the nature of the Spartan alliance, its history and development, is scanty and difficult to interpret, giving rise to a great diversity of opinion. The Spartan alliance was not a response to an external threat, like the Hellenic League, formed to fight the Persians in 481, or like the Delian League, formed to prosecute a war of revenge and liberation against Persia in 478/7. It was instead the product of a Spartan policy aimed at guaranteeing the security of Sparta and its domination of the Peloponnese.[4] By the beginning of the sixth century, Sparta's persistent problem—the suppression of her helots—was well under control, and she could turn to the northern Peloponnese.[5] Up to that time Sparta had followed the obvious policy pursued by a strong state toward her weaker neighbors. After defeating them, she incorporated their territory, treating some, the *perioikoi,* as subject freemen, and others, the helots, as something very much like serfs. In this way the southern and western regions of the Peloponnese had become Spartan territories without autonomy. The Spartans were now free to turn to their northern neighbor, Tegea. Not until the middle of the sixth century were the Spartans able to conquer this Arcadian city, for the Tegeans were tough fighters who put up a long and fierce resistance. At last the Spartans sought the advice of the oracle at Delphi and were told that they must acquire the bones of Orestes in order to take Tegea. A clever Spartan discovered the bones of a giant buried at Tegea, so we are told, and took them home. Shortly thereafter the Spartans took Tegea.[6]

The victory over Tegea was a turning point in Spartan policy. Instead of annexing the territory of the Tegeans, the Spartans con-

[3] Busolt and Swoboda, *GS,* 1330.

[4] Victor Martin, *La vie internationale dans la Grèce des cités* (Paris, 1940), 206; Ehrenberg, *The Greek State,* 118–119.

[5] G. L. Huxley, *Early Sparta* (Cambridge, Mass., 1962), 65.

[6] Hdt. 1. 66–68; Huxley, *Early Sparta,* 65–68; Ehrenberg, *PW, s.v.,* "Sparta," 1383.

cluded an alliance that was to prove lasting.[7] Among other things, the treaty provided that the Tegeans were not to harbor Messenian refugees and that Tegean supporters of Sparta would not be harmed. The major provisions are not mentioned, probably because they were so well known. They surely must have included the formula that was the basic ingredient of all future treaties between Sparta and her allies and that established the nature of Spartan hegemony: the allied states promised to "have the same friends and enemies and to follow the Lacedaemonians on land and on sea wherever they might lead." [8] Soon the rest of Arcadia came under Spartan control.[9] By 525 their influence extended to the Isthmus of Corinth, including all the Peloponnesians, with the exception of Argos and Achaea.[10] Each extension of the Spartan alliance meant that one more state had agreed to a treaty that turned control of its foreign policy over to Sparta. This was obviously agreeable to Sparta, but why were their allies willing to enter upon such agreements?

The Tegean experience, of course, offers one explanation. Beaten in the field, the Tegeans must have been glad to accept comparatively generous terms, for they retained their land, their freedom, and some degree of autonomy. Possibly other Arcadian states had a similar experience, but we know that not all the allies had first been defeated in combat, and many must have been glad to enter the alliance. To the conservative cities of the Peloponnese, Sparta's military might offered protection against enemies from within as well as from without. Fear of Argos, the other great Peloponnesian power, and fear of popular unrest which might result in the expulsion of oligarchies and the establishment of tyrannies provided these cities with a strong motive for accepting Spartan leadership.

[7] The alliance is mentioned and some of its provisions described in Plut. *Quaest. Graec.* 5. See also *Quaest. Rom.* 52. Eduard Meyer (*GdA* 2. 766) places the treaty in the sixth century, but Hiller von Gaertringen (*IG*, II, 3) puts it in 468, after the great Arcadian uprising. He is followed by Busolt and Swoboda (*GS*, 1320, n. 3). L. I. Highby (*The Erythrae Decree, Klio*, Beiheft, XXXVI [1936], 72–73) argues persuasively for a sixth-century date, which I accept.

[8] Xen. *Hell.* 2. 2. 20; Busolt and Swoboda, *GS*, 1320 and 1325.

[9] Busolt and Swoboda, *GS*, 1320; Herodotus (1. 68) tells us that by the time of the Tegean defeat the Spartans controlled the greater part of the Peloponnese.

[10] Ulrich Kahrstedt, *Griechisches Staatsrecht* (Göttingen, 1922), I, 28–29.

In the seventh century the Argives had dominated the Peloponnese, and even in the sixth they tried to control its northeastern section. To such states as Phlius, Sicyon, and Corinth they posed a continual threat. In 546 the Spartans defeated Argos in battle, gained control of the Thyreatis, a disputed area on the border between Laconia and the Argolid, and the island of Cythera off the southeastern Peloponnese.[11] The victory was important, for it extended Spartan influence to the northeastern Peloponnese and showed that the leadership of the entire Peloponnese had shifted from the Argolid to Laconia. It is important to notice, however, that from necessity or by design, Argos was neither captured or destroyed. For the time being she was weakened, but she remained a possible menace. The enemies of Argos were loyal to their Spartan allies not only from gratitude but perhaps from apprehension as well.

The sixth century was a period of tumultuous domestic strife in the Greek city-states. The growth of commerce, industry, and population had severely strained the political and social stability of the aristocratic republican governments of Greece. In the seventh century tyrannies had appeared in Argos, Sicyon, Corinth, and Megara, as well as in other cities outside the Peloponnese. Some of these persisted into the sixth century, but most had begun to outlive their popularity, while the upper classes had at last begun to regroup their forces and try to restore oligarchic rule. By the middle of the century, Sparta had taken the lead in the struggle against tyranny and in defense of oligarchy. Plutarch records a list of tyrants supposedly removed by the Spartans.[12] It includes tyrannies at Corinth, Ambracia, Naxos, Athens, Sicyon, Thasos, Miletus, Phocis, and in Thessaly. The list is not in chronological order, and some of the interventions are implausible, if not impossible. Still, Plutarch is surely reporting a reliable tradition when he says, "We know of no city of that time so zealous in the pursuit of honor and so hostile to tyrants as the city of the Lacedaemonians." [13] Sparta, like all ancient states with a "mixed constitution," was really an oligarchy, the natural refuge for exiled aristocrats and oligarchs. She did not merely

[11] Hdt. 1. 82; Huxley, *Early Sparta,* 70–73.

[12] *Mor.* 859 D.

[13] *Mor.* 859 C; see also Thuc. 1. 18. 1.

destroy the tyrannies, step aside, and let nature take its course.[14] Her policy was to promote oligarchy and defend it against its enemies. "The Lacedaemonians did not lead by holding their allies subject by the payment of tribute; instead they took care that they were governed by oligarchies in a manner conformable to Spartan interests." [15]

The alliance that Sparta led into the fifth century, the nucleus of the grand coalition that turned back the Persian invasion, was founded on Spartan military might and bound together by a mutual distrust of Argos as well as a common interest in defending oligarchy. But were there no other ties binding the members of the alliance, more formal and lasting than Spartan power or shared interests, both of which might be transitory? Were the members tied to one another or merely to Sparta? What were the rights and duties of Sparta and of the subsidiary allies? In short, what was the constitution of the Peloponnesian League? To this apparently simple question scholars have returned widely diverging answers. At one extreme is the view of Ulrich Kahrstedt:

> Membership in the league was based on perpetual treaties and indeed only with Sparta; there was no entry into the league by a decree of admission of all previous members, as in a federal union [*Verein*]. The league originated through the fact that Sparta made a pact with Tegea and grew because it did the same each time with almost every state of the neighboring territory. It is logical that, even later, states could not enter except by making a treaty of alliance with Sparta whose content either copied or was similar to that of the others which had been concluded earlier. The constitution of the league consisted merely of ties which ran from Sparta to the individual *poleis;* there were no ties that bound these to one another, no regulation of constitutional relations at all. . . . Thus, it is really wrong to apply modern terms like league, confederation, or confederacy to this political structure.[16]

At the other end of the spectrum stands Jacob Larsen, who believes that some time about 505 the equivalent of a constitutional convention of the allies of Sparta met to found the Peloponnesian League.[17] The purpose of that convention, he says, was to adopt two

[14] Huxley, *Early Sparta,* 75; H. T. Wade-Gery, *CAH,* III, 568–569.

[15] 1. 19.

[16] Kahrstedt, *op. cit.,* I, 81–82.

[17] Larsen's views may be found in a series of articles published in *CP:* XXVII (1932), 136–150; XXVIII (1933), 256–276; XXIX (1934), 1–19,

principles: Sparta must consult a league assembly before demanding support from the allies; and the allies must accept and abide by a majority vote of that assembly. The adoption of these principles "amounted to the adoption of a constitution and the transformation of what had been merely a group of Spartan allies into the organization known to us as the Peloponnesian League." [18] By using evidence from later periods and the historical analogy of other Greek alliances, Larsen tries to reconstruct the very procedure followed by the "constitutional convention." He suggests that first the representatives of Sparta's allies met in a congress and adopted the constitutional principles agreed upon in the form of a number of decrees. "These principles were then embodied in treaties ratified by means of an exchange of oaths." [19]

Larsen alone imagines such a formal arrangement, but others have occupied the middle ground between his view and the very loose organization pictured by Kahrstedt. Georg Busolt emphasized the dualistic nature of the Peloponnesian League, with the Spartans on the one side and the allies on the other.[20] He discerned some fine distinctions within the league:

> In the broader sense all states belonged to the allies of the Lacedaemonians with whom they had concluded a treaty, but the league included only those who took part in its union and in the forces of the league. The looser organization of the league rested in part on the treaties of the Lacedaemonians with the individual states, in part on common decrees which produced a law of the league.[21]

These fine distinctions are very difficult to perceive if one examines the entire history of the league, and they can be maintained only by explaining away exceptions to every rule or basing rules on unique examples. They arise from an unduly legalistic approach to the problem. Even so reasonable a scholar as Victor Martin is not altogether immune from this fallacy. Although he finds Larsen's arguments for the formal organization of the league unconvincing and agrees that

---

and in the third chapter of his *Representative Government in Greek and Roman History* (Berkeley and Los Angeles, 1955).

[18] *CP,* XXVII (1932), 140.

[19] *CP,* XXVIII (1933), 265.

[20] Busolt and Swoboda, *GS,* 1330.

[21] *Idem.*

in the beginning bilateral treaties prevailed, he believes that "with time customs were established that, by progressively specifying the rights and duties of the allies after collective undertakings, ended by becoming the same, in a certain degree, as a pact that in every case constituted a body of customs valid for all." [22]

If we are to understand the workings of the Spartan alliance, we must abandon the search for constitutional law, even for "a body of customs valid for all." Kahrstedt was right in seeing that the Peloponnesian League was nothing more than a collection of states, each tied to Sparta by a separate treaty, but even he was too legalistic when he sought general rules governing the relations between Sparta and the allies. The best way to see what difficulties can result from the pursuit of that method is to examine some of the attempts to discover the rules of the league. This is not the place to undertake a full analysis, but we can learn a good deal by examining one question whose importance and relative simplicity give some promise of success in the search for constitutional clarity and uniformity: Could Sparta or could she not order her allies to suppress rebellions within the alliance without consulting an assembly of the league?

The cases that provide evidence on this point occurred at the very end of the fifth century, but we have no reason to believe the alliance had altered in any way. In 403, King Pausanias led the Spartans and their allies against Athens, which had accepted a treaty with Sparta the year before but which was now judged to be in revolt.[23] The Corinthians and Boeotians refused to participate in the campaign, arguing that they would be in violation of their oaths if they attacked the Athenians, who had not broken their treaty. In 400, the Spartans decided to subjugate Elis after years of defiance, and they asked their allies to help against the rebellious state. This time all the allies, even the Athenians, obeyed, but once again the Corinthians and Boeotians abstained.[24] Larsen emphasizes that in both instances the abstaining member states were not punished.[25] He is eager to

[22] Martin, *op. cit.*, 205–206.

[23] Xen. *Hell.* 2. 4. 30.

[24] Xen. *Hell.* 3. 2. 21–25.

[25] Larsen (*CP*, XXVIII [1933], 269, n. 37) says that the Boeotians "are hardly to be counted as members of the League." He offers no support for his statement, and we must conclude that he has been influenced by the title

show that the league was a true federation which delegated important powers to its assembly, and so he interprets these events as demonstrating that, while Sparta could act against a rebellious member and ask allied support without first consulting the assembly, if the allies thought Sparta's case unjust, they had not only the right but the duty to refuse. The point is that only the assembly of the league had the right to decide on an expedition, even against rebellious members. "If Sparta acted without consulting the assembly, she ran the risk that members would refuse to support her." [26]

Busolt interpreted the evidence in a different sense. In his opinion, "The Lacedaemonians not infrequently summoned the allies to a campaign without a consultation of the assembly of the league. In this they must have been justified in certain cases, in case of a request for aid by an allied state under attack or of a rebellion by a member state." [27] But if that is true, how could Corinth and Boeotia refuse the Spartan appeal and get off scot free, as Larsen says they did? But the fact is that they did not ultimately escape the wrath of Sparta. The Spartans did not immediately punish them, it is true, but not because the defectors had constitutional right on their side. The Spartans had pressing business elsewhere; they were engaged in an Asian war against the Persians. By 395 the Spartans were at war with both Corinth and Thebes for several reasons, not least among them the fact that the Thebans had refused to join in the attack against Athens and had persuaded the Corinthians to do the same.[28] They went to war in 395 not because it had taken so long to convince them that their allies had acted unconstitutionally, but because they now believed that "it was a favorable time to lead an army against the Thebans and to put a stop to their insolence. Affairs in Asia were going well for them since Agesilaus was winning, and in Greece there was no other war to hinder them." [29]

We can see how arbitrary are all attempts to find regular consti-

---

"Peloponnesian League," which did not exist in antiquity. There is no better reason for doubting Boeotian membership in the Spartan alliance at this time than Corinthian.

[26] *Ibid.*, 269–270.

[27] *GS*, 1333–1334.

[28] Xen. *Hell.* 3. 5. 5.

[29] *Idem.*

tional procedures in the Spartan alliance by looking at Kahrstedt's treatment of the same cases. He does not see them as instances in which Sparta requested aid in putting down a rebellion within the league. Instead, he thinks of them as private wars conducted by Sparta, which, since they were not defensive, did not oblige the allies to help.[30] He believes that the individual members were pledged to support Sparta when she was attacked. When they themselves were attacked, they could expect support from Sparta in return, but the other allies were required to come to their aid only if a league war were declared.[31] Still wrestling with phantom legalities, Kahrstedt suggests that originally there may have been *pro forma* stipulations that required Sparta to abandon its private quarrels in case a league war was declared. But his belief that the alliance rested only on bilateral treaties forced him to the realistic conclusion that such stipulations would be meaningless. "Sparta could each time prevent the outbreak of a league war if it really did not wish to give up its own quarrel, since such a war could not be declared without a decree of the Spartan Apella, as well as a similar decree from the allies." [32]

The most important and unfortunate consequence of the search for constitutional regulations in the Spartan alliance is that it often leads scholars to seek an explanation for a particular historical action not in the immediate political or military situation or in the immediate interests of the participants, but rather in general, formal rules. Such rules must be constructed from what little evidence we have. To an extraordinary degree, most general discussions of the operation of the Peloponnesian League depend heavily on its behavior just before and during the Peloponnesian War. That is hardly strange, for Thucydides' account is the only detailed description we have of its workings. We shall analyze that account later on, but for the moment it is enough to say that the activities of the Spartans and their allies before and during the war could not have been typical. They were about to undertake what everyone knew might be a dangerous and difficult war. Special and unusual measures were taken to meet a special and unusual situation. The actions of the league in

[30] Kahrstedt, *op. cit.,* 92.
[31] *Ibid.,* 90.
[32] *Ibid.,* 92.

432, therefore, should not be considered characteristic, and it is wrong to generalize from them, as all the constitutional analysts do. The fact that they disagree as to the constitutional significance of what takes place is far less important than their common failure to recognize that constitutional analysis is beside the point. If we are to evaluate these and other critical events correctly, we must understand the essentially pragmatic nature of the alliance and try to understand the forces and interests that determined its behavior.

The Spartan alliance was a loose organization consisting of Sparta and her individual allies. Each state swore to have the same friends and enemies as Sparta in return for Spartan protection and recognition of its integrity and autonomy. Since each treaty was sealed by oaths, each state had what amounted to a perpetual alliance with Sparta. The distinction between offensive and defensive wars seems not to have existed, for even though we have many instances of Sparta or its allies refusing to fulfill a military commitment, the argument that an allegedly defensive war is really offensive never is offered as an excuse. This ambiguity was probably only one of many. The wording by which the allied state promised to have the same friends and enemies as Sparta might seem to indicate subservience on their part. In the beginning, when such states as Tegea or tiny Phlius were involved, this was surely true, *de facto,* but it is not clear that even then the obligation ran only one way. In fact, if the promise of Spartan protection meant anything at all, it must have meant that in some cases Sparta would make her ally's enemy her own. Later on, when such powerful states as Corinth and Thebes were included in the alliance, the bilateral nature of the treaty must have been still more apparent. The wording of the treaty, no doubt, was the same as in the treaties with the weaker states, but the mutual understanding of its meaning would be different. It is fruitless to wonder whether the theory behind the treaties implied equality between the signatories or the hegemony of Sparta. Their language was ambiguous, and reality, not theory, provided the interpretive principle.

When Sparta was strong and secure she could call the tune. She helped other states when it was profitable or unavoidable. She compelled others to help her when it was necessary and possible. They sent aid either in the hope of reciprocity, from fear of punishment, or in pursuit of their own interests. Sometimes states allied to Sparta fought wars against one another. Larsen would have us believe that the normal method for settling such disputes was to submit them to an assembly of the league. Unfortunately, he offers only one instance in support of this contention. Even in that unique case, the suggestion that the hostile states submit their quarrel to the league assembly was rejected, and a war ensued.[33]

The truth is that Sparta interpreted her inevitably conflicting responsibilities in accordance with her needs and interests. In 461/0, for instance, a boundary dispute caused a war between Corinth and Megara. At first the Spartans ignored the affair, but after the Megarians broke away from Sparta by seeking an Athenian alliance, Sparta and her allies supported Corinth because her hegemony and even her security were threatened.[34] In 423, on the other hand, even though the Spartans were temporarily at peace with Athens and so free to act, they chose not to intervene in a war between Tegea and Mantinea.[35] No doubt they found it more important to rest and recover their strength than to join in a war that posed no threat and offered no advantage. The situation was quite different, however, in 378. In that year the Spartans intervened decisively in a war between Orchomenus and Cletor, two small Arcadian towns. On this occasion the Spartans were engaged in a difficult war against Thebes and badly needed the mercenary troops who were fighting for Cletor. The Spartan king Agesilaus simply hired the mercenaries away from Cletor and ordered Orchomenus to desist from war so long as his campaign lasted.[36] On none of these occasions is there any evidence that anyone raised a constitutional issue, much less demanded a league assembly.

The fact is that we rarely hear of an assembly of the league. No meetings of the alliance could take place unless Sparta called them, simply because the only alliances that existed were bilateral treaties with Sparta. Meetings were called only if they were deemed neces-

[33] *CP*. XXVIII (1933), 274–275. The reference is to the quarrel between Boeotia and the Phocians in 395, which led to the Corinthian War. See *Hell. Oxy*. 13. 4.

[34] Thuc. 1. 103. 4; Diod. 11. 79. 1.

[35] 4. 134.

[36] Xen. *Hell*. 5. 4. 36–37.

sary or useful by the Spartans. Of course it would be absurd to think of launching a major war without the consent of the allies on whom success depended. Nevertheless, when King Cleomenes wanted to restore the aristocratic government of Isagoras to Athens in 507, he mustered an allied army not only without consulting an assembly but even without announcing the purpose of the expedition.[37] Only when the battle was about to begin did the Corinthians force a discussion, and their defection forced the Spartans to abandon their scheme.[38] A short time later the Spartans, fearing the vitality of the newly founded Cleisthenic democracy, tried to restore the tyranny of Hippias to Athens. Made cautious by their previous experience, they first called an assembly of their allies. Again they were rebuffed because of the general hatred of tyranny and perhaps because of a common fear of Sparta's growing ambition.

Throughout the fifteen years of the First Peloponnesian War, we hear of no meeting of the assembly of the league. In 432, of course, the Spartans had no choice but to call such a meeting before launching a war against the Athenian Empire. Even then, as we shall see, the assembly served an internal political purpose as well as an international one. In the fourth century Sparta was so powerful that she did not need to consult her nearer and weaker allies, while she often found herself at war against former allies who were stronger and more remote, Corinth and Thebes. As a result, we rarely hear of assemblies of the league. As an Athenian spokesman complained to the Spartans in 371, "You declare enemies for yourselves without consulting your allies whom you lead against them. The result is that often people who are said to be autonomous are forced to fight against their own friends." [39]

Even in this period of their greatest strength and arrogance, however, the Spartans called meetings of the league assembly when it was convenient. In 396, when they were about to launch a great and dangerous invasion of Asia,[40] and in 382, when asked to fight

[37] Hdt. 5. 74.

[38] Larsen believes that in 507 the Peloponnesian League did not yet exist, so an assembly would not be necessary. See *CP,* XXVII (1932).

[39] Xen. *Hell.* 7. 3. 8.

[40] Xen. *Hell.* 3. 4. 2.

against the powerful and distant Chalcidic League,[41] they called their allies together. They did so again in 376, immediately after a Spartan army was disbanded in discouragement after being prevented from entering Theban territory. At this moment of Spartan dejection and confusion it is not even clear who insisted on a meeting of the assembly.[42] The significant fact that arises from this brief survey is that on every occasion it was political or military reality, not constitutional regulations, which were decisive.

In other matters as well practical considerations ruled. The only formal regulation to which even lip service was paid was the one which demanded help for an ally who asked it, and there was no shortage of excuses for ignoring even that one. The only rules that counted were those imposed by military, political, or geographic reality. These realities enable us to see that Sparta's allies were not uniformly treated. We can discern three categories of allies, a division that was not formal but very meaningful. The first includes small states relatively weak and near enough to Sparta to be easily subject to her discipline. Phlius, Orchomenus, and, by the time of the Peloponnesian War, Tegea, are examples of such states. The second category is composed of states that were stronger, more remote, or both, but not so strong or remote as to avoid ultimate punishment: Elis, Mantinea, and Megara. When Sparta was strong she could and did demand obedience from them. When she was weak or distracted they could go their own ways, attack their neighbors, who might also be allied to Sparta,[43] adopt democratic constitutions,[44] and even make alliances with another state unfriendly to Sparta.[45] Such independence, however, was always temporary and sometimes costly.

The third category consists of states so remote or so powerful that their independence was rarely tampered with and whose conduct of foreign policy was rarely subordinated to Spartan interests. Only

[41] Xen. *Hell.* 5. 2. 11–23.

[42] Xen. *Hell.* 5. 4. 59–60.

[43] See Thuc. 5. 31, where Elis attacks Lepreum; 4. 134, where Mantinea attacks Tegea; 5. 29. 1, where the Mantineans subdue part of Arcadia; and 1. 104, where Megara fights Corinth.

[44] Elis: Arist. *Pol.* 1292 b; Xen. *Hell.* 3. 3. 27. Mantinea: Thuc. 5. 29.

[45] Elis and Mantinea with Argos, Thuc. 5. 29 and 5. 31; with Athens, 5. 43 and 5. 46; Megara with Athens, 1. 103. 4.

Corinth and Thebes belonged to this group. Thebes was a conservative agrarian state devoted to oligarchy in normal times. She probably joined the Spartan alliance at the end of the sixth century because of her fear of the Athenian democracy. Her remoteness from the Peloponnese and her powerful army guaranteed her independence. When her interests coincided with Sparta's, which usually meant when Sparta was hostile to Athens, she was a powerful and useful ally. When she believed her interests to be different, she had no hesitation in ignoring Sparta's wishes. A clear instance of Theban independence occurred in 421. On that occasion the Boeotians, under Theban hegemony, refused to accept the Peace of Nicias, which Sparta had made with Athens.[46] They refused to obey Sparta's request to give up their Athenian prisoners and surrender the border fort of Panactum, which had fallen into their hands.[47] This refusal made it impossible for the Spartans to carry out the terms of the peace and was a very serious blow to Spartan policy. In the fourth century, of course, Sparta's imperial ambitions outside the Peloponnese clashed directly with Theban interests, and from at least as early as 395 the former allies were bitter enemies. But even before that period the Spartans could never rely upon the Thebans for certain obedience.

Corinth was a still greater obstacle to unbridled Spartan hegemony. Astride the Isthmus, she could bar extra-Peloponnesian enemies of Sparta or permit them to invade the Peloponnese and threaten Sparta's security. Nor should we forget the critical role played by Argos in Peloponnesian politics. The Spartans knew that so long as the marchland of Thyrea-Cynuria was in their hands, so long as they claimed hegemony in the Peloponnese, the Argives would be hostile, waiting only a convenient opportunity for revenge. Just as Sparta was a guarantee to Corinth against Argive ambition, Corinth was no less a security for the Spartans. Sparta had good reason to fear a rapprochement between Argos and Tegea, a fear realized in 473/2.[48] In 421 the Corinthians threatened to create an alliance uniting Argos, Mantinea, Elis, and Corinth and even held out the possibility of bringing in Megara and Thebes. As a result

[46] 5. 17. 2.
[47] 5. 39.
[48] Edouard Will, *Korinthiaka* (Paris, 1955), 629–630.

they frightened the Spartans once again into a war they did not want.[49] In any war that required money and ships, Corinth was an essential ally. Her wealth was as proverbial as Spartan poverty. After the decline of Aegina, Corinth was the only ally of Sparta that could build, equip, and man a sizable and effective fleet.

For all these reasons Corinth's views could not be ignored, and her independent voice in matters of foreign policy was listened to with attention. It is not too much to say that on certain occasions a Corinthian veto could check a Spartan policy and even that sometimes Spartan policy was really determined at Corinth. In 525 the Spartans, with the enthusiastic support of Corinth, sent an army to Samos to bring down its tyrant, Polycrates.[50] We might think that Sparta's well-known hatred of tyranny was behind this unusual campaign, which took the Spartans not only out of the Peloponnese, but even across the sea. However, the Spartans' motive, at least according to Herodotus, was to avenge the theft of a bowl and a breastplate. Understandably, modern scholars have not been satisfied and have suggested that the expedition was anti-Persian, since Polycrates had become a Persian vassal. Others suggest that it was an attempt to extend Spartan hegemony to the Aegean.[51]

None of these motives is particularly persuasive, but the motive that Herodotus attributes to the Corinthians for participating in the campaign is even more dubious. He says that the Corinthians, like the Spartans, were fighting a war of revenge. Their complaint was that the Samians had given refuge to three hundred boys who were being sent by the tyrant of Corinth to the Lydian king Alyattes to be made eunuchs.[52] Now, by 525, this wrong was more than half a century old. It was a wrong, moreover, done not to the Corinthians, but to a tyrant whose memory they hated, and so it is hardly adequate to explain Corinth's action. What, then, was Corinth's true motive? We know that Corinth was an important commercial state whose products flowed from one end of the Mediterranean to the other in

[49] For a fuller account of these events, see Kagan, *AJP,* LXXXI (1960), 291–310 and *CP,* LVII (1962), 209–218.

[50] Hdt. 3. 47.

[51] These are the suggestions of Georg Busolt, Hans Schaefer, and J. Hasebroek, respectively. They are cited by Will (*Korinthiaka,* 634–635).

[52] Hdt. 3. 48.

the sixth century. Polycrates was a pirate-king who plundered the shipping of any state that sent its cargoes past Samos.[53] It is not hard to believe that the Corinthians were eager to attack Polycrates in order to clear the sea of his pirate ships, put an end to his thalassocracy, and make the Aegean safe for their own ships.[54]

Why did Sparta attack Polycrates? She was neither a naval nor a commercial state. We can find no satisfactory motive, and it is hard to avoid the conclusion that she was pushed into the campaign by Corinth.[55] The Spartan alliance was relatively new; the threat from Argos persisted; the danger of a union between Argos, Corinth, and Tegea was not to be ignored. "On the Peloponnesian chessboard the Argive pawn was a piece which Corinth could play against Sparta. . . . There we discern for the first time a new constant in Peloponnesian politics. . . ." [56]

In 507, as we have already seen,[57] the Corinthians showed their independence of Sparta and their decisive influence by preventing King Cleomenes from restoring the tyrant Hippias to power in Athens. The incident showed that Corinth could refuse to subordinate her interests to those of Sparta on certain occasions. An even more telling evidence of Corinth's influence in the Spartan alliance occurred in 461.[58] Relations between Sparta and Athens, correct, if not warm, since the end of the Persian War, began to deteriorate in 462. A great earthquake had struck Sparta a few years earlier, and it was soon followed by a revolt of the helots. Under the urging of the philolaconian Cimon, the Athenians went to Sparta's assistance, but shortly after their arrival they were unceremoniously invited to leave.

[53] Busolt, *GG,* II, 509–510.

[54] Such is the suggestion of Busolt (*ibid.,* 512) and Will (*Korinthiaka,* 636).

[55] This conclusion is well argued and ably defended by Will (*idem.*).

[56] *Ibid.,* 636–637.

[57] See above, p. 19.

[58] My chronology, for the most part, follows that of the authors of *ATL* (III, 158–180) and A. W. Gomme (*Hist. Comm.,* I, 389–413). Their accounts are not identical but not very far apart. The dating of the events between the end of the Persian War and the beginning of the great Peloponnesian War is difficult and uncertain. Although it has sometimes been necessary to depart from their guidance, especially in dating internal political events, I have found their accounts generally persuasive.

This produced a breach in the old alliance that had tied Athens to Sparta during the Persian War and a diplomatic revolution. Athens now allied itself with Argos, the traditional enemy of Sparta. When at last the helot rebels who had held out on Mt. Ithome surrendered under a safe conduct, the Athenians received them and settled them at Naupactus on the north shore of the Gulf of Corinth.[59]

By these actions the Athenians incurred Spartan hostility, but the Spartans were not yet moved to warfare. In 461, however, the Corinthians became embroiled with the Megarians in a quarrel over some border territory.[60] When the Megarians found themselves losing, they broke their treaty with Sparta and joined the Athenians. It is noteworthy that none of our sources suggest that Megara sought Spartan help or arbitration or asked for a meeting of the league. She must have known of Corinth's special position in the Spartan alliance and that Sparta would surely side with Corinth. After Megara's defection the Spartans led a Peloponnesian army against the Megarians, the Athenians sent their own army to defend Megara, and the first war between the two great alliances had begun in earnest.

Here we have a case where Corinthian and Spartan interests were similar if not identical but where the Corinthians pursued their own interests without first consulting their Spartan allies, even though their action strongly prejudiced the position of Sparta. At a time when war between Sparta and Athens seemed possible, the Corinthians were willing to pursue a private quarrel that not only precipitated a war but also guaranteed that the war would be fought under disadvantageous conditions. If the passes through the mountains of the Megarid were firmly in Peloponnesian hands, the Athenians could not invade the territory of their enemies but could be attacked by them. As Gomme has put it, "The cause of the quarrel between Corinth and Megara, περὶ γῆς ὅρων, is characteristic: Corinth was ready to risk the stability of the Peloponnesian League, not to mention the peace of the Greek world in general, rather than give up a claim to some strip of land."[61] The Spartans eventually might have fought the Athenians, but they would certainly not have chosen to

[59] 1. 102–103.
[60] Thuc. 1. 103; Diod. 11. 79.
[61] *Hist. Comm.*, I, 304.

do so in the circumstances forced upon them by Corinth. This was a clear example of the Corinthian tail wagging the Spartan dog.

Whatever the influence in the Spartan alliance of the several allies, it was Sparta that had to provide leadership and military power. If we are to understand the operation of the alliance, we must consider not only the relations between the allies but the problems within Sparta that affected them. In spite of her great military superiority, Sparta was usually reluctant to go to war. Her reluctance was always greater in proportion to the distance from home the Spartan army was compelled to go. The habitual caution at the root of Spartan policy is epitomized in a charming story told by Herodotus. In 499, Aristagoras of Miletus, who was planning an Ionian revolt against Persia, came to seek assistance. He had carefully planned his approach to King Cleomenes, promising him and his city great glory and immense wealth. Now Cleomenes was an unusually aggressive and ambitious king for a Spartan and might have been expected to yield to such temptation. He asked how many days' journey it was from the sea to the residence of the Persian king. Aristagoras was well prepared for this question and had even brought a map. It was here, says Herodotus, that he made his great mistake. He admitted that the journey inland would take three months. "At that Cleomenes cut off the rest of his speech telling of the journey and said, 'Milesian stranger, leave Sparta before sunset, for your words are unwelcome to the Lacedaemonians if you want to lead them on a journey of three months' distance from the sea.'" [62]

It has long been recognized that the chief source of such conservatism was Sparta's fear that the helots would take advantage of a long absence of the Spartan army and rebel.[63] The ratio of free Spartans to helots was in the neighborhood of one to ten,[64] and their relation-

[62] Hdt. 5. 50.

[63] The arguments are given by G. B. Grundy (*Thucydides and the History of his Age* [2nd. ed.; Oxford, 1948], I, 212–239). The same point of view is offered at some length in the first chapter of Georg Busolt's *Die Lakedaimonier und Ihre Bundesgenossen* (Leipzig, 1878) and is the basis of his interpretation of Spartan policy throughout.

[64] This is a conservative estimate, according to Grundy (*ibid.*, 219). Not even Guy Dickins (*JHS*, XXXII [1912], 1–42), who makes a powerful attack on Grundy's theory that population shortage and the helot threat were the major factors in Spartan policy, challenges this estimate.

ship was exacerbated by a long history of rebellions and cruel repressions. The ancient authors were perfectly aware of this threat to the security of Spartan rule and of its effects on Spartan policy. Thucydides tells us, "Most institutions among the Spartans have always been established with regard to security against the helots." [65] Listing Sparta's motives for seeking peace in 421, he emphasizes the desertion of the helots, which gave rise to the ever-present fear that those who stayed would join with those who fled and revolt, "just as they had done in the past." [66] As we might expect, Aristotle offers a general analysis of the problem. "It is agreed that leisure is one of the necessities for a state that is to be well governed; but in what manner this is to be provided is not easy to grasp. The class of serfs [*penestai*] in Thessaly often revolted against the Thessalians, and the same is true of the helots in Sparta, for they are like someone sitting in wait for disasters to strike the Spartans." [67]

Yet another problem continually affected the conduct of Spartan policy, this one arising from the constitution of the Spartan state. Ancient and modern students of constitutions have praised Sparta as a fine example of a mixed constitution. It balanced the monarchical, aristocratic, and democratic elements in such a way as to produce that rarest of flowers, political stability. The cycle of constitutions described by Plato, Aristotle, and Polybius was not to be found in Lacedaemon. From the middle of the sixth century, when the classical Spartan constitution seems to have reached its final form, until the third century, when it at last succumbed to the force of circumstances, Sparta's mode of government did not change. Her two kings served for life, led her armies, and performed religious and judicial functions; five ephors were elected annually, among other things to watch over the kings; the gerousia performed its senatorial functions, and the apella, the popular assembly, met on occasion to make or ratify important decisions. Such stability might appear to be the best guarantee of a consistent and well-conducted foreign policy. Compared to the constitution of democratic Athens, which in theory, and sometimes in practice, could adopt a policy on one day and its reverse on the next, which could adopt the policy of one man and put its

[65] 4. 80.
[66] 5. 14.
[67] *Pol.* 1269a.

execution in the hands of another, compared to such a constitution the Spartan polity would seem to have great advantages.

The course of Spartan history, however, shows that the stability of Sparta's constitution was not always matched by an equally stable policy.[68] In 506, Sparta, led by Cleomenes, set out on a campaign to put down the Athenian democracy. The Corinthians objected and refused to participate, but what really put an end to the attempt was a decision by Sparta's other king, Demaratus, to return to Sparta without a battle.[69] The Spartans learned the obvious lesson from this experience, and thereafter only one king was permitted to go on each expedition. This new law, however, did not prevent the kings from disagreeing on policy and intriguing against one another. Each could stand at the head of a faction within Sparta and try to advance his own policy while hindering his rival's.[70]

As an element producing instability in Spartan foreign policy, however, the rivalry between kings was far less important than the role of the ephors.[71] To be sure, their initial function may have been to serve as a check on the ambitions of the kings, but by the fifth

[68] For a cautious but incisive analysis of the way in which Sparta's constitution really worked in the classical period, see A. Andrewes, *ASI,* 1–20.

[69] Hdt. 5. 75.

[70] See, for example, the rivalry between Agesilaus and Cleombrotus in the fourth century, which is analyzed by R. E. Smith (*Historia,* II [1953–54], 274–288).

[71] The strongest statement in behalf of the importance of the ephors is that of Guy Dickins (*JHS,* XXXII [1912], 1–42): "From 550 onwards for nearly a century and a half the foreign policy of Sparta was dominated primarily by one consideration, and that not the population question, which did not arise at all until the beginning of the fifth century and only became of supreme importance in the fourth, but rather the issue of a conflict between the kings and the ephors lasting in an acute form for over fifty years and in a milder degree for almost the whole of Spartan history." Dickins' assertion is far too strong. The ancient evidence cited above makes it clear that the population or helot problem was of the greatest importance in the fifth century. Dickins himself admits that the earthquake of 464, which killed many Spartans and caused a helot rebellion, "permanently affected the offensive powers of Sparta," (*ibid.,* 35). His interpretation also goes too far in insisting upon alliances between ephors and a king where there is little or no evidence for them. It is further mistaken in imagining that the struggle was between the institution of the ephorate and that of the kingship. So it may have been at the outset, but by the fifth century it had become merely a factional struggle. In spite of these weaknesses, Dickins' essay is of great value in pointing out

century their role was more complex and even more decisive.[72] They and they alone, it appears, summoned the apella and conducted business before it. They sat with the gerousia, presented business to it, and were its executive officers. They had important judicial powers, notably, the right to try kings on a charge of treason. Chief among their responsibilities was the conduct of foreign affairs; they were, as Greenidge put it, the foreign ministry of Sparta.[73] They received foreign envoys, negotiated treaties, and ordered expeditions once war had been declared. The formula applied to decisions of peace and war was "It seemed good to the ephors and the assembly," [74] but Lysander did not exaggerate too much when he told the Athenians that the ephors alone had the authority in matters of peace and war.[75]

It is not only that these powerful officials often interfered with the pretensions of the kings, for the kings often differed from one another, and for long periods Sparta produced no ambitious kings. The problem was rather that there were five ephors, and decisions were made by majority vote. At any moment, therefore, a policy might be changed by the shifting of a single ephor's vote. Something of the sort happened in 403 when Pausanias persuaded three of the five ephors to order a Spartan army into Attica with himself at its head. The result was the deposition of the Thirty Tyrants, the restoration of the Athenian democracy, and thus the total reversal of Lysander's, and up to that time Sparta's, policy.[76]

Sometimes even a minority of ephors could affect Spartan policy. To be sure, the vote of the majority was supposed to be binding on

---

the important role of the ephors in making and unmaking policy. He is rebutted in the same number of the journal by G. B. Grundy (261–269). Dickins' response appears in the next number on pages 111–112. More recently, A. Andrewes (*ASI*, 8–10) has rejected the thesis of Dickins for similar reasons. In my judgment, however, he slightly underrates the importance of the ephors in shaping foreign policy and gives correspondingly greater weight to the apella.

[72] The discussion of the power of the ephors which follows owes much to the perceptive account of A. H. J. Greenidge in *A Handbook of Greek Constitutional History* (London, 1902), 102–106; see also Busolt and Swoboda, *GS*, 683–691.

[73] *Ibid.*, 106.

[74] Xen. *Hell.* 3. 2. 23 and 4. 6. 3.

[75] Xen. *Hell.* 2. 2. 18–19.

[76] Xen. *Hell.* 2. 4. 29.

the entire college of ephors, and Xenophon represents the Athenian oligarch Critias as asking the rhetorical question Wouldn't a Spartan ephor who opposed the policy of the majority be generally regarded as deserving punishment? [77] But we learn from Thucydides that in one case, at least, the minority might not quietly accept the majority decision. In the winter of 421/20, when the Peace of Nicias was in effect, Xenares and Cleobulus, two ephors, "who most particularly wanted to break the treaty, made private proposals to the Boeotians and Corinthians" to adopt a policy contrary to the official policy of the state.[78] This very instance illustrates another reason for the potentially disturbing influence of the ephors on Spartan foreign policy. The Peace of Nicias had been negotiated by ephors elected for the year 422/1, but in the following year, "the ephors who happened to be in office at Sparta were other than those under whom the treaty had been made, and some of them were even opposed to it." [79] The effect of all this was to produce a disconcerting vacillation in Spartan policy that baffled not only its friends and enemies but neutrals as well. During the early part of the Peloponnesian War, the Great King of Persia, it was reported, did not know what the Spartans wanted, "for though many envoys had come to him, no two said the same thing." [80]

The internal instability caused by conflicts between the Spartan kings, between ephors and kings, among the ephors themselves, and by the annual rotation of ephors could weaken Sparta's control of her alliance. An ally whose policy differed from that of Sparta could use Sparta's internal divisions to further its own ends. The paradox that the most stable of constitutions could produce a very unstable foreign policy added to the inherent difficulties of the Spartan alliance. Sparta's mighty army and her allies gave her enormous power, but if she used that power outside the Peloponnese, she ran the risk of losing its base by helot rebellion or Argive attack; if she did not use it when called upon by her more powerful allies, she ran the risk of losing them by defection. This dilemma severely vexed the Spartans in the course of the fifth century.

[77] Xen. *Hell.* 2. 3. 34.
[78] 5. 36. 1.
[79] *Idem.*
[80] 4. 50. 2.

2. The Origins of the Athenian Empire

The Athenian Empire resulted from Sparta's unwillingness or inability to extend her power, influence, and responsibility to the Aegean and its borders after the Greek victories at Plataea and Mycale in 479. Those victories had not ended the war against Persia, for the Persians could come again. Even if this were ruled out, the agreements made by the Greeks at the congress of 481 called for continued joint activities against the Persian Empire. That congress created a confederation of Greek states that greatly influenced the formation of the Delian League, which became the Athenian Empire, and we must examine its history.[1]

In 481, Xerxes, Great King of the Persian Empire, began his expedition, ostensibly to attack and punish Athens for her successful defiance of Persia at Marathon. The Greeks, however, had long known that his real purpose was the conquest of all Hellas,[2] so those of them who were not willing to submit met to consider what they should do.[3] The result was the formation of an offensive and defen-

[1] The best recent discussions of the Hellenic League of 481 are those of P. A. Brunt (*Historia,* II [1953/4], 135–163); *ATL,* (III, 95–105; 183–187), J. A. O. Larsen (*HSCP,* LI [1940], 175–213), R. Sealey (*ASI,* 233–256), and H. D. Meyer (*Historia,* XII [1963], 405–446).

[2] Hdt. 7. 138.

[3] Herodotus does not tell us where the meeting took place. Diodorus (11. 3) places it at the Isthmus of Corinth, while Pausanius (3. 12. 6) says it met at the Hellenion in Sparta. Most scholars accept the version of Diodorus, but as Brunt argues (*ibid.,* 148, n. 2), there is no reason to do so.

sive alliance, with Sparta at its head, made up of states bound together by a common danger and by solemn oaths. This was the organization that met again at the Isthmus of Corinth in the spring of 480 to plan the strategy that led to victory at Salamis and later to the decisive victories at Plataea and Mycale. Although Sparta was the leader, and most of the members of the Spartan alliance were also members of the new confederation, this was not merely an extension of the Peloponnesian League.[4] The new group included cities such as Athens, Plataea, Thespiae, and cities of the Aegean islands, which were not members of the Peloponnesian League previously. More important, the Spartans were given command of all the military forces only after a discussion whose nature was contrary to the very essence of the Spartan alliance.[5] The confederation against Persia had no official title, and its members are referred to variously as "the Greeks," "the Greeks who undertook the war against the barbarians," etc.[6]

At their first congress, the Greeks swore an oath whose exact nature we do not know. It is, of course, clear that they promised to fight the Persians "for the common freedom." [7] It is more than likely that they all swore to have the same friends and enemies, and this implied the cessation of quarrels among the allied states.[8] Athens and Aegina, in fact, put aside the conflict that had occupied them for

[4] The authors of *ATL* believe that it was (95–100), but the contrary arguments of Brunt (*loc. cit.*) are more persuasive.

[5] Herodotus (8. 3) tells us that the Athenians had claimed command of the navy but had yielded to the wishes of the allies. No such argument could be contemplated in the Peloponnesian League.

[6] The authors of *ATL* think its name was the "Lacedaemonians and their allies" (III, 97), which is consistent with their belief that it was merely an extension of the Peloponnesian League. Larsen (*op. cit.*, 177), on the other hand, thinks the new organization was called ἡ συμμαχία τῶν Ἑλλήνων. Brunt's arguments (*ibid.*, 145–146) seem decisive against both. It is hard not to agree with his statement that since the Serpent Column, which records the names of the members of the league against Persia, and is the only official document of that league that we have, has at its head merely "The following fought the war," we may conclude that no general name for the league was given, "because there was none to give." (146)

[7] Hdt. 7. 148; Diod. 11. 3. 4, περὶ τῆς κοινῆς ἐλευθερίας.

[8] Brunt, *op. cit.*, 157; Hdt. 7. 145 tells that the allies promised to "put an end to all their enmities and wars with each other."

some time. That the promise to fight for the common freedom included an obligation to free the Greek cities of the Aegean and its littoral is made clear by the admission of the Samians, Chians, and Lesbians into the league in 479 [9] and by the league's operations in the Hellespont under Pausanias. The question remains whether or not the alliance was meant to be perpetual. Our sources provide no positive statement that it was, but there is a good deal of evidence that in fact, and in the minds of the members, it persisted even into the Peloponnesian War. Almost twenty years after the formation of the league against Persia, when the Spartans were threatened with a helot rebellion, they called upon their allies for help. Among those who came were the Plataeans [10] and the Athenians.[11] When the Spartans became suspicious of the Athenians and sent them home, the Athenians "abandoned the alliance that they had made with them against the Mede." [12] As late as 427 the Spartans could justify their attack on Plataea by alleging that the Plataeans were in violation of the old treaty against the Persians in siding with the Athenians, who, they further argued, were enslaving Greeks. "Assert your own autonomy," the Spartans urged. "Help liberate the others who shared the dangers with you at that time [during the Persian Wars], swore the same oaths with you, and are now under Athenian rule." [13]

It is clear, then, that during the war against Persia the Greeks formed an alliance of unlimited duration for the purpose of defeating the enemy and winning and maintaining Greek freedom. The allies seem to have been bound to stay at peace with one another and to come to the assistance of a state under attack or in danger of

[9] Hdt. 9. 104.

[10] 3. 54. 5.

[11] 1. 102.

[12] *Idem.*

[13] 2. 72. 1. Larsen (*CP,* XXVIII [1933], 262–265 and *HSCP,* LI [1940], 175–213) believes that the continuing alliance was organized not in 481 but at Plataea in 479. He believes in the historicity of the Covenant of Plataea reported by Plutarch (*Arist.* 21. 1–2) and lately supported by A. E. Raubitschek (*TAPA,* XCI [1960], 178–183). The authors of the *ATL,* (III, 101–104) and Brunt (*op. cit.,* 153–156) regard the covenant described by Plutarch as spurious. For our purposes it is not important whether the continuing character of the Hellenic alliance originated in 481 or 479.

losing its freedom. Unlike the Peloponnesian League, the Hellenic alliance was not based on a series of separate treaties between the states and a hegemonal power. Instead, it was the product of a general covenant which was freely accepted but which did not permit secession. Sparta was chosen to be the hegemonal power, but her hegemony was of a different sort from that which she exercised in the Peloponnesian alliance. Although a Spartan was always commander in chief of any expedition, he needed the consent of the generals from the allied states to carry out his policy. On several occasions the Spartans were compelled to yield and carry out a policy that they did not approve. The covenant made no provision for regular meetings or for financial support. The league was a revolutionary innovation in the relations between the Greek states, made less shocking by the Persian emergency and certain similarities to the familiar Spartan alliance. Its goals and organization, however, were far vaguer than those of that alliance. Only experience would make clear what the true nature of the new league would be.[14]

Immediately after the Greek naval victory at Mycale, the Hellenic League was put to the test. The Ionian cities revolted from Persian rule and appealed to the league for support.[15] The challenge could not be avoided, for it was clear that the Greek force could not guard the rebels forever, yet if the Greeks departed, the Ionians would be left to face the vengeance of Persia. As early as this moment we can discern the disagreement among the Greeks that would soon split them into two hostile camps. The Peloponnesians argued that the Ionians should abandon their homelands and settle on land confiscated from Greeks who had sided with Persia. Even had this been possible, it could scarcely have appealed to the Ionians, who found a champion in the Athenians. The Athenians had an interest in the decision, for they had colonies in the area under discussion and were not eager to abandon them. They argued strongly against withdrawal and won their point. The rebellious islanders were sworn into the Hellenic League, and the Greeks set off for the Hellespont to destroy the bridges that Xerxes had built to connect Asia with

[14] For a discussion of the connection between this league and earlier types of organizations, see F. R. Wüst, *Historia,* III (1954–5), 129–153.

[15] Hdt. 9. 104.

Europe.[16] When the Greeks arrived they found that the Persians had broken the bridges. The Spartan king Leotychidas wasted no time in abandoning the campaign and returning to Greece. The Athenians, however, commanded by Xanthippus, remained to lay siege to the city of Sestus on the Chersonese.[17] It is at this point that Thucydides began his account of the growth of that Athenian power that he believed frightened Sparta into war. Sparta was still hegemon of the Hellenic League, but at the first test her traditional conservatism led her to abandon her responsibility. The new element was the demonstrated willingness of Athens to undertake the burden. The fall of Sestus within a few months proved her ability to do so successfully; Sparta was not the only state capable of providing leadership.[18]

Events in Athens now widened the schism. After the departure of the Persians, the Athenians brought back their families from Salamis, Aegina, and Troezen, where they had taken refuge, and began to rebuild their walls.[19] This was a perfectly reasonable action, for the destruction of their homes and temples would make any people eager to safeguard their city against a future attack. The Peloponnesians, moreover, had been reluctant to defend any cities north of the Isth-

[16] Hdt. 9. 106.

[17] Hdt. 9. 114.

[18] The change in leadership in the war against Persia after 478 is seen in quite a different way by H. D. Meyer (*Historia,* XII [1963], 405–446). In his view it was the result of an Athenian plot carried through in conjunction with Chios, Samos, and Lesbos. There is no space to refute his arguments here, but I find them unconvincing, for they take no note of domestic politics in Sparta and Athens and, most important, ignore the very real possibility that the threat from Persia was not ended and might at any time be realized by a new invasion. Another interesting study, which arrives at different conclusions from the ones offered here, is by R. Sealey (*ASI,* 233–255). In characteristically hardheaded fashion he cautions against an overly idealized view of Greek life. In his judgment, "the League of Delos was founded because of a dispute about booty and its purpose was to get more booty." Such a view is altogether too simple to fit the complicated motives of human actions. It is enough to point out that at least the Greeks of the Ionian mainland, who had just been freed from the Persians and were in imminent danger of reconquest, however many or few they may have been, were interested in something more than booty.

[19] 1. 89.

mus and gave little reason for confidence in a system of collective security based on unfortified cities. The Athenians had built walls round their city in the past without raising any complaints. The events of the Persian War, however, and particularly of the last winter, had changed the climate of Greek opinion. The Spartans, of course, generally preferred to see the Greek towns unwalled and thus more open to coercion by the threat of the Spartan phalanx.[20]

In their eagerness to put the war behind them and to return to normal conditions, the Spartans would probably have ignored the fortification of Athens, but their allies urged them to take action. The allies (Thucydides does not specify, but we may imagine they included Aegina and Megara, old enemies of Athens, and possibly Corinth as well) sent the Spartans to Athens to request that the Athenians should not rebuild their walls but should join them in a policy of razing all walls outside the Peloponnese. They gave the rather implausible grounds that this would deprive the Persians of fortified bases if they should undertake another expedition against Greece.[21] The real reason for the request was that the allies were afraid "of the size of the Athenian fleet, which had not previously been great, and of the daring that the Athenians had shown in the Persian War." [22]

The Athenians ignored the Spartan request and, thanks to the cleverness of Themistocles, were able to build their wall to a defensible height before anything could be done to hinder them. When word came that Athens was safely defended by her wall, Themistocles announced the fact to the Spartans and took the opportunity to apprise them of the new realities in the Hellenic world. Athens was now a walled city and able to protect its inhabitants. "If the Spartans or their allies wish to send embassies to us from now on, they must come with the understanding that we know very well what is in our own interest and in the general interest." [23] The wall was, in the judgment of Athens, advantageous to the Athenians and to all the

[20] 1. 90. 1.

[21] 1. 90. 1–2. As Gomme (*Hist. Comm.*, I, 258) puts it, "a poor excuse, for the possession of walled towns such as Thebes and Athens had not determined the strategy of the Persians."

[22] 1. 90. 1.

[23] 1. 91. 4–5.

allies, "for it is impossible to have an equal or similar weight in the common council except on the basis of equal military power." [24] This amounted to a declaration of independence from Spartan leadership and an assertion of equality in the conduct of the affairs of the Hellenic League. It opened the way for the foundation of the Delian League, but it also was the beginning of the suspicion and fear that would one day lead Sparta to make war on Athens. Up to that point the Spartans were very well disposed to Athens because of its role in the war against Persia. After the speech of Themistocles they showed no resentment and went home without making a formal complaint, "but they were secretly embittered." [25]

The assertiveness of Themistocles seems to have strengthened the influence of the Spartan faction, which favored continued Spartan leadership of the Hellenic campaign against Persia. In the withdrawal of Leotychidas after Mycale we may see the activity of the conservative faction, which was eager to give up extra-Peloponnesian adventures. No doubt they imagined that the Spartan withdrawal would mean the abandonment of the campaign and the return to tranquillity, whatever the cost to the Greek cities still under Persian rule. The Athenian assumption of command, the successful siege of Sestus, the fortification of Athens, and the bold declaration of equality by Themistocles must have damaged their cause among the people of Sparta. It must have been on a wave of anger and disillusionment that the war party came to power, reversed the policy that had recalled Leotychidas, and sent King Pausanias into the Aegean to reassert Spartan hegemony.[26] The immediate results were very pleasing. Spartan leadership was accepted by the Athenians without question, for among Pausanias' fleet were thirty ships from Athens. Pausanias attacked Cyprus, conquered most of it, and then took Byzantium from the Persians.[27]

At this point the influence of transcendent historical forces, whatever their weight at other times, yielded to the peculiarities of the individual. There is some reason to believe that the Spartans might have led the fight for freedom against Persia and maintained their

[24] 1. 91. 7.
[25] 1. 92. 1.
[26] 1. 94. 1.
[27] *Idem.*

undivided hegemony for some time had Pausanias' character been different. In fact, he was arrogant, tyrannical, and venal: "The commanders of the allies were treated with anger and harshness, while he punished the soldiers with whippings or by compelling them to stand all day carrying an iron anchor. No one could get bedding or food, or go down to the spring for water before the Spartans; their servants armed with whips drove away anyone who tried." [28] Small wonder that the Greeks from outside the Peloponnese, unaccustomed to Spartan arrogance, brought charges against Pausanias ranging from tyranny to treason. The Spartans were compelled to recall him and to put him on trial. For the Spartans this must have been more than merely an inquest into the alleged misconduct of a king. It could not avoid becoming a struggle over policy between the two factions. The war party was still strong enough to win an acquittal on the charge of treason and to have Dorcis sent out to replace Pausanias.[29] Their victory was less than complete, for Pausanias was held to account for the personal wrongs he had committed and, more important, the force sent with Dorcis was very small.[30]

The policy of the war party collapsed totally when the allies refused to accept Dorcis as their leader. He and his subordinates returned to Sparta, and the Spartans sent no substitute. Thucydides tells us that the Spartans feared a repetition of the Pausanias affair: "They also wanted to be rid of the Persian war and believed that the Athenians were competent to lead and were at the present time well disposed to the Spartans." [31] These must be the reasons offered by the peace party for the reversal of Spartan policy that they had brought about.

The Ionians and islanders who had been so affronted by Pausanias wasted no time in seeking a new leader. To understand the early history of the Delian League, we must remember that the initiative for its foundation came not from Athens but from those cities she would one day dominate. On the grounds of common Ionian kinship, they pleaded with the Athenians to take the hegemony and defend

[28] Plut. *Arist.* 23. 2–3.

[29] 1. 95. The argument in *ATL,* I, 192 that Dorcis was sent out to replace Pausanias immediately on the latter's recall in the summer of 478 is persuasive.

[30] Thuc. 1. 95. 6.

[31] 1. 95. 7.

them against Pausanias should the need arise.[32] Thucydides tells us plainly that Athens assumed the leadership by the will of the allies (ἑκόντων τῶν ξυμμάχων), and the evidence supports him.[33] It is clear that the Athenians required some degree of persuasion; leading the allies against Persia without Peloponnesian support, possibly in the face of Peloponnesian resentment, had some dangers. The Athenians could not know if the Ionians and islanders would prove loyal and willing to face the hardships and costs of the campaign. They were also wary lest the allies merely use them as a threat with which to persuade the Spartans to take a more vigorous role in the Aegean.

Such considerations must have shaped Aristides' reply to the Chians, Samians, Lesbians, and other allied captains who came to persuade the Athenians to accept the hegemony. He saw the need and the justice of their proposals, but insisted upon some action that would give the Athenians confidence in them and make it impossible for them to change sides again. Uliades of Samos and Antagoras of Chios immediately insulted Pausanias and drove him from Byzantium.[34] The die was cast, and the allies had proven their eagerness for Athenian leadership.

Their appeals did not fall on deaf ears. The Athenians were, in fact, glad to assume a leading role. It is plain that the tact and gentleness of the Athenian commanders, Aristides and Cimon, was calculated to exploit Pausanias' unpopularity to the advantage of Athens.[35] Herodotus spoke the simple truth when he said that the Athenians "offered the *hybris* of Pausanias as a pretext" when they took away the Spartan hegemony.[36] Their eagerness is not difficult to understand. The Aegean and its borders were outside the normal sphere of Sparta's interest, and involvement in that region was as dangerous to Sparta as it was inviting. For Athens the situation was quite different. Recent events had shown that in case of Persian attack Athens was vulnerable. The Athenian economy was increasingly dependent upon trade, a large part of it in the Aegean and in the Hellespontine region. A significant part of the grain eaten by the

[32] 1. 95. 1.
[33] 1. 96. 1. See Appendix A.
[34] Plut. *Arist.* 23. 4–5.
[35] Diod. 11. 46. 4–5; Plut. *Arist.* 23, *Cim.* 6.
[36] Hdt. 8. 3.

Athenians came from the Ukraine through the Hellespont and the Aegean. It was in large part for these reasons that Athens had planted colonies on the Chersonese in the sixth century. She could not allow the Hellespont and northern Aegean to remain in Persian hands or under threat of Persian control.[37] Athens, moreover, felt an emotional attachment to the Ionians, and their abandonment to Persian rule would have been difficult for Athenian politicians to justify.[38] Finally, coming on the heels of Marathon, Salamis could not fail to instill in the Athenians a new pride, confidence, and ambition, all of which are reflected in the speech of Themistocles to the Spartans. The needs of the allies, the conservative victory at Sparta, and the interests and ambitions of the Athenians all led to the formation of a new organization to fight Persia.

In the winter of 478/7 the allies met at Delos at what we might call a constitutional convention; Aristides the Athenian was probably chairman.[39] The assembly was probably made up of the commanders of the several allied contingents. The purposes of the new league were very much the same as those of the Hellenic League: to avenge Greek suffering by ravaging Persian territory [40] and to liberate those Greeks still under Persian rule.[41] But these were not the only goals, for the members swore to have the same friends and

[37] For a good recent account of Athenian economic developments in this period, see A. French, *The Growth of the Athenian Economy* (London, 1964), especially Chapter 3.

[38] Herodotus (6. 21) tells us that some time after the sack of Miletus by the Persians in 494, which put an end to the Ionian rebellion, Phrynichus presented a play on the subject which troubled the Athenians so much that the whole theatre broke into tears. They later fined the playwright "for reminding them of an evil that touched them so closely" and forbade the further presentation of the play. In the wake of the recent victory over Persia, no one could refuse to support the second Ionian rebellion.

[39] The convention (κοινὴ σύνοδος) is mentioned only by Diodorus (11. 47. 1). The discussion of the original constitution of the Delian League that follows depends chiefly on Larsen's article cited above and *ATL*, III, 225–233. Other useful accounts may be found in Victor Martin, *La vie internationale*, 145–185, and Busolt and Swoboda, *GS*, II, 1337–1360. Brunt (*op. cit.*) offers useful critical remarks on the views of Larsen and *ATL* as well as intelligent suggestions of his own. See also Raphael Sealey, *ASI*, 233–256.

[40] 1. 96. 1.

[41] 3. 10. 3.

enemies.[42] The permanence of the alliance was symbolized by the dropping of iron weights into the sea: the alliance was to last until the weights rose up again.[43]

It is important to notice that although the purposes of the Delian League were almost identical with those of the Hellenic League, the two leagues were not identical in membership, nor was the Delian League competent to act for the Hellenic League without Spartan consent.[44] The membership alone makes the difference very clear. The Hellenic League was composed of Peloponnesians, states from central Greece, and only later of states from the islands and Asia Minor. The Delian League included approximately twenty members from the islands, thirty-six from Ionia, thirty-five from the Hellespont, twenty-four from the region of Caria, and thirty-three from the region of Thrace.[45] It included no Peloponnesian cities but, "in the beginning, was primarily an organization of the Greek cities of the Aegean islands and the coast." [46] In the fourth century Aristotle could look back and see the formation of the Delian League as a "rebellion of the Ionians from the Spartan alliance," a judgment which was inexact but which indicates forcefully how completely independent the new league was from the old.

The true relation of the Delian League to the Hellenic League may be clearer to our generation than to an earlier one. It seems to have been General Alfred Gruenther who first compared the Delian League to NATO, and it is a useful analogy. As NATO is a regional organization, nominally within the principles of the United Nations Organization but really independent of it, composed of some UN members but very clearly excluding others, so too was the Delian League a regional organization, consisting of states who were also

[42] Arist. *Ath. Pol.* 23. 5.

[43] Arist. *Ath. Pol.* 23. 5; Plut. *Arist.* 25. 1. Larsen discusses previous opinion of the meaning of the ceremony in a footnote (*op. cit.*, 187, n. 5). Since Larsen wrote, Martin (*op. cit.*, 152, n. 1) has again doubted that it implied a permanent alliance. His arguments are refuted by Brunt (*op. cit.*, 150, n. 1). In this case the majority of scholars is certainly right in seeing the alliance as permanent.

[44] This is the view of Larsen, (*op. cit.*, 184). It is ably refuted in *ATL*, III, 231.

[45] The figures are calculated from the lists given in the *ATL*, III, 194–224.

[46] *ATL*, III, 224.

members of the Hellenic League but clearly excluding others. The Delian League no more required Spartan approval for its actions than NATO requires Russian approval for its. The Hellenic League might call on its Delian members for assistance and technically have the right to do so, just as the UN may call on its members for military or financial support. The hegemon of the former could not be confident of the response any more than the Secretary-General can today. After the foundation of the Delian League the Hellenic League had an increasingly shadowy existence and collapsed at the first real test.

The Delian League became increasingly significant because its purposes were essential to its members and because its organization was clearer, simpler, and more effective than either of the two interstate coalitions that had preceded it. The oaths that sealed the constitutional covenant were taken by Aristides for Athens, on the one hand, and by the Ionians, which means the allies,[47] on the other. From the beginning Athens was recognized as hegemon. The allies swore to have the same friends and enemies as Athens and also appointed the Athenian Aristides to assess the contributions of each state. They chose Athenians only as the financial officials of the league,[48] and Athenian generals commanded all league campaigns.

Hegemony was not domination. In the early period of the league, at least, the Athenians exercised what Thucydides called a "hegemony over autonomous allies who participated in common synods." [49] It is clear that sessions of the synod determined policy in the early history of the league and decided what should be done about recalcitrant or rebellious states. In this synod all members, including Athens, the hegemon, had only one vote.[50] In theory Athens was only an equal partner in the synod, no stronger politically than Samos, Lesbos, or even Seriphos. In fact, the system of equal votes, as the Mytileneans were later to point out, worked in Athens' favor.

[47] *ATL,* III, 227, n. 9.

[48] Walker (*CAH,* V, 46) believes that in the beginning the Hellenotamiae were not Athenian but Delian. For a convincing refutation of this argument, see *ATL,* III, 230, n. 26.

[49] 1. 97. 1.

[50] This is made clear by the speech of the Mytileneans in Thuc. 3. 10–11. The best discussions of the organization and operation of the synod may be found in Larsen, *op. cit.,* 192–197 and *ATL,* III, 138–141.

The greatness of Athenian naval and military power combined with Athens' enormous prestige guaranteed that the numerous small and powerless states would be under her influence, while the larger states such as Samos, Mytilene, Chios, and Thasos, who might have challenged Athenian domination, were easily outvoted. As the Mytileneans put it, "The allies were unable to unite to defend themselves because of the great number of voters."[51] From the beginning, then, Athens was in the happy position of dominating the Delian League without the appearance of illegality or tyranny.

Whatever the disadvantages of such an arrangement, it had one enormous advantage: the league could act swiftly and decisively. There could be no defection on the brink of a campaign such as the one by Corinth that had halted Cleomenes' attack on Athens. As Pericles implied, it was different from the Spartan alliance because it had a common political assembly that could quickly collect to take emergency action.[52] Athens, moreover, had and used the power to see that league decisions were carried out. The hegemonal power collected the contributions to the league treasury strictly and punished refusal to participate in campaigns.[53] The league, unlike its predecessors, even forbade private wars among its members, and Athens punished transgressors.[54]

The Delian League represented an advance over the Spartan alliance in another important aspect: its financial arrangements. Up to the conflict with Athens the Spartan alliance had little need for money. Campaigns were almost always on land, and the Spartans demanded from their allies only that they send the required military contingents. In the forth century the Spartans sometimes required money payments, but the character of their alliance guaranteed that these were for a special purpose and would not continue after the campaign was over. The Delian League, on the contrary, was chiefly a naval confederation whose purposes required that it maintain a fleet in being for an indefinite period. This was a costly undertaking and demanded a well-organized system for regular payments into the league treasury. Athens was given the responsibility of making the

[51] 3. 10. 5.
[52] 1. 41. 6.
[53] 1. 99. 1; 6. 76. 3.
[54] 6. 76. 3; Larsen, *op. cit.,* 188–190.

assessment and of collecting the money. Until 454/3 the treasury was at Delos; after that date it was transferred to Athens. From the beginning there was a distinction between those states who provided ships and manned them and those who paid money in lieu of serving themselves. The burden of providing, manning, and maintaining ships varied with necessity but was often heavier on those who did so than on those who merely paid money and received protection. Heaviest of all was the burden borne by Athens, which not only provided leadership but the largest fleet as well, which she manned and maintained. No doubt, booty collected from the Persians was expected to, and did, meet some of the cost, but the expenditure of time, effort, and lives was not insignificant. We can well understand why "most of the allies allowed their assessments to be changed from ships to money because of their reluctance to embark on military campaigns and so that they might not be away from home." [55] Of course, as the allies shrank from responsibility, the Athenians accepted more of it. This centralizing tendency helped make the league more effective against external enemies, but it led to a gradual but decisive change in the nature of the organization.

By the time of the Peloponnesian War, Athenian statesmen were willing to admit that the Delian League had become an empire and that Athens ruled it as a tyrant.[56] Although we may agree with Thucydides that "the allies themselves were responsible" [57] for the transition to empire, it is important to see how the change took place and by what means the Athenians imposed their will. The first recorded action of the league was the siege of Eion undertaken under the command of Cimon in the autumn of 477.[58] In the next year it was taken from the Persians, and its inhabitants were enslaved.[59] This action was clearly a legitimate step in the war against

[55] 1. 99. 3.

[56] 2. 63. 3.

[57] 1. 99.

[58] 1. 98. 1. For the date, see *ATL,* III, 175–179.

[59] 1. 98. 1. Since Thucydides uses the word ἠνδραπόδισαν, we may be confident that the citizens of Eion were literally enslaved. He often uses δουλεύειν, which can mean the same thing, but when he applies it to cities rather than individuals, it means political subordination, the absence of autonomy, rather than personal slavery. For a clear explanation of Thucydides' use of δουλεύειν, see *ATL,* III, 155–177.

Persia and must have caused no problem. In the same year the forces of the league captured the Aegean island of Scyros, which was inhabited by Dolopians. They were enslaved and an Athenian cleruchy was established on the island.[60] Although the Athenians profited from this expedition, the allies seem not to have objected, and in fact, they had reason to be pleased. The Dolopians who lived on Scyros were a semibarbarous people who made their living by piracy. When the Athenians expelled them, "they liberated the Aegean." [61] The establishment of an Athenian colony was a good way to guarantee continued freedom from piracy in that quarter of the Aegean.

Some time in the next few years the league launched an expedition against Carystus on the island of Euboea. This city was neither under Persian control like Eion nor a pirate state like Scyros, and, so far as we know, it had committed no action to merit an attack. On the other hand, the Carystians had fought on the Persian side in the recent war and so could expect little sympathy from the allies. The usual assumption is that Carystus had held aloof from the Delian League and that this expedition was undertaken to compel her to join.[62] This is supported by Thucydides' statement that the Carystians were not backed by the other Euboean states and finally capitulated on terms.[63] Carystus later appears on the tribute lists as a member making regular money payments. This is the first case of compulsion used to force a state into the league, and it surely had general approval. Apart from the unpopularity of the Medizing Carystians, there were other reasons for the campaign. It would scarcely seem fair that a city should benefit from the league's war against the Persians and its protection from piracy, while allowing its neighbors to bear the cost. The Athenians acted with the support of the league, but the use of compulsion was ominous.

About 470 the island of Naxos, an original member, rebelled from the league. Thucydides does not tell us the reason for this rebellion,

[60] Thucydides (1. 98. 2) says merely *ᾤκισαν αὐτοί*, but Diodorus (11. 60. 2) makes it clear that it was a cleruchy, the first that we know to have been established under the League.

[61] Plut. *Cim.* 8. 3–6.

[62] *ATL*, III, 198; Gomme, *Hist. Comm.*, I, 281–282.

[63] 1. 98. 3.

only that after it had been reduced by siege Naxos was "the first allied city to be subjugated [ἐδουλώθη] in violation of the covenant."[64] We are not told precisely what that means, but it seems likely that Naxos was forbidden a navy and thus would thereafter pay tribute instead of supplying ships and men. Perhaps she received a garrison; perhaps she had some land confiscated, as well as her ships; and possibly an Athenian cleruchy was settled on the confiscated land.[65] Once again we may be sure that Athens had acted with the approval of the league. Rebellion could not be allowed or the alliance would soon disintegrate. But once more Athens emerged stronger than before, having placed violent hands upon fellow Greeks.

Thucydides uses the attack on Naxos as the occasion for a general account of the change in the nature of the league that makes it clear that Naxos was not the only state in rebellion and that increasingly harsh treatment of rebels was the rule. The rebellions came about when members were unwilling or unable to pay tribute, supply ships, or do military service; the Athenians were strict in the collection of tribute and the exaction of service. The demeanor of the Athenian commanders changed as well. The Athenians had gained the hegemony, we are told, in no small measure because of the mildness and tact of such men as Aristides, Xanthippus, and Cimon. Cimon was still on the scene, but the behavior and manner of the Athenian commanders changed with the new circumstances. "The Athenians were no longer equally pleasant as leaders. They no longer behaved as equals on campaigns, and they found it easy to reduce states that had rebelled." [66] From the allied point of view, the rebellions and reductions produced a vicious circle. As each rebellious state was forced to give up her fleet and to pay tribute, it became weaker and Athens proportionately stronger. "The Athenian fleet was increased by their payments, while whenever they themselves revolted, they set about the war without preparation and without experience." [67]

The growing discontent of the allies must have been increased by Cimon's great victory over the Persians at the Eurymedon River on

[64] 1. 98. 4. I follow Classen in thinking that τὸ καθεστηκός means the covenant of the league. See also Gomme, *Hist. Comm.*, I, 282.

[65] *ATL*, III, 156–157.

[66] 1. 99. 2.

[67] 1. 99. 3.

the Anatolian coast in 469.[68] The victory was so decisive, the damage to the Persians so great, the booty collected so considerable, as to lead some to believe that the alliance against Persia, with its burdensome payments and service, might no longer be necessary. The Athenians thought otherwise, and they may have been right, for the Persians had certainly not abandoned the Aegean.[69] The allies nevertheless became increasingly restive, and more compulsion became necessary.

In 465 the island of Thasos, a charter member of the league and a rich and powerful naval state, revolted. The causes of this rebellion were quite different from those that seem to have brought on the Naxian uprising. The Thasians broke away because of a disagreement with the Athenians over some trading stations on the Thracian coast opposite Thasos and a mine that the Thasians owned in the same area.[70] These holdings were very rich and their control by Athens would be a great blow to Thasos. At the same time the Athenians were establishing a colony of ten thousand Athenians and their allies at Ennea Hodoi, the site of the future Amphipolis, near the Thracian coast across from Thasos. To be sure, this was an undertaking of the league and made good strategic sense as a base against the Macedonians, but it was probably the foundation of this colony, which would extend Athenian influence to the neighborhood of Thasos, that brought on the rebellion.[71] The colony was abandoned after the colonists suffered a serious defeat at the hands of the natives, but Thasos underwent a siege that lasted for more than two years. When the Thasians surrendered they were forced to take down their walls, give up their ships, the Thracian coast, and the mine to the Athenians, to pay an immediate indemnity, and thereafter to pay tribute.[72] This was the harshest treatment yet imposed; it obviously brought great profit to the Athenians and could not help adding to their unpopularity. It must have been not long after

[68] 1. 100. 1; Plut. *Cim.* 12–14; Diod. 11. 60–62.

[69] Diodorus (11. 62) tells us that right after the battle the Persians, "fearing the growing power of Athens," set about building a great number of new triremes.

[70] 1. 100. 2.

[71] *ATL,* III, 258.

[72] 1. 101. 3.

the fall of Thasos that the situation in the alliance began to reach the condition described by Diodorus:

> In general, the Athenians were making great gains in power and no longer treated their allies with decency as they had done before; instead they ruled with arrogance and violence. For this reason most of the allies could not bear their harshness and spoke to one another of rebellion; some of them even disdained the league council and acted according to their own wishes.[73]

The independence and open defiance implied by the last sentence was, of course, impossible so long as Athens was undistracted. By 462, however, the Athenians were embroiled in a struggle with Sparta on the mainland. Throughout fifteen years she would be involved in a war on land and sea, ranging from Egypt and the eastern Mediterranean to the mainland of Greece. In these circumstances some disaffection was inevitable; the "Crisis of Athenian Imperialism" [74] was at hand. Under the pressure of war and rebellion the Athenians turned to ever harsher means to assure their control of the league. In the process they converted it into an empire.

[73] 11. 70. 3–4.

[74] This apt description is the title of an important article by Russell Meiggs (*HSCP*, LXVII [1963], 1–36).

3. *Sparta after the Persian War*

The Spartan decision to abandon the leadership of the Aegean campaign against Persia had not been taken lightly. An unfortunate combination of circumstances had brought it about, and we may be sure that it left many Spartans dissatisfied. The Persian War had brought Sparta power, influence, and respect unprecedented among the Greek states, but it had also produced a formidable rival to its unique position of leadership. It had offered tempting opportunities for an extension of Spartan influence and power as well as a chance to gain great wealth, but it also brought the prospect of heavy military responsibilities far from the Peloponnese and the danger of corruption in its officials and in its very way of life. Not only the foreign policy of Sparta but its constitution and culture were at stake in the policy debates in the years following the war.

There were, in fact, three choices available to the Spartans. The most ambitious would be to strive for the absolute hegemony over the Greeks by land and sea which Sparta had enjoyed during the war. There can be no doubt that this policy had the support of many Spartans, but it was defeated, for the time being at least, by the disgrace of Pausanias. The most conservative policy would have been to act as though the war had not taken place, to give up all ambitions outside the Peloponnese, and to concentrate on consolidating the Spartan alliance and maintaining the ancestral constitution. The advocates of this policy certainly supported the withdrawal of Pausanias and Dorcis, but their strictly Peloponnesian policy was not immediately victorious. The pride and glory won at Plataea and

Mycale were too fresh in everyone's memory to be so totally abandoned. There was a third possibility: to abandon the war on the sea, for which Sparta was not well suited, and to seek a field for Spartan influence on the Greek mainland, among the Medizers of Thessaly and central Greece. Such a policy would tacitly accept a dualism in the Greek world: Sparta would dominate the mainland, and Athens would control the Aegean. Such an arrangement would not conflict with the continuance of the Hellenic League, in which Sparta could expect to retain her primacy. It was this last policy that the Spartans chose in the years immediately after the Persian War.

It was probably in the spring of 476 that the Spartans moved to put this policy into effect.[1] They sent an expedition to Thessaly under King Leotychidas, the victor of Mycale, to put down the reigning family, the Aleuadae.[2] It was the perfect method for implementing the continental program, for the Aleuadae were Medizers, and Sparta's campaign could be seen as a patriotic obligation for the leaders of the Hellenic League, which had sworn to punish the traitors. At the same time it offered a splendid opportunity to spread Spartan influence on the Greek mainland. Leotychidas was successful on the battlefield, deposing the Thessalian princes Aristomedes and Angelos. All Thessaly lay before him, but once again the venality of a Spartan king undid the success of Spartan arms. Leotychidas accepted bribes from the Aleuadae, was brought back to Sparta for trial, and went into voluntary exile in Tegea.

It was surely as part of the same policy that the Spartans proposed the exclusion from the Amphictyonic League of all states that had not fought against Persia.[3] Their chief targets were Thessaly, Thebes, and Argos, whose exclusion would guarantee Spartan domination of the important religious organizations of continental Greece. It would be a mistake to underestimate the political importance of these religious associations. We shall see that even Athens was con-

[1] It is not possible to establish the date of Leotychidas' expedition to Thessaly with absolute certainty, but I find the arguments of Busolt, *GG*, III: 1, 83, n. 1, and Grote (*A History of Greece* [4th ed.; London, 1872], IV, 349, n. 1) persuasive. Cf. Eduard Meyer, *GdA*, IV: 1, 489–490 and 490, n. 1.

[2] Hdt. 6. 72; Paus. 3. 7. 8; Plut. *De Mal. Herod.* 859 D.

[3] Plut. *Them.* 20. 3–4.

cerned to establish a religious basis for her imperial hegemony. This proposal of Sparta's was intended to provide a similar basis for her own ambitions on the continent. Unfortunately, Athens, in the person of Themistocles, intervened to thwart Sparta again. It is clear that his speech in behalf of the cities threatened with exclusion changed the course of the debate and defeated the Spartan motion. For this action especially, Plutarch tells us, the Spartans came to hate him and began to support his rival Cimon.[4]

The skill of Themistocles and the venality of Leotychidas had put a check to the expansion of Sparta into central and northern Greece, but the agitation for an active policy outside the Peloponnese was not yet silenced. The conflict over policy was in part a conflict of generations; the young Spartans who had thrilled to the joy of victory and had seen the opulence and comparative luxury of cities not bound by the laws of Lycurgus were not eager to subside into the austere confines of Laconia and the Peloponnese. Diodorus records a debate in Sparta in 475 that reveals the division in Spartan opinion.[5] There were many who thought that Sparta had lost the hegemony of the sea without any reason; they were angry with the states who had fallen away from them and joined the Athenian alliance. At a meeting of the gerousia they proposed a war against Athens to regain control of the sea, and at a meeting of the assembly to consider the proposal, the youth of Sparta and a majority of the other members were eager to regain naval hegemony. Diodorus outlines the reasons for their enthusiasm: as naval hegemon, "they would enjoy great wealth, Sparta would become greater and more powerful, and the houses of the private citizens would receive a great increase in their prosperity."[6] The appeal of these frankly imperialistic goals almost carried the day, but at the crucial moment Hetoemaridas, a venerable man of noble lineage and respected character, rose in opposition. We are told merely that he advised that Athens be allowed to keep her naval hegemony, "since it was not advantageous to Sparta to dispute over the sea."[7] Diodorus does not tell us what arguments he offered in support of this advice, but to

[4] *Idem.*

[5] Diod. 11. 50. See Appendix B.

[6] 11. 50. 3–4.

[7] μὴ συμφέρειν γὰρ τῇ Σπάρτῃ τῆς θαλάττης ἀμφισβητεῖν 11. 50. 6.

the general surprise it was adopted, and Sparta gave up all thought of a war against Athens.

The story is important, for it shows us clearly the strength and the purposes of the imperial party at Sparta, a party that never failed to play a role in Spartan affairs. The general conservatism of the Spartans should not blind us to the tension within the Spartan state. Strong discipline and tradition prevented the success of the imperial policy most of the time, but the pressure of the imperialists was constant and, on occasion, decisive. Normally the imperialists could not hope to succeed without the leadership of an able king who shared their views. A Cleomenes, a Pausanias, an Agesilaus, or, in unusual circumstances, an almost royal subject like Lysander was needed to defeat the powerful forces of tradition and inertia.

In 475, however, circumstances combined to support inertia. Both Spartan kings, Pausanias and Leotychidas, able generals and ambitious imperialists, had disgraced themselves and discredited their policies. The vacuum caused by their downfall was filled by the respected elders of the gerousia, who were suspicious of the dangers and the corrupting influence of an ambitious foreign policy. They trusted Athens because they had confidence in her leaders, men like Aristides and Cimon. If Themistocles had been in control of Athenian policy, it seems likely that he would have offered some provocation that would have played into the hands of the anti-Athenian forces at Sparta. But Cimon, supported by Sparta, was firmly in control at Athens, proof of the wisdom of the Spartan peace party.

Themistocles, of course, was a lingering threat to Sparta and to its friends in Athens. It was probably about the time when the Spartans were discussing their policy towards Athens or a little earlier that they tried to get rid of Themistocles.[8] They incited the

[8] The chronology of the career of Themistocles is a notoriously difficult question on which there is little agreement. Busolt (*GG*, III: 1, 112, n. 2) provides a useful and detailed discussion, but I believe that the evidence is not such as to produce certainty. With some hesitation I accept the chronology offered by Robert J. Lenardon (*Historia*, V [1956], 401–419 and VIII [1959], 23–48) whose discussion carefully considers all the evidence and analyzes the modern scholarship as well. For my purpose here, the absolute chronology is not very important; all that is required is the relation of the important events to one another. The sequence I advocate, a trial at Athens brought on by the Spartans in which Themistocles is acquitted on a charge

enemies of Themistocles to lodge an accusation of treason against him, providing them with money and with testimony that he was implicated in the crimes of Pausanias. Perhaps the Spartan involvement was too obvious or the recollection of Themistocles' great deeds too fresh; he was acquitted and his popularity enhanced.[9] This turn of events must have alarmed his enemies. They combined against him and succeeded in ostracizing him.[10] Far from putting an end to Spartan troubles, the ostracism only aggravated them. Themistocles went to live in Argos and visited other places in the Peloponnese as well.[11] As Beloch put it, "These were not pleasure trips"[12] and caused Sparta much anguish. In Argos itself a democracy was introduced to replace the oligarchy that had ruled since the Persian War.[13] The vigor produced by the new constitution soon made itself felt in foreign affairs. The Argive democrats determined to restore the power and prestige of their city, and within a few years they had, in one way or another, reduced Mycenae, Tiryns, Cleonae, Hysiae, Mideia and Orneae. The Argolid had been unified under Argive control, and Sparta was faced with a formidable threat on her eastern flank.[14]

At the same time the winds of change were blowing in the north-

---

of Medism and bribetaking, the ostracism of Themistocles, his activities in the Peloponnese, another Spartan accusation, and the flight of Themistocles to Persia, is supported by Grote, (IV, 370–372) and Lenardon, among others.

[9] Diod. 11. 54.

[10] Thuc. 1. 135. 3; Diod. 11. 55. 3; Plut. *Them.* 22, *Cim.* 10, *Arist.* 25; Nepos, *Them.* 8; Plato *Gorgias* 516 D. For a discussion of the political union against Themistocles, see Busolt, *GG,* III: 1, 110–112.

[11] 1. 135.

[12] *GG* ², II: 1, 146, n. 20.

[13] It is impossible to date the introduction of democracy into Argos with precision. We know merely that an oligarchy ruled in Argos up to the Persian War, and that by the time of the Peace of Nicias a democracy had replaced it. Most scholars agree that the democracy was introduced between the Persian War and the alliance between Argos and Athens in 461 (Busolt, *GG,* III: 1, 113–114 and 114, n. 3). With Glotz and Cohen (*HG,* 123), I associate the establishment of democracy with the arrival of Themistocles. Probably the democratic spirit spreading through the Peloponnese had already changed the Argive constitution, and this led him to choose Argos as a refuge. For a different interpretation and chronology, see W. G. Forrest, *CQ,* N.S., X (1960), 221–241.

[14] Diod. 11. 65; Strabo 8, p. 373; Thuc. 5. 47 and 77.

western Peloponnese. Elis, once a quiet region divided among several small villages, was now unified into a single state. The region thereafter grew in prosperity, population, and power.[15] It is clear that the unification was the result of a democratic movement that had made its way even to pastoral Elis.[16] The Eleian democrats, like their Argive equivalents, were ambitious and aggressive. Before long they had begun the conquest of Tryphilia on the border of Messenia. Unlike their oligarchic predecessors, they were not friendly to Sparta but sought friendship with states of similar constitutional organization, like Argos and Athens.

To these Peloponnesian disturbances around this time was added the unification of Mantinea in Arcadia, once again brought about by a democratic faction hostile to Sparta.[17] It is hard to believe that Themistocles, living in Argos and traveling to other Peloponnesian states, had nothing to do with these developments. It is not likely, however, that he had anything to do with bringing newly democratic Argos together with its old enemy Tegea. That unlikely alliance seems to have been the result of an assertion of Tegean independence in the face of Spartan disrepute and apparent weakness. The Tegeans had sheltered Leotychidas when he fled from Sparta, and they could not have won many Spartan friends in so doing. Perhaps they feared a Spartan reprisal; in any event, they concluded a treaty with the Argives. Sparta responded by attacking Tegea and, after a hard battle in which Tegea was supported by Argos, defeated the enemy.

Very shortly thereafter Spartan hegemony was tested by a revolt of all the Arcadian cities except Mantinea. Once again the Spartan phalanx was successful against a numerically superior opponent.[18] With the advantage of hindsight, we now know that this victory put an end to unrest in the Peloponnese for some time, but to the Spartans the extent of their success was not yet apparent. It seems very likely that they tried to strengthen their hold over the allies at this time by introducing the *xenagoi,* Spartan officials who supervised allied contingents, led them to the appointed rendezvous, and as-

[15] Diod. 11. 54; Paus. 5. 4. 3; Strabo 8, p. 336.

[16] Busolt and Swoboda, *GS,* I, 156 and n. 1; Busolt, *GG,* III: 1, 117.

[17] Strabo 8, p. 337; Busolt, *GG,* III: 1, 118–119.

[18] Hdt. 9. 35; Paus. 3. 11. 7; Busolt, *GG,* III: 1, 120–123 and 121, n. 1.

signed them to their battle stations.[19] This tightening of discipline within the Spartan alliance offered little protection against subversion within the allied cities, and so the Spartans directed their attention to a major instigator of revolutionary activities, Themistocles. They claimed to have evidence of his complicity in the treasonable activities of Pausanias and demanded that he should be tried before the Hellenic League. This was at once an attack on a dangerous enemy and a reminder to the Greeks that the Hellenic League was still alive and that a revitalized Sparta still claimed leadership over it. The Athenians were persuaded to surrender Themistocles for trial, which would have meant sure condemnation in a body always dominated by Sparta. Athenian officials, accompanied by Spartans, were sent out to arrest him and bring him to trial, but he was warned in advance and fled, first to Corcyra and ultimately to a position of honor and safety with the Great King.[20] From the Spartan point of view, Themistocles' exile was quite satisfactory, for it removed the fomenter of revolution from the Peloponnese and allowed Sparta to consolidate its military gains, restore its hegemony in the Peloponnese, and repair its damaged prestige.[21]

To the peace party, the events of the years since the great debate of 475 must have fully vindicated its conservative policy. There had been troubles enough in the Peloponnese to occupy the limited Spartan forces without begging for more in a struggle against Athens. The end to adventurous policies had also brought an end to corruption and immorality in the highest places. By no means least important, confidence in the Athenians had been fully justified. They had taken no part in the Peloponnesian uprisings, had given no aid to

[19] Busolt and Swoboda, *GS,* II, 1323 and 1335.

[20] Thuc. 1. 135–138; Diod. 11. 54–56; Plut. *Them.* 23–29.

[21] The foregoing account assumes, with Busolt, that the Spartan victories at Tegea and Dipaea took place in the late 470's. A. Andrewes (*Phoenix,* VI [1952], 1–5) places the Battle of Tegea shortly before the outbreak of the helot rebellion of 465 and Dipaea a short time after it. W. G. Forrest (*CQ,* N.S., X [1960], 229–232) puts Tegea in 469 and Dipaea after the helot rebellion. Although there can be no certainty, I continue to prefer Busolt's arguments, but even if both battles took place as late as 465, our main argument is not seriously affected. We would merely need to say that the Spartans moved against Themistocles before his work in the Peloponnese had taken full effect.

the new democracies, and had been quite ready to turn Themistocles over to Spartan vengeance. Sparta, it could be argued, might now look forward to a return to the peace and quiet of the prewar period, to its virtuous ancestral ways, to a secure Peloponnesian hegemony, defended from barbarian attack by a trusted and reliable Athens. The more militant Spartans might point out that it was an Athenian Themistocles who was at the root of many of their recent troubles and that it was the democratic movement begun in Athens that had revolutionized the Peloponnese. They might be jealous of Athenian prestige and chafe at the need for Athenian good-will to preserve Spartan security, but as long as friends of Sparta ruled at Athens, their cause was not hopeful. The hope of maintaining the new balance of power created by the Persian War rested on the Pnyx, the hill where the Athenian democracy chose its leaders and determined the policies of its state.

4. *Athens after the Persian War*

In Athens there had been no opposition to participation in the Delian League and to continued war against Persia. Themistocles, his political opponents Aristides and Xanthippus, and the rising young politician Cimon all played a leading role in the foundation and early growth of an active policy in the Aegean. If Themistocles was the father of the naval policy, it was Aristides who won over the allegiance of the allies and presided over the formation of the league and the assessment of the tribute, Xanthippus who took command of the first campaigns in the Hellespont, and Cimon who vigorously led the subsequent expeditions.

Like the Spartans, the Athenians could choose from three courses of action: they might refuse to involve themselves in any further action after Plataea and Mycale; they could try to exploit their new power and prestige to dominate all the Greek lands; or they might seek hegemony in the Aegean, leaving the mainland and the west to others. The first option had no supporters, but there was significant disagreement over the other two. The situation in Greece after the Persian War bears some resemblance to the condition of the victorious alliance after the Second World War. In each instance necessity had thrown together two states burdened with mutual suspicion. Differing opinions on war aims, strategy, and tactics had appeared during the war, but as long as there was a common enemy, these differences were muted. In each state some thought the differences transitory and hoped for a solution through mutual trust and accommodation. In each state others considered the differences impossible of settlement and conflict inevitable. They sought, if not to bring on war immediately, at least to achieve the best possible strategic position for the inevitable clash. In the more recent experience, the "cold warriors" won in both Russia and the United States; in Greece, "peaceful coexistence" was victorious in both Athens and Sparta.

Themistocles was the leader of the faction favoring an aggressive Athenian policy. He tricked Sparta into permitting Athens to build defensive walls and fortify the Piraeus. He continued to sponsor a program of shipbuilding and encouraged the immigration of foreign craftsmen to provide the necessary skilled labor.[1] He was the leading advocate and exemplar of a hard policy toward the allies. Even before Mycale he had ruthlessly extorted money from the islanders of the Aegean. By threat of force he obtained contributions from Carystus and Paros as well as other islands.[2] The plucky citizens of Andros resisted Themistocles' bullying. To his assertion that they must pay because Athens was aided by the two great gods Persuasion and Necessity, the Andrians replied that they too had powerful indigenous gods—Poverty and Helplessness: "Possessed by these gods, we Andrians will not pay, for the power of Athens can never be stronger than our inability." [3] If we interpret the lyrics of Timocreon correctly, Themistocles' exactions were felt as far as Rhodes, where he interfered in the internal politics of the island as well.[4]

It is possible that Themistocles, who certainly had personal connections in western Greece, Italy, and Sicily, had plans for extending Athenian influence to those regions,[5] and that he conceived a plan to make Athens not just the greatest, but the only, naval power in Greece by a single treacherous stroke.[6] The authority for both these conjectures is suspect, but there is little doubt that Themistocles' aim was unchallenged supremacy for Athens over all the Greeks, a policy hostile toward Sparta. We have seen that the arrogance of his reply to the Spartans' objection to the fortification of Athens and the

[1] Diod. 11. 43. 3.

[2] Hdt. 8. 112.

[3] Hdt. 8. 111; Plut. *Them.* 21. 1.

[4] Timocreon is quoted by Plutarch (*Them.* 21. 1).

[5] The little evidence we have is collected and probably exaggerated by Glotz and Cohen (*HG*, II, 55–56).

[6] Plut. *Them.* 20. 1–2.

Piraeus embittered the Spartans and that his success in frustrating Sparta's attempt to drive Medizing states from the amphictyony further enraged them. The continued supremacy of Themistocles would ultimately mean war with Sparta.

Whatever the differences among other Athenian politicians, there was general agreement in opposing Themistocles. It might be expected that Aristides and Xanthippus, old enemies of Themistocles who had suffered ostracism at his hands, might resume their rivalry after the end of the emergency, but they were joined by other powerful noblemen. Cimon, the son of that Miltiades who had been heavily fined by an Athenian court and had died in prison, leaving his children burdened with the unpaid debt, joined in the coalition with the same Xanthippus who had been his father's prosecutor.[7] He had married off his sister Elpinice to Callias, the son of Hipponicus, the richest man in Athens, and brought him into the coalition.[8] He himself married Isodice, an Alcmaeonid, and it was Leobotes, son of Alcmaeon, who brought the charge that sent Themistocles into exile.[9] This union of Philaids with Alcmaeonids and Kerykes, which united old enemies among the richest and most influential families, has led some scholars to believe that the social question was paramount in Athenian politics at this time. They see Themistocles as the champion of democracy and his downfall as the product of a conservative coalition.[10] The facts do not seem to warrant such a conclusion. The Alcmaeonid Cleisthenes founded the Athenian democracy, and the Alcmaeonid Pericles fostered its development; there is no reason to think that the intervening Alcmaeonids opposed it. Aristides was certainly no enemy of a democratic Athens.[11] Whatever his private feelings, Cimon worked within the framework of the Athenian democracy, thrived as a popularly elected leader, and opposed no democratic proposals until Ephialtes' attack on the Areopagus in 462. It is plain that an attempt to check or reverse the

[7] Hdt. 6. 136.

[8] Plut. *Cim.* 4. 7; Athen. 589e; Nepos *Cim.* 1. 3–4.

[9] Plut. *Cim.* 4. 9; 16. 1; *Them.* 23. 1. In *Arist.* 25, Plutarch erroneously calls Alcmaeon the accuser. See Busolt *GG,* III: 1, 110–111.

[10] Busolt, *GG,* III: 1, 110–111; Glotz and Cohen, *HG,* II, 122.

[11] Arist. *Ath. Pol.* 23. 3 and 24. 3; Plut. *Arist.* 22. 1.

development of democracy in Athens was not the major aim of the coalition against Themistocles.

Equally unpersuasive is the associated charge that the social consequences of Themistocles' naval policy produced opposition. Later critics might charge that by turning the Athenians toward the sea, "he increased the authority of the demos as opposed to the nobles and filled them with presumption, since power now had come to sailors and boatswains and pilots," [12] but we have seen that his opponents supported the naval policy. Even before the Battle of Salamis, when Themistocles was trying to persuade the Athenians to abandon Attica and fight the Persians on the sea, Cimon led a band of his friends up to the Acropolis and dedicated his horse's bridle to Athena as a symbol of his support of the naval policy.[13]

It is clear that the major issue dividing the coalition from Themistocles was the policy of Athens toward Sparta. It must have been apparent to all his opponents that the safe and expedient course was to maintain friendly relations with the Spartans and to encourage their acquiescence to the emergence of Athens as the hegemonal power in the Aegean and the leader of the war against Persia.

For this policy Cimon was the natural leader. Young and vigorous, a brilliant campaigner on land and sea, wealthy and of noble stock, he would in any case have been a natural candidate for high position in the state. His patriotism and devotion to an ambitious foreign policy in the Aegean were beyond question. His gentle and pleasant demeanor, as well as his generosity, endeared him to the people. But what especially made him influential was his special relationship with Sparta. In manner, speech, and training he resembled a Spartan more than an Athenian; he named one of his sons Lacedaemonius; he was the Spartan *proxenus,* their formal representative, in Athens. Small wonder that the Spartans, in spite of his youth, supported him as the leading opponent of Themistocles.

Plutarch is certainly right when he reports that the Athenians were happy to see the favor the Spartans showed Cimon, for they received considerable benefit from the friendly relations he maintained.[14] Athens was left in peace as her fleet went about the business

[12] Plut. *Them.* 19. 4.
[13] Plut. *Cim.* 5. 2.
[14] Plut. *Cim.* 16.

of converting the Delian League into an Athenian empire. At the same time the steady and reliable policy of Cimon enabled the conservative party at Sparta to control their more ambitious opponents. The victory of Cimon and the defeat of Themistocles meant that, for the time being at least, Athens was content with a division of Greece into two spheres of influence. Like the enemies of Athens at Sparta, the enemies of Sparta at Athens had been neither destroyed nor convinced. As long as nothing disturbed the supremacy of Cimon in Athens and the peace party at Sparta, they could only wait.

If we are right in thinking that Themistocles was ostracized in 473, then Cimon's supremacy met with no serious challenge for about a decade. At the end of that time a new generation of politicians emerged to challenge his leadership and his policies. The first hints of trouble appeared during the Thasian campaign. After the Thasians had been beaten by Cimon at sea, they were forced to undergo a siege. Perhaps they were encouraged to hold out by the destruction of the Athenian colonists who had recently been sent to Ennea Hodoi on the Thracian mainland. In any case, they appealed to Sparta for help and were not refused, for the Spartans promised to relieve the pressure by invading Attica.[15] A great earthquake at Sparta prevented the promise from being kept, and the secret agreement did not come to light for some years at least, but as Grote

[15] Thuc. 101. 1. Some scholars have rejected this statement by Thucydides. Glotz and Cohen (II, 135), for instance, doubt that the Spartans made such a promise, "car c'était la guerre ouverte avec la Ligue de Délos." Walker (*CAH,* V, 72) doubts it also and conjectures that the story may derive from Stesimbrotus. The fullest argument for rejecting Thucydides on this point is made by Raphael Sealey (*Historia,* VI [1957]). He warns that Thucydides "is not so reliable an authority on events that occurred before the Peloponnesian War," and that "the historian should beware of statements about secret undertakings and unfulfilled intentions" (p. 369). He appears to have a higher opinion of Thucydides' reliability for the events of the Pentacontaetia and for their interpretation in a more recent article on "The Origin of the Delian League" (*ASI,* 233–255). We have here a straight statement of fact offered by Thucydides on his own authority, and no one has offered a reason why he should have been either misinformed or biased on this point. Most scholars have accepted Thucydides without question. See Grote, IV, 398–400; Busolt, *GG,* III: 1, 203; Meyer, *GdA,* IV: 1, 501–502; Beloch, *GG,* II ^{2} : 1, 149; Bengtson, 189; Hammond *History of Greece* (Oxford, 1959), 290.

pointed out, the promise itself was very significant. "It marks the growing fear and hatred on the part of Sparta and the Peloponnesians towards Athens, merely on general grounds of the magnitude of her power, and without any special provocation. . . . The first intent of unprovoked and even treacherous hostility—the germ of the future Peloponnesian War—is conceived and reduced to an engagement by Sparta." [16] Ten years after its defeat by Hetoemaridas in the councils of Sparta, the war party was still strong enough to elect a majority in the ephorate willing to provoke a war with Athens. Had the secret agreement become public, it would have caused great difficulties for Cimon and his policy of friendship with Sparta, but his enemies were deprived of so useful a weapon.

When the attack came, it was on much weaker grounds than Spartan perfidy. In 463, in the third year of the siege, the Thasians surrendered on terms very favorable to Athens. Cimon must have been at the height of his popularity, yet his opponents took the opportunity to attack him on his return from Thasos. They charged that he had accepted bribes from King Alexander of Macedon not to invade that country, when he could have done so successfully.[17] We may dismiss the charge of bribery, as the Athenian jury did. Cimon's wealth and incorruptability were too well known for anyone to believe he would sacrifice his city's interest for money. The trial provided a forum for a debate on foreign policy. Cimon could be accused of lack of vigor in his pursuit of Athens' imperial interests in the northern Aegean, and at the same time, his Spartan policy could be attacked by implication. Cimon's defense shows that he clearly understood the intentions of his accusers. "I am not a proxenus," he said, "of rich Ionians and Thessalians, as some others are so that they may be courted and paid; I am proxenus of the Lacedaemonians and imitate and love their thrift and self-control, which I honor above any wealth, glorifying my city with wealth won from her enemies." [18] He successfully defended his policy of an aggressive war against Persia accompanied by friendship with Sparta and hurled the challenge back into the teeth of his accusers.

[16] Grote, IV, 399–400.

[17] On the surrender of Thasos, Thuc. 101. 3. On the attack on Cimon, Plut. *Cim.* 14. 2–3.

[18] Plut. *Cim.* 14. 3.

Among those accusers was Pericles, son of Xanthippus, a young man not much over thirty just making his debut as an important figure in Athenian politics. As the son of Xanthippus and Agariste, the niece of Cleisthenes, he was born into the aristocratic coalition that had opposed Themistocles and put Cimon into the position of leadership he still held in 463.[19] At first glance it might seem surprising to find him among the accusers of Cimon, but the situation had changed significantly since the leading men of Athens had combined to defeat Themistocles. For one thing, the object of the coalition had been accomplished. Themistocles had been gone from Athens for a decade and from Greece since 471. For another, relations between Athens and Sparta seemed to be going well, and the Spartan peace party appeared to be firmly in control. In the absence of an emergency, there was no reason why the great families of Athens should not return to their political rivalries, which went back at least to the beginning of the sixth century. If family rivalries meant anything at all, then Pericles was the obvious choice to oppose Cimon. His father, Xanthippus, had brought about the condemnation of Cimon's father and compelled Cimon to begin his career burdened by a heavy debt. Perhaps Cimon did not bear a grudge.[20] If not, he was an unusually forgiving man. More important, Pericles appears not to have forgotten the old rivalry. Tacitus was very shrewd when he said that it is human nature to hate those we have wronged. Pericles' election by the people to the role of accuser may have been prompted by the public recollection of his father's success in a similar role against Miltiades.

We would be mistaken, however, in thinking that Pericles' acceptance of the responsibility and his enthusiasm for it [21] resulted only from the old family feud [22] or from mere political opportunism. These certainly played a part in influencing his behavior. A man of his heritage, natural talents, and training could not fail to seek a career in politics and to aim for the highest position in the state.

[19] Plut. *Per.* 3 for his lineage. *Per.* 10. 4–5, *Cim.* 14–15, and Arist. *Ath. Pol.* 27 on the trial of Cimon and Pericles' debut.

[20] Such is the suggestion of Sealey (*Hermes,* LXXXIV [1956], 239).

[21] οὗτος γὰρ ἦν τῶν κατηγόρων ὁ σφοδρότατος. Plut. *Cim.* 14. 5.

[22] *Pace* C. Hignett, *A History of the Athenian Constitution* (Oxford, 1952), 253.

Cimon, the old family enemy, barred the way and seemed to have unquestioned command of the field, so long as the political game were played according to the rules developed since the Persian War. The growth of popular government represented by the reforms of the 480's and the domination of Themistocles posed the gravest threat to the political position of the old families. Hipparchus, Megacles, Xanthippus, and Aristides had all been ostracized, leaving Themistocles, a man of doubtful lineage and demagogic tendencies, in sole command. The Persian War had come just in time to submerge factional strife in the fervor of national defense. Their services in the war raised the prestige and influence of the restored nobles. At its close they were determined not to lose the support of the people and to unite so that Themistocles could not pick them off one by one, as he had in the decade before the war. The result was the political coalition we have described above and the "Areopagite constitution," that Aristotle believes reigned at Athens from 479 to 462.[23]

Some modern scholars have doubted that there was such an "Areopagite constitution." [24] They point to Aristotle's failure to mention any constitutional changes in detail. He says merely, "The council of the Areopagus again grew strong after the Persian War, gaining their hegemony not by a formal decree, but because they were responsible for the Battle of Salamis." [25] When Ephialtes later attacked the Areopagus, he simply took away the additional powers (*epitheta*) by which it had become the guardian of the state.[26] The vagueness of these statements has produced suspicion, but there is little cause for it. The historian of Rome would find it difficult to point to specific measures by which the potentially democratic constitution established by the Hortensian Law of 287 became the nar-

[23] Arist. *Ath. Pol.* 25. 1; 24. 3; 41. 2. For arguments in favor of the Aristotelean authorship of the *Athenaion Politeia,* which I accept, see James Day and Mortimer Chambers, *Aristotle's History of Athenian Democracy* (Berkeley and Los Angeles, 1962), 1–4. Cf. Hignett, *A History of the Athenian Constitution,* 27–30.

[24] Day and Chambers (*Aristotle,* 126), for instance, say, "The Areopagite constitution is palpably unhistorical: it was constructed by Aristotle to close the gap between the second democracy of Cleisthenes and the radical fourth democracy begun by Ephialtes."

[25] Arist. *Ath. Pol.* 23. 1.

[26] Arist. *Ath. Pol.* 25. 2.

row oligarchy that the Gracchi tried to destroy in 133. The upper classes, by means of the prestige gained in wars of survival, had merely accumulated unofficial powers, epitheta, one might say, by which they dominated the state. When the Gracchi attacked these usurped powers, the senate had no constitutional right to complain and was compelled to resort to violence. The "Areopagite constitution" had only seventeen years in which to establish itself before a split in the aristocracy brought it under attack, so no revolution was necessary to bring it down. Since Cimon was the unchallenged leader of the state by 463, motives of political ambition surely required that Pericles try to change the rules of the political game.

This was no simple task, for in spite of a reputation for Spartan dullness, Cimon was a shrewd and able man well deserving Plutarch's accolade: "It is agreed that he was not inferior in daring to Miltiades nor in intelligence to Themistocles and more just than either." [27] The traditional political system, where the scions of noble families vied with each other for eminence and the honors of state, had been overthrown by the genius and daring of Cleisthenes. Great nobles had counted on their clients, peasants awed by the wealth, religious influence, and military power of the local nobility, to win elections. The reforms of Cleisthenes had reduced the importance of local influence and aristocratic control of religious shrines.[28] Cleisthenes, moreover, had taken advantage of a new political factor that came to be more and more decisive: the demos, particularly those in and around the city of Athens. These people, in effect, became a part of Cleisthenes' clientele; joined with the traditional supporters of the Alcmaeonidae, they were enough to guarantee a reliable majority for Cleisthenes in the ecclesia. The tool of ostracism, which also depended on a reliable majority in the ecclesia and in the actual vote, protected Cleisthenes from hostile faction leaders and the new constitutions from subversion.[29]

Themistocles had used his talents to gain control of the Cleisthenic political machinery. His naval policy won the devotion of the demos, and his use of ostracism removed all his enemies from the scene.

[27] *Cim.* 5. 1.

[28] D. M. Lewis, *Historia,* XII (1963), 22–40.

[29] For this interpretation of ostracism, see Kagan, *Hesperia,* XXX (1961), 393–401.

The rule of Themistocles might have lasted a very long time, and the power of the noble families, whose leaders languished in exile, might have been permanently damaged were it not for the Persian War, whose political consequences we have already noted. Now Cimon devised a plan whereby an aristocrat might adapt himself to the new political conditions. He began with the inestimable advantage of a well-deserved reputation for heroism in the late war. To this he added an attractive appearance and a gentle and artless manner, both of which had great popular appeal.[30] His foreign policy of aggressive naval warfare against Persia was popular as a continuation of Themistocles' policy. The final ingredient in Cimon's recipe for political hegemony was money, in great amounts but judiciously employed. Cimon had acquired a good deal of money in the form of booty from his successful campaigns. Plutarch's description of how he spent it deserves quotation:

> He took away the fences from his fields, that strangers and needy citizens might have it in their power to take fearlessly of the fruits of the land; and every day he gave a dinner at his house, simple it is true, but sufficient for many, to which any poor man who wished came in, and so received a maintenance which caused him no effort and left him free to devote himself solely to public affairs. But Aristotle says (*Ath. Pol.* 27. 3) that it was not for all Athenians, but only for his own demesmen, the Laciadae, that he provided a free dinner. He was constantly attended by young comrades in fine attire, each one of whom, whenever an elderly citizen in needy array came up, was ready to exchange raiment with him. The practice made a deep impression. These same followers also carried with them a generous sum of money, and going up to poor men of finer quality in the market place, they would quietly thrust small change into their hands.[31]

It is of no great importance whether Plutarch or Aristotle is right as to the recipients of Cimon's bounty; the general picture is clear enough. He had found a way to build and maintain a clientele among the demos to rival that of Themistocles and men like him. Like the Irish political bosses of Boston and New York at the turn of the century, he won a loyal following among the poor voters by taking care of their personal needs and seeing to it that they voted

[30] Plut. *Cim.* 5. 3–4.

[31] Plut. *Cim.* 10. 1–3, translated by B. Perrin in *LCL.*

when they were needed. Another imperfect but revealing analogy is with the Tory democracy of Disraeli, who hoped to maintain the rule of the upper classes by voluntarily attending to the most grievous needs of the people.

Pericles was ill equipped to beat Cimon at his own game. He had no military reputation to match Cimon's; his personal appearance was far less pleasing, for he had an oddly shaped head that excited the ridicule of the comic poets.[32] His manner was unfortunate for a politician who hoped to win the masses away from their favorite. The contemporary poet Ion compared the presumptuous and arrogant manner of Pericles, his pride and disdain for others, with the tactful and easy manners of Cimon. Even if we disregard the poetic fancies of Ion, we must recognize that Pericles' austere and remote personality was a political liability.[33] Although wealthy, he could not compete with the riches of Cimon. For all these reasons he faced a gigantic task when he entered the lists against Cimon. Probably he did not expect to win, but wanted only to bring himself to public attention as a rising young member of the opposition. Since many of his father's supporters must have continued to support Cimon's foreign policy, the major subject of debate, it behooved Pericles to control the fury of his attack. At the trial he got up to speak only once and even then like a man who was merely fulfilling an obligation. Stesimbrotus attributes this mildness to the intervention of Cimon's sister Elpinice.[34] We may attribute it less romantically to prudence.

We have little reason, in fact, to believe that Pericles opposed Cimon's foreign policy. We know that it had been the policy of Xanthippus as well, and we hear of no Periclean statements or actions hostile to Sparta until well after the war with Sparta had begun. It is worth noticing that the man who later opposed Cimon's appeal to help the Spartans when they were endangered by a helot rebellion was Ephialtes.[35] No mention whatever is made of Pericles, and it is hard to believe that any recollection of his opposition would be omitted by later historians aware of his subsequent leadership of

[32] Plut. *Per.* 3. 2–4.
[33] Plut. *Per.* 5. 3–4.
[34] Plut. *Cim.* 14. 4.
[35] Plut. *Cim.* 16. 7–8.

wars with Sparta. In 463 the basis of Pericles' opposition to Cimon, if it was anything more than personal ambition, was domestic and not foreign policy.

The first events in which Pericles is definitely concerned are constitutional and legislative reforms to make the state more democratic. He was associated with Ephialtes in the attacks on the Areopagus that stripped it of its newly usurped powers, perhaps of some of its older ones as well.[36] He is specifically named as the first to introduce pay for jurymen,[37] and Plutarch charges him with the introduction of the theoric fund as well as the jury pay and other public largesses.[38] It is usual to suppose that the opening of the archonship to member of the zeugite class and the re-establishment of the thirty so-called local justices (*dikastai kata demous*), both usually taken to be democratic reforms, were Periclean.[39] To be sure, Pericles is not named as their author, and it is well to remember that the Pericles of the 450's is not the same man who dominated Athens after the ostracism of Thucydides, son of Melesias, in 443; it is not safe to suppose that everything that happened in Athens between the death of Ephialtes and the death of Pericles is the latter's doing. The fact remains that there is plenty of evidence that Pericles entered Athenian politics as a member of a democratic faction and as the champion of a democratic program.[40]

[36] Plut. *Per.* 9. 3–4; *Cim.* 15. 1–2; Arist. *Ath. Pol.* 27. 1. The ancient authors seem to have had conflicting versions of precisely what took place and the true relationship between Ephialtes and Pericles. Aristotle's story that Ephialtes was helped by Themistocles must be unhistorical. The evidence seems to indicate that Ephialtes was the leader of the opposition to Cimon and the Areopagite constitution, and Pericles his lieutenant.

[37] Arist. *Ath. Pol.* 27. 3.

[38] *Per.* 9. 3.

[39] Arist. *Ath. Pol.* 26. 2–3; see Busolt, *GG,* III: 1, 263–269.

[40] Raphael Sealey, *Hermes, op. cit.,* 234–247, has written a lively attack on the *communis opinio.* His warnings against unfounded assumptions are a useful tonic against attempts to read modern party politics and class struggles into the fifth century. His emphasis on "the family-politics of the great houses" is a necessary corrective, but it goes too far. The fact remains that some great houses or, at any rate, some members of the great houses favored more democratic policies, while others opposed them. The Alcmaeonids in general and Pericles in particular usually seem to have been in

It is the all but unanimous judgment of antiquity that Pericles was a champion of democracy. Plato, the enemy of Athenian democracy, considered him a typical demagogue and corrupter of the people. Aristotle says that when Pericles began his career the constitution became more democratic; because of the changes he and Ephialtes introduced, "the many became bolder and took the state more into their own hands." [41] The question arises chiefly because of the famous dictum of Thucydides that Athens in the time of Pericles "was in name a democracy, but in fact it was the rule of the first man." [42] Plutarch was troubled by it and set himself to resolve the apparent contradiction. He finally decided that Pericles was forced into his early democratic phase by the impossibility of defeating Cimon in any other way, but that after the ostracism of 443 had cleared the field of all rivals, he was able to employ the "aristocratic and royal statesmanship" of his later career.[43]

Some modern scholars have followed Plutarch's interpretation with only minor modifications, seeing 443 as the year in which the character of Periclean rule changed.[44] At least one has solved the problem by suggesting that Pericles never really was a democrat at all.[45] Perhaps the opposite solution is more persuasive. Thucydides' judgment on the Periclean constitution does not seem to accord with the facts he offers. Nobody denies that all questions of policy and all elections were decided in the ecclesia in 430 just as they had been in 450. Public officials underwent preliminary examinations and final audits; panels of citizens elected by lot had final jurisdiction in all matters. Each year Pericles had to stand for election to his office, and at each assembly he needed to win a majority of the voters to his policy. In 430 he was removed from office and fined by an angry citizenry. Even more telling is the fact that they sent a

the first group, while the Philaids in general and Cimon in particular seem to have been in the second.

[41] Plato *Gorgias* 515 E; Arist. *Ath. Pol.* 27. 1.

[42] 2. 65. 7.

[43] *Per.* 9 and 15.

[44] Busolt, *GG*, III: 1, 494–497; Hignett, *op. cit.*, 253–257; and Beloch, *Die Attische Politik Seit Perikles* (Leipzig, 1884), 19–21.

[45] Sealey, *Hermes, op. cit.*, 234–247.

peace mission to Sparta, in utter contradiction of his policy, while he was still in office. It is hard to deny that

> if democracy means and is government by the citizens, if the *ekklesia* decided policy by vote, if free elections persisted at their constitutional intervals, if Perikles was at all times responsible to the sovereign *demos,* and if an unoppressed political opposition survived, as it surely did, —if all this is so, then Athens was as democratic, not only in theory but in day-to-day practice, as government can conceivably be.[46]

Finally we have the evidence of Pericles' funeral oration. If any speech reported by Thucydides may be considered a close facsimile of what was actually said, it is this one. It is generally agreed to be the finest and most moving encomium of the democratic way of life ever spoken. It is altogether perverse to deny that the man who delivered it after a life in the service of Athens was a sincere believer in democracy. The allegation that he became a democrat out of political necessity need not detain us long. It is a commonplace employed whenever an aristocrat takes his place at the head of a popular movement; it was said of Cleisthenes in antiquity and of Franklin D. Roosevelt in recent times. In all three cases it is in conflict with the evidence.

All this is not to say that the young Pericles of the late 460's was a dreamy idealist unaware of the political significance of what he was doing. On the contrary, he must have known full well the nature of the revolution he was bringing about. We have seen that the rules of the political game made it impossible for him to win. He changed those rules to such good effect that he was ultimately able to dominate Athenian politics as no man had done before and none was to do again. The key to his success was surely the device that his ancient enemies castigated most vehemently: his use of state funds to pay Athenian citizens to perform their civic functions. This was attractive on theoretical grounds, for it made it possible for the Athenian democracy to fulfill its potentiality by allowing all its citizens to perform the duties and achieve the honors of citizenship (μετέχειν κρίσεως καὶ 'αρχῆς) as Aristotle put it, to hold office and to serve on juries, to rule and to judge.[47] It was no less attractive on

[46] Malcolm McGregor, *Phoenix,* X (1956), 93–102.
[47] *Pol.* 1275a. 23–24.

practical grounds, for it undercut a major base of Cimon's strength. No more need the poor seek the charity of Cimon and his political supporters; no more need they feel grateful for his largesse and express their gratitude at the elections and in the ecclesia. Now they could obtain a public support that was more regular, came to them of right and not by charity, and left them free to express the monumental ingratitude that democratic politicians must always expect.

The enemies of Pericles might argue that he had merely "offered the people what was their own," [48] but the people were nonetheless grateful and gave him their support. The ultimate effect was to destroy the revised system of patronage introduced by Cimon once and for all. As the New Deal of Roosevelt put an end to the fiefdom of the great cities, by taking patronage of the poor out of the hands of the local bosses and putting it under the control of the central government, so did the reforms of Pericles put an end to the clientage of the poor Athenian. Henceforth the opponents of Pericles must fight him on the new ground that he himself had chosen.

This domestic revolution was not easy to accomplish and might not have come about had it not been for developments abroad.[49] After the failure of their attack on Cimon's probity, the democrats changed their tactics. They now began a series of attacks on the very center of conservatism and the bulwark of aristocracy, the Areopagus. Ephialtes and Pericles took the lead in charging individual members of the council with mismanagement of the administration.[50] This was a useful softening-up tactic, but it probably would not have brought full success had not fortune intervened. In the summer of 464, Sparta suffered a terrible earthquake, which was soon followed by an uprising of the helots.[51] The effects of the disaster were not easily overcome, and by 462 the helots, who had taken refuge on Mt. Ithome, were still a threat. The Spartans appealed for help to their allies, among them the Athenians, who were particularly wanted for their reputed skill at siege operations. This, of course, led to a debate in Athens.

[48] Arist. *Ath. Pol.* 27. 4; Plut. *Per.* 9. 2; Aristophanes *Wasps* 684 ff.

[49] See Appendix C.

[50] Arist. *Ath. Pol.* 25. 2; Plut. *Per.* 9. 3–4; *Cim.* 15. 1–2. Aristotle has Themistocles helping Ephialtes, but that is surely impossible after 471.

[51] 1. 101. 1–2.

Ephialtes led the opposition to the Spartan request for help, urging the Athenians "not to help or restore a city that was a rival to Athens but to let the pride of Sparta lie low and be trampled underfoot." [52] The violence of the language is evidence of the hatred toward Sparta felt by Ephialtes and by at least some part of his faction. No doubt part of it derived from the traditional Themistoclean foreign policy, which sought to make Athens the sole leader of the Hellenes; another part of that hatred must have come from Sparta's consistent support of Cimon, the rival of Ephialtes. But the success of that support was even more detestable because Cimon was the great foe of the democratic constitutional reforms favored by the democrats. He tried to revive the powers that Pericles and Ephialtes had stripped from the Areopagus, and he was probably the first to use a return to the Cleisthenic constitution as a reactionary political slogan.[53] His enemies saw a close connection between his admiration for Sparta and his hostility to popular government, and they made good use of the people's dislike of Sparta, as well as Cimon's outspoken preference for Spartan character and manners.

In spite of the clamor and demagogy of his opponents, Cimon was still powerful enough to carry the day. He persuaded the Athenians to send him at the head of four thousand hoplites to help the Spartans, employing the effective exhortation "not to leave Hellas lame nor see their city deprived of its yokefellow." [54] It is more than likely that if the expedition had gone well and Cimon had returned from a successful campaign with the thanks of a grateful and friendly Sparta, the democratic tide might have been stemmed and even pushed back even then. Events, however, took a different turn.

The Athenians had not been on the scene long before the Spartans sharply changed their policy. For no apparent reason they singled out the Athenians among their allies and sent them home on the grounds that they no longer needed them. Thucydides tells us that the real reason for the Spartans' action was their fear of "the boldness and revolutionary spirit of the Athenians"; since they were

[52] Plut. *Cim.* 16. 8.

[53] Plut. *Cim.* 15. 2.

[54] Thuc. 102. 1–3; Plut. *Cim.* 16. 8–17. 4; Diod. 11. 64. 2–3. For the number of troops, see Aristophanes *Lysistrata* 1138–1144. For the possibly derivative quality of Cimon's remark, see Appendix B, p. 379.

Ionians and not Dorians, "if they remained they might be persuaded by the men on Ithome to change sides." [55] We need not doubt the accuracy of Thucydides' judgment. Even under the command of Cimon, four thousand Athenian hoplites, raised in the free air of democracy and proud of the power and glory of that democracy, must have seemed dangerous indeed to many Spartans. We may imagine the arrogance shown by at least some Athenians as they swaggered through the Peloponnese, called to aid a stricken Sparta. Even very moderate democratic ideas must have been both surprising and shocking to Spartan ears.

But if we penetrate below the general statement of Thucydides, it is possible to see the role that party politics may have played in the Spartan decision. The Spartans could not have failed to hear that the Athenian expedition had not been unanimously approved. They must have known of the opposition of Ephialtes and the hatred of Sparta it reflected. The war party, as we know, had always been suspicious and jealous of Athens, and in recent years it had regained enough power to influence Spartan policy. Perhaps, the frightening behavior and demeanor of the Athenians was enough to swing the balance in its favor. The Spartans may well have realized that to dismiss the Athenians would seriously compromise Cimon's position, probably lead to his overthrow, and the victory of his democratic opponents who hated Sparta. Their action might well lead to war, but they did not shrink from it. We may wonder whether Cimon appreciated the irony of the situation: the expedition that he had urged to guarantee friendship between Athens and Sparta provided the weapon with which his enemies in both states could destroy that friendship.

While Cimon was gone the democrats won a great victory over the Areopagus that stripped it of the additional powers it had gained over the years and left it merely a court with very limited jurisdiction. We may well believe that only the absence of Cimon and his four thousand hoplites made that victory possible.[56] On his return he made every effort to restore the political situation to what it had been before his departure. He tried to restore the lost powers to the Areo-

[55] Thuc. 1. 102. 3; Diod. 11. 63. 2 and Plut. *Cim.* 17. 2 seem to be based only on Thucydides and add nothing to the story.

[56] Hignett, 341.

pagus,[57] but his efforts were doomed to failure. The Spartans had destroyed his political credit. There can be no question that the Athenians regarded the dismissal of their army as a terrible insult, and they were angry with the man whom they held responsible for it. Dislike of Sparta was so deep and general that old friends of the Spartans found it expedient to renounce their association.[58] In such a climate it is hardly surprising that the Athenians withdrew from the alliance with Sparta made at the time of the Persian War. At the same time they made an alliance with Argos, Sparta's traditional enemy, and then brought in Thessaly to form a triple alliance clearly aimed at Sparta.[59] In the spring of 461 the Athenians ostracized Cimon, and the diplomatic revolution was complete.[60] A party hostile to Athens was in control of Spartan policy, and the enemies of Sparta were in command at Athens.

[57] Plut. *Cim.* 15. 2.

[58] For the Athenian reaction, see Thuc. 1. 102. 4; Diod. 11. 63. 3. I believe that Beloch's suggestion (*GG* ², II: 2, 1, 153) that Alcibiades, the grandfather of his notorious namesake, renounced his position as Spartan proxenus at this time is very plausible. See Thuc. 5. 43. 2.

[59] 1. 102. 4.

[60] Plut. *Cim.* 17. 2.

Part Two

The First Peloponnesian War

5. The War in Greece

Within two years of Cimon's exile the Athenians were allied with a state that had rebelled from the Spartan alliance and was engaged in combat with several Peloponnesian states. The First Peloponnesian War was on. After the Spartan rejection of Cimon's troops it could scarcely have been avoided. It is interesting to apply Thucydides' judgment of the "truest cause" of the later war to the outbreak of this one. "I think that the truest cause but the one least spoken of was that the Athenians had grown powerful, which presented an object of fear to the Spartans and forced them to go to war." In this case it appears to be right in every particular. The power of Athens had grown enormously since 479, when Thucydides begins his analysis. Fear of Athens was manifest in the debate in the Spartan gerousia of 475, in the promise to help Thasos in 465/4, and finally in the expulsion of the Athenian hoplites in 462/1. The expression of that fear, moreover, was internal and did not need outside goading. When the Spartans made the fateful decision to expel the Athenians, they needed and received no urging from Corinthians, Aeginetans, or Megarians. Always the impetus toward hostilities came from Sparta.

The Spartan attitude reflected an important fact about the condition of the Greek world from 479 to 461: Its stability was apparent only and not real. The alliance between Sparta and Athens was not an alliance of states but of factions. The faction of Cimon and the faction that would be headed by King Archidamus were prepared to accept limits to the hegemonal claims of their states, but in each state there were significant elements of the population who were not. The political positions of Cimon and the Spartan peace party were not strong enough to resist their enemies indefinitely. The Spartans simply were not yet prepared to share hegemony with Athens, nor were the Athenians prepared to accept Spartan checks on their ambitions. It is easy to believe that if the dismissal of the Athenians troops had not occurred, another *casus belli* might soon have been found. Probably no complex human event can be thought of as inevitable, but the First Peloponnesian War would have been hard to avoid after the formation of the Delian League.

The ostracism of Cimon left his enemy Ephialtes in control of the field, but he was not permitted to enjoy his victory, for an oligarchic plot brought about his assassination.[1] Now Pericles assumed the leadership of the democratic faction and of the state; he was to exercise a powerful influence upon both for more than thirty years. We have seen that although he and Cimon both came from the highest Athenian nobility, they could not have differed more in appearance, style, manner, habits, and prejudices. Their native differences were accentuated by the differences in their training. Cimon received the gymnastic training traditional for Athenian aristocrats. Although not without native wit, he was untrained in literature, rhetoric, and the liberal arts, disciplines that came to be thought of as characteristically Greek.[2] Pericles, on the other hand, was inclined to a life of the mind and was enough younger than Cimon to take advantage of the new intellectual currents that appeared in Hellas in the middle of the fifth century. His friends and teachers were such men as Damon, Zeno, and Anaxagoras, and his conversation of music, poetry, science, and philosophy. When Cimon worked to beautify and glorify his city, he planted plane trees in the agora and built new running tracks for the noble youths who exercised at the Academy.[3] Pericles built the Odeon, commissioned Mnesicles to build the Propylaea, Callicrates and Ictinus to plan the Parthenon, and Phidias to supervise its adornment and to create a statue of the goddess. To his native intelligence and excellent training he added remarkable rhetorical skill and a reputation for absolute

[1] Plut. *Per.* 10. 6–7; Arist. *Ath. Pol.* 25. 4.

[2] Plut. *Cim.* 4. 40.

[3] Plut. *Cim.* 13. 8.

incorruptibility.[4] The democratic measures he now put into effect provided the basis for a political strength that would one day be almost unassailable.

In 461, however, his position was far from secure. He was still a very young man, not yet thirty-five, who had come to power by a freak. He had to expect the friends of Cimon to oppose him, and he needed also to win the confidence of the party he led. He may not have approved of a policy of war with Sparta, but it had been the policy of the martyred Ephialtes, and Pericles had no choice but to pursue it. Some time in 461/60 the helot rebels on Mt. Ithome could hold out no longer and surrendered to the Spartans.[5] The conditions were not unduly harsh: the helots might leave freely provided that they did not return. No doubt the Spartans expected the helots and their families to scatter throughout the Hellenic world and never again to pose a threat to the security of the Peloponnese, but if so they were disappointed. Shortly before, the Athenians had taken possession of Naupactus, a town on the northern shore of the Gulf of Corinth, which had formerly belonged to the Ozolian Locrians. They offered it to the Messenian rebels, who happily accepted. The Athenians did this, says Thucydides, "because of their enmity toward the Spartans,"[6] and we may well agree with his judgment. To be sure, Naupactus would later prove a useful base from which to harass Peloponnesian shipping, and some Athenians might have thought about that, but the Athenian motive could have been less rational. Stung by the insult so fresh in their memory, they may merely have taken the opportunity to strike back at Sparta in any way possible.

[4] 2. 65. 8; Plut. *Per.* 15. 4–5.

[5] 1. 103. 1. The text says that this happened in the tenth year (δεκάτῳ ἔτει) of the rebellion, which had begun in 464/3. This would put the fall of Ithome in 454/3, and I agree with Gomme and the majority of scholars that such a date is impossible. An emendation of the text seems necessary, and the reading τετάρτῳ in place of δεκάτῳ seems attractive, if not certain. This would place the surrender in 461/0. For a detailed argument of this general view, see Gomme, *Hist. Comm.*, I, 401–408 and *ATL*, III, 176, notes 58 and 59. For a recent presentation of a minority view, as well as a review of the scholarship on the question, which has created much interest in the last quarter-century, see D. W. Reece, *JHS*, LXXXII (1962), 111–120, especially note 1 on page 111.

[6] 1. 103. 3.

A splendid opportunity for further revenge soon offered itself. The Megarians, who were engaged in a boundary dispute with Corinth, found themselves getting the worst of the war. No doubt they were aware of the special position Corinth held in the Spartan alliance and despaired of any help from Sparta. Instead, they withdrew from their association with Sparta and entered into an alliance with Athens. The Athenians took advantage of the opportunity to secure Pegae, the Megarian port on the Corinthian Gulf, and to build long walls connecting Megara to Nisaea. Nisaea was Megara's port on the Saronic Gulf, and the Athenians made it secure by garrisoning it.[7] This could only be interpreted as an act of war against the Spartans. Athens' acceptance of a rebellious ally into the Athenian alliance, her fortification of the vital route between the Peloponnese and the rest of Greece were acts that Sparta could not tolerate. The Athenians knew this quite well but did not shrink from the deeds. For them the war had already begun, and the Megarian offer of alliance was a god-sent opportunity to enter that war under favorable conditions.

Control of the Megarid was of enormous strategic value to Athens. It made the invasion of Attica from the Peloponnese almost impossible; the control of Pegae made it possible to supply Naupactus and control the Gulf of Corinth without making the long and dangerous voyage around the Peloponnese.[8] However, the Athenians paid a heavy price, for it was from the Athenian intervention in this Megarian quarrel that "the bitter hatred of the Corinthians for the Athenians first came into being." [9] Gomme thinks that this Corinthian hostility was important as a cause of this war as well as of the greater one some three decades later. "It required," he says, "the energy of Corinth, and some others, to push Sparta into the war; who, in spite of a desire to find every excuse for delay, could not afford to lose the valuable alliance of Corinth and could not fail to see that the Athenian empire really threatened the security of the Peloponnese as well as the rest of Greece." [10]

It is evident that Gomme was thinking more of the war that came in 431 than of its predecessor, for his remarks apply very well to the

[7] Thuc. 1. 103. 4; Diod. 11. 79.

[8] Gomme, *Hist. Comm.,* I, 304–305.

[9] 1. 103. 4.

[10] *Hist. Comm.,* I, 305.

later war but not to the earlier. As we have seen, Sparta required no push to persuade itself of the danger to the Peloponnese represented by Athens. The acceptance of the Megarian alliance was a direct blow at the Spartans, who understood it without Corinthian help. Gomme blames the Corinthians for risking the stability of the Peloponnese and the peace of Hellas in a quarrel over a strip of land, but his charge is unjust.[11] Corinth had no reason to expect that Megara would turn for help to Athens, her traditional enemy. She had less reason to believe that the Athenians, who had always had good relations with the Corinthians, would help their enemies. The Corinthians could not be blamed for failing to realize that they were in the midst of a diplomatic revolution and that the Athenian action was directed against Sparta rather than Corinth. The Athenians, to be sure, sowed dragon's teeth when they alienated Corinth over Megara, but the harvest would not come for almost thirty years.

While the Athenians were embroiled in the struggle between Megara and Corinth, their attention was drawn to events far afield. King Inaros of Lybia had led a revolt in Egypt against the Persian king Artaxerxes, who had ascended to the throne only a few years earlier. Realizing that he would need help, he called in the Athenians, who were already engaged in a campaign at Cyprus. They abandoned that undertaking, and with two hundred Athenian and allied ships they sailed up the Nile, having joined forces with Inaros.[12] It is not impossible that the Athenian expedition to Cyprus, whose origin and purposes we do not know, was sent out by Cimon before the break with Sparta had taken place.[13] There is no satisfactory way, however, to place the Athenian acceptance of Inaros' invitation before 460,[14] so we are forced to account for what appears a most reckless action on the part of the Athenians, who were willing to undertake a major commitment in Egypt at the same time that they faced a great conflict with the Peloponnesians.

This problem has troubled modern historians, particularly those eager to acquit Pericles of the charges of recklessness and imperial-

[11] *Hist. Comm.*, I, 304.

[12] 1. 104.

[13] Beloch, *GG* ², II: 2, 205; Nesselhauf, *Untersuchungen zur Geschichte der delischattischen Symmachie, Klio,* Beiheft, XXX (1933), 6, n. 1.

[14] *ATL,* III, 177, n. 60.

ism. They suggest that he really opposed the expedition, but since he was not yet in a position of strength and was still opposed by the shattered but ever present faction of Cimon, he was compelled to go along with Cimon's policy.[15] Beloch, certainly no friend of Pericles, is nevertheless unable to believe that he was responsible for the Egyptian expedition. "For the dispatch of a great fleet right after Cyprus fully conforms with the spirit of Cimon's policy, while it would have been obvious madness after the break with Sparta, which we may not attribute to such prudent statesmen as Pericles and Myronides." [16] Thus, he is forced to date the expedition to 462/1, which is not acceptable.[17]

There are many things wrong with this argument besides the date. Among the least of these is that none of our sources names Cimon in connection with either this Cyprian campaign or the Egyptian expedition, although they do name him in connection with the Cyprian campaign he led a decade later; nor is Myronides mentioned at all as an Athenian leader just at this time. Beloch, moreover, did not always consider Pericles a prudent statesman incapable of such foolishness, for he believes that he deliberately brought on the great Peloponnesian War merely to protect his political position at home.[18] Much more important, as Gomme has pointed out, is that this view leads to the improbable conclusion that Pericles, "incapable of supporting the Egyptian policy for its own sake, after being quit of Kimon by ostracism, meekly carried on his policy for six long years—in Egypt, though he reversed it in Greece—out of sentimental regard, I suppose, for his rival's name." [19]

Thucydides, as usual, does not allow us to see into the internal

[15] Franz Miltner, *PW,* XIX (1938), *s.v.* "Perikles," 754; Karl Dienelt, *Die Friedenspolitik des Perikles* (Vienna and Wiesbaden, 1958), 12.

[16] *GG* ², II: 2, 205.

[17] W. Scharf (*Historia,* III [1954–5], 308–325) takes a similar view. He believes that the campaigns in Cyprus and Egypt were both purely Cimonian. This leaves him open to the same objection that Gomme makes to Beloch's view (see below, n. 19). That objection seems to me insuperable.

[18] On Pericles as the cause of the war, see *Die Attische Politik,* 19–22. Beloch's judgment on Pericles as a statesman is "Wir können selbst zweifeln ob er ein grosser Staatsmann gewesen ist. . . . Aber er war, wie wir heute sagen würden, ein grosser Parlamentarier." *GG* ², II: 1, 155.

[19] *Hist. Comm.,* I, 307.

political situation, and in this instance our other ancient authorities seem to have had no independent source. Yet, if there can be no certainty about it, the historian must try to divine Pericles' attitude at this early date if he is to understand the later policy of Pericles when his policy was that of Athens. It is well to avoid the mistake of imagining that the policy that Pericles pursued after 450 must have been the same as that which he supported a decade earlier, that there was no development in his thinking, that like the Bourbons of the French Restoration, he learned nothing and forgot nothing. His vehement insistence that there should be no diversionary campaigns in the Peloponnesian War may well have resulted from the bitter memory of the disastrous end to the Egyptian campaign, which he had supported as a young man. Nor should we be surprised to find him supporting a policy of vigorous activity against Persia. His father had helped initiate such a policy; why should he not inherit Xanthippus' foreign policy as well as his domestic feud with the Philaids?

It is also wrong to imagine that only the friends of Cimon were eager for the Persian war. There had never been any disagreement among the factions in Athens as to the desirability of pressing the Persians hard and winning from them whatever profit was available. Themistocles was at least as aggressive in that direction as was Cimon. Ephialtes, as the inheritor of Themistocles' supporters, as the leader of the faction that would be the most imperialistic of all, must surely have urged the continuation of an aggressive policy against Persia. We have no reason to doubt that Pericles, his lieutenant and political heir, was at all reluctant to do the same. If we judge that this action of Pericles and the Athenian democracy was reckless and ill conceived, we should remember that both were young and sanguine, buoyed up by recent success, perhaps intoxicated with a bright new ideology whose glitter had not yet been tarnished by war and corruption. Like the young ideologues of the French and Russian revolutions, they may have felt that men who lived under a noble constitution embodying noble ideas would sweep all before them. If they were foolishly optimistic, it was not the last error they would make.[20]

[20] Grote (IV, 409) and Busolt (*GG*, III: 1, 303) do not raise the question of who was behind the Egyptian expedition. They apparently assume that there was no disagreement among the Athenians on this question, in which

In the spring and summer of 460 the Athenians took steps to secure their communications with their Argive allies. First they descended upon Halieis on the southern shore of the Argolic peninsula. It may be that they were able to gain control of Troezen at this time,[21] for they certainly controlled it later, and we know of no better opportunity. At Halieis, however, they were beaten by a combined force of Epidaurians, whose own territory was threatened, and Corinthians, who were eager to resist Athenian encroachment. But at about the same time, the Athenians won a naval battle off the island of Cecryphaleia, which lay between the Argolic peninsula and Aegina. The first battles of the war were ominous; the Athenians lost on the land and won on the sea.[22]

These Athenian attempts to gain a foothold on the western shore of the Saronic Gulf alarmed and angered the Aeginetans, who now joined the war against Athens. Aegina was an old enemy of Athens, long her rival in trade and now rapidly losing ground in the competition for naval supremacy. Pericles might call Aegina the eyesore of the Piraeus,[23] but the sight of Piraeus, fortified and issuing ever larger fleets of triremes, must have pained the Aeginetans even more. With the help of their allies they fought a great sea battle against the Athenians, who were also supported by their allies. The result

---

I think they are right. Walker (*CAH*, V, 77) says, "It may well have seemed to Pericles and the other leaders of the democratic party that here was a golden opportunity for teaching Persia the lesson that she needed. If Persia would not have peace with Athens, she should learn once more what war with Athens meant." He is arguing on the assumption that Athens had tried to obtain a peace with Persia in 461 and had failed. I am more in accord with the view of Glotz and Cohen (*HG*, II, 148) that Pericles played a leading role in the decision because he and his faction appreciated "les avantages qu'il tirerait d'une intervention en Egypte, grenier inépuisable, marché à enlever a ses fournisseurs phénicians, position militaire de premier ordre accrochée au flanc de la Perse." G. De Sanctis (*Atthis* [2nd ed.; Rome, 1904], 460) sees the strength of the analogy to the French Revolution and imagines that there were Athenians who were ambitious enough to hope for the unification of Hellas under Athenian leadership.

[21] Such is the suggestion of Grote (IV, 410).

[22] For the battles, see Thuc. 1. 105. 1–2; Diod. 11. 78. 1–2 pictures Athens as winning both battles, but there is no reason to prefer him to Thucydides here.

[23] Plut. *Per.* 8. 5.

was a great victory for the Athenians, who captured seventy enemy ships, landed on Aegina, and laid siege to the city under the command of Leocrates, son of Stroebus. The Peloponnesians withdrew three hundred hoplites who had been helping the Corinthians and Epidaurians and sent them to help Aegina. They tried to force the Athenians to break off the siege by starting diversionary campaigns, but all in vain. By the spring of 457, Aegina was forced to surrender and come into the Athenian league. The Aeginetans pulled down their walls, gave up their fleet, and were enrolled as tribute-paying members.[24]

Shortly after the Athenians had begun their siege of Aegina, the Corinthians invaded the territory of Megara, hoping to force the Athenians to give up the siege. It was a reasonable expectation, for not only was a sizable Athenian force engaged at Aegina, but a large contingent was still off in Egypt. The strain should have been too great, but the daring and resourcefulness of Athens was equal to the test. Myronides gathered together a motley army of men too old and boys too young for ordinary service. He marched them into the Megarid and won a smashing victory over the Corinthians.[25] We may get some idea of the pride the Athenians felt in their remarkable military achievements from an inscription, probably dating from the year 460/59: "The following men of the tribe Erechtheis died in the war in the same year in Cyprus, in Egypt, in Phoenicia, in Halieis, in Aegina, and in Megara." [26]

During all this time the Spartans had done very little, allowing their allies to carry the burden of the fighting. Remembering that they had declared themselves willing to invade Attica a few years earlier with infinitely less provocation, we may wonder why they waited so long to act now. For those who believe that the helot rebellion was still unsuppressed, the answer is obvious.[27] But the simplicity of this explanation is marred by the fact that the Spartans did

[24] Thuc. 1. 105. 2–3; Diod. 11. 78.

[25] Thuc. 1. 105. 3–106. 2; Diod. 11. 79. 1–4. See Gomme, *Hist. Comm.*, I, 307–311 for a discussion of the very memorable nature of this victory and its treatment by later historians.

[26] IG, I ^{2}, 929 = Tod, 26. The names of 177 men follow.

[27] Walker, *CAH*, V, 79.

undertake a major expedition in 458,[28] some three years before the surrender of Ithome by their own reckoning. It is hard to believe that by that spring the resistance of Ithome "was already breaking down," when we know that the siege was to last more than two years longer. Still, even if the helot rebellion was already finished, as we believe, we may well imagine that traditional conservatism, intensified by the recent terror, made the Spartans reluctant to take an army of any size out of the Peloponnese. It is possible also that politics may have played a role. Perhaps the victory of the war party had been only temporary; perhaps the unhappy consequences of the insult to Athens had produced a revulsion of feeling and restored the conservatives to power. About this we can only speculate, but whatever the political situation in Sparta, by this time no faction could fail to act. The Athenians were at war with Corinth, Aegina, and Epidaurus, three of the most important allies of Sparta. If she did not act now her hegemony was gone and her security in peril.

Still the Spartans did not invade Attica, the most obvious way to stop Athenian aggression. For this there was the best of reasons: they could not. The Athenian seizure and fortification of the Megarid barred a Spartan army from marching into Attica from the direction of the Peloponnese. For the time being Sparta was frustrated, but soon an unforeseen opportunity presented itself. The Phocians launched an attack on Doris, a small state in central Greece that had a special relationship with Sparta. Legend had it that Doris was the starting point from which the descendants of Heracles launched their successful attack on the Peloponnese, which led to its control by the peoples of Dorian stock. Sparta considered Doris its mother city. When the Spartans heard of the Phocian invasion, they immediately prepared to send help. Gathering a force of fifteen hundred Spartan hoplites and ten thousand allies under the leadership of Nicomedes, who commanded in place of the young King Pleistoanax, they made their roundabout way to the north, by way of the Gulf of Corinth.[29] This was obviously a far larger contingent than could possibly be needed for putting down the Phocians, a task that they accomplished quickly and easily. It is clear that the Spartan

[28] According to the *ATL* chronology; not later than 457 by anyone's account.

[29] Thuc. 1. 107. 1–2; Diod. 11. 79; Gomme, *Hist. Comm.*, I, 314.

strategy was to strike at Athens from the only vulnerable direction, the Boeotian frontier.

We are given a tantalizing clue to the mystery of Sparta's internal politics by the appointment of the commander of this expedition. Pleistoanax, to be sure, was too young for the responsibility, but why did the Spartans ignore their remaining royalty and turn to Nicomedes to lead the campaign? The answer must be that the other king was Archidamus. He had already shown and would show again that he was an able commander. We can only conclude that he was passed over because he opposed the expedition and the policy behind it. Perhaps he believed the expedition was too dangerous; perhaps he hoped that even now the Athenians might come to their senses and agree to an honorable peace. The peace party might not be able to impose its will, but it seems to have been able to disassociate itself from what it considered to be reckless policies.

Nicomedes and his supporters, however, had reason to think that their policy might be successful. Instead of returning directly to the Peleponnese by the sea route, they lingered in Boeotia. Thucydides tells us that they were encouraged to do so by "some Athenians who secretly invited them, hoping to put an end to the democracy and to the building of the long walls." [30] The Athenians, fearing an imminent attack by the Spartans, had already begun to build long walls connecting Athens to Phaleron and Piraeus. Later on a third wall, parallel to the Piraeus wall, would be built.[31] The completion of this construction would in effect turn Athens into an island unassailable by land and invincible so long as it retained command of the sea. A consequence of this policy, a direct descendant of the policy of Themistocles, would inevitably be to strengthen the Athenian democracy by emphasizing the navy at the expense of the more aristocratic cavalry. In the absence of Cimon his supporters were leaderless, frightened, and, in some cases, irresponsible. The result is one of the rare cases of treasonable conspiracy in Athenian history. Had Cimon been present, his good sense would have prevented these extremists from having any influence, and he would certainly have discouraged their activities. All our evidence shows him to have been a man comfort-

[30] 1. 107. 4.
[31] See Gomme, *Hist. Comm.,* I, 312.

able with the Athenian democracy, who could even live happily under the post-Areopagite constitution. He never allowed partisan considerations to interfere with patriotism; but he was in exile and could do nothing. It is possible that there had been communication between the Athenian oligarchs and the Spartan war party even before the Spartans had left the Peloponnese, but it is certain that their persuasion helped decide Nicomedes to stand and offer battle to the Athenians in Boeotia.

Nicomedes' hopes, however, did not rest only on the weak reed of Athenian oligarchy. The true source of his confidence was Thebes. It was a general rule in the world of the Greek city-states that neighbors were at least mutually suspicious and often hostile. In land-hungry Greece the source of conflict was usually a contest for desirable territory on the borders between neighboring states. For centuries, Sparta and Argos had contended for control of Thyreatis; a border dispute between Corinth and Megara had helped bring on the present general conflict; Athens and Megara had a history of conflict over border territory and over the island of Salamis, which lay between them; and such examples could be multiplied many times.

Athens and Boeotia, of which Thebes was the greatest city, shared a long border by Greek standards, yet until the end of the sixth century they appear to have lived in peace. In part, this demonstrated the dictum that good fences make good neighbors, for the Parnes mountain range made accidental border violations highly unlikely. Boeotia and Attica, moreover, were relatively large and prosperous regions where the pressure of want was not great. When conflict arose late in the sixth century, it was for political reasons. Whereas Athens had been able to unify Attica so successfully that every resident was a citizen of Athens and not of his locality, Thebes had not been able to do the same thing in Boeotia. At its strongest moments Thebes was only the leader of a confederation of autonomous towns with strong local loyalties and varying degrees of friendship for Thebes.

In 519 the Athenians became involved in Thebes' attempt to strengthen her control of Boeotia. They intervened on behalf of the Plataeans' struggle to maintain their independence against a Theban attack. Their success earned the undying friendship of Plataea and the hostility of Thebes.[32] The Thebans gave evidence of their feelings in 506 when Cleomenes took a Peloponnesian army into Attica to put down the Cleisthenic democracy. They joined with Cleomenes and the army of Chalcis to attack Athens from three sides, beginning the campaign by seizing the border districts of Oinoe and Hysiae. The plan failed when the Corinthians refused to cooperate and the Peloponnesian contingent retired from the field. Free now to turn against the Thebans and Chalcidians, the Athenians defeated them. Enraged by the turn of events, the Thebans turned to Aegina and helped bring on the first of a series of conflicts between Aegina and Athens, but to no avail. The Thebans suffered another defeat at Athenian hands, and their taste for vengeance was unappeased.[33] Plataea remained independent and closely attached to Athens.

The Persian War further estranged the now unfriendly neighbors. Athens fought valiantly for Greek freedom while Thebes Medized. The result was a serious diminution of Theban prestige and influence corresponding with the rise of Athenian power. The Boeotian confederation was dissolved and each city given its independence.[34] A moderate oligarchy seems to have replaced the "dynasty of a few men" who ruled Thebes tyrannically during the Persian War, and it managed to keep Thebes out of trouble until the outbreak of the First Peloponnesian War.[35] During the years of peace Thebes was able to retain her strength and to think again of regaining her prestige. It was under these circumstances that the Thebans invited the Spartan army to come into Boeotia and "to help their city to gain the entire hegemony of Boeotia." [36]

[32] For the events of 519, see Hdt. 6. 108 and Thuc. 3. 68. For a discussion of the date, which is debated by modern scholars, see Paul Cloché, *Thèbes de Béotie* (Namur, Louvain, and Paris, no date), 30–32. For the early history of Thebes, see Cloché, *ibid.*, 12–29 and F. Schober, *PW*, V: 2 (1934), *s.v.* "Thebai (Boiotien)," 1452–1459.

[33] Hdt. 5. 74–81.

[34] Diod. 11. 8. 13.

[35] The quotation is from Thuc. 3. 62. 3–4. I follow Busolt and Swoboda (*GS*, II, 1413, n. 1) in calling the Theban government a moderate oligarchy. Schober (1462) believes that a democratic government was installed after the war. His position is challenged by Cloché (*Thèbes*, 48–50), who is in essential agreement with Busolt and Swoboda, but calls the new Theban government "un régime aristocratique."

[36] Diod. 11. 81. 2. Justin (3. 6) says that the Spartans fought "ut Boeotiorum imperium his [sc. Thebanis] restituerent."

Diodorus provides us with the clue to Sparta's strange willingness to take a large army out of the Peloponnese to re-establish Theban supremacy in Boeotia at the same time that it was unwilling or unable to invade Attica. The Thebans promised that in return for Sparta's help, "They would themselves make war on the Athenians so that there would be no need for the Spartans to bring an army outside of the Peloponnese." The Spartans were delighted with such a prospect and agreed to the proposal, "judging that it was advantageous to them and thinking that if the Thebans became more powerful they would be a sort of balanced antagonist to the Athenians." As a result they helped fortify the city of Thebes and forced the Boeotian cities to become subject to Thebes.[37]

It is possible, as Thucydides implies, that the Athenians knew nothing of the Theban invitation. They did, however, know of a large Peloponnesian army in Boeotia, and they were suspicious of a plot to overthrow the democracy at Athens. As a result, they marched into Boeotia with the entire force available to them, accompanied by allied contingents including one thousand Argives. The entire force came to fourteen thousand men in addition to a detachment of Thessalian cavalry.[38]

The two armies met at Tanagra. The Athenian force was more numerous, but the Thessalians deserted to Sparta in the midst of the battle, and the Spartans won a victory in which both sides suffered heavy casualties. Although the Spartans controlled the field at the end of the day's fighting, their victory was somewhat Pyrrhic, for they were unable to follow it up and could do nothing but force their way through the Megarid and return to the Peloponnese. The

[37] Diod. 11. 81. 1–4.

[38] 1. 107. 5–7. Thucydides makes no mention of the Theban invitation, which affects his interpretation of the Athenian purpose in taking the field. He says that the Athenians thought that the Spartans 'απορεῖν ὅπη διέλθωσιν, suggesting that the Athenians hoped to take advantage of an opportunity to fight, which the Spartans would have been glad to avoid. He also speaks of the Athenians as going out against the Lacedaemonians, making no mention of the Thebans, yet Pausanias (1. 29. 6) tells us he saw a monument to two Athenian cavalrymen who died "fighting the Lacedaemonians and Boeotians on the borders of Eleon and Tanagra." He appears not to have known or not to have believed the story told by Diodorus, but that account appears to be more than plausible. For a discussion of the numbers of troops at the battle, see Gomme, *Hist. Comm.*, I, 315.

oligarchic conspiracy at Athens never came to anything, and within two months the Athenians were able to return and conquer a Boeotia that had been abandoned by its Peloponnesian allies.[39]

The Athenians had fought the Battle of Tanagra under peculiar conditions. Suspicion of treason was in the air, and it was natural to suspect that the friends of Cimon might be involved in the plot. Perhaps Cimon feared that some of his disgruntled followers might be tempted or perhaps he merely wanted to clear his friends' reputation and his own and to demonstrate their patriotism. In any event, Cimon appeared at Tanagra in full armor, ready to join his tribal ranks in the battle to come. The Athenian boulé, behaving with the panic that men show when there is rumor of treason in wartime, accused him of coming with treasonable intentions and drove him off.[40] Cimon was not embittered. Instead of sulking, he urged his friends to dispel the suspicion that surrounded them by their bravery in battle. They fought well and must have convinced their countrymen of their patriotism, for shortly after the battle Cimon was recalled from his exile, Pericles himself proposing the decree.[41] He soon was able to arrange a truce of four months with the Spartans and then may have gone off again to his estates in the Thracian Chersonnese to wait until conditions made possible a lasting peace with Sparta and a policy that he could honestly support.[42]

[39] Thuc. 1. 108. 1–2; Diod. 11. 82; Gomme, *Hist. Comm.*, I, 315–316.

[40] Plut. *Cim.* 17. 3–4. In his life of Pericles, Plutarch says that Cimon was driven off by "the friends of Pericles" (10. 1), but there is no real contradiction between the accounts. The same men are referred to in both passages: it was the proper duty of the councillors to send a man who had been banished away from the battle. The story that these men were the friends of Pericles is probably true; most councillors in 458/7 were likely to be friendly to Pericles, but Plutarch did not know precisely who they were, although he does have a rather precise knowledge of other things that happend at Tanagra. The tale that Cimon was driven off by "the friends of Pericles" instead of the boulé is merely a gloss by Plutarch or his source.

[41] Plut. *Cim.* 17. 4–6; *Per.* 2–3; Nepos *Cim.* 3. 3.

[42] Diodorus (11. 80. 5) tells us of the four-months' truce. Theopompus (*FGrH*, frg. 88) tells us of Cimon's recall and that he concluded a peace on his return. Busolt (*GG*, III: 1, 317–318) is the source of the suggestion that Cimon went off to the Chersonnese. Plutarch (*Cim.* 18. 1) seems to indicate that the peace Cimon made was the Five Years' Peace, which was not in fact concluded until 451/50.

Almost every element in the story of Cimon's recall has been questioned by modern scholars. The details of his actions at Tanagra have been called "an accumulation of absurdities"; [43] Plutarch's confusion of the four-months' truce with the Five Years' Peace of 451/50 has been taken as a reason for rejecting his entire story; the four-months' truce has been rejected as an invention, and, it has been pointed out, Diodorus does not even connect it with Cimon.[44] None of these objections is very weighty. Plutarch is often guilty of chronological confusion and artistic invention even when he is telling a story that is basically true.[45] The other objections need not detain us long; no one has yet imagined why Diodorus or his source Ephorus should invent anything like a four-months' truce on this occasion, and the omission of Cimon's name is hardly peculiar to this passage.[46]

A more serious objection to our account of events is political: "Why should the Spartans conclude a truce which left Boeotia at the mercy of Athens and secured to themselves no corresponding advantage? . . . Further, if Cimon was recalled in 457 B.C., why is there no trace of his presence at Athens until 451 B.C. Why, above all, was he not sent to the rescue of the Athenian force in Egypt?" [47] These questions make clear the true nature of the problem. Its solution requires an analysis of the political situation, which our sources do not

[43] Beloch, *GG* ², II: 2, 211.

[44] Walker, *CAH*, V, 468.

[45] As Gomme (*Hist. Comm.*, I, 326) has put it, "Beloch shows that the details of this story in Plutarch are impossible; but that is not reason enough for rejecting the whole. The details are embroidery."

[46] The story of Cimon's return is generally accepted. Grote (IV, 416–417), Glotz and Cohen (*HG*, II, 151–152), Busolt (*GG*, III: 1, 258, n. 1 and 316, n. 3), Meyer (*GdA*, IV: 1, 562), and Gomme, (*Hist. Comm.*, I, 326–327) all believe it, though each interprets the events somewhat differently. Raubitschek (*Historia*, III [1954–5], 379–380 and *AJA*, LXX [1966], 37–42) accepts the story but believes that the Five Years' Peace was concluded in 458/7, which I do not accept. Among modern scholars, only Beloch rejects the story outright. Walker, who is inclined to deny its truth, says, "There are only two alternatives: either Cimon was recalled after Tanagra, or he was not recalled at all, but came back when the ten years of his ostracism had expired. A recall, but at some other date than after Tanagra, may be left to those to whom compromise is dear" (p. 469). The interpretation offered here accepts the first of the alternatives.

[47] Walker, *CAH*, V, 468.

make explicit. Once again the historian who wishes to understand this difficult period must try to read between the lines.

It is not difficult for us to imagine the Athenian state of mind on the eve of the Battle of Tanagra. The long walls that would guarantee Athenian security were not yet completed; talk of treason was in the air. A strong Peloponnesian army was united with Athens' rejuvenated and implacable enemy Thebes. Corinth, which had intervened to save Athens from such a danger in the past, was now ranged among its most bitter enemies. A decisive defeat now could well mean the destruction of Athens and its recently acquired power. In such circumstances it was natural to fear treachery from Cimon's appearance. Cimon's behavior and the outcome of the battle changed all that. He and his friends had demonstrated their loyalty and patriotism. The battle, though technically a defeat, was a strategic victory, for the danger of invasion was past, for the moment at least, and the danger of treason seemed to be gone for good. The Athenians, however, could not relax. The Spartans had fought their way back to the Peloponnese by land; they might next fight their way back into Attica. The Athenians could not yet know that the Spartans were prepared to abandon their Theban allies, if, in fact, they had already decided to do so. The situation was still critical. The danger to Athens called for a cessation of factional strife, and the events at Tanagra made it possible.

Pericles, as we have seen, was not necessarily eager to fight Sparta. With others, he had carried on the war as vigorously as was necessary, but we have no reason to think that he was determined to carry it forward. If Cimon was now prepared to accept the reforms that Ephialtes and Pericles had introduced, and it appears that he was, there was no major policy difference between them. At any rate, there was no reason why the Athenians should not use Cimon's unique qualities to win a respite and perhaps an ultimate settlement. The time could be used to further the completion of the walls and to make Athens secure in case the war should continue. Athens had everything to gain and nothing to lose by agreeing to a truce of four months.

It is, of course, more difficult to understand why Sparta was willing to make such an agreement. The problem becomes a bit simpler if we look at the results of Tanagra from the Spartan point of view.

In a battle in which they had risked a sizable army, the Spartans had won a narrow victory that had turned out to be strategically useless. They had, moreover, suffered heavy losses, and the entire course of Spartan history shows how seriously they took the loss of Spartan soldiers. They might very well have re-evaluated their agreement with Thebes, which promised them freedom from extra-Peloponnesian expeditions but which had delivered instead a costly battle in Boeotia that profited Thebes alone. In these circumstances, the idea of a negotiated peace must have seemed more attractive.

It was at this time that news of Cimon's recall came to Sparta. If we are right in thinking that the advocates of peace were already gaining ground, the news could well have turned the tide in their favor. The return of Cimon to Athens might mean a return by Athens to a conservative policy in mainland Greece and a restoration of the friendly relations between Athens and Sparta. It must already have been very clear that the expulsion of Cimon and his troops from Sparta had been a costly mistake, expensive to both the Spartans and Cimon. What could be more fitting than to correct that error through the agency of Cimon himself?

The conclusion of a four-months' truce, far from arousing suspicion, is a reason to have confidence in the historicity of the account. In the first place, it accords well with the necessarily cautious nature that negotiations would have after Tanagra. More telling still is the analogy to a similar truce concluded by the Spartans with the Argives in 418. On that occasion the Spartans and their allies were about to engage the Argives in a great battle on the Argive plain. Just as the armies were ready to come to grips, King Agis of Sparta concluded a truce for four months with one of the Argive generals and with an Argive who was proxenus of the Spartans. The Argives said they would be willing to submit complaints to arbitration and "for the future to make a treaty and keep the peace." [48] This was a clear attempt to win a victory by diplomacy and thus avoid a battle that it appeared the Spartans could win, although at a cost. The Spartans accepted the truce after Tanagra for the same reasons; the peace party must have urged its acceptance in the hope of restoring Spartan policy to its traditional paths.

[48] Thuc. 5. 58–59. For the interpretation of these events, see Kagan, *CP*, LVII (1962), 207–218.

The Athenian victory at Oenophyta shattered all such hopes. The truce was strictly between Athens and Sparta and did not include Boeotia. On the sixty-second day after Tanagra, Myronides took an Athenian army to Oenophyta in Boeotia, where he defeated the Boeotian forces. The Athenians pulled down the walls of Tanagra and became the masters of all Boeotia except for Thebes itself, newly fortified with the aid of Sparta. The Athenians quickly overran Phocis and Locris and would have done the same to Thessaly had they not been checked by the walls of Pharsalus.[49] Democracies were established in the cities of Boeotia, perhaps even in Thebes itself.[50] Suddenly, at one stroke, Athens had become the master of central Greece.

While all this was going on, the Athenians completed the building of their walls. From then on they were invulnerable to Spartan attack. This had all taken place in the period from the late summer of 458 down to the end of the next winter. In the spring of 457 this *annus mirabilis* was capped by the surrender of Aegina and its reduction to a tribute-paying member of the Delian League.[51] All this success could not fail to dampen Athenian ardor for peace. Negotiation could only succeed if Athens were willing to abandon some of the fruits of her victory. Elated by their victories, the Athenians were certainly not willing to make any sacrifices and were prepared to prosecute the war until their enemies should sue for peace.

There is good reason to think that Pericles was not in favor of the second expedition to Boeotia that produced the Battle of Oenophyta. He is nowhere mentioned in connection with that campaign, and here the argument from silence is worth something, for it was common for later writers to attribute anti-Spartan actions to him. It is further true that we have very clear reports of later campaigns that

[49] Thuc. 1. 108. 1–3; Diod. 11. 81–83.

[50] Thuc. 1. 113. 2; 3. 62. 5; Arist. *Pol.* 1302 b 29; Pseudo-Xenophon, *Ath. Pol.* 3. 10–11. See the discussions of Gomme, *Hist. Comm.*, I, 317–318 and Cloché, *Thèbes,* 68–69 and 49–50.

[51] Thuc. 1. 108. 3–4; Diod. 11. 78. 4. It is not clear whether Aegina was a member of the Delian League before this war. It is generally assumed that it was not, but was rather a member of the Peloponnesian League. D. M. Leahy (*CP,* XLIX [1954], 232–243) argues in favor of this traditional view. Douglas MacDowell (*JHS,* LXXX [1960], 118–121), however, presents the case for early membership in the Delian League.

he himself led against the Spartans.[52] If he is not named, we have good reason to think he was not involved; if he was not involved, we may suspect that he disapproved.

It is well to keep in mind that in 458/7, Pericles was still under forty and far from the unchallenged master of Athens. For instance, Myronides, the victor of Oenophyta, was a veteran of the Persian War and a man of immense prestige. It is clear that he favored an aggressive policy, and he was not alone. The likelihood is that the warlike faction at Athens simply outvoted Pericles without rejecting what he had done, for the four-months' truce, as we have seen, gave Athens a free hand in Boeotia. The attack may have violated the spirit of that truce but not its letter. When the war policy proved so incredibly successful, the policy we have attributed to Pericles was finished. Pericles could do nothing but bow to circumstances and accept what he could not alter. It must have been at this time that Cimon decided that the political climate in Athens was not to his liking and withdrew until a more favorable season. His efforts to restore peace would not be welcomed by the ebullient Athenians. He would return when the fortunes of war had made them more sober.

In the following summer Athenian daring won additional victories. Tolmides took an Athenian fleet around the Peloponnese. He burned the Spartan dockyards at Gytheum, captured Chalcis, a Corinthian colony on the north shore of the Gulf of Corinth, and inflicted a defeat upon the army of Sicyon.[53] The unbroken series of Athenian successes continued, and the Athenian strategy appeared to grow ever more aggressive.

By the autumn of 457 the Athenian forces were troubling the Persians in Egypt to such a degree that they were compelled to seek relief. As usual, the Great King tried to make use of Greek quarrels to further his own interests. He sent Megabazus to Sparta, supplied with money, to persuade the Spartans to invade Attica and so to draw off the Athenians from Egypt. Megabazus soon found that the money brought no results and returned to Persia with the remaining

[52] Thuc. 111. 2–3; Diod. 11. 85. 1–2; Plut. *Per.* 19. 2–4.

[53] Thuc. 1. 108. 5; Diod. 11. 84 gives a somewhat confused account of this expedition, including activities omitted by Thucydides and placing the settling of Naupactus, which happened earlier, in this year. See also schol. Aeschin. 2. 75.

funds.[54] The Spartans were clearly not ready to risk a major campaign when Athenian power was at its acme. The Persians now had no choice but to undertake a major offensive of their own in Egypt. Megabyzus was sent overland with a very large army to put an end to the uprising. The Egyptians and their allies were quickly defeated in battle. The Greeks were driven from the city of Memphis, which they had held, and shut up on the island of Prosopitis in the Nile. The siege lasted for almost eighteen months, but at its conclusion in 454 the entire Greek force was destroyed, and Egypt was restored to Persian control.[55]

This was a disaster of the greatest magnitude for Athens. The account of Thucydides suggests that almost all of a fleet of two hundred and fifty ships and their crews of forty to fifty thousand men were lost. Even if we reject these figures as too large, the lowest estimate is that of Ctesias, which speaks of forty ships, meaning something like eight thousand men.[56] Even assuming that a good part of the force was not Athenian, such a destruction of Athenians and their allies was nevertheless a tremendous and unprecedented defeat. Its psychological impact must have been even more damaging than the loss of men and ships. It broke an uninterrupted series of Athenian victories over Persia, caused serious unrest in the Aegean, and forced a curtailment of the Athenian efforts on the mainland. A second attempt to win control of Thessaly had already failed, and Pericles' campaigns in the Gulf of Corinth, which took place in the same summer, were Athens' last military activities in Greece until 447. The Athenians were forced to abandon their expansion on the continent to meet the challenge of their first great imperial crisis.[57]

[54] Thuc. 1. 109. 2–3; Diodorus (11. 74. 2) says the Spartans refused the money.

[55] Thuc. 1. 109–110; Diod. 11. 75 and 77. 1–5; Ctesias 32–34.

[56] See Gomme, *Hist. Comm.*, I, 321–322 for a discussion of the literature on the size of the Egyptian expedition.

[57] Although Thucydides mentions the Egyptian disaster (1. 110. 5) immediately before he speaks of the Thessalian campaign and the Periclean expeditions (1. 11. 1–3), I believe that these activities took place before news of the Egyptian defeat reached Athens, and Thucydides tells of the defeat when he does merely to complete his narrative of the Egyptian campaign. In this I accept the chronological suggestion of Meiggs, *HSCP*, LXVII (1963), 3–4 and n. 12.

6. The Crisis in the Aegean

The disastrous defeat of the Egyptian expedition seriously challenged Athens' hegemony in the Aegean. The Athenian response took them a long way towards converting their hegemony into frank and open domination. Thucydides is tantalizingly silent on the details of the transition from the Delian League to the Athenian Empire, but we are able to fill in some of the gaps by using the evidence of ancient inscriptions. With their aid we can piece together the steps in the evolution of the Athenian Empire and flesh out the bare statements of the ancient authors.

In the early 450's, Athens was fighting a war on two fronts, against Sparta and her allies on the one hand, and Persia on the other. This put an unprecedented strain on her purse and on her manpower, which, of course, resulted in heavy demands upon the allies. The allies may have been happy to fight against Persia and to join in a campaign against Egypt that promised to bring them great wealth, but they were unlikely to favor the more difficult, less profitable, and emotionally less acceptable prospect of fighting against their fellow Greeks. Perhaps encouraged by Persian intrigue, some of the allies, such as Erythrae and Miletus, took advantage of the terrible defeat suffered by the Athenians in Egypt to revolt.[1] Erythrae

[1] The authors of *ATL* date the rebellions of Erythrae and Miletus before the destruction of the Athenian forces in Egypt. They believe that the allies were reluctant to fight in Egypt, that the Athenians tried compulsion, and that rebellion ensued (III, 253). I have preferred the version of Meiggs (*HSCP*, LXVII [1963], 2), which sees the revolts as a consequence of the Egyptian disaster.

and Miletus were two states on the coast of Asia Minor. The evidence of inscriptions allows us to see how the Athenians dealt with these rebels after the suppression of their revolts.

Our knowledge of the revolt of Erythrae comes from an Athenian decree copied by Fauvel early in the nineteenth century which is now lost. Subsequent work by epigraphers has improved the text to the point where it can now be dated with relative security to the year 452.[2] The decree provides regulations for the control and government of Erythrae following her return to the Delian League after a revolt. The rebellion appears to have been undertaken by an Erythraean tyrant supported by Persia, for each member of the newly established council had to swear not to receive exiles who had fled to the Persians, while the death penalty was prescribed for anyone betraying the city to the tyrants.[3] The new government was a democracy, probably on the Athenian model, certainly supported and supervised by Athens. The decree speaks of Athenian civil officials (*episkopoi*) and a commander of the Athenian garrison (*phrourarchos*). It further requires that the Erythraeans should supply sacri-

[2] The date and the text that establish it are those of the *ATL,* II, 54–57 (D10). It is accepted by Meiggs (*loc. cit.*) and by most epigraphers. In recent years the date of this decree and of many Athenian inscriptions of the third quarter of the fifth century have come under vigorous attack from H. B. Mattingly. His thesis is expressed in the following articles: *Historia,* X (1961), 148–188; *JHS,* LXXXI (1961), 124–132; *CQ,* N.S., XI (1961), 154–163; *CQ,* N.S., XVI (1966), 172–192; and *ASI,* 193–224. In brief, he argues on epigraphical and historical grounds that the decrees that show Athens tightening her grip on the allied states and taking harsh measures belong not in the 450's but in the period of Cleon's eminence in the 420's. The orthodox view is defended by Meritt and Wade-Gery in two articles, *JHS,* LXXXII (1962), 67–74 and LXXXIII (1963), 100–117 and also by Meiggs, *HSCP,* LXVII [1963], 24–30. As Mattingly graciously admits, his argument "seems to have won no adherents. I cannot really complain of this, since my arguments were inevitably far from cogent" (*CQ,* N.S., XVI [1966], 172). He has won no adherent to his general theory in me, but he has made it clear that the dating of each inscription must be carefully examined without prejudice. As Meiggs has put it (*JHS,* LXXXVI [1966], 87), "Mattingly has performed a very useful service in compelling us to examine more rigorously judgments which we have accepted at second hand." Not the least of his services was to provoke the splendid article of Meiggs, which supports the traditional dates in a persuasive fashion.

[3] Lines 25–34.

ficial animals for the Panathenaic Games. If all this seems evidence of naked imperialism, it should be pointed out that the decree is careful not to slight the interests and significance of the league. The councillors swear an oath of loyalty not only to Athens but to the league, and exiles from Erythrae are banished from the entire confederacy. The Erythraeans also retained at least a degree of judicial autonomy.[4]

The revolt of Miletus seems to have taken place about the same time. The absence of Miletus from the first two tribute lists and its presence on the third, the list of 452/1, indicate that the Milesians had been in rebellion but were subdued and returned to the league. We do not have the decree, precisely parallel to the Erythrae decree, which brought the rebellious state back into the league; instead we have a document that gives evidence of a subsequent intervention by Athens into the government of Miletus, dated to the year 450/49. The Regulations for Miletus, as the document is usually called, both resembles and differs from the rules established for Erythrae.[5] The Regulations do not establish a democratic government in Miletus, but they do provide for five Athenian officials, *archons,* not *episkopoi,* who are to govern in partnership with the magistrates of Miletus. Judicial autonomy is smaller than in Erythrae, and some cases, at least, are to be heard in Athenian courts. An Athenian garrison is established, and it is possible that the Milesians were compelled to supply military and naval help as well as to pay tribute.

It is very instructive to trace the history of Miletus from the rebellion down to the decade before the Peloponnesian War.[6] During the early 450's, Miletus was governed by an oligarchy friendly to Athens. A tyranny, supported by Persia, seized power and revolted. After the

[4] Line 29. L. I. Highby (*The Erythrae Decree, Klio,* Beiheft, XXXVI [1936], 10–33) emphasizes the friendliness of the relations between Athens and Erythrae implied by this decree. A necessary nuance to that interpretation is provided by Meiggs, (*JHS,* LXIII [1943], 23–24).

[5] The text of the decree (Dll) is that of *ATL,* II, 57–60. For the date and interpretation see *ATL,* III, 255–258; Meiggs, *JHS,* LXIII (1943), 25–27; *HSCP,* LXVII (1963),5, *JHS,* LXXXVI (1966), 95; and J. P. Barron, *JHS,* LXXXII (1962), 1–6. I accept Barron's interpretation of Milesian history for this period.

[6] Barron, *JHS,* LXXXII (1962), 1–6. He builds on and develops a thesis established by A. J. Earp, *Phoenix,* VIII (1954), 142–147.

suppression of the revolt, the oligarchy, which had remained loyal in exile, was restored to power. The restored government was shored up by an Athenian garrison and Athenian officials. In 446/5, troubled by the increasing openness of Athenian imperialism, and taking advantage of Athens' preoccupation with a Spartan invasion and the Euboean rebellion, the Milesian oligarchs massacred their democratic opponents and rebelled from Athens. The revolt was crushed, the tribute collected, the oligarchs outlawed, and a democracy on the Athenian model established. As an act of conciliation and encouragement to the new democracy, the tribute was cut in half.[7]

One of the Athenian responses to the crisis caused by the disaster in Egypt was the removal of the treasury of the league from Delos to the safety of Athens in 454/3.[8] Whether fear was the true reason or merely a pretext we cannot know, but the Athenians wasted little time in turning the event to their own advantage. Beginning in that year, they began to collect one sixtieth of the tribute paid by the allies as an *aparché,* first fruits, to Athena Polias, patron of Athens and now patron of the reorganized league.[9] The money collected in this way would soon provide temples on the Acropolis, support the Athenian fleet, provide work for the citizens of Athens, and accumulate as a reserve fund.

So important and radical a change required some justification, and there is reason to think that at this time Athens tried to change the concept behind the league and its very nature. From the beginning, many of the members of the league were colonies that had been sent out by Athens. The Athenians, moreover, had long claimed to be the founders of Ionia, a claim that the Ionians accepted.[10] The year of the transfer of the treasury happened to be one in which the Great

[7] The foregoing account is admittedly only a reconstruction and may not be right in all details, particularly in the attribution of motives. It seems to be very plausible, nonetheless, and explains all the evidence more satisfactorily than any other theory.

[8] Plut. *Per.* 12. 1.

[9] For the replacement of the Delian Apollo by Athena Polias as patron of the league, see Meritt and Wade-Gery, *JHS,* LXXXII (1962), 69–71; J. P. Barron, *JHS,* LXXXIV (1964), 35–48; and A. E. Raubitschek, *AJA,* LXX (1966), 37–41.

[10] Barron, *JHS,* LXXXII (1962), 6 and n. 40 and LXXXIV (1964), 46–47.

Panathenaic Festival, held every four years, took place. The coincidence appears to have produced the idea "that the league be assimilated into a system of colonies, with the four-yearly Great Panathenaia as their common feast." [11] It seems clear that the Athenians placed some stress on the status of their allies as colonies, for colonial status among the Greeks implied not inferiority and shame but equality and pride. Ties between colony and mother city were normally warm and solemnized by common religious observances.[12] Within a few years of the transfer of the treasury, the allies were asked to send a cow and a full suit of armor to the Great Panathenaic Festival, "symbolizing food and military assistance to the mother-city." [13] The burden was not heavy, and the honor of participating in the grand procession to the image of Athena was not insignificant, so "we may suppose it was thought less a burden than a privilege, and so was not a unilateral Athenian fiat but a resolution of the League." [14]

These changes in the nature of the league may or may not have pleased its members, but they certainly did not put an end to the danger to Athens. An inscription dated to 451/0 indicates that the Athenian colony of Sigeum on the Hellespont was threatened by other Greeks encouraged by the Persians.[15] There is good reason to believe, moreover, that many important island members of the league were refusing to pay tribute in the years between 454 and 450.[16]

[11] Meritt and Wade-Gery, *JHS,* LXXXII (1962), 71.

[12] Raubitschek (*AJA,* LXX [1966], 37) points out that the allies of Athens took part in the Dionysian and Eleusinian festivals as well as the Great Panathenaic Festival.

[13] Barron, *JHS,* LXXXIV (1964), 47.

[14] Meritt and Wade-Gery, *JHS,* LXXXII (1962), 71.

[15] *IG,* I², 32; Meiggs, *HSCP,* LXVII (1963), 6.

[16] No payments at all are recorded for Chalcis, Eretria, Hestiaea, Cythnos, Siphnos, Styra, Tenos, Paros, and Naxos for these years, while Ceos, Seriphos, and Andros appear for the first time in 450. These would make up an important part of the total. Although the lists preserved are fragmentary, Meiggs is surely right in saying, "Statistically it is extremely unlikely that a state which has left no trace in the fragments of four lists, from each of which approximately a half is preserved, was paying regularly" (*idem*). The absence of these islands from the lists has been explained in two ways. A. B. West (*AHR,* XXXV [1930], 267ff.) and the authors of *ATL* (III, 267ff.) believe that these islanders supplied ships and not money in this period. Nesselhauf

The troubles Athens faced in securing and reorganizing her empire are enough to explain the absence of any reports of Athenian actions against the Peloponnesians in the years from 454 to 451. In 451, Cimon returned to Athens, the ten years of his ostracism having passed. Whether or not the suggestion that Pericles had already sought to make peace with Sparta through Cimon in 458 is correct, conditions now certainly pushed the Athenians in that direction. The tightening of Athenian control over rebellious cities made them more secure, but it may well have made other cities resentful and restive. The Athenians could not be sure they would not be confronted by a series of rebellions that might threaten the existence of their Aegean empire. Persia, moreover, was once again a serious threat and might bring a fleet into the Aegean to match the mighty army that had triumphed in Egypt. For all these reasons Pericles and the Athenians must have been glad to have Cimon back to negotiate a peace with Sparta for them.[17] Plutarch says that Elpinice negotiated a reconciliation between Pericles and Cimon whereby the former would control the city and the latter command the war against Persia. But at this point there was no need for an intermediary between the two men, who agreed in all matters of policy; the division of responsibility was inevitable in view of the talents of both men and the need for Pericles to retain control of the political base on which his power rested.

In this year Pericles introduced a law limiting Athenian citizenship to those who had two citizen parents.[18] This measure is often seen as a demagogic attempt to please the masses, who were jealous of their privileges, since pay for public duties had made citizenship a precious possession.[19] It is likely that the opposite is true. The expansion of the citizen body was a tradition among democratic politicians. Cleisthenes had increased the citizenry by enfranchising metics. Themistocles had advocated measures to attract emigrants to Athens. In the fourth century it was possible for Aristotle to theorize that democracy itself went hand in hand with a large and growing population. Demagogues habitually created more citizens of the lower

(*Untersuchungen,* 11ff.) and Meiggs (*ibid.,* 6–9) argue that they were disaffected and refused to pay. I find the latter view more persuasive.

[17] Thuc. 1. 112. 1; Diod. 11. 86. 1; Plut. *Cim.* 18. 1; *Per.* 10. 4.

[18] *Ath. Pol.* 26. 3; Plut. *Per.* 37.

[19] E.g., Walker, *CAH,* V, 86.

class, since "a large population generally preserves democracy." [20] Conservatives and oligarchs, on the other hand, always tried to limit citizenship and to maintain the purity of the citizen body. The new advantages of citizenship that had been created by Pericles would have made the lower classes less hostile to a limitation on citizenship. Pericles himself had already achieved political control; further extension of the citizen body was not necessary for his continued eminence. By proposing a law to limit citizenship, he could make a gesture of reconciliation to the supporters of Cimon and to the conservatives in general that would cost him little or nothing. It was a move toward the center of the Athenian political spectrum to match the step taken by Cimon in accepting the reforms of Ephialtes and Pericles. Hignett is certainly right when he says, "Both statesmen were patriotic enough to subordinate their private quarrels to the welfare of Athens. If this was the setting of the citizenship law it must have been either a concession to the conservatives or a measure on which both they and the radical leaders were in agreement." [21]

Such agreement paved the way for the Five Years' Peace, that Cimon concluded with Sparta in 451. Athens had good reason to seek such a peace, but it remains to explain why the Spartans should have been willing to give up a splendid opportunity to roll back the Athenian gains and restore her own former hegemony. In part the answer lies in the return of Cimon and the hope which he always inspired in Sparta, particularly in the hearts of the peace party, that Athens would come to its senses. But Athens was not the only one in trouble. The Athenians had proven themselves a formidable, tenacious, and indefatigable opponent at Tanagra, Oenophyta, on the coast of the Peloponnesus, in the Megarid, and in the Gulf of Corinth. The danger from Argos, moreover, still threatened. If the war persisted, it could not be long before Sparta's old enemy would try to regain the lost provinces of the Thyreatis, the Alsace-Lorraine of

[20] For Cleisthenes and the increase in the citizenry, see Aristotle, *Pol.* 1275b; *Ath. Pol.* 21. 4. For Themistocles, see Diod., 11. 43. 3. For Aristotle's theory, see *Pol.* 1319b and 1321a and James Day and Mortimer Chambers, *Aristotle*. The historicity of the Cleisthenic enfranchisements has been doubted by Day and Chambers and also by J. H. Oliver (*Historia,* IX [1960], 503–507). It is defended in my article in *Historia,* XII (1963), 41–46. See also D. M. Lewis, *Historia,* XII (1963), 37, n. 135.

[21] C. Hignett, *A History of the Athenian Constitution,* 347.

Argive-Spartan relations. The Spartans, too, could see some advantage in a peace on the basis of the *status quo,* if they could be freed of the danger from Argos. It must have been as a condition of the peace that Athens abandoned her alliance with Argos. The Argives had no choice but to make a Thirty Years' Peace with the Spartans, which they observed faithfully.[22] The Spartans abandoned Thebes, and in return the Athenians deserted Argos.

Athens had reverted to a Cimonian foreign policy: peace with Sparta and aggressive war against the Persians. Very soon Pericles would show that the Egyptian disaster had made him more cautious and more eager to conserve the empire Athens had already won than to risk it by trying to extend it. For the moment, however, his interests were the same as those of Cimon; the empire could not be preserved without a blow to render the Persians harmless. As a result, he surely supported the despatch of a grand armada of two hundred ships under the command of Cimon to gain control of Cyprus. Of these, Cimon sent sixty to help the Egyptian rebels who were still holding out against the Persians. The remaining ships settled down to a siege of Citium on the southeastern coast of Cyprus. There Cimon died, either of wounds or disease.[23]

For almost thirty years he had played a leading part in Athenian affairs. With Themistocles and Aristides, he was a founding father of the Athenian empire. A conservative in temperament, an aristocrat by birth, training, association, and inclination, he nevertheless could adapt himself to a democratic society. An able politician and faction leader, he put Athens before faction. Until his ostracism and the rise

[22] 5. 14. 4; 22. 2; 28. 2. Gomme (*Hist. Comm.,* I, 328) points out that the sequence of events offered here is not the only one possible, that we do not know what was the relationship between the Spartan-Athenian peace and the Spartan-Argive treaty. He is quite right, but where certainty is unattainable, the historian must make do with likelihood. The situation is understood in much the same way as I understand it by Walker (*CAH,* V, 86–87); Beloch (*GG* ², II: 2, 209–210) and Gaetano De Sanctis, (*Pericle* [Milan and Messina, 1944], 125–126). De Sanctis expresses it most neatly: "la tregua di Cimone dovette essere pagata dagli Ateniesi a prezzo abbastanza caro. Essi cioè ebbero a rinunziare all'alleanza di Argo che dava loro il modo d'intervenire a tempo opportuno nel Peloponneso. Ma questo era il prezzo minimo che gli Spartani potessero chiedere. . . ."

[23] Thuc. 1. 112. 1–4; Diod. 12, 3–4; Plut. *Cim.* 18–19. 1.

of Pericles to supremacy, he was the most important man in the state. Even in his absence, like the ghost of Hamlet's father, he haunted the minds of his followers and moved them to action. His appearance at Tanagra may well have avoided treason and a devastating defeat for Athens. His influence played a great part in reconciling the aristocracy to the Athenian democracy and avoiding the bloody civil wars that shattered the tranquillity of other Greek states. Small wonder that Plato, who had rejected the Athenian democracy as a place where a noble soul could practice political virtue, should condemn him as a man indistinguishable from demagogues like Pericles and Themistocles.[24] But Cimon, of course, was not a demagogue. He was a politician who lived in the real world and who tried to restrain the worst inclinations of extremists on the right as well as the left. Unlike Callicles, the young man in Plato's dialogue, he could give an affirmative answer to the question "Have you made your fellow citizens better?" He was a great soldier and a great patriot; Athens would miss him.

After the death of Cimon the Athenians abandoned the siege of Citium, but at the end of the same summer (450) they encountered a combined force of Cypriotes, Phoenicians, and Cilicians at Salamis, a city on the island of Cyprus. The result was a decisive victory for the Athenians on both land and sea. The victorious fleet, joined by the ships that had gone to Egypt, returned to Athens, leaving Cyprus in the possession of Persia, but the main purpose of the expedition had been accomplished. The Athenians had demonstrated that they still controlled the sea and that they were willing and able to resist any Persian attempt to return to the Aegean.

The victory at Cyprus, combined with the removal of Cimon from Athenian politics, gave Pericles a free hand to pursue his own policy. It was then that he freed himself from the past and formulated the foreign policy that he pursued until the end of his life. Themistocles' policy of waging aggressive war against Persia had accomplished all that it could. Athens had profited from it, and her empire was the proof. But the Egyptian defeat had shown clearly that all these gains could be lost by a reckless policy of expansion. The rebellions of Erythrae and Miletus proved that the subject states would rebel if Athens were distracted. This led Pericles to prefer a policy of peace

[24] *Gorgias* 515 d-e.

with Sparta as well. Whatever he may have thought of the Athenian expansion on the mainland—and we may believe that he was less than enthusiastic about it—it too had accomplished all that was likely. Two failures in Thessaly had shown that the northern limit of Athenian influence had been reached. An attack on the Peloponnese would be difficult and dangerous in itself and would surely embroil Athens in a war serious enough to encourage rebellion in the Aegean. In 450, Athens was what Bismarck might call a saturated power. She sought no additional territory, but would take the necessary measures to insure the security of what she already held and the continued splendor of her prestige. The Periclean program, then, was peace with both Persia and Sparta, the defense of Athenian dignity, and firm control of the empire.

In the spring of 449, Athens concluded a treaty of peace with the Great King of Persia.[25] The terms negotiated by Callias, the son of Hipponicus, are reported by Diodorus: "All the Greek cities in Asia are to be autonomous; no Persian satrap is to come closer than a three-

[25] The authenticity of this peace, usually called the Peace of Callias, is one of the most debated questions in Greek history, along with the date of the fall of Ithome and now the authenticity of the Themistocles Decree. In my opinion, the state of the evidence does not admit of certainty. The defenders of authenticity depend on less than excellent ancient authorities. The doubters depend on interpretations of witnesses at least as untrustworthy plus the argument from silence. In this unhappy situation, I prefer the version of Ephorus in Diodorus to the doubtful epigraphical arguments of Theopompus and so am led to accept the historicity of a formal peace. It is important to point out, however, that the debate between doubters and believers is less one of substance than of form. All agree that the fighting between Athens and Persia came to an end and that Pericles immediately felt free to use league funds for his building program. Whether the peace was formally negotiated or not, it was clearly enough understood to be a fact, so that the Athenians were able to divert funds from military purposes to peaceful uses within the same year as the alleged peace. Defenses of the authenticity of the Peace of Callias include H. T. Wade-Gery, *HSCP*, Suppl., I (1940), 126ff.; Gomme, *Hist Comm.*, I, 331–335; *ATL*, III, 275–300; J. H. Oliver, *Historia*, VI (1957), 254–255; A. Andrewes, *Historia*, X (1961), 15–18; Meiggs, *HSCP* LXVII (1963), 10–13; and K. Kraft, *Hermes*, XCII (1964), 158–171. Arguments against are in Walker, *CAH*, V, 469–471; Raphael Sealey, *Historia*, III (1954–1955), 325–333; H. B. Mattingly, *Historia*, XV (1965), 273–281; and the best of all of all the critical accounts, the witty and vigorous article by David Stockton in *Historia*, VIII (1959), 61–79.

days' journey from the sea; no Persian warship is to sail in the waters between Phaselis and the Cyanean rocks; if the King and his generals respect these terms, the Athenians are not to send any expedition against the country over which the King rules." [26] The language and perhaps even some of the terms may have been changed by fourth-century rhetoricians, but there is no doubt as to the meaning of the peace. The Persians gave up their claim to control Greek states in the Aegean, on its coast, and in the Hellespont as well. In return the Athenians agreed to abandon their aggression against the Persian Empire. The Persian War was now truly over. Athens had completed the victory that Sparta had left unfinished after Mycale.

It is not without significance that the peace was negotiated by Callias, the brother-in-law of Cimon. As the husband of Elpinice, he was proof that the friendship between Pericles and Cimon lived on after the latter's death, and he must have done a good deal to allay the suspicions of the Cimonian faction and to win them over to the new policy. Callias was most useful to Pericles as a symbol of unity, and he employed him several times to negotiate important agreements.[27] He is not the only one to give evidence of the extent to which Pericles had drawn close to Cimon and his friends. Cimon himself had married Isodice, a member of the Alcmaeonid family, as was the mother of Pericles. After Pericles had divorced his wife, he gave her to Hipponicus, a relative of Callias. In 433 it is likely that Pericles was behind the appointment of Lacedaemonius, the son of Cimon, to the command of the first expedition to Corcyra. Finally, it is worth pointing out that Pericles gave great influence to his friend Metiochus; Cimon had a half brother called Metiochus. It is well to remember that "behind the public politics of the Athenian state was the family-politics of the great houses; here Pericles was an adept." [28]

But a masterful touch in managing the factions within the aris-

[26] Diod., 12. 4. 5–6.

[27] He negotiated the treaties with Rhegium and Leontini and the Thirty Years' Peace with Sparta in 446/5. The authors of *ATL* (III, 276) distinguish him from Callias, the son of Calliades, who moved the financial decrees of 434 and died at Potidaea, whom they call Callias the Financier. Callias, son of Hipponicus of Alopece, husband of Elpinice, they call Callias the Treaty-Maker.

[28] The quotation is from Raphael Sealey, *Hermes,* LXXXIV (1956), 247. On page 239 he has gathered the prosopographical material reproduced here.

tocracy was not enough in a democracy. Athens in the mid-fifth century was neither the Roman republic nor eighteenth-century England. So radical a change in policy must be explained, justified, and made palatable to the man in the street. Pericles' ancient enemies called him a great demagogue, and the most fervent of his modern enemies has called him not a statesman, but merely *"ein grosser Parliamentarier."* [29] Without prejudice, it may be agreed that he was a brilliant democratic politician who knew that in a democracy it is not enough to conceive and formulate good policies; it is equally necessary to persuade the electorate of their excellence and desirability. Plutarch tells us that he was a brilliant speaker who "showed that rhetoric, as Plato said, is the winning of men's souls," but the speeches in which he must have expounded and defended his program are not preserved.

What is preserved is the description of a dedication that the Athenians made to the god in thanks for the victory at Cyprus. They offered a tenth of the booty of that battle and ordered an inscription by Simonides in honor of the great victory over Persia. It "praised the struggles on Cyprus as the most glorious deed that the world had ever seen. At the same time it was a monument to the whole Persian War, the inclination to which had been embodied in the person of Cimon." [30] Pericles, of course, was behind this propaganda, which sought to demonstrate that the war had been concluded by a glorious Athenian victory instead of a negotiated peace and which seemed to tie Cimon to the new Periclean policy. At the same time this unprecedented generosity to the memory of Cimon could not fail to draw his followers closer to Pericles.

There could hardly be a more suitable occasion for unity at home, for Pericles was faced with extremely difficult tasks in establishing his new foreign policy. On the one hand he must find a justification for the Athenian Empire and the continuation of tribute payments after the original purpose of the league and the tribute had been abandoned. A related problem was his need to justify the diversion of funds from the league's treasury to purely Athenian uses, for Pericles had great plans for the artistic and cultural development of his city. This imperial side of Pericles' problems was very serious, as

[29] Beloch, *GG* ², II: 1, 154.
[30] E. Meyer, *Forschungen,* II, 19.

the epigraphic evidence clearly shows. In the assessment of 454/3, 208 cities were assessed over 498 talents. By 450/49 the figure had dropped to 163 cities paying less than 432 talents, a drop of over 13 per cent in assessed revenue. In addition, there is evidence that some cities made only partial payments and some paid late.[31] The picture is one of a good deal of resistance to Athenian control on the part of some cities and of hesitation and uncertainty on the part of others. If the empire was not to disintegrate, firm action was needed, and quickly.

The other half of Pericles' assignment was the establishment of a clear policy in regard to Sparta. The peace negotiated by Cimon was plainly only a truce in which time was gained to negotiate a permanent settlement. The death of Cimon intensified the need to conclude such a settlement quickly, for he had been the man Sparta trusted. Pericles would be required to produce deeds instead of words. This presented a serious problem, for between Athens and Sparta there stood a barrier that would have taxed the diplomatic talents and good will of even Cimon: the land empire Athens had acquired on the Greek mainland from Megara to Thessaly. Plainly, the Spartans could not permit this enormous change in the balance of power to become permanent. The likelihood is that the peace party, who surely had negotiated the Five Years' Peace with Cimon, had expected him ultimately to concede at least Megara in the permanent settlement, as he had immediately abandoned the Argive alliance. It is hard to believe that they could have won the Spartans over to their position without such an expectation. The Athenians, on the other hand, had seen the great value of Megara as a barrier to Spartan invasion, and it is hard to imagine any statesman with the will or ability to persuade them to surrender it. Pericles might be eager for peace with Sparta, but he was unable to pay the price the Spartans would surely ask.

In the spring of 449, Pericles boldly attacked both his major problems at once. He introduced a bill

to invite all Greeks, wherever they lived, whether in Europe or in Asia, whether small cities or large, to send representatives to a congress at Athens, to deliberate about the holy places that the barbarian had destroyed, and about the sacrifices that they owed, having promised them to

[31] *ATL,* III, 28–36; 52–59.

the gods when they fought against the barbarians, and about the sea, so that all might sail it without fear and keep the peace.[32]

Twenty messengers with the maturity and dignity of men over fifty were sent to deliver the invitations, five to Asia and the Aegean islands, five to Thrace and the Hellespont, five to Boeotia, Phocis, Acarnania, Ambracia, and the Peloponnese, and five to Euboea, the regions across from it, and Thessaly. The invitations urged them to come and "share in the plans for the peace and common interests of Greece." [33] The implications for the empire were plain. In this respect the Congress Decree, as it is called, was an attempt to set the claim of Athens to leadership of the Greeks on a new foundation. Religious piety, Panhellenism, and the common good were now to justify continued loyalty and sacrifice. While war had brought the Greeks together originally, let the maintenance of peace and security cement their union henceforth.[34]

There is some disagreement as to what response Pericles expected from Sparta. Some have believed that he was entirely disingenuous, that he anticipated a Spartan refusal, which would allow him to claim the hegemony of Greece by default.[35] At the other extreme is the view that the plan was offered with total sincerity in the hope of establishing a general and lasting Panhellenic peace. In this view the invitation to the congress was evidence of Pericles' honest attempt to restore peace to the Greeks; we should not assume that he expected or even provoked a Spartan refusal as a means of justifying Athenian imperialism. "To assume such a degree of political unscru-

[32] Plut. *Per.* 17. 1.

[33] *Ibid.*, 2–3.

[34] Nesselhauf, *Untersuchungen*, 32 has put Pericles' message particularly well: "Hatte bisher der Krieg die Griechen geeint, so wurde an seiner Stelle jetzt in schlagwortartiger Programmatik die Sicherung des Friedenzustandes als neues Ziel verkündet."

[35] Beloch (*GG* ², II: 1, 177) thinks that Pericles concluded the peace with Persia in the belief that a war with Sparta was inevitable. Miltner (*loc. cit.*, 763–764) believes that the invitation to the congress was an "Akt von grösster aussenpolitischer Tragweite, indem die Durchführung der einzeln verhandlungspunkte die Anerkennung der Hegemonie Athens in Griechenland, die damals zum ersten Male von Athen beansprucht wurde, bedeutet hatte. . . . Der Plan scheiterte, wie zu erwarten war und wie auch P. vorausgesehen haben muss, an der strikten Ablenhnung Spartas."

pulousness appears . . . misleading." To say that Pericles foresaw the failure of his proposal "really means that he feared it." [36]

If we are to understand the purpose of the Congress Decree, we must eschew both extremes, for each is too simple and fails to reckon with the complexities of the situation. The cynical view neglects the fact that Pericles had already given evidence of his eagerness for peace with Sparta by recalling Cimon and accepting the Five Years' Peace. The picture of Pericles as a disinterested devotee of Panhellenic peace and unity neglects the marvelous advantages to Athens of such a peace as the congress would establish. We may imagine that when Pericles made his proposal he thought there was at least a chance that Sparta's peace party, always anxious to avoid war, and perhaps made more trusting by Pericles' *rapprochement* with Cimon and his faction, would accept the change in the balance of power as a new fact of life and persuade the Spartans to do the same. If this should happen, nothing could please Pericles more, for it would be a diplomatic triumph that would crown his new policy of "pacific imperialism" with success at one stroke.

If the Spartans should refuse, and any realist must have understood that there was a good chance that they would, then nothing would be lost and much would be gained. Athens would have shown its Panhellenic interests and concerns and gained a moral advantage over Sparta.[37] The situation is not altogether different from the one facing the United States after the Second World War. Europe was already well along the road toward being divided into two spheres of influence. The Americans conceived the Marshall Plan with somewhat similar considerations. Their primary political goal was to strengthen western Europe, their own sphere of influence, which faced the threat of dissolution through communist accessions and the secessions from the American camp that would surely follow. On the other hand, it is altogether too cynical to say that the United States was not also moved by sympathy for the suffering people of Europe, by the desire to rebuild that war-shattered continent and return it to peace and prosperity. As it happened, the fulfillment of the second purpose would also help to accomplish the first, and so benefit the

[36] I have paraphrased the words of Dienelt, *op. cit.*, 21. The quotation is from note 28 on that page.

[37] For a similar interpretation, see De Sanctis, *Pericle*, 131–132.

Americans. They did not offer the plan in the confident expectation that it would be rejected by the Russians and their satellites. Acceptance would have pleased the United States, for it would have called off the cold war, which had already begun, in circumstances favorable to the Americans. The Russians' refusal was certainly not startling, but it was far from inevitable. The rejection, however, was a moral victory for the United States and put Russia in a bad light. It also helped justify further steps by which America tried to strengthen its leadership of the West in a world that was now more firmly split.

Like the Russians, the Spartans declined the invitation to participate and wrecked the congress.[38] The Spartan refusal, however, was a great propaganda victory for Athens, for the Athenians could now brand their rivals as indifferent to the welfare of Greece and unwilling to fulfill their sacred vows and duties. Even though the congress never met,

> It emphasized to all the world the claim of Athens to play the dominant role in the religious leadership of Greece, and its failure gave Athens the excuse for considering the reconstruction of her own temples, at least, out of funds collected against the barbarian, as part of an imperial plan which had fallen short of a more nearly perfect consummation through no fault of hers.[39]

Now Pericles was free to restore order to the empire and to guarantee the regular payment of tribute. It is the opinion of the leading historians of the Athenian Empire that Athens accepted a moratorium on tribute payments after the Peace of Callias, that is, for the year 449/8.[40]

> No doubt there had been a spontaneous reaction to the news of the peace in which the allies expressed their conviction that tribute was no longer needed. This attitude of the allies was natural and intelligible. The evidence is that Athens consented and that in the brief hiatus between Confederacy and Empire no collection of tribute was made.[41]

[38] Plut. *Per.* 17. 3.

[39] *ATL,* III, 280.

[40] *ATL,* I, 133 and 175, reaffirmed in *ATL,* III, 278–299 and note 16 on p. 278. The same view is held by Meiggs (*HSCP,* LXVII [1963], 14–15), although with less confidence.

[41] *ATL,* III, 278–279.

The evidence for this conclusion is the tribute lists, for, as usual, the literary sources are silent on the details of imperial rule. Only three quota lists are preserved for the four-year period from 450/49 to 447/6. The first of these, as we have seen, reflects the disturbances in the empire after the Egyptian disaster.[42] There are incomplete payments and states listed with balance due. There is no better way to comprehend the situation than to quote Meiggs' concise account:

> Only two other lists are preserved from this second assessment period, and their numbers do not survive. The first is at the bottom of the front face of the stele, the second on the right side. The second follows closely the order of the first, is complementary to it, and must surely belong to the next year. No fragments survive from the top of the back face. The next list of which the number survives is the list of the tenth year, 445/4, but the list immediately above it on the back face is from the same assessment period, and is almost certainly the list of 446/5. It follows from the evidence either that there is one list missing from the series or that there was a very short list at the top of the back face, providing room for less than 70 cities from an expected total of over 160. This list would be the list of 447/6 and in that year Megara and Euboia revolted. But such a large reduction in numbers from 447 to 446 is not credible, and had this space been occupied by a quota list some fragments would surely have survived and been identified. We should agree with the authors of the *Athenian Tribute Lists* that the space at the top of the back face was unoccupied and that the year in which no *aparchai* were recorded was 449/8.[43]

This reconstruction has been challenged on epigraphical grounds, and it cannot be regarded as decisively demonstrated.[44] But even if we grant that no quota list was inscribed on the stele for 449/8, we need not believe that none was demanded or collected. It is possible that "no *aparchai* were listed, because the whole tribute of the year was given to a special purpose." [45] Another possibility is that domestic opposition by Thucydides, son of Melesias, or someone of the

[42] Meiggs (*HSCP*, LXVII [1963], 14) thinks that it is evidence for the conclusion of the Peace of Callias in 450 instead of 449. In my opinion, it is evidence of the same kind of unrest which we know in Erythrae and Miletus before the peace.

[43] Meiggs, *ibid.*, 15.

[44] See Appendix D.

[45] Meiggs, *HSCP*, LXVII (1963), 15. This is essentially the suggestion made by Meritt ("Athens and the Delian League," in *The Greek Political*

same views may have prevented the payment of the quota to Athena on the grounds that the purpose for which it would be used, the adornment of Athens, was not proper. In this view the tribute would have been collected, but there would be no quota list, since, "our records are of the quota paid to Athena, not of the whole tribute. . . ."[46] Whether or not these explanations are probable, nothing could be less likely than that Athens would take the occasion of the conclusion of peace with Persia to encourage her allies to think that tribute payments might no longer be required. That would only make it more difficult to justify a resumption of payments. It was precisely the purpose of Pericles to maintain and to justify continuity in his imperial policy, to make it clear that the peace did not alter its essential nature. The justification would be different, but the procedures must remain the same. We may be sure that Pericles did not initiate or acquiesce in a temporary halt in tribute payments.[47]

Soon after the failure of the congress the Athenians began to tighten their control over their empire. A papyrus now located at Strasbourg, which seems to be a commentary on one of the speeches of Demosthenes or an epitome of such a commentary, mentions a decree that Pericles proposed in the summer of 449. The papyrus is somewhat mutilated, but the decree has been restored:

the appropriate officials are, [to carry up] at [the Panathenaia for Athena]

Experience, Studies in Honor of William Kelly Prentice [Princeton, 1941], 53) during a period when he was less confident that no tribute was collected in 449/8. At that time he said, "In the present state of knowledge it would perhaps be best not to claim that the absence of the quota list in 449/8 means that no tribute was collected. There are too many uncertain elements entering into the problem of the missing list. A more probable view is that Athens collected some tribute, and that she may have transferred all of it, not merely a quota, to Athena." So far as I can see the uncertain elements have not been significantly reduced since 1941.

[46] Gomme, *CQ*, LIV (1940), 67. Gomme's views on the whole question are on pages 65–67.

[47] For a brief but shrewd evaluation of the problem, see Victor Ehrenberg, *Sophocles and Pericles* (Oxford, 1954), 126, n. 1. I can only agree with him that "whatever final answer the epigraphists will find, there can never have been in any one year an official communication to the cities that there was no need to pay."

the money lying in the public treasury [which has been collected from the cities,] a sum of 5000 talents, according to Aristeides' [assessment, and to carry up] to the Acropolis after that [a further 3000] during the period of [construction; and in order to] maintain [control of the sea] the Council to [care for the] old triremes [so as to] hand them over [sound] and to build new ones in addition each [year, besides those already on hand to the number of] ten.[48]

If this version is correct in its essentials, then we have evidence of the beginnings of Pericles' use of league funds for purely Athenian purposes, not necessarily connected with military matters. Five thousand talents were to be taken immediately to begin construction, and after that, a sum of two hundred talents was to be paid each year for fifteen years, to reach the total of the additional three thousand talents. "Athens, at any rate, would rebuild her own temples." [49] The building program, however, would not interfere with the maintenance of the fleet, which would guarantee the freedom of the seas and keep the peace to justify the payment of tribute. The boulé would see to it that the old ships were kept in good repair and that ten new ships were added annually. If we may believe the report of Diodorus that Themistocles had persuaded the Athenians to build twenty new ships each year and that they continued to do so after 477, then the Papyrus Decree of Pericles shows that the peace with Persia made it possible to cut naval costs sharply.[50]

At the same time as the Athenians were laying a moral foundation for their continued hegemony, they were also taking steps to ensure the obedience of their allies. Three epigraphical documents are enough to give us a good picture of the nature of Athenian policy.[51] In 449/8 the Athenian Clearchus moved a decree to close

[48] See Appendix E.

[49] *ATL*, III, 281; Wade-Gery, *HSCP*, Suppl., I (1940), 150–151.

[50] The shipbuilding program of Themistocles is mentioned in Diodorus 11. 43. 3.

[51] The Monetary Decree of Clearchus, *ATL* D14, the Kleinias Decree, D7, and the Treaty with Colophon, D15, are dated by the *ATL* 449/8, 447 and 446 respectively. The first two were once thought to belong to the 420's, and Mattingly, in the articles cited above, would like to keep them in that context, when the evidence for tight Athenian control is undeniable. The thesis advanced here is that a tightening of control was already evident in the 440's as a response to the mid-century imperial crisis. With Meiggs and against Mattingly, I believe that the epigraphic criteria support the early date for the inscriptions.

mints in the allied states and impose Athenian weights, measures, and coins on the allies. The decree was to be posted in each city, by the Athenians if the natives failed to do so. The measures ordered in the decree were to be carried out by Athenian officials in the allied states unless there happened to be none, in which case the local magistrates were to see to their enforcement. To be sure, the Athenians were unable to enforce this decree with total success,[52] but the harshness of the language, the absence of reference to the alliance, the cool assumption that Athenian officials would be present in most cities shows how far things had come since the settlement of Erythrae.

In 447, Cleinias, possibly the father of Alcibiades, moved a decree dealing with the collection of tribute. The "archons in the cities" and the *episkopoi* were to see to it that the tribute was collected annually and brought to Athens. The cities were to record the amount of tribute they sent on separately sealed tablets, and their couriers were to hand over the tablets to the Athenian boulé with the seals intact. Presumably, previous shortages in the tribute payment had been blamed on the couriers. The inscription goes on to speak of the punishment for violations of the tribute regulations:

If any Athenian or ally does wrong concerning the tribute which the cities must send to Athens, having inscribed the amount on a tablet for the couriers, let anyone of the Athenians or allies who wishes charge him before the prytanies. Let the prytanies bring the charge that someone has brought before the boulé, or else each of the prytanies must pay a fine of ten thousand drachmas. If the boulé condemns the accused wrongdoer, it does not have the authority to fix the punishment but must immediately bring the case before the court of the heliaea. And when the court has judged that a wrong has been committed, let the prytanies give judgment as to what the convicted man should suffer or pay. And if someone commits a wrong concerning the payment of the cow and panoply, the charge and the penalty are to be treated in the same way.[53]

Once again we have evidence of Athenian officials established throughout the empire, in this case supervising the collection of the tribute. The procedure for punishing violations is very careful and implies the right of appeal, but initial charge, appeal, and sentencing

[52] E. S. G. Robinson, *Hesperia,* Suppl. VIII (1949), 324–340.

[53] Lines 31–43. My translation considerably expands the terse and legalistic language of the decree in order to make clear my understanding of its meaning. It should be checked against the text, *ATL,* II, 51.

all take place in Athens under the control of Athenians, whether in the boulé or the courts. Finally, by now the payment of a cow and a panoply for the Athenian festivals is universal. As we have seen, this implied that all tribute-paying allies had the status of Athenian colonies.

An inscription embodying an Athenian treaty with Colophon dated in 447/6, combined with what we learn from the tribute lists, gives us more evidence of what was happening to the relationship between Athens and her allies. The tribute quota list for 454/3 shows Colophon paying three talents, but from 450/49 through 447/6 the city appears to be absent from the lists and so to have paid no tribute. From 446 on, the tribute is reduced to one and one-half talents and is paid regularly.[54] The treaty inscription helps us interpret these facts. Its last section deserves quotation, if only for the extraordinary language in which it is couched:

Let the secretary of the boulé inscribe this decree and the oath on a stone stele in the city within the boundaries of the Colophonians; and let the colonists who have been settled in Colophon inscribe it and the oath on a stone stele in the market place within the boundaries of the Colophonians. And let the Colophonians swear the following: I will do and say and plan whatever good I can with regard to the people [*demos*] of the Athenians and their allies and I will not revolt from the people of the Athenians either in word or deed, either myself or in obedience to another. And I will love the people of the Athenians and I will not desert. And I will not destroy the democracy at Colophon, either myself or in obedience to another, either by going off to another city or by intriguing there. I will carry out these things according to the oath truly, without deceit and without harm, by Zeus, Apollo, and Demeter. And if I transgress may I and my descendants be destroyed for all time, but if I keep my oath may great prosperity come to me.[55]

It appears that the Colophonians had refused to pay tribute for some years, and when the Athenians were free to attend to them, they located a colony either of loyal allies or of Athenians on Colophonian territory. As was their custom when they confiscated land from an allied state, the Athenians reduced its cash contribution. Whatever the government of Colophon had been before, it was now a democracy. Loyalty, it should be noted, was sworn not to the alliance, but to "the demos of the Athenians and their allies." The lan-

[54] *ATL,* III, 282.
[55] *ATL,* II, 69.

guage of the oath was inconsistent with what a Greek would call autonomy.

By 450, of course, the Delian League had been transformed from a collection of autonomous Aegean states under the hegemony of Athens, with its center and treasury at Delos, into an organization of Athenian colonies, still nominally autonomous, but whose center and treasury was now at Athens. Desertions, rebellions, and refusals to serve had reduced the number of naval states and increased the number of those who paid tribute. That tribute now served to widen the disparity in power and influence between the Athenians and their allies.

One of the most useful weapons in maintaining Athenian control was the establishment of cleruchies on allied territory. In 450 cleruchies were sent to Naxos, Andros, and Lemnos. In 447/6 others were established on Imbros, the Thracian Chersonese, Chalcis, and Eretria.[56] A cleruchy, unlike an *apoikia,* or colony, was a settlement of Athenians on land taken from another people. The settlers did not make up a new independent city but remained Athenian citizens, often living side by side with the natives. Plutarch makes the advantages to Athens of such establishments very clear: Pericles sent out the cleruchies "to relieve the city of the lazy mob which took too much interest in public affairs because of its idleness, and to repair the poverty of the people. He did this also to establish a garrison as an object of fear to the allies to prevent them from making a rebellion." [57] The reduction of tribute that went along with the establishment of a cleruchy was more than made up for by the security that Athenian cleruchs, like early Roman colonists, gave to the empire.

The tribute was being paid, although some states were recalcitrant still. It appears that the Hellespontine region was particularly reluctant to pay, and it is likely that Pericles himself led an expedition to Thrace and the Hellespont in 448/7 to "show the flag" and to demonstrate to the more remote members of the empire that the peace with Persia had not ended Athens' hegemony or their own obligation.[58] By 447/6 the tribute lists already show the effects of the tightening Athenian control.

[56] For Naxos and Andros, see Plut. *Per.* 11. 5 and Paus. 1. 27. 5. For Imbros and Chersonese, see *ATL,* III, 289–294. For Chalcis and Eretria, see Diod. 11. 88. 3 and Paus. 1. 27. 5.

[57] *Per.* 11. 5.

[58] Plut. *Per.* 19. 1; for the date, see *ATL,* III, 299.

7. The End of the War

For the time being at least, the imperial part of Pericles' policy was going well. The other half, relations with Sparta, was not equally successful. In 449, soon after their rejection of Pericles' invitation to the Panhellenic Congress, the Spartans embarked upon the so-called Sacred War, in which they took control of the temple of Apollo at Delphi away from the Phocians and turned it over to the Delphians.[1] The Phocians were allies of Athens by virtue of a treaty concluded in 454/3. It is likely that they had gained control of the sanctuary because of this alliance and the Athenian victory at Oenophyta.[2] By their action the Spartans were not violating the letter of the Five Years' Peace, but in attacking an ally of Athens, they were certainly violating its spirit.

The attack is evidence of the restoration to power of the Spartan war party. Any hope that Pericles might have been fully converted to a Cimonian policy, that he might be willing to abandon at least part of his continental empire, was shattered by the Congress Decree. That decree, on the contrary, might appear a manifesto declaring the Athenian intention to claim religious and political hegemony over all Greece. The Spartans, already embarrassed by Athenian successes in central Greece, had suffered a further blow to their prestige as a result of the Periclean maneuver which forced them to

[1] Thuc. 1. 112. 5; Plut. *Per.* 21; Philochorus, frg. 88. I follow the *ATL* for this date and for the date of the Athenian counterattack which Thucydides reports in the next clause (3. 178, notes 64 and 65). Cf. Gomme, *Hist. Comm.*, I, 337 and 409 with note 2.

[2] *IG*, I [2], 26 = Tod, 39; Gomme, *Hist. Comm.*, I, 337.

reject an offer to participate in a religious and Panhellenic crusade. The attack on the Phocians and the restoration of independence to the priests of Delphi was a natural result of Sparta's disappointment and anger.

By now Sparta had overcome the effects of the helot rebellion. The peace with Argos guaranteed security on her eastern flank, and the end of Athens' war with Persia freed her from all fear of seeming to do the Mede's work.[3] It is interesting to notice that Sparta, under the control of her bellicose faction, once again took the initiative in bringing on hostilities. The campaign at Delphi could very well bring on a renewal of the war with Athens, for the Athenians had fought at Tanagra with even less formal reason. Here again, the Thucydidean judgment that the growth of Athenian power drove Sparta to war seems quite justified.

In fact, Athens did not immediately respond to the challenge. It was not until the summer of 447 that an Athenian army went to Delphi and restored possession of the sanctuary to the Phocians,[4] by which time the situation had changed. In 449, however, Pericles still hoped to avoid war with Sparta. As we have seen, he was faced with a difficult task of imperial organization which could cause unforeseeable trouble. With the memory of the Egyptian campaign so fresh, Pericles was far from eager to commit Athens to a war on two fronts, especially with its financial condition far from satisfactory. Perhaps he also hoped that his restraint would persuade the Spartans of his pacific intentions and lead them to accept the *status quo*.

It speaks well for Pericles' ability to control Athenian passions that he was able to maintain this policy for two years, during which anti-Spartan feeling must have been great. Perhaps the troubles in the empire helped persuade the Athenians of the need for restraint, but by 447 the situation had become relatively stable, the tribute was once again pouring in, and the more aggressive Athenians were ready for action. Eager to punish Sparta for her attack on their Phocian allies, the Athenians recovered Delphi for the Phocians, and for themselves the honor of the *promanteia,* the right of preferential treatment in consulting the oracle.[5]

[3] De Sanctis, *Pericle,* 135–6.

[4] See note 1 above.

[5] Plut. *Per.* 21.

Plutarch attributes this campaign to Pericles himself, but in this instance we may question his accuracy. It was common by Plutarch's time to attribute a permanent and inflexible hatred of Sparta to Pericles. He introduces the Athenian part of the Sacred War with a typical general remark: Pericles "considered it a great achievement to hold the Lacedaemonians in check, and set himself in opposition to these in every way, as he showed by his actions in the Sacred War." This attribution conflicts not only with the general tenor of Periclean policy in this period, but with Plutarch's own report of Pericles' reluctance to fight in Boeotia in the same year.[6] We cannot be sure, however, that Plutarch is wrong. If he is not, I think it likely that Pericles took command of the expedition under duress or to avoid having it led by a more reckless commander, in very much the same way that Nicias accepted the command of the Sicilian campaign. Whatever Pericles may have thought of this campaign, he certainly tried to check the confident aggressiveness to which it gave rise.

In the spring of 446, Boeotia, where the Athenians had driven out oligarchical governments and replaced them with friendly democracies, experienced an oligarchic revival. Orchomenus and Chaeroneia in particular were recaptured by the oligarchic exiles. Other oligarchic exiles from Locris and Euobea as well as other Boeotians were ready to join in a movement to drive out the friends of Athens and re-establish "autonomy," that is, oligarchic rule free of Athenian interference.[7] Athens was faced with the loss of its newly won land empire in central Greece. Tolmides, one of the most daring and aggressive Athenian leaders, wanted to launch an immediate expedition into Boeotia to recover the lost cities and to restore Athenian influence. Plutarch tells us that Pericles "tried to restrain and persuade him in the assembly, making his famous remark, that if he would not listen to Pericles, he would not go wrong in waiting for time, the wisest of counselors." In this case we may believe that Plutarch is passing on an accurate account, for he reports a famous public remark that is clearly and unambiguously associated with a specific event.[8]

[6] *Per.* 18. 2–3.

[7] Thuc. 1. 113. 1–2; 4. 92. 6; Diod. 12. 6.

[8] The story is told in *Per.* 18. 2–3. Many scholars have doubled Plutarch's story. Busolt (*GG*, III: 1, 421, n. 2) for instance, suggests that this may be

Pericles may have had few supporters for his policy of avoiding conflict with Sparta before the rising in central Greece, but once it had taken place the situation was different. There must have been many men who realized that it would be impossible to hold an area of that size in the face of general hostility.[9] When we find that Orchomenus was now on the same side as Thebes, her traditionally bitter enemy, we get some idea of the strength of feeling that united the class that counted in Boeotia, the landholding citizenry that made up the hoplite phalanx, a strength that could not have escaped the notice of the clearer-thinking Athenians.[10]

In the event, Pericles was unable to stop the expedition to Boeotia. Tolmides took one thousand Athenian hoplites, along with contingents from the allies, to liberate the Boeotian cities in oligarchic hands. The number of Athenians seems quite small in comparison with the four thousand who accompanied Cimon to Sparta in 462 and the thirteen thousand who seem to have been present at Tanagra. It appears that the bold and confident Tolmides considerably underestimated the power of the Boeotian oligarchs. His first campaign was successful, for he captured Chaeroneia, selling its population into slavery and planting an Athenian garrison in it. On the way back, however, disaster struck. At Coronea an oligarchic army from Orchomenus, Locris, Euboea, as well as other Boeotians, ambushed the Athenian army and won a smashing victory. Many Athenians were killed, among them their general, Tolmides. Many others were cap-

merely an example of Plutarchian invention to contrast the foresight of Pericles with the recklessness of Tolmides. He quotes with approval Duncker's remark that delay would only make the danger from Boeotia greater. I have argued above that the public and specific nature of the story makes it unlikely to be an invention or the mere excuse for the treatment of a familiar *topos.* It is quite true that delay would make the danger of losing Boeotia greater, but that only tells against the veracity of Plutarch's account if we assume that Pericles was unwilling to give up Boeotia at this time. I argue below that the opposite is true.

[9] Gomme (*Hist. Comm.,* I, 339) says: "Doubtless there is some truth in Plutarch's view which implies that Perikles was (by this time at least) against the attempt to hold Boeotia altogether, and that there had been many in Athens, even before the defeat, who felt it was beyond their powers—that it was exhausting rather than adding to their strength."

[10] See the shrewd analysis of De Sanctis (*Pericle,* 134), who speaks of this class as "certo la più potente, e meglio organizzata, la classe della borghesia abbiente che poteva fornirsi di armi proprie."

tured. This one battle put an end to the continental empire of Athens. The Athenians came to terms very quickly; they agreed to evacuate all of Boeotia in return for the repatriation of the captured Athenians. Without Boeotia, Phocis and Locris were untenable.[11]

The defeat at Coronea proved even more costly. Perhaps it helped shatter the Athenians' aura of invincibility; perhaps it was only that the time for a reaction had come. In any case, the Boeotian defeat was rapidly followed by other rebellions. In the summer of 446, Euboea revolted. For Pericles this rebellion was something quite different from the Boeotian uprising. Euboea was a rich and important island containing several cities which paid a sizable tribute. It was located directly on an important route to the Hellespont. Its possession by hostile forces would place an intolerable strain on the Athenian Empire. For these reasons he did not hesitate but immediately crossed the Euripus to put down the revolt. He had scarcely arrived when frightening news compelled his return. Megara, Athens' barrier against a Peloponnesian invasion, had revolted and, with the aid of Corinth, Sicyon, and Epidaurus, had destroyed the Athenian garrison except for those who had escaped to Nisaea. With this barrier removed, a Peloponnesian army was on its way to invade Attica. The Five Years' Peace had just expired, and it looks very much as if the Spartans had planned a concerted attack to coincide with its expiration.[12]

Pericles, of course, had no choice but to defend Attica, and so he took his army back to meet the Peloponnesians, who were engaged in ravaging Eleusis and the Thriasian plain. A decisive battle appeared imminent, but just as it seemed about to take place, the Peloponnesian army, led by Sparta's King Pleistoanax and his advisor Cleandridas, turned around and went home. The ancients explained this strange behavior in the simplest and most obvious way: Pericles bribed Pleistoanax and Cleandridas to abandon their attack.[13] Mod-

[11] Thuc. 1. 113; Diod. 12. 6; Plut. *Per.* 2–3.

[12] Thuc. 1. 114. 1–2; Diod. 12. 5; Plut. *Per.* 22. 1–2.

[13] Plutarch (*Per.* 22–23) says that after the withdrawal the Spartans were furious with both men. Pleistoanax was fined so heavily that he was unable to pay and was compelled to leave Sparta. Cleandridas, says Plutarch, went into voluntary exile and was condemned to death *in absentia.* He caps his story with the tale that Pericles listed in his accounts for that year an item εἰς τὸ δέον. He also reports Theophrastus' story that every year thereafter Pericles sent ten

ern scholars have found that explanation, even if true, to be inadequate. It is perfectly clear that in the conversation that Pericles held with Pleistoanax and Cleandridas more was offered than money. Pericles was prepared to offer peace terms too good to reject in return for a Spartan withdrawal. They must have been very similar too, if not exactly the same as, the terms that would form the basis of the Thirty Years' Peace. Central Greece was lost irrevocably; Megara, supported by a Peloponnesian army and governed by a hostile oligarchy, could only be recovered by an enormous effort, and even then success was not assured. In any case, with the empire in danger, Athens could not afford such an effort. Athens had everything to gain by recognizing the new realities and nothing to lose.

The Spartans, too, had good reasons to avoid a battle. Even if they should win, their experience at Tanagra showed them that an encounter with Athenian hoplites would be costly. It is further true, as De Sanctis has pointed out, that "if Pericles spent money to induce Pleistoanax and Cleandridas to retire from Attica it was money spent uselessly,"[14] for all the Spartans could accomplish by a victory was the destruction of a number of Athenian soldiers and the destruction of the Attic countryside. As the Peloponnesian War that began in 431 would show, this would not destroy the Athenian Empire or bring Athens to its knees. If Pericles were prepared to abandon Athenian claims on the Greek mainland, what need was there of a costly battle? No reasonable Spartan could ask for more. To be sure, not all Spartans were so reasonable. The more aggressive shared a hatred of Athens going back to the Athenian challenge to Spartan hegemony in 478. For them nothing but the humiliation of Athens was satisfactory; to accept anything less was treason. Their

---

talents to Sparta to conciliate Spartan magistrates and buy time with which to prepare for war. It is worth noticing that Ephorus (frg. 193) says only that the Spartans suspected (ὑπολαβόντες) that their leaders had taken bribes. The Theophrastus story can easily be dismissed as an invention to illustrate the common opinion of his time that Pericles was the implacable foe of Sparta. Some scholars have refused to reject the story of the bribe outright, e.g., Walker, *CAH,* V, 90 and E. Meyer, *GdA,* IV, 586. Some believe it to be an invention or ignore it altogether, e.g., Beloch, *GG*², II: 1, 183–185; Busolt *GG,* III: 1, 429. All agree that it is not enough to explain what happened. See especially De Sanctis, *Pericle,* 139.

[14] *Pericle,* 139.

success in winning a condemnation proves only that hatred for Athens was a powerful force in Spartan politics at the moment when the Athenians seemed helpless. A short period of reflection soon restored Sparta to its senses.[15]

The Spartan withdrawal gave Pericles the respite he needed. He returned to Euboea with fifty triremes and five thousand hoplites and quickly subdued it. The settlement of Euboea completed the process by which the Athenians quelled the unrest that had begun after the Egyptian disaster, and at the same time it also completed the reorganization of the league into an Athenian Empire. Tolmides had already established a cleruchy on Euboea, perhaps at the time of the Boeotian rebellions, possibly to prevent oligarchically inclined Euboeans from helping their Boeotian neighbors.[16] Pericles' settlement after the rebellion was firm, to say the least. The Hestiaeans, because they were accused of atrocities, were altogether expelled, and their land was given to Athenian settlers.[17] The rest of the Euboean cities were allowed to negotiate a settlement, but the terms were hardly generous. At Chalcis, for instance, what must have been the best land, in the Lelantine plain, was taken away from the noble Hippobotae. Some of it was assigned to Athena and leased for rental, and the rest was given to Athenian cleruchs.[18] It is likely that a similar cleruchy was established at Eretria. An inscription has been preserved bearing the agreement that the Athenians made with Chalcis. A fragmentary inscription indicates that the treaty with Eretria was very similar.[19]

[15] Compare this experience with the one undergone by King Agis in 418. He too broke off an impending battle to negotiate a truce. The Spartans responded by fining him ten thousand drachmas, burning down his house, and passing a law forbidding him to lead an army out of Sparta without the consent of ten *xumbouloi* especially appointed (Thuc. 5. 63).

[16] Diod. 11. 88. 3; Paus. 1. 27. 5; *ATL,* III, 294.

[17] Thuc. 1. 114. 3; Plut. *Per.* 23. 2.

[18] Aelian *V.H.* 6. 1; Plut. *Per.* 23. I follow the interpretation of the *ATL,* III, 288–297. Cf., however, Nesselhauf, *Untersuchungen,* 135–138 and Gomme, *Hist. Comm.,* I, 344–346, who believe that cleruchies were not established after the rebellion, but that the land was rented both to Athenians and to native Euboeans.

[19] *ATL,* D16 and D17, II, 69–72. For commentaries, see Tod, I, 82–86; Gomme, *Hist. Comm.,* I, 342–345; and the bibliography in *ATL,* II, 69 and 70.

The Chalcidian treaty is not as harsh as it might have been. Chalcis was to retain control over her own magistrates just as the Athenians controlled theirs, "the true mark of autonomy."[20] In other respects, however, the treaty is a very tough document indeed. Even the competence of Chalcidian magistrates was limited, for it did not cover charges of treason or cases in which exile, death, or loss of citizen rights were the penalties. In such cases provision was made for appeal to an Athenian court. The Athenians promised to stand by the treaty and not take arbitrary measures against Chalcis or its citizens, but the Chalcidians had to promise to pay such tribute as would be fixed. For the time being an Athenian garrison would remain on the scene, and Chalcidian hostages would be kept in Athenian hands. Finally, each Chalcidian swore an oath very much like the one that had been imposed on Colophon:

> I will not revolt from the people of Athens by any manner or means, in word or in deed, nor will I obey anyone else who is in rebellion; and if anyone rebels I will denounce him to the Athenians; and I will pay the tribute which I persuade the Athenians to assess, and I will be an ally to the Athenian people as best I can and as justly as I can, and I will help and defend the people of Athens, if someone harms the people of Athens, and I will obey the people of Athens.

The settlements at Chalcis and Eretria are all we need to complete our picture of the condition of the Athenian Empire at the end of the First Peloponnesian War. It was not much different at the beginning of the Great Peloponnesian War a decade later. What had begun as a voluntary alliance of autonomous states had become an imperial organization in which the hegemonal power exacted military support, financial contributions, and religious deference from her colonies. Whatever autonomy might mean, it was plainly incompatible with garrisons, cleruchies, foreign officials, imposed constitutions, and the kind of language found in Athenian imperial decrees. The original aim of war against Persia had been replaced by a more general program that emphasized Panhellenic unity, religious piety, freedom of the seas, and the preservation of peace.

We cannot doubt that most of the members received many advantages from the alliance, but in many cases it was not interest but

[20] Gomme, *Hist. Comm.*, I, 342. The inscription reads: *τὰς δὲ εὐθύνας χαλκιδεῦσι κατὰ σφῶν αὐτῶν εἶναι ἐν Χαλκίδι καθάπερ 'Αθήνησιν 'Αθηναίοις.*

compulsion that held the alliance together. By 445 the only states that had significant fleets and were truly autonomous were Lesbos, Chios, and Samos. The next great test of the security of the Athenian Empire would come with the defection of one of these powers. We shall see that Athens met that challenge without changing her imperial policy. We shall also see that her domestic situation between the wars was far more stable than that of her great Peloponnesian rival and could not be successfully exploited by recalcitrant allies. Unlike Sparta, Athens embarked on the years between the wars as the master of her alliance, free to adopt and pursue whatever policy suited her, secure in the knowledge that her leadership would remain firm so long as her fleet was powerful and her treasury full.

In the late summer or early autumn of 446 the Spartans and the Athenians concluded a Thirty Years' Peace, and the oaths that ratified it were taken in the following winter. We do not have a copy or a report of the entire peace, but we can piece its provisions together from scattered references. The Athenians agreed to abandon all their holdings in the Peloponnese. Since there is no mention of Naupactus, Athens was allowed to keep this important strategic location. These were the only territorial provisions. They meant that Athens agreed to abandon her continental empire, which she had, in any case, already lost. In return she got what amounted to official recognition of the Athenian Empire, for Sparta and Athens each swore on behalf of its allies, and the further provisions of the treaty recognized that Greece was now divided into two blocs. Members of each alliance were not permitted to change sides. Neutrals could join either side if they wished. A special arrangement was made for Argos. Although it was joined to Sparta by the Thirty Years' Peace which it had made in 451, it was not included in this peace, which now expressly allowed Argos to make a treaty with Athens if it chose. Such a treaty, of course, could not be directed against Sparta until 421, when the Argive-Spartan treaty expired. Finally, there was a provision that disputes were to be submitted to arbitration.[21]

History provides us with many kinds of peace treaties. One kind concludes a war in which one side has completely destroyed the

[21] For the date of the treaty, see *ATL*, III, 301–302; for its provisions, see Thuc. 1. 35. 2; 40; 44. 1; 45. 3; 67. 2; 67. 4; 78. 4; 140. 2; 144. 2; 145; and 7. 18; Diod. 12. 7; Paus. 5. 23. 3.

other. This is less a treaty than a statement to the relatives of the deceased as to disposal of the body. An example is the treaty concluding the last war between Rome and Carthage. A second variety comes after a war in which one side is clearly victorious and imposes very harsh terms on the loser, who has been defeated but not destroyed. Such was the peace that Rome imposed on Carthage after the Second Punic War, the peace that Germany imposed on France in 1870, and, some have argued, the peace imposed upon Germany at Versailles in 1919. Such a treaty often contains in it the seeds of another war, for it humiliates the loser without destroying his capacity for revenge. A third kind is the treaty that concludes a war in which both sides have been made aware of the dangers and costs of war and the virtues of peace. Such a treaty has as its aim not the destruction and humiliation of one side or the other, but the guarantee of stability and security against a renewal of war. Examples of this variety appear to be the Peace of Westphalia and the settlement with which the Congress of Vienna ended the Napoleonic Wars. Two elements are required for the success of this last variety of peace treaty: it must accurately reflect the military, political, and ideological realities of the situation; and it must be backed by a sincere desire on the part of the signatories to make it work, to look upon it as a lasting peace, not merely a truce during which they can prepare for the next battle.

The peace concluded in 446/5 clearly belongs in this last category, if it is regarded as a true peace at all. Neither side was sufficiently victorious to impose its will on the other, so there could be no question of destruction or humiliation. The question is whether it was intended to be or possibly could be anything more than a truce. It is customary to answer this question in the negative, to consider the First Peloponnesian War merely as a prelude to the decisive contest that must inevitably follow.[22] But this is to judge by the event, to assume that something was inevitable because it happened. If we examine the Thirty Years' Peace without preconceptions, we will find that it contained at least the first element necessary for a

[22] See, for example, the remarks of Busolt, *GG,* III: 1, 438: "Das langjährige Ringen war ein Vorspiel gewesen, in dem die Gegner ihre Kräfte erprobt und an Übung und Erfahrung für den unvermeidlichen Entscheidungskampf gewonnen hatten."

lasting peace: realism. In recognizing Spartan hegemony on the mainland and Athenian control of her empire, the peace took a long step toward eliminating a major cause of unrest in the Greek world since the Persian War. The events of 479–477 had created a split in the leadership of Greece. Until Cimon's dismissal from Sparta in 462, the fiction of unity under Spartan hegemony had been maintained with much difficulty. The war of 461–446 would either make unity a reality, whether under Spartan or Athenian hegemony, or compel both states to recognize dualism as the new reality. Since neither proved strong enough to defeat the other in its own element, a peace that recognized dualism conformed to the facts and so gave hope of future stability.

Like any settlement, this one had elements of potential instability. Mutual distrust had by no means disappeared. Many Athenians had not given up their dreams of Athenian domination, of unchallenged hegemony, of expansion in all directions. Many Spartans and Peloponnesians continued to fear these ambitions, and perhaps others felt that the very existence of a powerful Athens threatened the safety and independence of the Greek states and the prestige and power of Sparta. Athenians may well have feared that Spartan jealously awaited only the right moment to destroy the Athenian Empire. Corinth could not have been delighted to find Athens retaining a foothold on the Corinthian Gulf at Naupactus. There was potential trouble in the fact that the Athenian Empire included states with special claims on the friendship of Sparta, like Aegina, and on Corinth, like Potidaea. There was a chance that the right of neutrals to join either side might lead to conflict. All these were possible sources of danger and instability, but they need not lead to a renewal of war if all parties were truly willing to keep the peace and to avoid adventurous policies. This willingness would be tested in the next decade.

Part Three

The Years of Peace

8. Athenian Politics: The Victory of Pericles

One of the great dangers to peace in a world divided into mutually suspicious powers is political instability within each state. We have seen how internal political conflicts in both Athens and Sparta contributed to the outbreak of the First Peloponnesian War. If a renewal of that war was to be avoided, each side must pursue a steady policy of restraint and mutual reassurance, and such steadiness is very difficult to achieve under any constitution. It was the good fortune of Athens, however, that within a few years after the conclusion of peace, she attained a degree of political stability that enabled her to conduct her foreign affairs with consistency and restraint.

If we have interpreted events correctly, the policy of aggressive war on land that produced the defeat at Coronea was not the policy of Pericles, but of the more ambitious element led by Tolmides, which he had not been able to control. The death of Tolmides and the disastrous consequences of his policy freed Pericles from this source of political opposition. The left, to use an anachronistic but useful term, would not trouble him for some time. Without losing the devotion of the demos, whose loyalty was guaranteed by his domestic program, Pericles relied very heavily on the moderates who had supported Cimon and followed him into the coalition with Pericles. Their fondness for Pericles could only have grown as the memory of Cimon faded and as Pericles became more and more the voice of moderation among the democrats. It is no coincidence that the trusted Callias, symbol of the alliance between Cimon and Pericles, was one of the negotiators who concluded the Thirty Years' Peace.[1]

But the very forces that destroyed the opposition on the left raised up a new opposition on the right. It was led by Thucydides, son of Melesias, probably the brother-in-law of Cimon.[2] This relationship has led some scholars to think that he inherited the mantle of Cimon and simply carried on as leader of the aristocrats (*kaloi kagathoi*), and again Plutarch is preserving an important and accurate tradition,[3] but not everyone has been convinced. Hignett's view of the nature of the opposition to Pericles is typical.

> Plutarch calls them the aristocratic party, but his views on Athenian political history are distorted by the conditions of his own day, and he habitually fails to realize that in the fifth century there were not two but three parties in Athens. The new leader of the opposition, Thucydides the son of Melesias, is called Kimon's κηδεστής and may have been his brother-in-law, and his adherents were probably composed in the main of Kimon's old following, the hoplite class.[4]

Plutarch may well have failed to understand fifth-century politics, but Hignett's own understanding lacks nuance. The evidence seems to show that there were, broadly speaking, two major political groups in Athens. One took its roots in the agitation against the Areopagus carried on by Ephialtes and Pericles beginning in 463. At its inception it would have deserved the title radical, but the passage of time, the success of its program, and the experience of power had tamed it, so that in modern terms we might call it liberal. It is not in the nature of all men to mellow with age; nor do all members of a political group agree as to its aims. No doubt some followers of Ephialtes had been attracted more by his attacks on Sparta than on the Areopagus. Their ranks may have been swelled during the First Peloponnesian War. Tolmides seems to have been one of them, and his death deprived them of leadership. Yet there remained this radical wing of the old Ephialtic group that was dissatisfied with the new Periclean policy of peace and accommodation with Sparta. The

[1] Diod. 12. 7.
[2] Wade-Gery, in *Essays in Greek History* (Oxford, 1958), 246–247.
[3] *Per.* 11. 1.
[4] Hignett, *Athenian Constitution,* 256.

other major political group sprang up after the Persian War in the coalition against Themistocles. It created the Areopagite constitution and fought against the reforms of Ephialtes under the leadership of Cimon. We might call it a conservative party.

Cimon had adapted himself to the new conditions, joined with Pericles in his policy of maintaining the empire and seeking an understanding with Sparta, and brought most of his followers along with him. There had always remained, however, a number of diehards who would not accept the new democracy. They had planned treason before Tanagra but had been thwarted by Cimon. His death made it possible for them to organize as an opposition to Pericles. In all this time the moderate wings of both parties had grown closer together as their community of interest became more apparent. Thus, it could appear that there were three parties, radical, moderate, and oligarchic, but in fact there were two major groupings, one liberal and the other conservative, each with a radical wing. When the aggressive radicals of the left were discredited by the debacle of 446, the entire political spectrum shifted to adjust to their departure from the scene. The moderate coalition led by Pericles appeared to have moved to the left, although its policy was unchanged. The vacuum that was created to its right was filled by the oligarchic faction, which now emerged from the disgrace that their suspected treason had produced a decade earlier.

The group led by Thucydides consisted of those oligarchs who had refused to come to terms with the Periclean democracy. His political genius converted it from a suspected political faction to a respectable party that could present itself as a loyal opposition and come close to defeating Pericles and his policies. One of his great innovations was in the realm of political organization. Heretofore we have used the term party to describe political groups in Athens, but it should be clear that it is used loosely for lack of a more accurate description. Of political organization along party lines there was very little. Even after the Cleisthenic reforms the old politics of the great families and their clients had continued. The reforms of Ephialtes, to be sure, had crystallized political life along ideological, and perhaps along class, lines for a time, but the moderation of Pericles and the cooperation of Cimon had helped blur them again. The political position of Pericles was not very different from the one enjoyed by Cimon during his period of ascendancy; both relied on a combination of personal popularity, largesse to a clientele, and combinations with powerful noble families. The great difference was that Pericles paid his largesse out of public instead of private funds and so had an immensely larger clientele. Neither had anything that might be called a political party or the disciplined following and organization that go with it.

These were the invention of Thucydides. Party politics in Athens were so undeveloped that up until this time political groups did not even sit together at meetings of the assembly. Thucydides changed this, "for he did not allow the men called *kaloi kagathoi* to be scattered and mixed with the people as they had been before, their merit being eclipsed by numbers, but selecting them out separately and bringing them together into a single body, he made the power of all of them weighty, like a counterweight in a balance." [5] This organization was not only effective in itself but was also valuable in bringing to light the conglomerate nature of Pericles' political support. The marriage between Periclean liberals and Cimonian conservatives was one of convenience, and many differences remained that Pericles would have preferred to leave obscure. The new political organization, with its policy of concerted opposition, made ambiguity difficult. Plutarch's description of the new situation is very persuasive:

> From the beginning there had been a sort of flaw under the surface, as there might be in a piece of iron, which hinted at a difference in the popular and aristocratic policy, but the rivalry and ambition of the opponents cut a very deep wound in the state and caused one part of it to be called "The People" [δῆμος] and the other "The Few" [ὀλίγοι].[6]

Organization alone is not enough to destroy as powerful a coalition as Pericles commanded. The *oligoi* needed a political program to lure the moderates away from Pericles. What Thucydides would have liked to proclaim was a program to roll back the democratic revolution of Ephialtes. This is a bold statement, but the scanty evidence we have seems to support it.[7] We know that he was an

[5] Plut. *Per.* 11. 2–3.

[6] *Per.* 11. 3–4.

[7] For a list of the ancient references, see Fiehn, *PW*, VI A, 1937, *s.v.*

aristocrat of the bluest blood. In Plato's *Meno,* Socrates praises him for giving his sons a good general education and for making them the best wrestlers in Athens, and uses him as an example to show that even the best men cannot pass on virtue to their sons. He had many friends in Athens and among the allies; he "came from a great house and possessed great power in Athens and in the rest of Greece." [8] Wrestling, of course, was the most aristocratic of activities, and Plato himself was a famous wrestler. The palaestra served as a splendid meeting place for the noble youths of Athens, their trainers, admirers, and friends. If the conversations Plato reports in his dialogues are typical, little good was spoken of democracy. If Wade-Gery is right, Melesias, Thucydides' father, was the greatest wrestling master of his time, the subject of an epinicion by Pindar, and the subject also of "the last words of praise for any Athenian" uttered by that most aristocratic of poets. We must agree that "no one who knows much of Pindar or indeed of the structure of early fifth-century Greek society will doubt that poet, trainer and athlete alike belong to the same class, the international aristocracy of Greece." [9] To that same class, of course, belonged the son of Melesias.

Aristotle also had a good opinion of him. He says that the best statesmen Athens had, after remote antiquity, were Nicias, Thucydides, and Theramenes. About Nicias and Thucydides almost everybody, says Aristotle, agreed that "they were not only gentlemen [*kaloi kagathoi*] but also statesmen and ruled the state in all matters as a father rules his household [*patrikos*]." [10] We can get some idea of Aristotle's idea of good statesmanship from his inclusion of Theramenes and the defense he offers for him. Whatever we may

---

Thukydides (2), 625–627, who also includes what amounts to a survey of modern German scholarship on the subject up to his time. The most important and interesting study of Thucydides is Wade-Gery's article, cited above. Although I disagree with most of its conclusions, it is a pioneering work which has helped us to a better understanding of the man and his political milieu. See also A. E. Raubitschek, *Phoenix,* XIV (1960), 81–95.

[8] 94 c-d.

[9] For Melesias, see Wade-Gery, *Essays,* 243–247.

[10] *Ath. Pol.* 28. 5, πάντες σχεδὸν ὁμολογοῦσιν ἄνδρας γεγονέναι οὐ μόνον καλοὺς καγαθοὺς ἀλλὰ καὶ πολιτικοὺς καὶ τῇ πόλει πάσῃ πατρικῶς χρωμένους. For my translation of *patrikos,* see J. E. Sandys, *Aristotle's Constitution of Athens* (London, 1893), 114–115.

think of his motives, we must not forget that Theramenes was involved in the oligarchic revolution of the Four Hundred in 411, that he invented the strategem whereby the Athenians were starved into accepting unconditional surrender from Sparta in 404, and that he saw fit to join the Thirty Tyrants before falling victim to their excessive zeal. None of the evidence seems to contradict Plutarch's belief that Thucydides led a party of aristocrats who pursued an aristocratic program and were called "The Few" as opposed to "The People," not a party of moderate democrats.

There is another document that may give us an insight into the ideas and wishes of Thucydides and his party. It has come down to us under the title *Athenaion Politeia* and the manuscripts attribute it to Xenophon. Everyone agrees that it cannot be by Xenophon, but there agreement on authorship ends, and it has been customary to speak of the anonymous author as the "Old Oligarch." Several scholars have believed it to be written by Thucydides, son of Melesias, himself. Such an assertion is impossible to prove, and the best course is to admit that we do not know the author.[11] Still, it is noteworthy that scholars have seen fit to associate the ideas of the Old Oligarch with those of Thucydides. If we compare those ideas with the program Thucydides put forth, we shall see that there is some reason to agree with that association.

The precise intention of the pamphlet and the circumstances of its composition are far from clear, but we may dismiss the suggestion that it is ironic or intended as a joke. It is a serious work written by an oligarch for oligarchs, but the author enjoys the paradox of an oligarch explaining to other oligarchs that the Athenian democracy is really a very sensible apparatus when viewed from the democratic point of view. He begins,

> As for the constitution of the Athenians, I do not praise them for having chosen it, because in choosing it they have given the better of it to the vulgar people (πονηροί) rather than to the good (χρηστοί). That is why I do not praise it. But since they have made such a choice I want to demonstrate that they preserve that constitution well and that they also

[11] For the best discussions of the questions of authorship, date, and interpretation, see Gomme, *HSCP* Suppl., I, 1940, 211–245 and Hartvig Frisch, *The Constitution of the Athenians* (Copenhagen, 1942), with an extensive bibliography. My quotations come or are adapted from Frisch's text and translation.

do well in other matters in which the rest of the Greeks think they blunder.

From this point of view it is perfectly understandable that "the vulgar, the poor, and the people are given preference over the distinguished and the rich," because it is the navy that gives Athens its power and the lower classes who man the ships. They employ election by lot for positions that are safe and pay a fee, but leave the dangerous posts of general and commander of cavalry to "the best qualified men" (δυνατοτάτους). Some may wonder that the Athenians give the greater share of government to the mob than to the aristocrats, for

> in every country the aristocracy is contrasted to the democracy, there being in the best people the least licentiousness and iniquity, but the keenest eyes for morals; in the people, on the other hand, we find a very high degree of ignorance, disorder, and vileness; for poverty more and more leads them in the direction of bad morals, thus also the absence of education and in the case of some persons the ignorance that is due to the want of money.

But it is plain to the Old Oligarch that to prefer talent and virtue would soon lead to the destruction of democracy. The fact is that rather than be subordinate in an ideal constitution, the people prefer to live under a constitution where they are free and sovereign. "Whether the constitution is bad or no, they do not care very much. For what *you* think is no ideal constitution," he says to his oligarchic audience, "is just the condition for the people being in power and being free."

He makes very clear what he and his friends would consider a good constitution. The word which is translated ideal or good constitution is *eunomia,* a name given by Tyrtaeus to the ancestral constitution of Sparta and by Pindar to the oligarchy of Corinth and almost always associated with oligarchy or aristocracy. In the Old Oligarch's opinion such a constitution will see to it that the best and most qualified men will make the laws. The aristocrats (οἱ χρηστοί) will punish bad men (τοὺς πονηρούς); only the worthy (οἱ χρηστοί) will deliberate concerning affairs of state and will not allow madmen (μαινομένους 'ανθρώπους) to serve in the council or to speak in the assembly. In such a constitution the people, of course, will sink into slavery (τάχιστ'ἂν ὁ δῆμος εἰς δουλείαν καταπέσοι).

The Old Oligarch objects, too, to the free and easy life of Athens in which metics and slaves walk about freely, refuse to stand aside in the street, dress no worse than other Athenians, and are not to be beaten with impunity. The demos of Athens has destroyed the reputation of the old aristocratic training in gymnastics and music, replacing them with dramatic festivals, athletic contests, and naval expeditions in which the poor may participate since the rich are made to bear the cost.

A major subject of complaint is the Athenian treatment of the allies. The allies are forced to come to Athens for judgment in cases between Athenians and allies. This makes it more likely for the Athenians to win the case. It also enriches the Athenians who are paid for jury service, not to mention the profit to the tourist trade of Athens and the tax collected at the Piraeus. "Now every one of the allies has to cringe to the Attic people . . . and in court anybody is obliged to beseech and stretch out his hand to the casual person entering. Consequently the allies have more and more been made slaves of the people of Athens." As in their own state, the Athenians support the worst elements in the allied states because aristocrats everywhere oppose them while the worthless mob alone supports them.

Perhaps the central message the Old Oligarch wishes to convey to his oligarchic audience may be found in the following paragraph:

> The people itself I personally forgive its democracy; for everybody must be forgiven for looking to his own interest. But anybody who without belonging to the people prefers living in a town under democratic rule to living in one ruled oligarchically has prepared himself for being immoral, well knowing that it is easier for a bad person to remain unnoticed in a town under democratic than in one under oligarchic rule.

This paragraph seems to provide the clue to the intention of the author of the pamphlet and to the purpose of the oligarchic party at Athens. At another time, in Rome, the aristocratic Tacitus would use the experience of his illustrious father-in-law to show his fellow nobles that a good man can live even under a bad emperor. But by the time of Tacitus, many aristocratic plots had failed and monarchical rule seemed inevitable. In the Athens of Thucydides, however, the unbridled democracy was relatively new and had not been effectively challenged. Cimon had shown that subversion need not be the only way for the Athenian aristocrats to rule. Intelligent political management combined with charismatic leadership could make what was a democracy in name into an aristocracy in fact. It would, of course, be utter folly to make any of these attitudes and aims public. Issues must be found which were acceptable to a democratic people, which would discredit Pericles, and which would attract support to the party of Thucydides.

The son of Melesias had a keen understanding of the nature of democratic politics, and he must have learned the lessons of the recent past well. To destroy a politician in a democracy it is well to discredit him personally, to attach to his name and person attributes that are generally disliked, distrusted, and feared. In Athens the most damaging charge that could be made against a democratic politician was that he aimed at tyranny. The memory of the Peisistratid dynasty had been blackened by the treason of Hippias, who brought a Persian army to Marathon to conquer his native land. Athenian drama abounds with attacks on tyranny as the polar enemy of democracy.

Pericles was peculiarly vulnerable to charges of tyranny. As a young man, we are told, he was reluctant to face the public because of his resemblance to Peisistratus. "Very old men, noticing the sweetness of his voice and his glib and swift tongue in debate, were amazed by the similarity." [12] His wealth and nobility, coupled with his espousal of the popular cause, also brought to mind the demagogic tyrant of the sixth century. As we have seen, Pericles was not the man to win the love and personal affection of the masses as Cimon had. He won no great military glory; he was proud and unbending rather than affable and friendly. He avoided public occasions, was the least convivial of men, and rarely made public speeches, delegating the responsibility of carrying out his program to his associates.[13] He associated with suspicious intellectuals, held uncommon religious views, and consorted regularly with foreign men and women. He was the sort of man whom the comic poets called Zeus or the Olympian, which indicate at the same time the stature of his reputation and the aura of arrogance that surrounded him. It was easy enough to persuade some people that such a man

[12] *Per.* 7. 1.
[13] *Ibid.* 7. 4–6.

was on the way to establishing a tyranny, and it is clear that when the son of Melesias set out to oppose him he had come forth "to blunt the edge of his power so that it might not be absolutely a monarchy." [14]

These personal attacks on Pericles were useful, but a more general program was also necessary. It is a credit to the acumen of Thucydides that he selected one that was politically effective, could be combined with the charge of Periclean tyranny, and gave promise of accomplishing the purposes of the oligarchic party: an attack on the use of imperial funds for the Periclean building program. Plutarch reports at least a reasonable approximation of the complaints made at meetings of the assembly:

> The demos is dishonored and in bad repute because it has removed the common money of the Hellenes from Delos to Athens. Pericles has deprived it of the most fitting excuse that it was possible to offer to its accusers, that it removed the common fund to this place out of fear of the barbarian and in order to protect it. Hellas certainly is outraged by a terrible arrogance [*hybris*] and is manifestly tyrannized when it sees that we are gilding and adorning our city like a wanton woman, dressing it with expensive stones and statues and temples worth millions, with money extorted from them for fighting a war.[15]

The shrewdness of this attack is made clear when we observe the subtlety and breadth of its appeal. The attack, we should notice, is not against the empire itself, which would have alienated the majority of Athenians. It is not even aimed at the tribute, which would have had much the same effect. Instead, it complains of the misdirection of that tribute from its proper use in the war against Persia to the domestic program of Pericles. This was a clever stroke aimed at the Cimonian element in Pericles' moderate coalition. It was a reminder of how the original Cimonian policy had been perverted if not altogether abandoned. It tried to split off the old Cimonians by suggesting to them that Cimon would not have sanctioned the continued collection of tribute without a Persian war to excuse it. The

[14] *Ibid.* 11. 1; ὥστε μὴ κομιδῇ μοναρχίαν εἶναι.

[15] *Per.* 12. 2; E. Meyer (*Forschungen*, II, 86) supports the view that Plutarch gives us a reliable account of the entire debate: "die von beiten Seiten vorgebrachten Argumente sind uns bei Plut. *Per.* 12 in authentischer Fassung bewahrt."

attack, moreover, took a high moral tone, employed the language of traditional religion and old-fashioned morality, and contrasted it not with the immorality of democracy, which would have been offensive, but with the arrogance of tyranny.

Nor was the attack on the abuse of imperial revenues chosen merely for its propaganda value. The son of Melesias was surely aware that the supremacy of Pericles rested on the loyalty of the demos, which was guaranteed by the expenditure of public money among the poor. The cost of such welfare programs always rises, as the modern world has learned. It may be that ordinary income might have been enough to sustain Pericles' program in the 450's, but rising expectations, and perhaps growing numbers, made that inadequate by the '40's. It is possible that Pericles was thinking of such things when he proposed the law restricting citizenship in 451/50. In any case, the welfare program depended on the tribute by the time that Thucydides challenged Pericles. If the oligarchs could put a stop to the use of imperial money for domestic Athenian purposes, at one stroke they would help their aristocratic friends among the allies who carried the major burden of paying the tribute and deprive Pericles of the resources that helped keep him in power. That accomplished, they might hope to defeat him as Cimon had defeated Themistocles and restore the state to the condition it had enjoyed under the Areopagite Constitution.[16]

There can be no doubt that the plan was effective. Thucydides was a formidable speaker and debater, whose attacks forced Pericles

[16] For an interesting discussion of the purposes and activities of Thucydides and his faction, see H. D. Meyer in *Historia,* XVI (1967), 141–154. Meyer rejects the interpretation of the political events offered by Plutarch and largely accepted here. Putting aside the possibility that the party of Thucydides might really have been anti-imperialist, he suggests that there was no real opposition to the empire, and that the dispute was over means rather than ends. He does not give great weight to the possibility that the oligarchs were eager to overthrow the democracy established by Ephialtes. In his judgment they were chiefly interested in defeating Pericles and the building program which would have guaranteed his supremacy. After his fall, they presumably would have continued the imperial policy. The evidence discussed above seems to me to point in another direction altogether. Meyer's argument is weakened somewhat by his overly simplified view of Athenian politics, which sees only two sharply defined parties. As we have seen, Athenian politics were more complicated.

openly to defend his policy. The result was a great debate between two brilliant orators. Unfortunately, only Plutarch reports it, and even he quotes just a few fragments of what must have been incomparable rhetoric. We get some idea of the spirit and fierceness of the competition from an anecdote reported by Plutarch. King Archidamus of Sparta once asked the son of Melesias whether he or Pericles was the better wrestler and received this reply: "When I throw Pericles in wrestling he argues that he has not been thrown and wins by persuading the very men who have seen the whole thing."[17] Thucydides, of course, was no mean wrestler himself, whether in the palaestra or in debate. He was not a military man like Cimon, but more of a parliamentary and political man (ἀγοραῖος δὲ καὶ πολιτικὸς μᾶλλον), who "by wrestling matches with Pericles on the bema soon brought the political situation to a state of equilibrium."[18]

Thucydides, however, had underestimated the political talents of his opponent. In answer to the main complaint Pericles offered no apology but rather a spirited defense. The Athenians, he said, need make no account of the money they receive from the allies so long as they protect them from the barbarian:

> They furnish no horse, no ship, no hoplite, but only money, which does not belong to the giver but to the receiver if he carries out his part of the bargain. But now that the city has prepared itself sufficiently with the things necessary for war, it is proper to employ its resources for such works as will bring it eternal fame when they are completed, and while they are being completed will maintain its prosperity, for all kinds of industries and a variety of demands will arise which will awaken every art, put in motion every hand, provide a salary for almost the entire city from which it may at the same time be beautified and nourished.[19]

It was a brilliant rebuttal. The first part answered the moral attack and was directed chiefly at the Cimonian element in the moderate group who were most susceptible to it. The use of imperial funds for Athenian purposes was not analogous to tyranny, Pericles suggested, but to the untrammeled use of his wages or profits by a man who had entered into a contract. If there were any breach of morality,

[17] *Per.* 8. 4.
[18] *Per.* 11. 2.
[19] *Per.* 12. 4.

it must be on the part of such allies who shrank from paying the tribute, although Athens continued to provide protection as always. But the second part is even more masterly. It was aimed at the lower classes who benefited from the empire most obviously and directly and reminded them in the plainest terms what it meant to them. It stripped the veil from the arguments of Thucydides and showed what his program implied: the end of the use of allied money for Athenian programs, which meant the end of the Periclean welfare state. In this crisis he reminded the masses who formed the hard core of his political support that their interests were at stake and he expected them to vote for their interests.

Events proved his expectation sound. Hard pressed by charges of corruption in the handling of funds for his building program, he brilliantly turned the tables on his opponents. Did the people think, he asked in the assembly, that he had spent too much? Altogether too much, was the reply. "Well then," said Pericles, "let the expense of the buildings be mine and not yours. But the name inscribed on the monuments will be mine as well." The result was all that Pericles could have wished; there was a general outcry in his favor, and he was urged to spend whatever was needed from public funds.[20] It was, of course, a remarkably effective rhetorical trick. No one man could afford to pay for the buildings, and everyone knew it. To admit this, however, is not to dismiss the importance of the gesture and the meaning of the rhetoric. Perhaps it is not too imaginative to see in this story a message that Pericles meant to convey to any of his democratic supporters who might have forgotten the nature of his opposition. These buildings, he implied, are yours, not the property of a wealthy nobleman; they are symbols of your glory and evidence of the greatness of your democracy. Do you want to return to a time when the great nobles were all and the people nothing? Perhaps some of his audience thought back, in contrast, to the story of Miltiades, who in an earlier time asked merely an olive crown as a reward for his victory in battle. A certain Sophanes of Decelea is said to have risen in the assembly and said, without grace, "When you have fought and conquered the barbarian alone, Miltiades, then you may

[20] *Per.* 14. 1–2.

ask to be honored alone." [21] Such was the old democratic spirit that Pericles was able to evoke.

In this way Pericles was able to check the swift growth of the opposition party. The danger was by no means passed, but he still retained a reliable majority, and the Athenian constitution presented him with a means for restoring tranquillity to Athenian politics: ostracism. It was a weapon originally designed by Cleisthenes to protect the democracy against subversion while it was still in its infancy. It also gave the leader of the democracy a weapon with which he could rid himself of a leader of the opposition who had become too dangerous. It was, however, a double-edged sword and could only be used with safety if the proposer of an ostracism were confident of a majority. It had been of enormous value to Cleisthenes, who had never needed to use it, for the very threat was enough to cow his enemies. It had been employed to good effect by Themistocles in the 480's to rid himself of all his rivals. It had been turned against him by the coalition of Cimon in 474, and Cimon had been its victim in the democratic surge of 461. We must realize that no politician used the weapon of ostracism unless he was altogether confident that his opponent would be ostracized and not himself. The exception that tested the rule was the ostracism of Hyperbolus in 417. His ostracism was the only one that produced a surprise, for neither of the obvious candidates, Nicias and Alcibiades, was ostracized but instead a relative nonentity. This was precisely because both major candidates felt that the vote would be too close for comfort and joined forces against Hyperbolus. The experience showed the weakness of the institution, and it is no accident that it is the last ostracism of which we hear.[22]

These considerations support Plutarch's clear and unequivocal statement that it was Pericles who introduced the proceedings that ostracized Thucydides, probably in the spring of 443, and removed him from Athenian politics for ten years.[23] Athenian political parties

[21] *Cim.* 8. 1.

[22] On the origin and purposes of ostracism, as well as my interpretation of its history, see Kagan *Hesperia,* XXX (1961), 393–401. The standard monograph on ostracism is that of Jérôme Carcopino, *L'Ostracisme athénien* (2nd ed., Paris; 1935), but the discovery of many ostraca and a good deal of recent scholarship has made it somewhat out of date.

[23] It is surprising that such shrewd historians as Grote (IV, 506) and Busolt (*GG*, III: 1, 495, n. 3), among others, should have believed that it was Thucydides who brought on the ostracism. No persuasive argument is put

tended to be groups clustered around a leader, and the removal of that leader usually had serious consequences for the party. The son of Melesias more than most was the heart and soul of his party, which he had led from the political wilderness into a position close to victory by the force of his rhetoric, organizational skill, and personality. When he was ostracized, his faction was totally shattered.[24]

It is customary to date from the ostracism of Thucydides the change in the character of Pericles from demagogue to aristocrat, from champion of the poor to defender of property, from party leader to statesman.[25] But if we have understood him correctly, there was no great transformation either in the character or policy of Pericles. He was both a demagogue, which is to say a skillful politician in a democracy, and an aristocrat, both before and after the ostracism. Thereafter he continued to be the champion of the poor as he had been from the beginning of his career, but he also defended the property of Athenian citizens, which he had never dreamed of attacking. His success was based on the fact that he had always been both party leader and statesman, and he continued to be both. It is possible, even likely, that in his youth his foreign policy had been more aggressive, that he believed it possible for Athens to expand her empire, her influence, and her wealth by warfare, but if so, he had abandoned that policy and that belief well before the final struggle with Thucydides. The recall of Cimon, the Five Years' Peace, the

---

forth to support that view, the nearest thing to it being Grote's remark: "Probably the vote was proposed by the party of Thucydides, in order to procure the banishment of Pericles, the more powerful person of the two, and the most likely to excite popular jealousy." But this is to misunderstand the nature of the institution, which operated less by popular jealousy than by political power. If Thucydides thought that the more powerful man was more likely to be ostracized, he was more naive than the rest of the record shows. The words of Plutarch, moreover, are altogether unambiguous: τέλος δὲ πρὸς τὸν Θουκιδίδην εἰς ἀγῶνα περὶ τοῦ ὀστράκου καταστὰς καὶ διακινδυνεύσας ἐκεῖνον μὲν ἐξέβαλε (*Per.* 14. 2). Adcock (*CAH*, V, 166–7), De Sanctis (*Pericle*, 157) and Ehrenberg (*Sophocles and Pericles*, 137) are among those who believe Pericles initiated the ostracism.

[24] *Per.* 14. 2.

[25] The first transformation is noticed by Plutarch (*Per.* 9. 1–2 and 15. 1–2), the second by Beloch (*Die Attische Politik*, 19–21), the third by Hignett (*op. cit.*, 253–257). Raphael Sealey (*Hermes*, LXXXV [1956], 234–247) argues against the reality of such a major shift.

Peace of Callias, and the Thirty Years' Peace are all proof enough of that. Before the ostracism Pericles had decided on a conservative foreign policy, which meant the abandonment of expansion, coupled with the firm maintenance of control in the empire, and a democratic welfare state for Athens. The ostracism of Thucydides amounted only to a popular ratification of those decisions.

The removal of the son of Melesias did, of course, improve the political situation of Pericles and, for the moment, made him more independent of his supporters. But political victories in a democracy, no matter how overwhelming, are never permanent. A clever politician will begin planning for future troubles the day after his victory. Although Plutarch tells that the resolution of its political quarrels had unified Athens and made it "like a smooth surface," some ripples had not yet receded. The moralistic, anti-imperial propaganda of Thucydides could not have failed to make an impression on the Cimonian supporters of Pericles. The idealistic, Panhellenic appeal of Thucydides' complaints about Athenians tyrannizing over other Greeks must have been a major reason for the support many of them gave him. To win them back to his moderate coalition, Pericles must appeal to such sentiments. The destruction of the right wing, moreover, strengthened the left. To defend his imperial policy, Pericles had appealed to pure self-interest; he had emphasized the empire as a source of profit. For the moment he was in firm control of the aggressive imperialists, but one day they might insist on payment for their services in saving Pericles from defeat. Finally, the allies themselves might present a problem. The hopes of the many friends of Thucydides scattered throughout the empire must have rested on his success. No doubt they expected him to succeed and then to end, or at least reduce, tribute payments. The disappointment of his defeat could well lead them to revolt, as many of them had done only a few years earlier.

It was to this last problem that Pericles immediately turned. The tribute lists give evidence that troubles in the empire had not been completely ended by the suppression of the Euboean rebellion and the measures that followed it. In the year 447/6 some 171 cities are listed. The following year shows only 156 and the year after that 158. The year of the ostracism finds 163 cities on the lists, which climbs to 165 in 443/2. In 442/1 there is a rather marked increase to 173. This drops to 164 in 441/40 but rises again to 172 in 440/39.[26] The rise from a low of 156 in 446/5 to 165 in 443/2 is evidence of the undramatic but steady tightening of imperial control that followed the Euboean rebellion, but the increase from 165 to 173 between 443/2 and 442/1 is striking, and it appears that the new higher figure became normal, for the dip of 441/40 may very well be the result of the Samian revolution of that year.[27] It seems very much as if something significant happened in the realm of imperial organization in 443/2. The rest of our evidence confirms this judgment. In the normal course of events a reassessment of the tribute was due for the year 442/1, but instead such a reassessment took place a year earlier. Not only was there an early reassessment, but for the first time the empire was formally divided into five districts: Ionia, the Hellespont, Thrace, Caria, and the Islands. Such a division was already implicit, but now it was made explicit and appears inscribed on the stones. It is also clear that significant changes were made in the tribute paid by some of the cities. In some cases substantial reductions took place; in others there was a restoration of a previous, probably normal, figure after fluctuation; in still others some intermediate figure between previous highs and lows was fixed. None of these changes were large enough to compare with the more important adjustments of 446/5, which often resulted from the establishment of cleruchies. They appear rather to be minor readjustments, part of a general but not radical reorganization.

Another fact that emphasizes the unusual character of the year 443/2 is that for the first time a co-secretary (*xyngrammateus*) is chosen to serve the board of Hellenotamiae. His name is Satyrus, and he is chosen for the same job in the following year, the only instance of a secretary of any kind ever chosen for consecutive years. Finally, it is worth noticing that the man elected chairman of the board of Hellenotamiae for the same year was Sophocles of Colonus, the tragic poet.[28] From all this information several questions arise:

[26] See the table provided by Ehrenberg, *Sophocles,* 130.

[27] *Idem.*

[28] The evidence for the foregoing account is collected and interpreted by Ehrenberg in the sixth chapter of his *Sophocles and Pericles,* (117–140). I have in general followed his interpretation. The texts of the relevant tribute lists are in the second volume of *ATL,* 13–22; *ATL,* III, 67–68 and 306–307 add some pertinent remarks. An argument for 443/2 as a year of reassess-

What were the purposes, nature, and results of this imperial reorganization? Why was the reassessment made a year earlier than usual? Why was it necessary to choose a second clerk and keep him on an unprecedented second year? Finally, what, if anything, is the significance of the appearance of the famous Sophocles as chairman of the board of Hellenotamiae?

The answers to most of these questions can only come from a proper understanding of the political situation in the aftermath of the ostracism of Thucydides. The first task for Pericles was to maintain imperial control where it existed and to restore it where it had been cast off. A closer analysis of the tribute lists shows that in the Hellespontine, Thracian, and Carian districts, particularly the more remote inland towns, there had been considerable defections.[29] It was imperative to act immediately to recover lost ground and to deter further defections. It must have been chiefly for this reason that Pericles moved the reassessment up a year and used the occasion for a thorough reorganization.[30]

But it was not enough to tighten up imperial control; it was also necessary to win back the moderates who had been impressed by the arguments of the son of Melesias. For this reason the reassessment and reorganization were gentle and, we must imagine, scrupulously fair. We hear of no new cleruchies, no harsh measures, but only of readjustments of tribute, usually downward. It was as though Pericles were harking back to his campaign speeches and refuting the charge of tyranny. Athens, he was saying, does not wish to dominate

ment is made by Meritt in *AJA,* XXIX (1925), 247–273. See also Nesselhauf, *Untersuchungen,* 36ff.

[29] See Ehrenberg's table (*Sophocles and Pericles,* 130).

[30] The authors of *ATL* (III, 306) believe that Pericles intended to make the Great Panathenaea of 442, the normal occasion for a reassessment, "a demonstration that Athens was the center of the civilized world," and that he advanced the reassessment to the summer of 443 "to keep this celebration clear of business." Even if the evidence for Pericles' intentions were far better than it is, this explanation would be a very weak one. Ehrenberg also rejects it and offers one far more persuasive. "Pericles had finally silenced the opposition of the oligarchs who had been voicing the complaints of the allies. What was more natural than to remove some causes of discontent and thus secure the tribute from reluctant states, when concessions could no longer be regarded as a sign of weakness?" (*Sophocles and Pericles,* 129–130).

and exploit her allies, but merely to see that they observe the bargain they have made. If they did so they would find Athens fair in financial matters and careful of their rights. The reorganization required a good deal of work in addition to the usual labors of the committee, and so a second secretary was needed. When one year proved insufficient, Satyrus, who had no doubt become indispensable, was reappointed to finish the job. The reorganization was clearly effective, especially in the more difficult regions. Between 444/3 and 440/39 the number of cities paying tribute in the Hellespont went from twenty-five to thirty-two, in Thrace from thirty-eight to forty-three, and in Caria from thirty-five to forty-six. Although the Carian district ultimately proved untenable, the rest was saved.

The question of Sophocles remains. What are we to make of his chairmanship? To begin with, it is important to recognize that Sophocles came from a wealthy and respected family. By the time of his election he was about fifty and had been an important and popular public figure at least since 468, when he had won his first victory as a tragedian. There is a story that the prize was awarded by a jury composed of Cimon and his fellow generals.[31] However that may be, we may well imagine him to be a typical Cimonian. That he was in favor of Pericles and his program, like many other Cimonians, is made more than likely by his willingness to serve as chairman of the board of Hellenotamiae at such an important moment. Further evidence is provided by his election to the strategia in 441/40. It is possible to argue that he was elected to the board of Hellenotamiae before the ostracism of Thucydides, and so need not have been a Periclean candidate. Possibly one might even argue that so popular a man as Sophocles could have been elected to the generalship against the wishes of Pericles, even though the evidence shows such situations to be rare. Yet it is worth mentioning that Sophocles is one of only two men in the time of Pericles who held both positions, and the other's being a Hellenotamias is uncertain.[32] It is surely impossible to believe that Pericles, at the height of his power, would have been unable to stop the election of a political opponent to the generalship.

But there is even better evidence of the friendly relationship be-

[31] *Cim.* 8. 8.

[32] Ehrenberg, *Sophocles and Pericles,* 133.

tween Sophocles and Pericles. Ehrenberg has offered us a brilliant and persuasive interpretation of the epigraphic and historical data. He points out that the tribute list for 443/2, number 12 in the series, is the first to name a chairman of the board. Like all the previous lists, it has a prescript in wide-space large letters giving the number of the list and the name of the secretary. At the bottom of the list, the name of the second secretary and the chairman are inscribed in letters smaller than the prescript and only a little larger than the list itself. The prescript of list 13, which follows immediately, is written in the same smaller letters. "We get the impression that these three lines are somehow pressed into narrow space, perhaps as a result of an afterthought, after the spacing of the whole reverse side of the stele, which contains the lists 9–13, had been done." The prescript for list 13 contains the names of all three officials, two secretaries and a Hellenotamias. In future lists the Hellenotamias is always mentioned and the prescripts are once again inscribed in large, widely spaced letters.[33] Now the general opinion is that the Hellenotamiae were elected at the same time as the strategoi, in the seventh month of the Athenian year. The decision to have an ostracism was taken in the sixth, and the actual ostracism in the eighth. Thus, Sophocles stood for his office at the hottest moment in the struggle between Pericles and Thucydides, when it was clear that one of them would be ostracized. Whether or not he correctly anticipated the outcome, it is clear he did not suffer by it. The evidence seems to show that his selection as chairman came late.

It is easy to believe that the idea for this innovation came from Pericles after he was rid of his opponent. His influence over Athenian affairs could never have been greater than at the moment of his victory over the son of Melesias. It was then that the idea must have come to him of moving up the reassessment and using it for a significant reorganization of the empire. But it was not enough that the reorganization should be fair and equitable. As an experienced democratic politician, he knew that it was at least equally important that it should *seem* fair and honorable and should be recognized as such by one and all. It was no less important that it should seem to have the support not only of the radical imperialists but of the respectable, conservative elements as well. Nothing could have served his needs

[33] *Ibid.,* 132–133.

better than to have Sophocles available to head the board of Hellenotamiae at such a time. Whether by chance or design, he had been elected. It was certainly no chance that the position of chairman was first given a prominent listing at this moment and Sophocles chosen to fill it. In one stroke Pericles could accomplish the necessary imperial reorganization and demonstrate the respectability and moderation of his policy to the more restless element among his supporters. Perhaps they were not yet fully convinced, but this brilliant improvisation could not fail to help. Soon developments in the west would give him another opportunity to convince them.

9. Athens and the West: The Foundation of Thurii

Although the Athenian Empire lay to the north and east, Athens was not altogether uninterested in the west. As we have seen,[1] there were rumors that Themistocles had ambitions of western expansion, and it is not too much to believe that at the height of their success the more sanguine Athenians may have cast covetous eyes on the wheat fields, harbors, and precious metals of the Greek cities of Sicily and southern Italy. In the year 458/7, at any rate, when the victorious Athenians had not yet been sobered by the Egyptian disaster, they concluded a treaty with Egesta in western Sicily.[2] It is

[1] See above, Chap. 4, p. 58.

[2] The date is established by the name of the archon on the very fragmentary inscription *IG*, I [2], 20. It was formerly read as Ariston and dated to 454/3. Most epigraphers now read it as Habron and so date it to the year 458/7, but W. K. Pritchett has pointed out that there is reason for caution (*CP*, XLVII [1952], 263 and *AJA*, LIX [1955], 58–59). It is his judgment that the stone does not justify any reading of the archon's name. "Wear on the surface has obliterated the name of the archon, and the epigraphist and the historian must accept this fact" (*AJA*, LIX [1955], 59). I have accepted the majority opinion for the date of the treaty, in part because it seems to me to make good historical sense, but I am fully aware it is not much more than an educated guess. No important interpretation should be made to rest on it.

For a brief discussion of the problem and a full and up-to-date bibliography, see Hermann Bengtson, *Die Staatsverträge der griechisch-römischen Welt von 700 bis 338 v. Chr.*, II (Munich and Berlin, 1962), No. 139, 41–42. See also *SEG*, X, 7; XII, 6; XIV, 1; XXI, 10; XXII, 3.

possible that similar alliances were made about the same time with Rhegium on the toe of Italy and Leontini, a Sicilian town to the northwest of Syracuse.[3] If these dates are correct, they may give evidence of Athenian ambition during this most ambitious period in Athenian history, but even then it is not clear that Pericles was in favor of this policy. We have seen that he was by no means in full control of Athens in the fifties and that he was unable, on occasion, to restrain the more aggressive Athenians. There is a long standing suggestion that these alliances were, in fact, made by the radicals.[4] Such a suggestion cannot be confirmed, but it seems no less likely than any other.

However one judges these cases, they cannot be understood as anything but isolated instances of Athenian involvement in the west. There is no reliable evidence for a pattern of continued active Athenian political interest in Italy and Sicily. Certainly there is not a shred of evidence to connect Pericles with an ambitious western policy.

The first clear instance of a serious Athenian interest in western affairs is its leading role in founding a colony in southern Italy. Sybaris had been destroyed by its neighbor Croton late in the sixth

[3] The evidence for the date of these alliances is even worse than that for the treaty with Egesta. It is to be found on two stelae carrying inscriptions of the treaties *IG*, I², 51, 52 = Tod, 57–58. In each case the heading has been inscribed on a part of the stone where a previous heading had been erased. These are plainly instances of renewals in which an old treaty is being reaffirmed. The date of the renewal is firmly fixed by the archon's name to 433/2. The problem is to decide when the original treaties were made. Suggestions have ranged from about 460 (S. Accame, *Riv. di Fil.*, N.S., XXX [1952], 127ff.) to 439 (H. Wentker, *Sizilien und Athen* [Heidelberg, 1956], 70–71; 89ff.) Bengtson once again provides a full bibliography (*Staatsverträge,* 82) as well as a simple and accurate description of the historian's plight: "Wann dieser geschlossen wurde, ist unbekannt." For additional remarks, see *SEG,* X, 48; XII, 20; XXI, 35. I have ventured to date them in the early fifties because they seem to me to fit the adventurous mood that prevailed in Athens between the ostracism of Cimon and the Egyptian disaster. Once again, no great weight should be placed upon any date for these treaties.

[4] H. Droysen, *Athen und der Westen vor d. sizil. Expedition* (1882), 17ff., cited by Ehrenberg, *AJP,* LXIX (1948), 159, n. 27. I have been unable to see the book. Ehrenberg says, "It seems no longer necessary to refute" this view. It seems to me impossible to refute, just as it is impossible to prove.

century and again in the middle of the fifth. Shortly after this second destruction, dated by Diodorus five years after the second founding of 453/2, the surviving Sybarites sought help in rebuilding their city.[5] From this appeal there ultimately resulted the foundation of the city on a new site, which was called Thurii. We have no contemporary source for its foundation. We must rely chiefly on Diodorus and a few reports from scattered late authors, which often seem to contradict his version of the events. The result is a rather confused picture in which the chronology is far from clear and from which many very different interpretations have arisen. In spite of the difficulties, and although it is impossible to reach absolutely certain conclusions, we must try to understand what happened at Thurii and what it meant, for its foundation was an event of the greatest importance in the history of the relations of the Greek states in the critical years between the two Peloponnesian wars.

Diodorus places all the events connected with the foundation in the year 446/5,[6] but there is another strong tradition which places the foundation in 444/3.[7] Most scholars accept the later date, but the fact is that both dates seem relevant.[8] It is likely that it was in 446/5 that the Sybarite survivors sent ambassadors to Sparta and Athens asking help in resettling their city and inviting the Spartans and Athenians to join in the colony. Probably the request was made after the conclusion of the Thirty Years' Peace, for it is highly unlikely that such a request could be made while Sparta and Athens were at war with one another, but it was natural to apply for help to the two hegemonal states of Greece after the peace. The Spartans characteristically refused, but the Athenians agreed to take part.[9] This is as much as we may say about the first part of the Athenian involvement. Although Diodorus continues on to give details of the

[5] The text of Diodorus reads πέντε ἔτεσιν ὕστερον τοῦ δευτέρον συνοικισμοῦ. F. Vogel, the editor of the Teubner edition, brackets this passage, saying only *delevi*. He is followed by C. H. Oldfather in the Loeb edition, where it has been dropped to a footnote. There seems no satisfactory reason for rejecting the text of the manuscripts.

[6] 12. 7; 10, 3.

[7] Plut. *Mor.* 835c; see also Ehrenberg, *AJP*, LXIX (1948), 150, and n. 6.

[8] For good discussions of the chronological problems, see Busolt, *GG*, III: 1, 523 n. 3 and Ehrenberg, *loc. cit.*

[9] Diod. 12. 10. 3–4.

foundation, most of them clearly belong to the later date and the second phase of Athenian participation, and none can be confidently assigned to 446/5.[10] All we know, then, is that when the Sybarites asked the Athenians to provide settlers for re-establishing their city, Athens complied.

Let us be clear that this action did not amount to the establishment of an Athenian colony or cleruchy. We cannot be sure what was the purpose of Pericles, who was surely in command in 446/5, in agreeing to this migration, but we should not lose sight of the fact that in the previous year Athens had sent cleruchies to Imbros, the Chersonese, Chalcis, and Eretria. In 446/5 colonies were sent to Colophon, Erythrae, and Hestiaea, and new cleruchies were sent to Chalcis and Eretria after their rebellions were put down.[11] To be sure, these settlements were aimed, in part, at making the empire more secure, but they also reflect the need to rid Athens of excess population. The burden of providing a living for the poor placed a great strain on the Athenian treasury, particularly when the future of imperial tribute was in doubt. It is not necessary to see great imperial or commercial ambitions in this agreement to send supernumerary citizens to a city that was not an Athenian colony and that the Athenian settlers could not control.[12]

Athenian participation did not put an end to the troubles of the Sybarites. After a while, they "were destroyed by the Athenians and other Greeks, who, although they had come to live with them, despised them so much that they not only killed them but moved the city to another place and called it Thurii." [13] Diodorus provides some additional details. The old Sybarites, it seems, claimed special rights for themselves: political, social, and economic. This enraged the other settlers and led to the slaughter and expulsion of the Sybarites.[14]

[10] Ehrenberg thinks that the Athenian invitation to the Peloponnesians to join them in founding the colony belongs to 446/5, but he admits that this is not certain (*AJP,* LXIX [1948], 153 and note 18).

[11] *ATL,* III, 299–300.

[12] See Appendix F.

[13] Strabo p. 263, 6. 1. 13.

[14] 12. 11. 1–2. Diodorus places these events after the foundation of Thurii, but his chronology throughout is muddled. Strabo's account speaks only of Sybaris and Sybarites. He tells a clear and simple story that is preferable.

These events took place after the signing of the Thirty Years' Peace in the spring of 445. We must allow at least a year for the development of the strife and the final clash, so that by the spring or summer of 444, possibly a bit later, the word of what had happened must have reached Athens. It is generally agreed that some time in the year 444/3 the Athenians organized a colonizing expedition under the leadership of Lampon and Xenocritus to found a city on a new site near Sybaris. They sent messengers to the cities of the Peloponnese as well as other parts of Greece, many of whom accepted; this was to be not an Athenian, but a Panhellenic colony. The site was chosen in accordance with the instructions of the Delphic oracle. The land was divided equally among the settlers, regardless of their place of origin. A democratic constitution was established, and the Thurians were divided into ten tribes, organized into three groups. There was a Peloponnesian group made up of a tribe each for the Arcadians, the Achaeans, and the Eleians. Another, made up of extra-Peloponnesian Dorians, consisted of tribes called Boeotia, Amphictyonis, and Doris. Finally, there were four other tribes, one each for Ionia, Athens, Euboea, and the Islands. The lawgivers and founding fathers of the constitution were Charondas and Protagoras, and among the illustrious colonists were Hippodamus of Miletus, the famous city-planner, and Herodotus, the father of history.[15]

So much is generally accepted, but the interpretation of these facts has led to much disagreement. Since the meaning of the foundation of Thurii is of the greatest importance to our understanding of Athenian policy, we must look carefully at the more important interpretations before suggesting our own. It has often been assumed that the Athenian establishment of Thurii on a Panhellenic basis was a conciliatory gesture towards Corinth, the state most suspicious of Athenian ambitions in the west.[16] Wade-Gery agrees that such was at least part of the purpose, but asks why the Athenians made such a gesture. To his mind, Pericles never abandoned a policy of aggres-

[15] This common ground is established by putting together the account of Diodorus 12. 10–11 with the article of Ehrenberg cited above and that of P. Cloché, "Périclès et la Politique Extérieure d'Athènes entre la Paix de 446-445 et les Préludes de la Guerre du Péloponèse," *AC,* XIV (1945), 95–103.

[16] E.g., O'Neill, *Ancient Corinth* (Baltimore, 1930), 196, and F. E. Adcock, *CAH,* V, 169.

sive imperialism. "Perikles meant the Sparta-Athens dualism to be provisional. The years 445–431 were not, nor were meant to be, a milennium: Athens had recoiled to jump better." [17] The period between the peace of 446/5 and 431 was one of "relentless pressure westwards . . . aimed directly at Korinth, indirectly at Sparta: Korinth was to be forced out of the Spartan League or, if necessary, ruined." Thus, since the establishment of Thurii on a Panhellenic basis was not an aggressive action but quite the reverse, Pericles could not have supported it. To be sure, he had proposed the settlement of Thurii and employed his friends Lampon and Xenocritus as founders, but he intended it purely as an imperial undertaking.

In 444/3, says Wade-Gery, Pericles was not elected general, and the planning of the expedition fell to Thucydides, son of Melesias, the archfoe of Pericles. A member of the international aristocracy of Greece, "he was the true Panhellenist: and . . . Perikles, in the Congress Decree, stole his thunder. To Perikles, Panhellenism was a thing which could be made to serve Athens: to Thucydides, it meant equality of all Greek states, the renouncement of Athenian domination." [18] It was Thucydides who invited the Peloponnesians to share in the colony and set it on its Panhellenic path. Unfortunately, Thucydides was ostracized in the spring of 443, and the result was a "mongrel policy" for Thurii. With the return to power of Pericles, Athens turned its back on peaceful Panhellenism and resumed its imperial ambitions. The tightening of Athenian control of the empire, the treaties with Rhegium and Leontini, which Wade-Gery thinks may belong to this year, possibly the alliance that Phormio concluded with Acarnania, were all stages in an uninterrupted process leading to Athens' treaty with Corcyra in 433 and the Peloponnesian War.

Now this is as forceful a statement as we have of the proposition that Pericles and Athens were undeviatingly committed to an aggressive and expansionist policy not only in the north and east, but in the west as well, from the very moment that the Thirty Years' Peace was made. If it is correct, it renders absurd any claim that the Peloponnesian War could have been averted, for Sparta and Corinth could certainly not stand idly by forever while Athens increased its

[17] *Essays,* 253.
[18] *Ibid.,* 256.

power at their expense. The fact is, however, that the entire theory is gossamer and disintegrates at the first touch.[19]

The argument for Thucydides as the sponsor of the Panhellenic colony rests in the first place on two paragraphs (6–7) in the anonymous *Life of Thucydides,* which comes down to us in the manuscripts. This purports to be a life of the historian, not the son of Melesias. It tells a highly confused story of Thucydides going to Sybaris before he was condemned and ostracized. The source is universally regarded as altogether untrustworthy, and this particular tale is absurd and incoherent even by its low standard.[20] The second basis for Wade-Gery's interpretation is the argument that Pericles was out of power in 444/3 and could not have initiated the plan for a Panhellenic colony in that year. This argument rests on a passage in Plutarch's *Life of Pericles* (16.3): "After the overthrow and ostracism of Thucydides, Pericles for no less than fifteen years acquired a position of authority and domination that was continuous and unbroken because of his election as general each year."[21] Wade-Gery takes this to mean that from 443/2, the year after the ostracism, to 429/8, the year of his death, Pericles held the generalship

[19] So far as I know it has won no adherents, though it seems to linger in the minds of those who share its general belief in unceasing Athenian imperialism on all fronts. In part this is no doubt due to a proper respect for the erudition and wisdom of its author and for the daring brilliance of the concept, which draws on a remarkably scattered and disparate body of evidence. Scholars who have written on Thurii since Wade-Gery, however, have not accepted his theory. See De Sanctis, *Pericle,* 169–170, Gomme, *Hist. Comm.,* I, 386–387, Cloché *AC,* XIV (1945), 100, n. 1, Ehrenberg, *AJP,* LXIX (1948), 159–163, and Wentker, *Sizilien und Athen,* 86–87 for explicit rebuttals. The authors of *ATL* (III, 305, n. 20), of which Wade-Gery is one, had by 1950 come to the conclusion that the earlier view of Wade-Gery "needs certain modifications." These include a complete rejection of the idea that Athens put "relentless pressure" on Corinth. They continue to believe "that the plan for Thouria [*sic*] was strongly coloured by the opposition to Perikles," a view they alone hold, so far as I can see. With their main conclusion, however, I agree fully: "We think, then, that between 446 and 433 Athens avoided overt provocation of Korinth. . . ."

[20] Gomme, *Hist. Comm.,* I, 386–387; Ehrenberg, *AJP,* LXIX (1948), 160–161.

[21] *μετὰ δὲ τὴν Θουκυδίδου κατάλυσιν καὶ τὸν ὀστρακισμὸν οὐκ ἐλάττω τῶν πεντεκαίδεκα ἐτῶν διηνεκῆ καὶ μίαν οὖσαν ἐν ταῖς ἐνιαυσίοις στρατηγίαις ἀρχὴν καὶ δυναστείαν κτησάμενος.*

without interruption. In the first place, as Wade-Gery recognizes, Pericles was removed from office in 430/29 and died in the midst of his term in 429/8, so that the terms continuous (διηνεκῆ) and unbroken (μίαν οὖσαν) hardly seem applicable. If we interpret the passage strictly, we should have to begin the series of elections in 445/4.[22] But the fact is that we have no warrant to take these figures seriously at all. It is perfectly clear that Plutarch is talking in very general terms and that his figures are round, to say the least. Earlier in the very same sentence he says, "For forty years Pericles stood first among such men as Ephialtes, Leocrates, Myronides, Cimon, Tolmides, and Thucydides. . . ." If we take this claim seriously, we must believe that Pericles was paramount in 469, when he was no more than twenty-five years old. That is absurd, and no one does take it seriously, yet we are asked to believe in the accuracy of the figure of fifteen years that appears in the same context.

Scholars have pointed out yet another flaw in the argument: the assumption that if Pericles was not general he was out of power.[23] It is clear that a continuous run of generalships was the exception rather than the rule in fifth-century Athens. "If Perikles was strategos 6 or 7 times between 460 and 443, that was remarkable. . . . If he was not reelected in 445–444 and 444–443, that was normal, and we must not infer from it any change or upset in Athenian policy."[24] Finally, we should recognize that the notion that Pericles was out of power in 444/3 rests on a fundamental misunderstanding of the institution of ostracism at Athens. We have seen that the vote on ostracism was introduced by Pericles, not his opponent. No politician ever did such a thing without full confidence in the support of a comfortable majority. Whether or not he was general in 444/3, Pericles was in command of the political situation and must bear full responsibility for the dispatch of a colony to Thurii and the form that it took.

Ehrenberg rejects the notion that Thucydides was responsible for the Panhellenic nature of Thurii, yet he seems to believe in a modified version of the "relentless pressure" theory. For him the foundation of Thurii is a continuation of that peaceful imperialism of the

[22] This is precisely what Beloch does (*GG* ², II: 1, 185 and n. 3).

[23] Gomme, *idem.*; Ehrenberg, *op. cit.*, 162–163.

[24] Gomme, *idem.*

Congress Decree which would have supported Athenian political imperialism with religious hegemony. In the case of Thurii, "The aims were both more modest and more realistic. But the spirit was the same. Pericles founded a colony on a Panhellenic basis, a colony led by an Athenian οἰκιστής and intended as a stronghold of Athenian influence in the West."[25] This view has a good deal of support and deserves careful consideration. In the first place, it is well to clear the ground by eliminating unfounded suppositions. There is absolutely no reliable evidence for Athenian involvement in the west between 445 and 435 except for the colonization of Thurii.[26] If we are to believe that Athens meant to extend her influence to the west in the years between the Peloponnesian Wars, we must confine our search for proof to that event.

At Thurii, Ehrenberg has tried to find such proof. His most important argument is that the colony was not really Panhellenic, that its Panhellenism was merely a cloak to hide the truth, that Thurii was founded by Athenian friends of Pericles and dominated by Athenians and their allies in the "well-founded expectation of Athenian leadership." It was given a democratic constitution and filled with the friends of Pericles. The whole policy was Periclean, "that is to say, democratic and imperialistic."[27] An investigation of the ten Thurian tribes shows that Athens was the only single city represented by a tribe. It is further plain that with the tribes Eubois, Nesiotis, and Ias, Athens and her allies controlled four of the ten tribes. All the Dorians, including Corinthians and Spartans, were placed in a single tribe, so they could have been neither numerous nor influential. Ehrenberg takes this as evidence for Athenian machinations to control and dominate the colony. But surely this is to read too much into the tribal names or perhaps to read their significance too simply. If the constitution of Thurii was like that of Athens, then the tribes, like the original tribes of Cleisthenes, had to be roughly equal, for in Athens, at least, they provided regiments for the army and could not be too different in size. Thus, the Athenians could not have decided in advance how the Thurian tribes would be organ-

[25] 163.

[26] See above, pp. 154–156, and Appendix G.

[27] 160.

ized and named; first they had to discover who would come to join their colony.

We must keep in mind that the several Greek states did not appoint contingents of settlers to leave home and join the colony. The colonists were individuals who were attracted by the Athenian invitation. Until they gathered in Italy, no one could be sure how many there would be or what would be the number of settlers from each region. That there were few Spartans and Corinthians is hardly surprising. Sparta had no population to spare and had not sent off a colony for centuries. Corinth was a rich, exciting, and flourishing city with a mixed economy and many sources of entertainment. So far as we know she was not troubled by overpopulation in this period. Arcadia, Elis, Achaea, the Aegean Islands, Euboea, and many parts of Ionia and Boeotia, on the other hand, were far from prosperous and generally had more people than they could support. Athens, as we have seen, had a rapidly expanding population. The assignment of settlers to tribes thus seems less a part of an Athenian plan of domination than a reflection of the nature of the new body of citizens.

Perhaps it is also a bit naive to believe that the presence of three tribes of settlers from states in the Athenian Empire guaranteed the Athenians' control. There was enough resentment towards Athens in the empire to make it equally likely that the Euboeans, Islanders, and Ionians might be very touchy and resentful of any Athenian attempt to assert superiority in any way. This is only conjecture, but so is the suggestion that the tribal organization makes a mockery of the notion that Thurii was a Panhellenic colony. The hard fact is that Athenians seem to have made up only about one-tenth of the population and to have been confined to a single tribe. If the Panhellenism of Thurii was a fraud, we need other evidence.

But the argument over Panhellenism is only a minor issue in comparison with the basic question: Did Athens use, or intend to use, Thurii as a base for her western ambitions? The best answer to this question can be found by examining the history of the colony. Very soon after its establishment, the new city became involved in a war with the old Spartan colony of Taras. Diodorus assigns the fighting to the year 444/3, but we have seen that his chronology is not reliable at this point. Perhaps we should understand him to mean that it took place two years after the foundation of the city, which he places in

446/5. If so we may guess that 442/1 is the proper date, but in any case some date in the forties is appropriate.

Diodorus gives us a rather vague account of continuous fighting on land and sea with mutual plunderings but no clear result.[28] Once again Strabo has a clearer, fuller, and more reliable account. He is following Antiochus of Syracuse, a fifth-century writer who composed a history with one book devoted to southern Italy. We have reason to believe Strabo when he gives the following account:

> Antiochus says that when the Tarantines were at war with the Thurians over who should possess Siris, and Cleandridas, who was in exile from Sparta, was their general, they agreed to establish a joint colony in common, but the colony was judged to belong to the Tarantines. . . .[29]

It is not hard to put the two accounts together. For Diodorus the war is indecisive because neither side annihilates the other. Both our authors are describing the same event with different degrees of detail. Finally, we have the evidence of a dedication inscribed at Olympia in old Laconic letters, which reads: "The Tarantines offered a tenth of the spoils they took from the Thurians to Olympian Zeus." [30] The main point is indisputable: only a short time after its foundation Thurii fought a war with a nearby Spartan colony and lost.

It is at this point that the believers in the theory that Thurii was an outpost of Athenian imperialism must contend with the curious behavior of the Athenians. Athens took no action. Is it possible that so soon after the foundation of the colony, after going to such unusual lengths to set it up, that an imperialistic Pericles should make no move to support it? The defeat at Siris was the beginning of a decline of Athenian prestige in southern Italy that was never checked, yet Pericles permitted it without so much as a gesture or a word. Such behavior ill accords with a policy of aggressive imperialism or "relentless pressure." One of the first things the new colony of Thurii had done was to make peace with the traditional enemy of Sybaris, Croton.[31] Is it too daring to see in this and the refusal of

[28] Diod. 12. 23. 2.

[29] Strabo 6. 1. 15, p. 264.

[30] W. Dittenberger, *SIG*, Number 6. Σκῦλα ἀπὸ Θουρίον Ταραντῖνοι ἀνέθεκαν Διὶ 'Ολυμπίοι δεκάτον. Dittenberger dates it ca. 440, "non multo post Thurios conditos."

[31] Diod. 12. 11. 3.

Pericles to intervene in the war between Thurii and Taras, a contrary policy of peaceful Panhellenism and nonintervention?

The attitude of Athens towards Thurii was put to an even sharper and more direct test. In 434/3 factional strife broke out at Thurii.[32] The date is of some importance for an understanding of the situation, for it is after the outbreak of hostilities between Corinth and Corcyra, but before the Athenian alliance with Corcyra. It is fair to say that at that moment a conflict between Athens and Sparta seemed possible, and to some even inevitable. It was in these circumstances that the Thurians split on the question of whose colony Thurii was and the related question of who was its οἰκιστής. There can be little doubt that the question arose as a result of the tense international situation, which soon led almost all Greeks and some barbarians to choose one side or the other in the impending struggle. The Athenians asserted that the colony was Athenian, alleging that "the greatest number of citizens had come from Athens." [33] The Peloponnesians countered that since a "great many" (οὐκ ὀλίγους) of them had been among the founding fathers, the colony should be regarded as Peloponnesian.

Unfortunately we do not have anything from Antiochus of Syracuse to clarify the nature of the dispute, but we shall not be far from the truth if we summarize the argument in the following terms: The dispute was important because its outcome might determine the attitude of the state in the forthcoming war. The Athenians argued that Thurii was Athenian because the single city with the greatest number of original colonists was Athens. The Peloponnesians argued that the colony was Peloponnesian because there were more Peloponnesians than Athenians, or indeed than any other geographical group. The upshot of the affair was that the Thurians sent to Delphi to ask, "Who shall be called the founder of the city?" The god replied that he himself should be considered the founder. That settled the matter. Thereafter Apollo was declared the founder of Thurii, and peace was restored. "The Panhellenic character of the colony was made clear,

[32] The date is established by Diodorus (12. 35) and has not been challenged so far as I know. It is accepted both by the conservative Busolt (*GG*, III: 1, 537) and by the daring Beloch (*GG* [2], II: 1, 202).

[33] Diod. 12. 35. 2: ἀποφαινόμενοι πλείστους οἰκήτορας ἐξ Ἀθηνῶν ἐληλυθέναι.

but the way was paved for the dissolution of the connection with Athens." [34]

Once again Athens did absolutely nothing. But this time her silence is even stranger, for now there was a very good chance that war would come, and if it did, a colony in the west would be helpful, while a hostile state could be dangerous. Yet Pericles did not intervene, even though Delphic Apollo was a friend of Sparta, and his acceptance as founder of Thurii meant that it would be more likely to side with the Peloponnesians if war came. It appears that in 434/3, Pericles still hoped to avoid war and was reluctant to take any steps in the west that might frighten or anger Corinth or Sparta. There seems to be no reason to believe that Thurii was anything other than what it seemed to be, a Panhellenic and not an Athenian colony. There should be no doubt, furthermore, that it was a project supported by Pericles from the beginning, or that he remained firm in his determination to leave it independent down to and into the Peloponnesian War.

If all this is true, we need to explain why Pericles pursued the policies he did, when he did, and precisely in the way that he did. Our sources, of course, do not provide us with much information as to Pericles' thinking, but the interpretation of his political situation that we have offered makes the following reconstruction not altogether unlikely. Some time in the year 444/3 the Athenians received word of the civil war in Sybaris by which the Athenian and allied settlers had ejected the Sybarites. Their situation was perilous, for a certain number of citizens was necessary, not only for the ordinary functioning of a city-state, but for its defense. The settlers had either to receive reinforcements or come home. Now, in the circumstances it must have been no easy task to persuade Athenians to go off to Thurii. Southern Italy was very far from home, and the average Athenian knew very little about that part of the world, as the Sicilian expedition would later show. Even in 446/5 there could not have been too many who went, for Athenians only made up about 10 per cent of the population. By 444/3 the attraction was less and the supply of Athenians smaller. The troubles of the first contingent did

[34] Busolt, *GG*, III: 1, 537. He goes on to say that this was "eine Niederlage der athenischen Kolonialpolitik," for he is of the school that believes Thurii to have been intended as a base of Athenian imperialism.

not serve to encourage further settlement. At the same time, the great number of Athenians who had gone overseas in colonies or cleruchies since the foundation must have come close to draining the city of potential emigrants. If Pericles wished to reinforce Thurii, he would be hard pressed to find enough Athenians for the job.

In this way necessity compelled Pericles to broaden the base of the new colony and seek settlers outside of Attica. But it was by no means necessary for him to extend his invitation throughout the Greek world, including the Peloponnese, and to create a Panhellenic colony. In 437/6 he undertook to found the colony of Amphipolis at the site of Ennea Hodoi in Thrace. On that occasion, too, there were not enough Athenians available, so he was compelled to turn to foreigners. To begin with, these additional settlers were collected from the neighborhood of Amphipolis without any Panhellenic fanfare. Beyond that, even though the Athenians were only a fraction of the populace, there was never any question that Amphipolis was an Athenian colony.[35] The comparison is very illuminating. There were several reasons why the two colonies were treated so differently. If we have understood the Periclean policy rightly, geography was one consideration. Amphipolis was located within the Athenian sphere of influence, in the neighborhood of Athenian allies, subjects, and colonies. In that location there was no reason to display unusual modesty and restraint. Thurii was a unique Athenian settlement in Italy, in a region foreign and not vital to Athenian interests, but an area of great sensitivity for the Corinthians and even the Spartans. The very appearance of undue ambition in that part of the world might destroy the policy of disengagement with the great Peloponnesian powers that Pericles was trying to follow.

But foreign relations alone do not explain the nature of the Thurian colony. In 444/3 the political threat that the son of Melesias posed to Pericles was at its height, and the rhetorical weapon that was doing the most damage was the combination of anti-imperialism and Panhellenism that was the overt program of the *oligoi*. We may suppose that Pericles saw this at least as clearly as we do and seized upon the opportunity of the appeal of the Athenians at Sybaris to steal his opponents' thunder. It is likely that some time in 444,

[35] Thuc. 4. 106. 1; 4. 103. 3–4; Diod. 12. 32. 3; schol. Aeschines 2. 34; *ATL*, III, 308–309.

before the decision to hold an ostracism, Pericles announced his intentions for the new colony and sent out his invitations to the Greek world, including the Peloponnese. In one stroke he had taken the wind out of his opponents' sails. He had demonstrated his moderation, his lack of imperial ambition, and his Panhellenic sentiments. Perhaps this strategem turned the political tide and gave Pericles the confidence to bring on the ostracism that finally rid him of Thucydides.

His choice of the leadership of the expedition showed the same acumen and the same response to the political realities of the moment that would characterize his selection of Sophocles as chairman of the board of Hellenotamiae in the next year. The leading founding father was Lampon. He is referred to sometimes as a seer (μάντις), sometimes as an interpreter of oracles (ἐξηγητής or χρησμολόγος).[36] Plutarch tells the story of his association with Pericles: a unicorn was brought to Pericles. Anaxagoras dissected the skull and explained the phenomenon rationally and scientifically. Lampon, however, interpreted it as a cosmic message that showed that the split between the parties of Pericles and Thucydides would be resolved by the victory of Pericles and the consequent unification of the state.[37] We may deduce from this tale that Lampon was favorably disposed to Pericles and his cause, but it is also clear that Pericles, himself a coldly rational and highly educated man, understood the importance of religious orthodoxy for the masses. Ehrenberg has clearly seen the significance of Lampon for the colony at Thurii:

It is evident that the activities of prophets such as Lampon were essential for the whole enterprise. This is not surprising, for our sources give us many examples of the genuine and fervent belief of the Greeks, the Athenians as well as others, in oracles, prophecies and mantic evi-

[36] The references to Lampon in these religious capacities are contained in the following passages: Athenaeus 344e; Hesychius, *s.v.* ἀγερσικύβηλις; Eupolis, frg. 297 (Kock); Photius, *Lexicon, s.v.* Θουριομάντεις; Suidas (or The Suda) *s.v.* θουριομάντεις; schol. Aristoph., *Peace* 1084; and *Birds* 521. In the fragment of Hesychius it is explained that Cratinus called Lampon a mountebank (ἀγύρτης). These passages have been collected with some comments as testimonia by James H. Oliver, *The Athenian Expounders of the Sacred and Ancestral Law,* (Baltimore, 1950), 124–125.

[37] *Per.* 6. 2.

dence. . . . Every leading politician, whether he himself believed in these things or not, had to make use of them, and so had Pericles.[38]

The allegiance of Lampon brought more than religious orthodoxy to the Periclean cause. It also provided an aura of political and social respectability for the Thurian undertaking. In later years Lampon headed the list of the signers of the Peace of Nicias. He alone prepared recommendations for the regulation of the first fruits of the olive crop offered at Eleusis. "The man came obviously from one of the eupatrid families which dominated the political life of the period and which with the help of adoptions and adlections dominated the religious life throughout the whole history of Athens to the fifth century after Christ." [39] In the political crisis of 444/3, it must have been very useful to Pericles that the expedition to Thurii gave public prominence to such a supporter of his policy. He was living evidence, as was Sophocles, that a man could be *kalos kagathos* without joining the *oligoi*.

Whatever the domestic considerations surrounding the foundation of Thurii, its later development carried forward its initial intention in the realm of foreign policy without deviation. No doubt Pericles was disappointed when Thurii seemed to turn away from Athens, but it is wrong to say, "The foundation of Thurii reflects and confirms the greatness of his mind and the failure of his policy." [40] The policy was a great success at home, where it helped Pericles achieve political supremacy. It can be considered a failure in foreign policy only if we assume that he intended the colony as a spearhead for western imperialism, but we have seen that there is no basis for such an assumption. If, on the other hand, it was intended to sooth and conciliate Athens' recent enemies, the events of the next few years proved it altogether successful.

[38] *AJP*, LXIX (1948), 164–165.

[39] For Lampon as signer of the peace, see Thuc. 5. 19. 2 and 5. 24. 1. His role in the Eleusinian offerings is described in an official Athenian inscription, *IG*, I ^{2}, 76 = Tod, I, 74, line 60. The quotation is from Oliver, *op. cit.*, 12. Ehrenberg (*op. cit.*, 164–165) seems to underestimate or to be unaware of the social and political prominence of Lampon apart from his association with Pericles.

[40] Ehrenberg, *op. cit.*, 170.

10. The Samian Rebellion

Late in the summer of 440 a war broke out between Samos and Miletus over the control of the town of Priene.[1] The quarrel presented a difficult imperial problem to the Athenians. Samos was a completely autonomous state, paying no tribute, one of only three states that possessed a navy, and that a very powerful one. Her constitution was oligarchic. Miletus, on the other hand, had revolted in the 450's and been subdued. It paid tribute and had been deprived of a navy. A few years earlier, in 446/5, a second rebellion resulted in the establishment by Athens of a democratic constitution.[2] Some scholars believe that subsequent events stemmed from the fact that Samos was oligarchic while Miletus was democratic.[3] But something more important than constitutional preferences was at stake. If Athens deprived states of their means of defense, as she had been doing ever since the siege of Naxos more than three decades earlier, she had an obligation to see that they were not maltreated by their neighbors. Apart from their preferences and advantage, the Athenians could not simply ignore a war between two members of their alliance, particularly if one was strong and the other weak.

When the Milesians, supported by some private citizens from Samos who wanted to overthrow the oligarchy, complained to Athens that they were being beaten by Samos, the Athenians could not

[1] Thuc. 1. 115. 2; Diod. 12. 27. 1; Plut. *Per.* 24. 1. For the date see Gomme, *Hist. Comm.*, I, 390.

[2] See above, pp. 100–101.

[3] E.g., Glotz and Cohen, *HG*, II, 207; Busolt, *GG*, III: 1, 542–543 and n. 1 on 543.

refuse to take action. They sent to the Samians, asking them to break off the war and to submit the dispute to arbitration.[4] The Samians refused, perhaps because they knew they were in the wrong, perhaps because they expected Athens to favor Miletus in any case, perhaps merely as a denial of Athens' right to intervene in Samian affairs. Diodorus says that the Samians fought the Milesians because they "saw that the Athenians inclined toward the Milesians," but it is hard to know just what that means. Even if his report is accurate, we do not know whether the Athenians favor towards the Milesians was based on the facts of the dispute or on prejudice and their own advantage. None of our sources tells us the rights and wrongs of the dispute over Priene. Whatever the truth may be, the Samian refusal of arbitration was an act of defiance that left Athens no choice. If she could not defend the weak members of her alliance from attack by the strong, her claim to leadership was a mockery.

Pericles responded promptly and decisively. He sailed to Samos with forty ships and replaced the oligarchy with a democracy. He took fifty boys and fifty men as hostages and deposited them on Lemnos. He imposed an indemnity of eighty talents on the Samians and withdrew as swiftly as he had come, leaving a garrison behind.[5] The settlement was far from harsh in comparison with others imposed on rebellious states. Samos retained her autonomy, kept her walls, fleet, and land, and paid no tribute. It was nonetheless decisive, making it abundantly clear that Athens meant to maintain her hegemony even over large and powerful naval states.

The ease with which Pericles subdued the island gives ample evidence that the Samians had not expected such a reaction from Athens. Perhaps the reasonable and gentle policy of Pericles after his struggle with the son of Melesias had led them to believe that his

[4] Thuc. 1. 115. 2; Plut. *Per.* 24. 1 and 25. 1. Thucydides does not mention the demand for a truce and arbitration, another of the many curious omissions in his account of the Pentecontaetia. Nothing in his version contradicts it however, and there is no reason to doubt its authenticity. See Cloché, *AC,* XIV (1945), 105, n. 2 and Busolt, *GG,* III: 1, 542–543.

[5] Thuc. 1. 115. 3–4; Diod. 12. 1–2; Plut. *Per.* 25. 1–3. Busolt suggests that since the tales Plutarch reports of bribes unsuccessfully offered to Pericles by the hostages, the oligarchs, and Pissuthnes, the Persian satrap of Sardis, speak well for the integrity of Pericles, they may not have originated with that notorious miso-Athenian and liar, Duris of Samos.

imperial attitude had softened. Perhaps they meant to test his resolution. In any case, they had certainly not expected such swift retaliation. The defeat did not cow them; it infuriated them. Up to this point the Samian quarrel with Miletus and the resulting defiance of Athens was a very limited challenge. Now it turned into a great revolution with grandiose goals. When they resumed their rebellion, the Samians "contested the supremacy of the sea." [6] Before it was over they had come "within a very little of taking the control of the sea away from Athens." [7]

Immediately upon the withdrawal of the Athenian fleet, some of the Samians, after plotting with the leaders of the upper classes, fled to the continent to seek the aid of Pissuthnes, satrap of Lydia, who permitted them to collect seven hundred mercenary troops and stole for them the Samian hostages from Lemnos. This last act was of the greatest importance, for until they were freed of anxiety for their loved ones, the Samian oligarchic leaders could not join in open rebellion.[8] The mercenaries, aided by their friends on Samos, made a night crossing to the island and caught the democratic government and the Athenian garrison by surprise. Some democrats were captured and some exiled. As a final and irrevocable act of rebellion and defiance, the victorious Samian oligarchs seized the Athenian imperial officials and garrison and turned them over to Pissuthnes. After that, rather superfluously, the Samians publicly declared themselves enemies of Athens.[9] The magnitude of the threat to Athens was immediately made clear by the simultaneous rebellion of Byzantium. It appears that there were also defections in Caria, Thrace, and the Chalcidice.[10] At the same time, Mytilene, the major city of Lesbos, was planning to join in the uprising, awaiting only promise of support from Sparta before beginning the revolt.[11]

[6] *ἀντιλαμβάνεσθαι τῆς θαλάττης* (Plut. *Per*. 25. 3).

[7] Thuc. 8. 76. 4, also quoted by Plut. *Per*. 28. 6: *παρ' ἐλάχιστον δὴ ἦλθε τὸ Ἀθηναίων κράτος τῆς θαλάσσης, ὅτε ἐπολέμησεν, ἀφελέσθαι.*

[8] For a good account of the factional politics at Samos in this period, see Ronald P. Legon, *Demos and Stasis: Studies in the Factional Politics of Classical Greece,* unpublished doctoral dissertation, Cornell University, 1966, 127–148.

[9] Thuc. 1. 115. 4–5; Diod. 12. 27. 3; Plut. *Per*. 25. 2.

[10] Busolt, *GG,* III: 1, 544 and n. 5; Meyer, *GdA,* IV: 1, 713.

[11] Thuc. 1. 115. 5 is the only certain reference to the Byzantine uprising,

We must not allow hindsight to obscure the danger that these events presented to Athens. Samos was in itself a powerful opponent, but the rising at Byzantium made it more than possible that the Samian rebellion would ignite a general revolution throughout the empire. The actions of Pissuthnes, moreover, made it seem likely that the Persians were prepared to take advantage of the opportunity to break the peace they had made with Athens, whether formal or informal, and try to regain their lost position in Asia Minor and the Aegean. Finally, the Samians made overtures to Sparta and the Peloponnesians, asking for assistance against Athens. If Sparta responded favorably and the other two possibilities became realities, Athens would be faced with precisely the combination of enemies that ultimately defeated her and destroyed her empire in 404. Everything, in fact, depended on the attitude of the Peloponnesians, for the Great King would not commit himself to a war, nor would most of the Athenian subjects risk a rebellion without the promise of support from the Spartans. The attitude of Sparta, in turn, was very much influenced by that of Corinth, not only because of the special relationship between them, but because much of the navy needed for the war must come from the Corinthians. The test of Pericles' policy since 446/5, then, was at hand. If that policy, particularly in the west, appeared to Sparta and Corinth to be aggressive, ambitious, and frightening, we should expect them to seize this "incomparable opportunity . . . to make a sudden attack on Athens while her sea power was seriously engaged." [12]

The deliberations of the Peloponnesians are reported to us in the speech that the Corinthian envoys made in the Athenian assembly

---

but the name of Byzantium has been plausibly restored in an inscription listing Athenian expenses for the Samian War in 441/0 and 440/39. See *SEG*, X, 221. The Mytileneans spoke of their request for Spartan support of their rebellion in their speech to the Spartans in 428. There can be no certainty about the date of this request, for the passage reads only, βουλομένος μὲν καὶ πάλαι, ὅτε ἔτι ἐν εἰρήνῃ ἐπέμψαμεν ὡς ὑμᾶς περὶ ἀποστάσεως (3. 13. 1). Yet no one has suggested a better context for it, indeed few scholars have tried to place it at all. Eduard Meyer, one of the few to notice it, places it "in eins der folgenden Jahre," (*GdA*, IV: 1, 714, n. 2) but gives no reason. Grote (V, 1, n. 1) places it before the affair at Corcyra. Only Busolt (*GG*, III: 1, 545 and n. 3) has seen that the Mytilenean unrest is best placed in this year.

[12] Meyer, *GdA*, IV: 1, 713.

in 433. They were there to persuade the Athenians not to accept the alliance that Corcyra was offering them, which would probably lead to a war with Corinth. There is no doubt that the Corinthians tried to put themselves and their actions in the best light, but we have every reason to believe their account accurate. Since Thucydides was in Athens when the speech was delivered to the Athenian assembly, we may be sure he heard it, and if he ever accurately reports what the speaker really said, he must be doing so on this occasion. The Corinthians, moreover, could not have told the Athenians anything untrue or unlikely, for it would have destroyed their credibility and damaged their case. This account, therefore, is as good evidence as we have for any event in the fifth century. At the time of the Samian rebellion, then, the Spartans called a meeting of the Peloponnesian League to discuss the Samian request for aid. The Peloponnesians were of two minds, but the Corinthian response was clear and decisive: "We did not vote against you," the Corinthians told the Athenians, "when the other Peloponnesians were divided in their voting as to whether they should aid the Samians, but openly we argued that each side should be free to punish its own allies." [13]

The Corinthian decision sealed the fate of Samos. The Peloponnesians gave no aid, the Persians drew back, a general conflagration in the empire never took place. Athens, as we shall see, was left free to chastise her rebels and did so, although it proved no easy task. But the Corinthian reply and the reasoning behind it is a priceless bit of evidence on the question of greatest concern to us: Was there a real chance for a lasting peace between Athens and the Peloponnesians? We have already seen that a large part of the answer to that question depends on whether or not the interested parties truly accepted the settlement of 446/5, which recognized the Athenian empire and the division of the Greek world into two spheres of influence. The Corinthians believed that the Athenians had honestly accepted that settlement and sought no further aggrandizement at the expense of the Corinthians; they interpreted Athenian actions in the west as we have done, as inoffensive and unambitious, for if they did not, their behavior at the debate concerning aid to Samos is inexplicable. At the same time, their own statement shows that the Corinthians, too, accepted the division of the Greek world into two

[13] Thuc. 1. 40. 5–6; see also 41. 1–3.

parts as a lasting and workable arrangement. Their actions at the critical moment show that they meant what they said. The Spartans, by their silent acquiescence, showed that they agreed. In 440, at least, a major war was far from inevitable, for both sides understood the rules and were willing to abide by them. There was even reason to expect that the restraint shown on this occasion might make the possibility of such a war more remote.

The details of the fighting in the Aegean need not detain us long, but several matters deserve our attention. For one thing, it was Pericles himself who set out with a fleet of sixty ships when he heard of the rebellion of the Samians, just as he had led the first expedition. He plainly regarded this as a matter of the most vital importance which he would entrust to no one else. Another interesting fact is that Sophocles the tragedian was elected general for the year 441/40 and so was one of the men who went with Pericles to put down the Samians. There is probably something to the story that he was elected by the Athenians because of their admiration for the *Antigone,* which had been performed the previous year. It is clear, in any case, that the choice of Sophocles was not based on his reputation for military skill. His contemporary, the poet Ion, was probably right in saying that Sophocles was not particularly able in matters of state, but "just like anyone among the upper classes of Athens." [14] When he was elected there was no reason to expect a war, but when one broke out, Pericles shrewdly put Sophocles to the best possible use. His wealth, nobility, and fame gave him entrée into the aristocratic houses of the Greek world. No envoy from Athens could be more certain of a friendly welcome and a thorough hearing from the upper classes in the empire. This could be very useful for Athens at a time when there was good reason to expect restlessness and possible treachery from these very people. Thus, while Pericles awaited reinforcements from Athens before attacking the island of Samos, he sent Sophocles to Chios and Lesbos. At Chios he was given a memorable banquet by his Chian friend Hermesilaus, who was proxenus of the Athenians. Ion was present and gives a full report of the behavior of the Athenian poet-general at a typical gathering of *kaloi kagathoi*. Sophocles must have been successful, for not only did

[14] Ath. 603d.

Lesbos and Chios fail to rebel, they ultimately provided contingents of ships and helped the Athenians in their siege of Samos.[15]

Although they put up a good fight and at one time cleared the sea near the island of Athenian ships for a fourteen-day period, the Samians were beaten at sea. Still resisting fiercely, they compelled the Athenians to organize and maintain a costly siege, but in the ninth month, in the spring or summer of 439, they were forced to capitulate. The terms were necessarily harsh, but not so harsh as might be expected. The Samians pulled down their walls, gave up their fleet, accepted a democratic regime, and agreed to pay a war indemnity of 1,300 talents in twenty-six annual installments.[16] On the other hand, they paid no tribute and were compelled to receive neither garrisons nor cleruchies.[17] Perhaps Pericles thought that the establishment of a friendly democracy and the example just given of the alertness and competence of the Athenian navy was enough to guarantee the future loyalty of Samos. Perhaps the comparative mildness of the settlement was part of his program to show the moderates in Athens that moderation and security, not greed and ambition, were the bases of his imperial policy.

Soon after the Samian surrender, the Byzantines, too, came to terms. They were permitted to return to their place in the empire

[15] Thuc. 116–117; Ath. 603f–604b.

[16] Thuc. 1. 117. 3. The amount of the tribute and the terms of payment are established by *ATL*, III, 334–335. Cf. Gomme, *Hist. Comm.*, I, 355–356. The basic document is the inscription at Athens of the cost of the revolt (*IG*, I², 293 = Tod, 50). Fragments of the decree regulating the settlement at Samos are recorded in *IG*, I², 50. Thucydides does not mention the establishment of a democracy at Samos. Our information comes from Diodorus (12. 27. 4) and is accepted by most scholars but rejected by Beloch (*GG*², II: 1, 197). Legon (*op. cit.*, 139–148) provides a useful discussion of the problem in the light of later events at Samos and concludes that the settlement of 439 provided for at least a nominal democracy rather subservient to Athens.

[17] Nesselhauf (*Untersuchungen*, 138–139) supports the view of Ulrich Kahrstedt that Samos is absent from the tribute lists because the Athenians confiscated her lands and established cleruchies. This opinion is ill founded and is refuted by Gomme (*Hist. Comm.*, I, 355). Busolt (*GG*, III: 1, 553) and Miltner ("Perikles," 772) believe that the peace removed the island of Amorgus from Samian control, but as Gomme (*Hist. Comm.*, I, 356) points out, since it did not pay tribute until 434/3, it was probably not organized separately until then.

under the same conditions as before. In 442 and 441, just before the rebellion, they had paid an annual tribute of 15 talents and 4,300 drachmas. In 432 we find them paying only 18 talents and 1,800 drachmas, a very modest rise for so prosperous a city. Byzantium had put up very mild resistance and was a good place to show the same moderation that had characterized the Samian settlement.[18] So ended the rebellion that had threatened to become a great war and to dismember the Athenian empire. Pericles came out of the affair with his personal prestige at its peak. His military exploits had been crowned with success. The diplomatic support afforded him by the Peloponnesians, active on the part of the Corinthians, tacit as befits the Spartans, completely vindicated his policy towards them. The moderation of his treatment of the rebels and his employment of such respected men as Sophocles and Lampon in his projects must have gone a long way towards dispelling the misgivings of the moderates which the son of Melesias had aroused.

Pericles was chosen to give the funeral oration over the men who had fallen at Samos and delivered a memorable speech. When he came down from the bema, the aged Elpinice chided him, saying, "These are wonderful deeds you have performed, Pericles, for you have destroyed many good citizens, not fighting Phoenicians and Persians, like my brother Cimon, but subjecting an allied and kindred city." Her attack was unjust in every detail, for Cimon had subdued Greeks at Naxos and Scyros and Thasos, while in defeating Samos, Pericles had also put down a threat from Persia. Yet Pericles was content to reply mildly. There were not many in Athens who would share her views. In 439, Pericles not only stood without a rival, for no one had arisen to take the place of Thucydides, but he had also gone far towards creating a consensus the like of which Athens had never seen.

The affair at Samos also strengthened the Athenian Empire, for it showed the Athenian capacity to suppress rebellion and the great risk inherent in depending on support from Sparta or Persia. In this, the Samian War resulted in a growth of Athenian power, but it was a growth in security, not a growth in extent. It served to confirm a situation that had already been accepted by the Peloponne-

[18] See Appendix H.

sians. There was nothing in it to alarm any power that accepted the *status quo* established by the Thirty Years' Peace, and the actions of Corinth and Sparta showed that they accepted it. There is every reason to think that a lasting peace was more likely after the Samian rebellion than before.

11. The Consolidation of the Empire

The rebellions of Samos and Byzantium demonstrated that the imperial reorganization of 443/2 had not been completely successful. They had been accompanied by troubles in Thrace and defections in Caria. During 440/39, the years of the rebellion and siege, several Carian towns had already disappeared from the tribute lists. Caria had always been a difficult region to control because of its remoteness and because many of the towns were inland and practically within the Persian Empire. The revenue from these Carian towns was not great, and the cost of coercing them was hardly justified. At the same time, Caria had little strategic importance, and a military expedition inland might well bring on unnecessary trouble with the Persians. As a result Pericles chose retrenchment in place of coercion. In the assessment of 438 about forty Carian cities were permanently dropped from the tribute lists, and Caria was merged with Ionia into a single tribute district.[1]

The troubles in the Hellespont, however, represented a far more serious problem requiring different treatment. By the fifth century, Athens did not produce enough grain to feed herself but relied on imports for her subsistence. Of the four great granaries that served the Mediterranean world, the littoral of the Black Sea, chiefly the Ukraine, was the most important for Athens, and this could be

[1] *ATL,* III, 114–117 and 308; B. D. Meritt, *AJA,* XXIX (1925), 292 ff.; F. E. Adcock, *CAH,* V, 172.

reached only through the Hellespont and the Bosporus. Egypt was again safely under Persian rule and not available for Athenian use; North Africa was a Carthaginian preserve. Sicily and southern Italy were open to Athenian trade, but they were a long way off and very much under Peloponnesian influence. Thus, the Hellespontine route to the Black Sea was the life line of Athens. It not only led to the nearest and potentially most secure source of grain, but it also supplied dried fish, a staple of the Athenian diet.[2] The importance of this region to Athens is often seen in purely economic terms, but its economic significance was subordinate to its strategic role. The entire security of Athens rested on its independence of local food supplies. The long walls turned Athens into an island obtaining all its requirements by sea. An enemy who could cut off her access to the food supply of the Black Sea could bring her to her knees. It was vital that the route to the Black Sea be secured for Athens.

In 439, Pericles had pacified Byzantium by a combination of force and moderation, but he had reason to think that greater efforts were needed to secure the entire area. The natives could not fail to know that a Persian satrap had assisted rebels from the Athenian Empire, had accepted Athenian prisoners from them, and had suffered no punishment either from the Great King or from Athens. They might well believe that Persia was ready to help any who wished to rebel or, at least, that the power of Athens was waning and might in the future be disregarded in the regions more remote from Attica. It was probably in 437 that Pericles undertook his famous expedition to the Black Sea.

He sailed to the Pontus with a large and brilliantly equipped fleet. He accomplished what the Greek cities asked of him and treated them humanely. At the same time, to the neighboring barbarian peoples and to their kings and dynasts he showed the greatness of the Athenian power and the security and boldness with which the Athenians sailed wherever they wished and made the entire sea their own.[3]

[2] For the Pontic region as a source of grain, see H. Michell, *The Economics of Ancient Greece* (Cambridge, 1957), 20, 228; Victor Ehrenberg, *The People of Aristophanes* (Oxford, 1951), 326; A. French, *The Growth of the Athenian Economy* (London, 1964), 108–113. For the importance of fish, see Ehrenberg, 130–132; Michell, 286–289; and French, 127.

[3] Plut. *Per.* 20. 1.

In this way Pericles showed the flag and impressed upon these remote people the wisdom of friendship with Athens. Not content with mere display, he helped the people of Sinope drive out their tyrant and sent six hundred Athenian settlers to take the place of the Sinopians who had supported tyranny. Another colony was placed near Sinope at Amisus. At the same time Pericles appears to have established friendly relations with Spartocus, a dynast who had just taken power in the kingdom of the Cimmerian Bosporus, near the entrance to the Sea of Azov, and founded an Athenian colony at Nymphaeum, near by. It is possible that the same expedition was the occasion of the foundation of an Athenian colony at Astacus, at the extreme eastern tip of the Sea of Marmora. When Pericles returned to Athens, he had reason to be confident that the vital northeast was secure east of Byzantium.[4]

To the west of Byzantium lay the kingdoms of Thrace and Macedon, and on their southern borders were many subjects of the Athenian Empire. During the Samian and Byzantine rebellions there had been a good deal of unrest in these regions. As we have seen, some towns failed to pay tribute, and an Athenian casualty list that has been preserved shows that there was fighting in the Thracian Chersonese and possibly in the Thracian territory beyond it.[5] But the security of the Athenian Empire was not merely a matter of repressing rebellious subjects, for Thrace and Macedonia, although the latter had not yet reached the position of power that would enable Philip II to conquer Greece, were powerful and dangerous neighbors. Thucydides tells us, "Of all the kingdoms between the Adriatic and Black Sea, the Thracian was the wealthiest and most prosperous, though in military power and size of army it came a long way second to the Scythian." [6] Of the Thracians, the Odrysians, ruled by Sitalces, were the most formidable and dominant tribe. In the time of Teres, the father of Sitalces, the Odrysians had allied themselves with the Scythians. By the time of the Peloponnesian War, Seuthes, who succeeded Sitalces, was powerful enough to take advantage of

[4] See Appendix I.

[5] For the text and dating of the stone, see *IG*, I [2], 943; *SEG*, X. 413; Tod, 48. See now D. W. Bradeen, *Hesperia*, XXXVI (1967), 321–328, especially 325.

[6] 2. 97. 5.

Athens' distraction to collect tribute from members of the Athenian Empire; his rule extended from the Bosporus to the Strymon and from the Aegean to the Danube.[7]

Macedonia was a backward country by Greek standards, but its numerous men were fierce fighters with particular skill as horsemen. In the first half of the fifth century, Alexander I had pushed the borders of his kingdom to the west bank of the Strymon.[8] In 465 the Athenians had unsuccessfully tried to establish a colony on the Strymon, almost certainly to exploit the neighboring timber forests, so vital for the Athenian fleet, and to work the mines that produced precious metals near by.[9] In 463, Cimon had been accused of accepting bribes from Alexander not to conquer part of his territory; we may imagine that part of that territory included the silver mines near the Strymon.[10] By the time Perdiccas succeeded Alexander, the Macedonians were surely working the mines and adding financial resources to their growing power. The coast of Thrace and Macedon, and even more importantly, the Chalcidic peninsula between them, constituted a major source of tribute. The same region was also vital as a source of timber for the fleet. It was strategically located, for a hostile power that controlled it could march to the Hellespont and the Bosporus and cut the Athenian life line. For all these reasons Pericles could not hesitate in securing it for Athens.

Thrace and Macedon were basically continental powers and could not be easily reached by the Athenian fleet. If the flag was to be shown and Athenian power fortified in these regions, something more permanent than a naval cruise was required. Soon after the Samian and Byzantine rebellions had been put down, Pericles fixed on a policy aimed at establishing Athenian power more permanently and more securely. Probably in 438 he established an Athenian colony at Brea on or near the coast of the Thermaic Gulf, to the west of the Chalcidice. A year later a colony was established to the east of the Chalcidice, on the Strymon, at a site called Ennea Hodoi, which the Athenians named Amphipolis. Although we have no textual authority, it looks very much as if the two colonies were

[7] Thuc. 2. 97.

[8] Thuc. 2. 99; *ATL,* III, 313 and 309, n. 47.

[9] Thuc. 1. 100.

[10] Plut. *Cim.* 14. 3; *ATL,* III, 313 and n. 60.

part of a plan to defend the vital areas of the Chalcidice and the coastal regions to the east and west of it. If so, these colonies had much the same function as the Roman colonies: to deter rebellion of allies and incursions from enemies outside the empire by the presence of garrison-colonies close enough to the scene for swift preventive action or retaliation.

The evidence for the colony at Brea is not so good as we should like. All the information we have is a single inscription,[11] and there is disagreement both as to the site and the date of foundation; but good arguments on grounds altogether different from those given above have been offered for the site and date accepted here.[12] The Brea decree is the best evidence we have for the way in which the Athenians established and organized a colony for imperial purposes and deserves quotation in full:

The adjutants for the oikist shall make *provision for the sacrifice* in order to obtain favourable omens *for* the colony, as they shall decide. Ten distributors of land shall be chosen, one from each tribe. These shall allot the land. Democlides shall establish the colony with full powers to the best of his ability. The sacred precincts that have been set apart are to be left as they are, but no further precincts are to be consecrated. The colony is to make an offering of a cow and panoply to the Great Panathenaea and a phallus to the Dionysia. If anyone attacks the territory of the colonists, the cities are to bring help as quickly as possible according to the treaty which was made when . . . was first secretary to the council, concerning the cities of the Thraceward Region.

This decree is to be written on a stele and placed on the acropolis; the colonists are to provide the stele at their own cost. If anyone puts a motion to the vote contrary to the stele, or speaks against it as a public orator, or attempts to persuade others to rescind or annul in any way any of the provisions decreed he shall be deprived of civil rights together with his sons and his property shall be confiscated, and one tenth shall go to the goddess, unless the colonists themselves make some request *on their own behalf*.

Those in the army who are enrolled as additional colonists shall settle at Brea within thirty days of their arrival in Athens. The colonial expedition is to set off within thirty days, and Aeschines shall accompany it and pay the expenses.

[11] *IG*, I ^{2}, 45; Tod, 44; B. D. Meritt, *Hesperia*, XIV (1945), 86 ff.
[12] See Appendix J.

Phantocles proposed: Concerning the colony at Brea, let it be as Democlides proposed, but the prytaneis of the Erechtheid tribe shall introduce Phantocles to the council in its first sitting. The colonists to Brea shall be from the Thetes and Zeugitae.[13]

The settlement of Brea shows many features typical of Athenian colonies and others which resemble the arrangements at Thurii. Like all Athenian colonies, Brea is to send appropriate offerings to the great Athenian festivals. The provision for the publication of the decree and the penalties for changing the terms of settlement without the agreement of the colonists are probably also typical.[14] The "adjutants of the oikist" (ἀποικισταί) are very reminiscent of the seers and other religious men who took part in the foundation of Thurii to please orthodox opinion. But far more striking than these similarities are the many differences which show that the colony at Brea was something special. It is perfectly clear that it was to be "a bulwark in the important Thraceward region." [15] Its precarious position as a dangerous outpost on the barbarian frontier is made clear by the provision for aid in case of attack by the allies of Athens, for "the cities" means the allied cities, which "seems to show that the Athenians had agreed with the allies in the Thraceward region to found a colony, and bound these allies to support it in case of need." [16] We know of no parallel provision.

There is more than a little reason to think that the danger was so well understood that Athens had to make the terms of settlement especially attractive in order to win recruits. On the one hand, the terms are so advantageous to the colonists that they are expected to pay for the publication of the colony's charter. On the other hand, the Athenians are willing to pay some expenses for the beginning of the colony, possibly even the traveling expenses of the colonists. The special item regarding the enrollment of soldiers still on duty as

[13] The translation is by Graham, *Colony and Mother City in Ancient Greece* (Manchester, 1964), 228–229. It begins with the first complete sentence, which is line 3 of the inscription, since the beginning is mutilated. The words in italics are not clear on the stone and are restored. I am indebted to Graham's important study for much of my interpretation of the implications of the decree.

[14] Graham, *Colony and Mother City,* 60–63.

[15] *Ibid.,* 34.

[16] *Ibid.,* 34–35.

additional colonists (ἔποικοι) is also interesting in this regard. These troops were probably still engaged in mopping-up operations in Thrace and the Thracian Chersonese. The possibility of barbarian incursions in the wake of the Samian and Byzantine rebellions, perhaps magnified by nervous Athenian allies in the Thraceward regions, made it urgent to establish the new colony as quickly as possible, which may account for the provision requiring the colonists to set out in thirty days. But the Athenian soldiers in Thrace were the very men wanted for the colony at Brea, both because of their experience in the general area and their military ability, so a special dispensation was inserted for the Thracian veterans, whereby they could join the colony late, presumably on equal terms, provided that they set out within thirty days after their demobilization at Athens. Finally, it is most significant that the founder of the imperial colony of Brea was neither Apollo nor a seer, but an Athenian general for the year 439/8. We cannot be sure, but it would not be surprising if Democlides had done his service for that year in the region of Byzantium and Thrace.[17]

Another element that strikes a note very different from that of the foundation of Thurii is the extremely close control Athens exercised over the colony of Brea. There could be absolutely no confusion over its founder, such as troubled Thurii in 434/3, for he was an Athenian named formally and in advance, and his name was engraved on a stele set up for all to see on the Athenian acropolis. Although he is given full power (αὐτοκράτορα), this must be merely a formal authorization, for the nature of the colony and the detailed regulations for its settlement are provided in the charter. We have already seen that Athens guaranteed its protection. It established procedures for distributing the land, dealt with religious matters, set the time limit for departures, provided for the only means of amending the charter, provided for late settlers, and decided what classes of

[17] The evidence for Democlides as general is provided by fragments of an inscription added to *IG*, I², 50, the regulations for Samos after the revolt, by Wade-Gery, *CP*, XXVI (1931), 309–313. Wade-Gery dates it to 440/39, but Meritt has shown (*Athenian Financial Documents* [Ann Arbor, 1932], 48–53) that the following year is better, and his date is accepted by R. Meiggs and A. Andrewes in their new edition of G. F. Hill's *Sources for Greek History Between the Persian and Peloponnesian Wars* (Oxford, 1951), n. 62.

people were eligible to join. This last provision, limiting membership to the two lowest classes in Athenian society, shows that even now Pericles used colonization for social and political as well as strategic purposes. What Bury called the palladium of aristocracy could also be the safety valve of the Periclean democracy.

The colony of Brea seems not to have been a great success, for it left only a vague memory of its existence in the literary tradition, and although fighting took place throughout the Chalcidic peninsula during the Peloponnesian War, we hear nothing of it in the sources. Perhaps it was absorbed into the recolonized city of Potidaea in 429. In any case, it probably did not last long after the beginning of the war, for Potidaea became the main Athenian base in the region, so that Brea lost its strategic importance.[18]

In 437/6, not long after the foundation of Brea, the Athenians founded the colony of Amphipolis. The site was a very desirable one and had provoked at least two previous attempts at settlement by Greeks. In 497, Aristagoras of Miletus had tried to colonize the place, but he had been driven off by the Edonians, a Thracian people of the region. In 465 the Athenians had made a major attempt, but were destroyed by the Thracians at Drabescus.[19] The site was attractive to the Athenians as a source of timber for shipbuilding and of revenue, probably from the working of nearby silver mines, and perhaps from the collection of tolls for crossing the Strymon at a convenient spot.[20] It is clear, however, that the strategic position of Amphipolis was its most important feature from the Athenian point of view. The loss of the city to Brasidas in 424 was seen as a disaster by the Athenians, and the same considerations that made it important then explain its colonization thirteen years earlier. Until the fall of Amphipolis, "the Spartans had access to the allies of Athens as far as the Strymon . . . but so long as they did not control the

[18] The few literary references to Brea are collected by Tod (p. 89). Scholars who believe that Brea was located to the east of the Chalcidice think that Brea may have been absorbed by Amphipolis. Both the western site that I believe in and the date of foundation that I think correct argue against that. The suggestion of Brea's absorption by the Athenian colony of Potidaea, which seems to me very likely, is made by Woodhead (CQ, N.S., II [1952], 62).

[19] Thuc. 4. 102. 2–3.

[20] Thuc. 4. 108. 1; Graham, *Colony and Mother City,* 200–201.

bridge . . . they were unable to go further. But now [that the city and bridge were in Spartan hands] it had become easy and the Athenians feared that the allies would revolt." [21]

In 437 the Athenians may not have contemplated a Spartan expedition into Thrace, but they did have reason to fear allied defections and incursions by the Thracians and Macedonians, so they established the colony of Amphipolis as an impregnable fortress to prevent rebellion and guard the vital land route to the Hellespont. The founder of the colony was another general who had proved his skill in the Samian War, Hagnon, son of Nicias.[22] Hagnon is mentioned, along with Phormio and Thucydides, as one of the generals who brought forty ships to reinforce Pericles at the siege of Samos,[23] and he chose his site with a keen eye for its defense. It was located on a bend in the river, so that the city projected out into the river and was bounded by water on two sides. On the landward side he built a long wall connecting the two points on the river, so that the city was something like a triangle. Protected by triremes and a sufficient garrison, it would be all but impossible to storm or besiege.

To serve as a satisfactory bulwark of Athenian power in Thrace, the new colony must have been a sizable one, but once again few Athenians were willing to settle in a far-off frontier garrison surrounded by barbarians. The Athenians handled the problem in two ways: they tried to make the colony attractive to Athenians, as they had done at Brea; and they made it a mixed colony, as they had done at Thurii. We know that Amphipolis never paid tribute.[24] If we had

[21] Thuc. 4. 108. 1.

[22] Thuc. 4. 102. 3.

[23] Thuc. 1. 117. 2.

[24] Franz Hampl (*Klio,* XXXII [1939], 1–60) has argued that Athens took the land for the city of Amphipolis away from the Thracians and regarded it as their own. "Die Bürger von Amphipolis bebauten danach athenischen Boden, bildeten somit . . . eine polis ohne Territorium" (p. 5). From this it follows that the Amphipolitans must have paid rent for the land, which explains both why Amphipolis was a source of revenue to Athens and why it was not on the tribute lists. His conclusions are accepted by Fritz Gschnitzer (*Abhängige Orte in Griechischen Altertum* [Munich, 1958], 91–92) and H. D. Westlake (*Hermes,* XC [1962], 280). Hampl's arguments, for Amphipolis at least, have been totally demolished by Graham, *Colony and Mother City,* 201–206. Graham says, "We do not know why Amphipolis and other colonies of Athens founded after the Persian Wars did not pay tribute,

the foundation decree of Amphipolis we would very likely find that the settlers received special benefits similar to those granted the colonists at Brea. Perhaps the settlers were given especially large or desirable plots of land. We know that the neighboring town of Argilus supplied many settlers for Amphipolis. We know too that the tribute of Argilus, which had been one talent in 438/7 and before, had been reduced to one-sixth of that by 433/2, and that she may even have been altogether excused from tribute payments for some of the intervening years. Perhaps the dislike that the Argilians later showed toward Amphipolis was caused by the confiscation of some of their land for which they did not feel adequately compensated by a reduction in tribute.[25]

Whatever special conditions Athens may have offered, there was no way it could attract enough Athenians to guarantee the security of Amphipolis. When Thucydides speaks of the Amphipolitan population in 424, he speaks of it as a "mixed multitude" (πλέον ξύμμεικτον), in which there were few Athenians and many Argilians and others.[26] But unlike Thurii, Amphipolis was very clearly an Athenian colony. There was no question that the Athenian Hagnon was its founder, and memorials to him as *oikistes* stood in Amphipolis until they were torn down by the rebels who had betrayed the town to the Spartans and driven out the Athenians.[27] The settlers were either Athenians or people from the neighborhood. No invitations were broadcast throughout Hellas, and there was no question of a Panhellenic colony. The Thracian coast included important parts of the Athenian Empire and was very clearly a part of the Athenian sphere of influence. The Aegean Sea and its borders was regarded by Pericles as *mare clausum,* and no outsiders were welcome.

The location and function of Amphipolis made its later history

---

though we can conjecture that a payment made by formal allies was considered inappropriate for Athens' own colonies" (p. 201). My suggestion is that Amphipolis, and probably other Athenian colonies such as Brea, were exempt from tribute because of the service they rendered the mother city as garrisons, and in order to make them attractive to Athenians, who were needed to man them.

[25] *ATL,* III, 308–309.

[26] 4. 103. 3–4; 106. 1.

[27] Thuc. 5. 11. 1; Graham, *Colony and Mother City,* 37–38, 199.

altogether different from that of Thurii. While Pericles allowed the latter to drift away from Athens shortly after its foundation, he and his successors made every effort to hold Amphipolis. During the war it was protected by two generals: one made the city his headquarters for the defense of Thrace, and the other guarded the river with a fleet based downstream at Eion.[28] There can be no doubt that the Athenians considered Amphipolis vital. Thucydides the historian was condemned and exiled for his failure to bring up the fleet he commanded in time to save the city from Brasidas. Cleon was killed in a battle trying to recapture the city. A critical clause in the Peace of Nicias required Sparta to restore the city to Athens, and her failure to do so was one of the reasons for the failure of the peace.

The establishment of colonies at Brea and Amphipolis, like the suppression of the revolts of Samos and Byzantium, strengthened the Athenian Empire and in so doing produced a growth in Athenian power. But once again it was a growth in security, not extent; it confirmed the *status quo* established in 445 and did not alter it. It should have contributed to the sense of security that makes lasting peace possible. It is wrong to say that Athens "had never been . . . as powerful," as she was in 433.[29]

Before the Egyptian disaster, the return of Megara to the Spartan alliance, and the oligarchic rebellions of central Greece, Athens had the prospect of an inexhaustible grain supply, enormous wealth, control of central Greece, and absolute security against invasion. All of that was lost by 445, and Athens was incomparably weaker on the eve of the Peloponnesian War than she had been at her acme in the early 450's.[30] Her actions after the Thirty Years' Peace were all consistent with an acceptance of the end of her greater ambitions. Her actions in the Aegean and the northeast were merely the necessary steps to allow Athens to live within the terms of that peace. She needed a safe route to the Black Sea to guarantee her grain supply. She needed peaceful and obedient allies to guarantee her financial position. She needed to establish strategic colonies in Thrace to defend both these interests. None of her actions threatened the Pelo-

[28] Thuc. 4. 102–108; Graham, *Colony and Mother City,* 199–200.

[29] Glotz and Cohen, *HG,* II, 213.

[30] E. Meyer, *Forschungen,* II, 313–314. "Thatsächlich dagegen hat die Zeit von 460 den Höhenpunkt der Macht Athens gebildet" (p. 314).

ponnesian states in any way. The establishment of a Panhellenic colony at Thurii and Athens' subsequent refusal to interfere with its development, however disappointing, was intended as a gesture of renunciation toward the Peloponnesians, and particularly the Corinthians. Their behavior in the Samian crisis shows that they understood it as such. By 433, Athenian power had grown in comparison with its low point in 446, when a Spartan army was poised to ravage Attica. It had achieved a degree of security after a difficult and troubled time, but it did not approach the heights it had reached a quarter of a century earlier.

Pericles has been called an imperialist, and so he was, if by that term we mean that he favored maintaining Athenian control over the allies and exploiting them to the advantage of Athens. The ambiguity of the word, and perhaps the influence of transcendental theories on the nature of imperialism, have led some to think that he never abandoned the hope of dominating all the Hellenic world and more. We should remember, however, that not all empires, and certainly not all imperial rulers, have suffered from an insatiable desire for more. Many have seen that further expansion would only endanger the safety of what was already held. Augustus believed that about the Roman Empire, and most of his successors agreed, eschewing further aggression almost always. Bismarck, after he had conquered what he thought was enough, seems to have been satisfied, deeming further conquests not worth the bones of a Pomeranian grenadier. His later policy seems to have been devoted to maintaining the *status quo* without war, if possible. England in 1914 was a great imperial power, yet it seems not to have been eager for further growth. In making alliances with Russia and France, her two greatest imperial competitors, she put security before imperial ambition.

It might be argued that a city like Athens, whose democracy and domestic tranquillity depended on imperial revenues, could not long remain quiet, but must expand. There were certainly contemporaries who felt that way, both within Athens and without, but Pericles was not one of them, as his internal and foreign policies from 445 to 433 show. On the one hand, he had sharply limited the growth of the citizen body through the absorption of aliens with his citizenship law of 451/50. He had removed great numbers of supernumerary and indigent Athenians by his establishment of cleruchies and colonies.

We have seen that by the 430's, Athens was so far from being overpopulated that she found it difficult to provide enough settlers for vitally needed colonies. At the same time, Pericles had taken steps to assure that the necessary funds from the empire would be forthcoming regularly. If anything, the economic and social realities of democratic Athens argued for a cautious policy to guarantee imperial revenue rather than a reckless one that might jeopardize it.[31]

Some have argued that a glorious dream of Hellenic unity under Athenian leadership, with all the states bound together by a common democracy, underlay the Periclean policy, which was warlike in the east, pacific in the west, but always aimed at total supremacy.[32] Our examination of his early career should make us hesitate to attribute such grandiose plans to Pericles at any time, but his actions plainly show that it is fanciful to burden him with such ambitions after 446/5. The disaster in Egypt had shaken the foundations of the empire and compelled a major reorganization. The attempt to establish a land empire in mainland Greece resulted in the defeat at Coronea, the defection of Megara, the revolt in Euboea, and the invasion of Attica. Once again the safety of the empire, and this time of Athens itself, had been imperiled by the overextension of Athenian resources and the failure to limit Athenian ambitions. It took Athens many

[31] This point is well made by G. B. Grundy (*Thucydides and the History of his Age,* [2nd ed., Oxford, 1948], I, 169–211). Grundy's appreciation of Pericles' policy, particularly the change it underwent in emphasis after 446/5, seems to me largely correct, but for the wrong reasons. He believes that the economic question was paramount and reasons of commerce the most important element in it. I think that economics were important but subordinate to political considerations and that commercial interests had only a small influence on policy.

[32] The view is widespread and is held by Cloché (*AC,* XIV [1945], 93–128), who says, "de l'Italie méridionale au Pont-Euxin, impérialisme 'pacifique' et impérialisme 'armé' ont servi l'un et l'autre à propager la gloire et la domination d'Athènes. . . ." (p. 128), and by Ehrenberg (*AJP,* LXIX [1948], 149–170), who considers the foundation of Thurii "typical of Periclean policy. It was he who pursued a determined, if sometimes unrealistic, policy of powerful expansion and imperialism" (p. 170). The best statement of this position, too long to quote here, is given by De Sanctis (*Pericle,* 192–193), who pictures Pericles as moved by the great ideal described above but prevented from achieving it by his inability to overcome, "la limitatezza egoistica della polis. . . ."

years, many lives, and a great expenditure to restore the security and tranquillity she enjoyed before she embarked on an adventurous policy. From these experiences Pericles learned a bitter lesson that he never forgot; it guided his plans and policies to the day he died. On the eve of the war, and in response to the Spartan ultimatum, he explained his strategy to the Athenian people. He told them that he was confident of victory "if you are willing not to try to extend your empire at the same time as you are fighting the war and not to add self-imposed dangers, for I am more afraid of our own mistakes than the strategy of our opponents." [33] His policy during the years of peace was much the same: to preserve and strengthen the empire Athens already held but not to endanger it by expansion.

[33] Thuc. 1. 144. 1.

12. *Athenian Politics on the Eve of the War*

The frankness, even bluntness, with which Pericles addressed the Athenians in the months before the war broke out and in the period of the war before his death bears testimony to the special position he had in their regard. This position he held because they respected and admired him for his political, military, and aesthetic achievements, for his long experience, and for his remarkable incorruptibility. Most important, the political situation in Athens gave him a very secure base of power.

When the crisis at Corcyra erupted, Pericles stood without a rival. The opposition on the right had been leaderless for ten years, and the program that had brought it to the brink of success had lost its appeal to any broad section of the people. The moderation, peacefulness, and success of Pericles' foreign policy, coupled with his consistent employment of men from the leading families of Athens as his lieutenants and coadjutors, had firmly won the respectable moderates to his side. At the same time, the continuing effects of his economic and social program at home guaranteed the support of the masses. From time to time they might grumble about a particular policy or the "brains trust" with which he surrounded himself. Perhaps they were somewhat put off by his haughty demeanor, his remoteness, and his philosophical interests, but there was never any possibility that they would desert his standard. It is even possible that they were devoted to Pericles for more than the tangible benefits they received from him and his programs. The achievements of a long and glorious career, the dignity of his bearing, the nobility of his character, the loftiness of his speech, and the disinterestedness of his public service surrounded him with an aura that must have performed political magic. Modern democracies, at least, have shown that the masses may be moved not always, certainly not solely, by vulgar material self-interest. Extraordinary men may be attractive to them even without demagogic proposals, if only they be sufficiently outstanding in the political virtues. We may well believe that Periclean Athens was a democracy of the same character.

It would be wrong, however, to believe that Pericles' political troubles ended with the ostracism of the son of Melesias in 443. Shortly after the Samian War he was confronted with a series of attacks, indirect but not insignificant, from a new and potentially dangerous source. The date and origin of these attacks have been hotly disputed, and we must examine the debate before assessing their effect on Athenian politics.[1] Our sources mention Pericles' political troubles in connection with the allegation that he brought on the Peloponnesian War to escape these attacks. Plutarch says that the worst charge of all, but the one with the most support, is that Phidias, a close friend of Pericles and the sculptor and contractor of the great chryselephantine statue of Athena on the acropolis, was charged with embezzlement. Behind the accusation, says Plutarch, were men jealous of Phidias' influence, but also those who wanted to use the prosecution as a test case to see how the juries would act in a trial touching Pericles. The accusation was brought by a certain Menon, who worked with Phidias. Although Phidias was able to prove his innocence, he was later condemned for including his own and Pericles' portraits in the sculptures on the Parthenon. A decree was passed giving the informer Menon immunity from taxation and personal protection.[2]

[1] My own view, already indicated in the second sentence of this paragraph, depends chiefly on the arguments of Eduard Meyer (*Forschungen,* II, 299–301, 327–333), F. E. Adcock (*CAH,* V, 477–480), Felix Jacoby (*FGrH* 3B Suppl., 484–496, commentary to Philochorus 328 frg. 121), and especially to two recent articles by F. J. Frost (*JHS,* LXXXIV [1964], 69–72, and *Historia,* XIII [1964], 385–399).

[2] *Per.* 31.

At the same time, Aspasia was tried for impiety, and Diopeithes introduced a bill that provided that atheism and "teaching about the heavens" were public crimes. This proposal, says Plutarch, aimed at "directing suspicion against Pericles through Anaxagoras." The people were pleased by these activities, and while they were still in the mood, Dracontides moved that Pericles be required to deposit his accounts with the council and that his case should be decided by jurors voting with specially sanctified ballots. Hagnon amended the bill so that any suits arising from the investigation should be tried in the ordinary way before a jury of fifteen hundred. Plutarch tells us that Pericles was able to save Aspasia by weeping at her trial, but he was forced to send Anaxagoras away out of fear for his safety. Finally, fearing for his own safety in the trial to come, he passed the Megarian Decree and launched the war to save himself. All this Plutarch reports as one explanation of the coming of the war; he himself says that the truth is not clear.[3]

Ephorus tells much the same story, adding one fine tale to it. In his version Pericles was guilty of misusing the imperial funds for his own purposes. When called upon to account for them, he worried about what to do. His nephew Alcibiades advised him not to seek a way to render his accounts, but rather a way not to render them. Then came the prosecutions of Phidias, Aspasia, and Anaxagoras. To save himself Pericles brought forward the Megarian Decree and brought on the war.[4] From Plutarch's remark that his version had the most support, and from its persistence through the centuries, it is clear that this interpretation of the cause of the war became fixed in the popular mind.[5] It is clear that a major reason for the popularity of the tradition was its appearance in the works of the comic poets, particularly Aristophanes. In the *Peace,* produced ten years after the start of the war, in the spring of 421, he presented a comic explana-

[3] *Per.* 32.

[4] Diod. 12. 38–39.

[5] It may be found so late as the fourth century of our era in Aristodemus (*FGrH* 104, frg. 1) and in the *Suda, s.v.,* "Pheidias." A survey of the history of the question of responsibility for the Peloponnesian War in antiquity is provided by H. Brauer (*Die Kriegsschuldfrage in der geschichtlichen Überlieferung des Peloponnesischen Krieges,* Inaugural Dissertation, Emsdetten, 1933).

tion for the coming of the war, which was remembered and taken seriously in later centuries. His chorus asks:

But where has Peace been all this long time, tell us, Hermes, most benevolent of the gods.

Hermes replies:

O, you very wise farmer, listen to my words if you want to hear why she was lost. The beginning of our trouble was the disgrace of Phidias; then Pericles, fearing he might share in the misfortune, dreading your ill nature and stubborn ways, before he could suffer harm, set the city aflame by throwing out that little spark, the Megarian Decree.[6]

The charge that the Megarian Decree had caused the war and that Pericles was responsible was surely no novelty by 421, but there is a very good chance that Aristophanes invented the connection between the trial of Phidias, a charge against Pericles, and the deliberate use of the Megarian Decree to bring on war and prevent embarrassment. Certainly, the simple farmers to whom Hermes explains the events seem never to have heard that version before. Trygaeus says:

By Apollo, no one ever told me that! nor did I think there was any connection between Phidias and Peace.

The chorus is equally surprised:

Nor did I, until just now. That is why she is so beautiful, since she is related to him. My, how many things escape our notice.[7]

The whole thing is comic invention that adds a new and absurd element to an old and well-known story. Its absurdity and humor are made all the clearer by what follows, for it turns out that the Spartans entered the war for money, bribed by the Athenian allies who were anxious to cease paying the tribute (619–627).

This comic interpretation was taken seriously in the ancient world, and at least one modern scholar has succumbed to its attractions.[8] Thucydides, of course, was a contemporary and knew better. He wrote, in no small measure, to set right the question of how the war began and what were its real causes. But it is likely that the joke of

[6] 601–609.

[7] 615–618.

[8] Beloch, *Attische Politik,* 19–22; *GG* ², II: 1, 294–298.

Aristophanes would be taken more seriously today were it not for an unusually careful commentator on the *Peace* who investigated the basis for Aristophanes' charge. He found some important evidence in two passages from the *Atthis* of Philochorus, a writer on Athenian history who lived in the third century B.C. Philochorus says that in the archonship of Theodorus (438/7) the statue of Athena was dedicated. Phidias was accused of stealing ivory from it. He was condemned and is said to have fled to Elis, where he worked on the statue of Zeus in Olympia. In the archonship of Pythodorus (432/1), which was seven years later, the Megarians complained to the Spartans that the Athenians were wronging them by barring them from the markets and harbors of their empire.[9] Attempts have been made to explain away the evidence of Philochorus in several ways,[10] but the essential matter of the interval between the attack on Phidias and the Megarian complaint cannot be challenged. Since we know that the latter took place in 432, the former must have happened in 438.

Our knowledge of the attack against Aspasia is far less clear. It is altogether possible that the story of her trial and acquittal were late inventions in which real slanders, suspicions, and ribald jokes were converted into an imaginary lawsuit. But if it happened, we have better reason to believe that it happened in 438 than at any other time. Plutarch, whose habit of arranging events topically makes his chronology less than reliable, says that the trial of Aspasia took place "about the same time" as the trial of Phidias.[11] Beyond that, we have reason to believe that Aspasia was particularly unpopular in the years immediately following the Samian War. It had been a long and difficult war begun by Athens' intervention in a quarrel on behalf of Miletus. Aspasia came from Miletus, and it did not take

[9] *FGrH* 328, frg. 121. The names of the archons are corrupt, but as Jacoby says, "It is annoying that the names of the archons are corrupt in both excerpts, but not more than just annoying, as the interval between the two archons is preserved in the first excerpt; the alteration made by Lepaulmier (Πυθώδορον to Θεοδώρου, and Σκυθοδώρου to Πυθοδώρου) are slight and certain." (3B Suppl., 486).

[10] D. Kienast, *Gymnasium*, LX (1953), 212; O. Lendle, *Hermes*, LXXXIII (1955), 284–303. For a brief discussion and rejection of their views, see Frost, *Historia*, XIII (1964), 395.

[11] *Per.* 32. 1.

long for the slander to get abroad that Pericles had brought on the Samian War to please her.[12] In 438, when the war was over but its memory still fresh, an attack on the mistress of Pericles would have the greatest chance of success. Whether or not there was a formal accusation or trial, we need not doubt that the enemies of Pericles launched some kind of attack against his consort at about the same time as the trial of Phidias.

The problem of Anaxagoras is even more difficult, for it is beclouded by all kinds of stories invented later to illustrate the fate of the philosopher in an ungrateful world. We should ignore these tales and deal only with the decree of Diopeithes, which did not name Anaxagoras but clearly exposed him to attack in the likely event that anyone should wish to bring charges against him. In this situation, Pericles chose to avoid the dangers inherent in the public debate on matters concerning traditional beliefs and religious opinions: "In this crisis, the spirit of Galileo rather than that of Socrates prevailed, and the scientist was sent out of town." [13] The suggestion has been made that the attacks on Anaxagoras all date from the 450's, but Wade-Gery is quite right in saying that we should not move it from where Plutarch puts it, "about the same time" as the attacks on Phidias and Aspasia.[14] To the charges of dishonesty and impiety against Phidias and responsibility for the war, immorality, and impiety against Aspasia, the enemies of Pericles added suspicions of impiety and atheism against Anaxagoras. Pericles could not fail to be tarred by the same brush, and perhaps there was even talk of bringing an accusation against Pericles of collusion, in his role of supervisor of the project, with the peculation of Phidias.[15] We cannot be sure about the details of the attacks, but the evidence points to the fact that there were such attacks, that they were intended to strike at Pericles, and that they took place in 438/7.

We are left to determine the source of the opposition to Pericles. The date rules out attempts to blame a rejuvenated oligarchic party,

[12] Plut. *Per.* 24. 1; 25. 1.

[13] Frost, *op. cit.*, 396.

[14] The argument for the 450's is made by A. E. Taylor, *CQ* (1917), 81ff. Wade-Gery (*Essays*, 259–260) argues against such a date but believes that all the trials took place in 433/2 after the return and under the leadership of Thucydides, son of Melesias.

[15] Frost, *JHS*, LXXXIV (1964), 72.

restored to life by the return from exile of its leader, Thucydides, son of Melesias.[16] The style and nature of the attacks, too, suggest a different source. Attacks on probity and virtue of individuals had been the means by which Ephialtes had undermined the power of the Areopagus and opened the way to greater democracy. Pericles himself had taken part in a trial in which the incorruptible Cimon was charged with taking bribes. Attacks on advanced opinions in art, science, and philosophy were more likely to find favor with the uneducated masses than with the aristocrats who supported the sophists. These considerations lead to the suspicion that the attacks on the friends of Pericles originated not on the right but on the left.

We have seen that there were Athenians during the First Peloponnesian War who found Pericles and his policies insufficiently aggressive. The likelihood is that their numbers grew after the ostracism of 443 had removed the threat of Thucydides and ended the need to rally round the democratic and imperial cause. Pericles' moderation may well have irked them. If the rebellious Euboeans deserved to have their lands confiscated and cleruchs settled among them, they might have argued, why should not the Samians suffer the same? The Byzantines, too, had been treated too gently. At the very least their tribute should have been sharply raised. Coddling the rebels would only encourage further defections. We have no evidence for such discussions in the 430's, but it is interesting, at least, that in the 420's, when Pericles was dead and Cleon in power, the Athenians sharply raised the imperial tribute. It is likewise interesting to notice that when Mytilene revolted in 428/7, it was Cleon who urged the ultimate punishment as a deterrent to future rebels.

In 438/7, Cleon himself had probably not yet become the leader of the faction that attacked Pericles, although by the first years of the war, he was already making demagogic attacks upon him and his conduct of the war, which he found insufficiently aggressive.[17] But he was not the first demagogue to come before the people of Athens. In the *Knights* of Aristophanes, Demosthenes speaks of an oracle that tells how Cleon, "the villanous Paphlagon," will be destroyed:

[16] That view is championed by Wade-Gery (see note 14) and Kienast (*Gymnasium,* LX [1953], 210–229).

[17] Plut. *Per.* 33. 6–7.

How, the oracle says clearly that first will come an oakum-seller who will govern the affairs of the state. . . . Second, after him, comes a sheep-seller. . . . He will rule until a greater rascal than he appears; then he is destroyed. In his place will come a leather-seller, Paphlagon, the thief. . . .[18]

The scholiast identifies Eucrates as the oakum-seller. A scholion to Plato's *Menexenus* speaks of a certain sheep-seller, Lysicles, who was an orator and a demagogue in the time of Pericles, and he must be the general who was killed in action in 428/7.[19] Such, very likely, were the men who assailed Pericles, in 438/7, helped, no doubt, by the up-and-coming dealer in hides, Cleon. The professions of these opponents makes it clear that they were of a totally different background from previous Athenian politicians. With the possible exception of Themistocles, all the political figures in Athenian history up to this point, regardless of their views, came from the upper class, indeed from the very best families; they were all *kaloi kagathoi.*

Pericles was pre-eminently such a man, and we have seen that he was careful to choose similar men to carry out his policies. The growth of the Athenian Empire and the prosperity that went with it had created, or at least encouraged, a prosperous class of businessmen who were decidedly not *kaloi kagathoi.* Since Athens was a democracy, there was no way to prevent these "new men" from taking an active part in public affairs, from serving on juries, on the boulé, as minor officials. Few—if any—of them, however, rose to the highest positions in the state. The masses might be content to remain deferential to their social betters, to leave, as the Old Oligarch said, the more dangerous posts of *strategos* and *hipparchos* to the *dynatotatoi,* but these rising men were rich enough and ambitious enough to seek their place among the rulers of their city. As Pericles had attacked Cimon, in part at least, because the old soldier stood in the way of his political advancement, so, I think, did Eucrates, Lysicles, and Cleon attack Pericles. No doubt dissatisfaction with his imperial policy had something to do with it, but social dissatisfaction and personal ambition may have counted for even more.

Whatever the motives behind them, and whatever success they

[18] Aristophanes, *Knights,* 128–137. I have omitted the interlocutory lines spoken by Nicias.

[19] The passage in the *Menexenus* is 235 and the source of the scholion is Aeschines Socraticus. The death of Lysicles the general is reported by Thucydides 3. 19.

may have had in discomfiting and embarrassing Pericles, these attacks failed in their major purpose. Even if we believe some of the far from reliable stories, the picture that emerges from the events of 438/7 reveals little damage to Pericles. Phidias was acquitted and went off to work for the greater glory of Olympian Zeus, hardly a suitable assignment for a man recently convicted of impiety. Aspasia was unharmed, with or without the help of the only recorded Periclean tears. Anaxagoras seems not to have come to trial at all.[20]

Pericles, of course, was never troubled by any public accusation which questioned his probity in financial matters. There can be no question that the investigation launched by Dracontides aimed at embarrassing Pericles seriously; perhaps its supporters even hoped for a conviction. The unusual legal procedure he proposed suggests that the enemies of Pericles tried to use the prejudices of religious orthodoxy aroused by the other trials in the case of Pericles himself. The official charge, according to Ephorus, was "stealing sacred property." [21] The decree of Dracontides provided that all suits arising from the investigation of Pericles' accounts should be tried on the acropolis with ballots taken from the altar. The likelihood is that "using sacred ballots taken from the altar of Athena would make superstitious jurymen almost duty-bound to find Pericles guilty." [22] When Hagnon amended the decree to provide for a more normal procedure, the entire plan fell through. Nowhere in Athens could one find a duly selected jury of fifteen hundred who would convict Pericles, and we may be sure that no suit was ever brought. The fact that Hagnon was given the honor of founding Amphipolis the next year may be more than a coincidence. His selection for that honor, of course, is evidence enough, if evidence were needed, to show that Pericles was firmly in command at Athens. It may also have pleased him to have a public occasion to display the gratitude he felt towards men who supported him and his policies.

In the last years before the Corcyrean crisis, the political situation in Athens was more stable than it had been at least since the time of Cleisthenes. Pericles had beaten off challenges from the right and from the left. In a political environment in which the role of individual leadership was vital to the success of a policy or a party, there

[20] *FGrH* 3B Suppl., II, 167, n. 29.
[21] Diod. 12. 39. 2.
[22] Frost, *JHS,* LXXXIV (1964), 72.

was no politician of stature who opposed him. On more than one occasion the people had shown their trust and confidence in him and their preference for him over any rival. He had, moreover, won over the influential upper classes, who, with few exceptions, supported him and shared the burdens of government. Until the situation was radically changed by the war and the plague, and the sacrifices they demanded, his power was as secure as a democratic statesman's can be. Only one hand guided Athenian policy, and that hand belonged to Pericles. If it be true that he was responsible for steering Athens into the war, we may be sure, at least, that he did not do so out of fear for his political position.

Part Four

The Final Crisis

13. *Epidamnus*

It is not uncommon for great wars to arise from incidents in remote places. The Second Punic War broke out as a result of a quarrel over the unimportant Spanish town of Saguntum. The Great War of 1914 was the consequence of an assassination in the Bosnian city of Sarajevo. But Saguntum was located near the frontier between Carthaginian territory and an area under Roman protection. Bosnia was in a region which had long been the subject of dispute between Russia and Austria, and it is common to speak of the Balkans as a cockpit where several wars had taken place in the years before the Great War. The metaphor of a powder keg awaiting a spark is not strained when applied to both situations.

Epidamnus, however, where the events took place which ultimately led to the Peloponnesian War, was even more remote from the center of things than either Saguntum or Sarajevo. It was located on the eastern coast of the Adriatic, over one hundred miles to the north of Corcyra. In antiquity it was also called Dyrrachium, although in the fifth century Epidamnus was more common. The modern town of Durazzo occupies its site and is part of Albania.[1] It was well beyond any conceivable sphere of Athenian interest, for even if we believe in continuing Athenian ambitions in Italy and Sicily, Epidamnus was far to the north of the route leading there. It was also, of course, well beyond the limits of Spartan concern. One could hardly imagine a less likely spot to provide the occasion for a great conflict between Athens and Sparta.

[1] Gomme, *Hist. Comm.*, I, 158.

Epidamnus was founded in the last quarter of the seventh century by Corcyra. Since Corcyra was itself a Corinthian colony, it followed customary procedure and chose a Corinthian, Phalius, as the founder. From the first the colony was made up of some Corinthians and other Dorians, as well as the Corcyreans, but there was absolutely no question that Epidamnus was a Corcyrean colony.[2] The city grew and prospered. Although surrounded by barbarians (an Illyrian people called the Taulantians) and distant from the centers of Greek culture, the Epidamnians were by no means cut off from the other Greeks. Early in the sixth century one of their citizens was rich and important enough to contest for the hand of Agariste, the daughter of Cleisthenes, the powerful tyrant of Sicyon. A flight of exiles from Elis to the coast of Illyria probably contributed to the growth in the wealth and population of Epidamnus.[3] By 516 the city was wealthy enough to produce a citizen who not only won the chariot race at Olympia but dedicated statues of himself, his horses, and chariot as well.[4]

It is natural that the early constitution of the state should have been aristocratic, and there is reason to believe that the aristocrats had special privileges in the trade with the barbarians, which may have led to especially friendly relations between the aristocrats and the native Illyrians.[5] It is possible that the Epidamnian aristocrats were the descendants of the first settlers from Corcyra, but this does not necessarily mean that Corcyra was more closely attached to them than to the commoners.[6] As time passed and the population and

[2] Thuc. 1. 24. 1–2; the date of foundation comes from the *Chronicles* of Eusebius and is generally accepted as approximately correct. See Gomme, *Hist. Comm.*, I, 158, Will (*Korinthiaka,* 371) and Graham, *Colony and Mother City,* 30–31, the last of whom demonstrates that Epidamnus was unquestionably a Corcyrean colony.

[3] Thuc. 1. 24. 3. For the early history of Epidamnus, my chief source is R. L. Beaumont, *JHS,* LVI (1936), 159ff., especially 166–168. The story of the wooing of Agariste is told in Hdt. 6. 127, and the tale of the Elean exiles comes from Strabo, p. 357.

[4] Paus. 6. 10. 5.

[5] Thuc. 1. 24. 5; Plut. *Quaest. Graec.* 29. 297F; Beaumont, *op. cit.,* 167.

[6] Wentker, *Sizilien und Athen,* 11, makes more of the special relationship between the first settlers of a colony, who become its nobility, and the mother city than the evidence warrants. He believes that the mother city established a position of hegemony based on a bond of service between the noble colonists

prosperity of the town grew, the usual economic, social, and political developments took place. Thucydides tells us that social conflict was particularly severe in Epidamnus and that there was civil strife lasting for many years. To this was added a war against the barbarians of the neighborhood which devastated the city and deprived it of its power. In the year or two before 435 the democratic faction drove out the aristocrats, who immediately joined with the barbarians and attacked the city by land and sea. Under great pressure the democrats in the city sent ambassadors to Corcyra, the mother city, where they sat down as suppliants in the temple of Hera. The request they made was that the Corcyreans "should not look on at their destruction but reconcile them with the exiles and put an end to the war with the barbarians." [7]

What the Epidamnians were asking of the Corcyreans was the kind of help a colony might expect of its mother city. It was very much like the help Corcyra, in cooperation with Corinth, had given to Syracuse in 492, when Hippocrates of Gela had defeated the Syracusans in battle. Corinth and Corcyra intervened on that occasion on behalf of their colonial kinsmen.[8] The Epidamnian democrats did not ask the Corcyreans to take their part in a factional struggle, but merely to put an end to that struggle and help them against the barbarians. The Corcyreans, however, were unmoved by the appeal and refused. When the democrats of Epidamnus realized that they would get no help from their metropolis, they turned for help to the gods. Sending to the oracle of Apollo at Delphi, they asked whether they should give their city over to the Corinthians as their founders and try to get some help from them. The god answered affirmatively, and the Epidamnians went to Corinth. "They handed over their colony and, pointing out that their founder was from Corinth and revealing the oracular response, they asked the Corinthians not to look on while they were destroyed but to help them." The Corinthians accepted the invitation.[9]

---

and the metropolis (p. 13). I agree with Graham (p. 151) that Corinth's support of the Epidamnian democrats shows that the idea is "somewhat far-fetched."

[7] Thuc. 1. 24. 5–7.

[8] Hdt. 7. 154; Graham, *Colony and Mother City,* 143–144.

[9] Thuc. 1. 25. 1–3.

The question immediately arises as to why the Corcyreans refused to aid their beleaguered colony, and the silence of Thucydides makes it difficult to give a confident answer. Corcyra had other colonies, or shares in colonies, in the Greek northwest. She shared with Corinth in the colonies of Anactorium, Apollonia, and Leucas, and we have reason to think that she made an effort to maintain her influence in them during the fifth century.[10] One would think that the Corcyreans would be glad of a chance to increase their influence in Epidamnus, so that their refusal is somewhat puzzling.

One explanation that has been offered is that the Corcyreans remained aloof because they favored the aristocrats and expected them to win if there were no interference. This arises from one of two assumptions or a combination of both: that the Epidamnian aristocrats, and they alone, were related by blood to the Corcyreans, and that Corcyra itself was an oligarchy. The support for the first assumption comes from the fact that when the Corinthians agreed to support the Epidamnian democrats, the aristocrats went to Corcyra, pointed out the graves of their common ancestors, made claims on the kinship of the Corcyreans, and obtained their help.[11] This proves nothing; for the aristocrats to make such claims does not show that the democrats could not or did not. The fact is that Diodorus informs us that the democrats did ask the Corinthians for help, "on the grounds that they were kinsmen." [12]

The second assumption, that the government was oligarchic, though made by many scholars, rests only on the incident at Epidamnus. The argument is that if Corcyra helped aristocrats, its own constitution must have been aristocratic. Not only is this argument intrinsically dubious, as oligarchic Corinth's help to the democrats of Epidamnus shows, but we have good reason to think that Corcyra was, in fact, a democracy. In 427, when civil war broke out at Corcyra, the government of the island was democratic.[13] A change from aristocracy to democracy could hardly have come about so swiftly without a serious struggle. Since none of our sources says a

[10] Graham, *Colony and Mother City*, 128–153.

[11] Thuc. 1. 26. 3; Graham, *Colony and Mother City*, 149–150.

[12] Diod. 12. 30. 3: ἀξιοῦντες τοὺς Κερκυραίους συγγενεῖς ὄντας βοηθῆσαι.

[13] Thuc. 1. 70.

word about such a civil conflict, although a lengthy and detailed account of the civil war of 427 such as Thucydides gives would demand an account of such recent troubles, we must believe that the government of Corcyra was democratic in the years before 435 as well. We may not, therefore, explain Corcyra's behavior toward Epidamnus by oligarchic or aristocratic sympathies.[14]

Another suggestion is that the Corcyreans stood aloof because of cynical self-interest. Perhaps they expected both sides to wear each other out and leave Epidamnus so helpless that it would become a Corcyrean protectorate.[15] This appears to come closer to the truth. We must remember that civil war at Epidamnus had been going on for some time, and the Corcyreans had looked on complacently. If they favored the aristocrats out of kinship, political sympathy, or advantage, they should have intervened before they were exiled. If they favored the democrats for similar reasons, they should have helped them crush their opponents. The fact is that Corcyra seems to have been remote not only in geography but in attitude. Her foreign policy was one of "splendid isolation," and she seems to have been little interested in the affairs of her colony some distance to the north; it is her ultimate involvement rather than her aloofness that requires explanation.

It is hardly surprising that Epidamnus should have turned in her desperation to Corinth after her refusal by Corcyra, and the Corinthians responded quickly and vigorously. They issued an invitation to colonists to reinforce the city and immediately sent off a garrison of Corinthians accompanied by their allies from Ambracia and Leucas. The quickest, easiest, and most usual way to go was by sea, but the expedition set off to Apollonia on land, "fearing that the

[14] For an oligarchic or aristocratic rule at Corcyra, see Busolt, *GG,* III: 2, 766 and 774–5; Bernhard Schmidt, *Korkyraeische Studien* (Leipzig, 1890), 67; Meyer, *GdA,* IV: 1, 566; IV: 2, 6; Glotz and Cohen, *HG,* II, 615. Those who believe Corcyra was democratic include Grote (IV, 537) and Bürchner (*PW,* XII, 1413). Legon (*op. cit.,* 8–12) presents a useful discussion of the problem and arrives at the cautious conclusion that before the war Corcyra was either a democracy or a moderate oligarchy which could easily move in the direction of democracy without trouble. He rules out, however, the kind of aristocracy that would be automatically sympathetic with Epidamnian aristocrats.

[15] Beaumont, *op. cit.,* 167.

Corcyreans would prevent them if they went by sea." [16] The Corinthians, it is clear, undertook their expedition in the full expectation that Corcyra would object and that a war with Corcyra might ensue. Why were they willing to take the risk? It is customary in our time, and not always wrong, to seek an economic answer to such questions. It has been suggested that Illyria was a Corinthian trade center where they obtained the materials for the perfume that they exported in their beautiful aryballoi. More important is the suggestion that the silver for the ubiquitous coins of Corinth came from the mines of Damastium in Illyria.[17]

Now the evidence for Corinthian trade in Illyria is almost wholly archaeological and very slender. By any standards it was not large in comparison with the Italian and Sicilian trade. The evidence for Corinthian silver mines in Illyria is not much better. It depends on an obscure passage in Strabo, which says there were silver mines at Damastium, but no one knows precisely where Damastium was located.[18] It is by no means clear, moreover, that Illyria was the source of Corinthian silver at all. Some have suggested that the Corinthian pegasi were made of silver from Spain by way of Samos or came to Corinth by way of Euboea, but the truth is that we simply do not know where the silver came from.[19]

[16] Thuc. 1. 26. 2–3: *δέει τῶν Κερκυραίων μὴ κωλύωνται ὑπ' αὐτῶν κατὰ θάλασσαν περαιούμενοι.*

[17] The case for Corinthian economic interests in Illyria is made best by Beaumont, *op. cit.*, 181–186 and accepted by Michell, *Economics*, 244–247.

[18] Strabo, 326, placed it "somewhere near [*πλησίονδένου*]" some Illyrian peoples far to the north of Epidamnus and Apollonia. O. Davies (*Roman Mines in Europe* [Oxford, 1935], 239) says the mines were located too far from the coast to have been controlled by the Greeks, although Beaumont points out that Strabo tells us that one of the local tribes was ruled by a Corinthian Bacchiad (p. 182). According to J. M. F. May (*The Coinage of Damastion and the Lesser Coinages of the Illyro-Paeonian Region* [London, 1939], viii ff., 2ff.), the coinage of Damastium, which is not known before the fourth century, was current to the west, in the Chalcidice. Thus, if Corinth got her silver from the mines of Damastium at all, she very likely got it by way of Potidaea. It is, of course, possible that Corinth received its silver through the Illyrian colonies, but what little evidence there is does not point in that direction. See J. G. Milne (*JHS*, LVIII [1938], 96), who agrees with May's conclusions.

[19] M. Cary (*Mélanges Glotz* [Paris, 1932], I, 138) favors the Spain-Samos theory, and Milne (*loc. cit.*) suggests Euboea as a source. In 1943, C. H. V.

We cannot, of course, be sure that Illyria was not the source of Corinthian silver, and the seekers for an economic motive for Corinthian intervention at Epidamnus point to a passage in Thucydides that seems to support their view. It comes in a speech that the Corinthians made at Athens to counter the Corcyrean request for an alliance. They point out that their geographical position has made the Corcyreans haughty and independent. They are accustomed to be judges in the cases in which they are themselves involved, "because they sail to the harbors of others very little, but chiefly receive others who come to them by necessity." [20] From this Beaumont argues as follows:

Why was it a "necessity" (ἀνάγκη) for the Corinthians to make frequent voyages to Corcyra? The voyage to Sicily need not have taken a Corinthian merchantman within fifty miles of the island, and Corinthian trade with the Adriatic, which must indeed have passed near Corcyra, was, apart from the possibility of silver, in luxuries, and on the available evidence it can hardly be ranked as a vital interest. Thucydides I, 37, 4 is clear evidence that Corcyra lay on some vital Corinthian trade route. Corinth simply had to make the voyage to the north. What was it, if it was not silver, that made the Adriatic trade so valuable? [21]

It is very important to analyze this argument, for on it rests the whole case for an economic interpretation of Corinth's behavior at this time, and Beaumont is its most authoritative proponent. Since he himself dismisses the trade with Illyria as not vital, we need only concern ourselves with the question of silver.

The entire argument rests on the assumption that the Corinthians found it "a necessity" to make frequent stops at Corcyra and that these stops were on voyages to the north. This assumption, however, is not supported by the evidence. To begin with, it may be true that the Corinthians *need* not stop at Corcyra on their way to Italy and Sicily. In theory they could have sailed directly across the open sea as the ferry does today. But that is not the way the ancient Greeks

---

Sutherland examined the claim for Illyria and concluded that "the evidence must be accounted as conjectural" (*AJP*, LXIV [1943], 134, n. 20.) Nothing has happened since to alter the validity of that judgment.

[20] Thuc. 1. 37. 3: διὰ τὸ ἥκιστα ἐπὶ τοὺς πέλας ἐκπλέοντας μάλιστα τοὺς ἄλλους ἀνάγκῃ καταίροντας δέχεσθαι.

[21] Beaumont, *op. cit.*, 183.

sailed the seas. They feared the open sea, and particularly the dangerous Adriatic. The normal procedure was to cling to the coast and only venture away from it when absolutely necessary. The usual route from Corinth would be to sail along the northern shore of the Gulf of Corinth, where the Corinthians had sensibly planted colonies, to the Corinthian island colony of Leucas. From there one would sail along the coast of Epirus to Corcyra, and thence make the shortest possible crossing to Italy. Ships aiming for Sicily would move on along the Italian coast and cross to Sicily near the narrow Straits of Messina. When the Athenians made the trip to the west during the war, and from Leucas on it was the same route as the Corinthians would take, they proceeded in this way. As Thucydides points out, one of the reasons the Athenians chose to accept the Corcyrean alliance was because "it seemed to them that the island was well situated for a coasting voyage to Italy and Sicily." [22]

Thus, if it was a necessity for the Corinthians to sail frequently to Corcyra, it is far more likely that it was to break a trip to the west, where Corinth certainly did have vital economic interests, than as a stopping place on the way north. But it would be wrong to exaggerate the importance of Corcyra even for Corinth's western trade. Even if we assume that Corinthian merchants were occasionally irritated by their treatment in Corcyrean courts when commercial disputes arose, which is at best an unsubstantiated speculation, this was hardly a matter of vital interest to Corinth, one which would justify a war. If things were really bad at Corcyra, the Corinthians could have sailed north along the coast not too far to the friendly colony of Apollonia and used it as the stopping place on the way to Italy. In fact they did no such thing, surely because they had no reason to do so. Finally, it should be emphasized that it was not Corcyra's unfriendliness to visiting merchants that brought on the crisis, but the opportunity for Corinthian intervention at Epidamnus. The former complaint is barely mentioned by the Corinthians in their speech at Athens and never referred to again. It was merely a device used by the Corinthians to counter the Corcyrean charges that Corinth was in the wrong because she refused arbitration.[23]

[22] 1. 44. 3.

[23] This section was composed before I had seen M. I. Finley's excellent contribution on ancient Greece to the first volume of the *Second International*

The setting of their speech at Athens is very important for our interpretation of it. The Corinthians were speaking in the Athenian assembly. Their purpose was to blacken the character of the Corcyreans and to demonstrate their own rectitude. Nothing could be less useful than to indicate that the Corinthians were arguing in behalf of a selfish interest. As we shall see, the one complaint they made against Corcyra on their own behalf is of a violation of decency and religious practice, not of material interest. What they are saying is that the Corcyreans take advantage of their geographical location and the necessity of others to use their harbors. The victims, if there really were any, might well include Athenian merchants, and it may be that the Corinthians were aiming their remarks, which are not emphasized, at such Athenians, among whom they might find sympathetic ears. All this is conjecture, but what is clear is that the passage provides no evidence of vital Corinthian interests in the north. The question has been asked, "What was it, if it was not silver, that made the Adriatic trade so valuable?" We have no good reason to think that there was a silver trade in the Adriatic, so we may answer that nothing made it valuable; therefore it was not valuable and certainly not vital. It is also clear that Corinth's western interests, although both valuable and vital, were not threatened by Corcyra, but far more important, had nothing whatever to do with Epidamnus, and may not be used to explain Corinthian intervention there.

If we turn away from the realm of economic interests and examine the history of the relations between Corinth and Corcyra, we may find a more plausible motive for the Corinthian intervention at Epidamnus. Corcyra was a Corinthian colony, founded by the Bacchiads late in the eighth century. It is possible that, along with Syracuse, which was founded about the same time, it was intended to serve as an outpost for Corinthian trade with the west and thus to be closely attached to the metropolis, although it seems more likely that important Corinthian trade in the west followed rather than preceded the

---

Conference of Economic History entitled *Trade and Politics in the Ancient World* (Paris, 1965), 11–35. It is pleasant to learn that my conclusions as to the value of the evidence for economic motives in the modern sense agree with his.

[24] For a discussion of the date of foundation and the theories of the original

foundation of these colonies.[24] Whatever the original intentions, there is no doubt that both Corcyra and Syracuse became altogether independent states, in no way under the control of Corinth; each colony had its own special development. Syracuse remained on very good terms with the mother city, but between Corcyra and Corinth a deep hostility sprang up very early. Herodotus tells us that there were differences between them from the foundation of the colony.[25] As early as 664, Corinth and Corcyra fought a naval battle, the first one among Greeks, according to Thucydides.[26] We do not know the cause of that early war, but it was clearly a war between two sovereign and independent states and not a war of independence.[27]

The enmity between metropolis and colony was intensified by the accession of the Cypselid dynasty of tyrants in Corinth. Without delay the Corcyreans received the exiled Bacchiads whom Cypselus had driven from Corinth.[28] Since Corcyra had been hostile to Bacchiad Corinth, we have no ready explanation for this action, but it early set the tone for relations between Corcyra and the Corinth of the Cypselids. There is good reason to think that under the Cypselids Corinth for the first time undertook to establish what we might call a colonial empire in the northwest of Greece. This is not to say that the colonies they founded were subject states, but unlike Syracuse and Bacchiad Corcyra, they were probably under close Corinthian supervision. An examination of the geography of these Cypselid foundations shows that their location was not haphazard or determined by the usual agricultural considerations. Molycreium and Chalcis were on the north shore of the Gulf of Corinth, opposite Patras; Sollium, on the Acarnanian coast and Leucas, the island opposite it; Anactorium, on the south shore of the Ambracian Gulf and Ambracia on a river a few miles from the north shore; finally, there were Apollonia, Epidamnus, and Corcyra itself, all at some time under the control of Cypselids. The distribution is ideal for

purposes of the colonies, see Graham, *Colony and Mother City,* 218–223.

[25] 3. 49. 1.

[26] 1. 13. 4.

[27] Graham, *Colony and Mother City,* 146–147.

[28] Nicolaus Damascenus, *FGrH,* 90, frg. 57, 7.

securing coastal shipping to the north and west and for asserting Corinthian influence in the entire region.[29]

The trouble between Corinth and Corcyra was intensified by Corcyra's own interests in much of the same region. We have already seen that at a moment when their hostility was muted, the Corcyreans followed custom in employing a Corinthian founder for Epidamnus, which was, however, a purely Corcyrean colony, very remote from most of the Corinthian foundations. Corinthian interests met those of Corcyra head on in the colony of Apollonia. The ancient authors are divided as to whether it was a joint colony of the two cities or had been founded by Corcyra.[30] We cannot be sure about the foundation of Apollonia, but the numismatic evidence points to Corcyra as founder. The first coins of Apollonia that we possess date from the middle of the fifth century. Like the contemporary coins of Epidamnus, they are nothing more than Corcyrean coins stamped with the first letters of the name of their town. It is no coincidence that at this time inscriptions first appear on Corcyrean coins. We must agree with Graham: "It appears likely that the three cities had all used Corcyra's coins before this time, and it was only necessary to put an inscription on Corcyra's coins when the colonies began to issue identical coins for themselves." [31] We may go beyond Graham in suggesting that the reason Apollonia and Epidamnus began inscribing the names of their towns on the Corcyrean coins is that they had begun to pull away from Corcyrean control and were asserting some degree of independence. It is not too much to believe that this movement toward independence may have been supported by Corinth, which hoped to supplant Corcyrean influence with its own.

The colonies of Anactorium and Leucas seem to offer evidence

[29] For a discussion of the Cypselids and their colonial policy, see Edouard Will (*Korinthiaka* 521–539), who offers useful discussions of the problems and controversies. See also E. Will, *La Nouvelle Clio,* VI, 413–460 (1954) and Graham, *Colony and Mother City,* 118–153.

[30] Strabo (316) and Ps.-Scymnus (439) speak of it as a joint colony, while Pausanias (5. 22. 4) calls it a Corcyrean colony. Stephanus Byzantinus, *s.v.,* "Apollonia," speaks only of Corinthian settlers. Thucydides (1. 26. 2) calls it a Corinthian colony (Κορινθίων οὖσαν ἀποικίαν), which it had certainly become by 435, but his evidence does not bear on the question of the origins of the colony.

[31] 130.

that the experience of Apollonia was not unique. Two of our ancient sources speak of Leucas as a Corinthian colony founded by a son of Cypselus, but they do not agree on which son.[32] Plutarch says that it was founded by Periander.[33] All are very remote from the event, and their disagreement makes it likely that little was known of the foundation of Leucas by the first century. In the fifth century, however, a dispute over Leucas took place between Corinth and Corcyra. The argument seems to have been very much like the one that occurred in 435 over Epidamnus; there was a disagreement over which was the true metropolis of the colony. Themistocles was called in to arbitrate and settled the affair by deciding that Corinth should pay an indemnity of twenty talents and thereafter treat Leucas as the common colony of Corinth and Corcyra. The solution was highly pleasing to Corcyra, where Themistocles was thereafter considered a public benefactor.[34] The story is confirmed by Thucydides, who characteristically offers no details but makes it clear that Themistocles was considered a benefactor (εὐεργέτης) by the Corcyreans.[35]

If we try to reconstruct the events from the meager description of Plutarch, we find the parallel with the Epidamnian affair most striking. The payment of an indemnity to Corcyra plainly indicates that there had been some fighting, and Corinth was judged sufficiently culpable to pay the costs. The pleasure of the Corcyreans may seem to indicate that the settlement was fully in accord with their own wishes and claims, but that seems unlikely. Arbitrators rarely award full satisfaction to one side, and it is incredible that the Corinthians would have accepted the decision without receiving at least part of their own demands. It seems more than likely that Leucas had been founded by Corcyra, perhaps through a Corinthian. Over the years the island may have moved toward independence and sought aid from Corinth, which was glad to offer it in return for the recognition of its claims as founder. The war must have come when Corcyra challenged those claims. The decision of Themistocles gave Corinth half a loaf by recognizing her as co-founder; it pleased the Corcyreans

[32] Strabo, 452; Nic. Dam. *FGrH,* frg. 57, 7.
[33] *Moralia* 552E.
[34] Plut. *Them.* 24. 1.
[35] 1. 136. 1.

because it prevented a total Corinthian victory, such as Corinth seems to have won at Apollonia, and awarded them an indemnity.[36]

Anactorium seems to present a similar experience. In 433, Thucydides speaks of it as a place common to the Corinthians and Corcyreans,[37] but in 425, when the Athenians captured the town, he calls it a "city belonging to the Corinthians." [38] Later authors speak of it as being founded by a son of Cypselus, although they do not agree on which son.[39] The evidence of the coins is different from what we find at Apollonia and Epidamnus, which first used Corcyrean coins and then stamped them with a local inscription. Like Leucas, Anactorium used Corinthian coins engraved with its own initial. This appears to suggest that the city had initially been a Corinthian colony. Perhaps it is correct to conjecture that a Corcyrean element had been added to the population by Periander when he controlled Corcyra,[40] although it seems more likely that the Corcyreans had been there from the first.

There can, in any case, be no doubt that there was a Corcyrean population of some strength in Anactorium at the outbreak of the Peloponnesian War. We have seen that Thucydides considered it common to Corinth and Corcyra, and its actions in the succeeding years make it clear why he thought so. At the Battle of Sybota in 433, the nearby towns of Ambracia and Leucas supplied a total of thirty-seven ships, while Anactorium supplied only one. Even if we

[36] Graham (*Colony and Mother City,* 129–130) considers it possible that Leucas was originally a joint colony of Corinth and Corcyra. This seems to me possible, but unlikely for the reasons offered above and because of the long-standing enmity between the states. The best argument in his favor is that Leucas originally used Corinthian coins, which points to a Corinthian foundation. I cannot explain this inconvenient fact away, but find it less decisive than the evidence of Plutarch's story. We simply know too little about the early history of western Greece to be sure that Leucas was not an exception to the rule that the use of another city's coinage generally implied some close political relation. Whatever the truth in this matter, we agree that "Corinth was trying to gain sole control of Leucas in the early fifth century, and had succeeded in doing so by the time of the Epidamnus dispute."

[37] 1. 55. 1: *κοίνον Κερκυραίων καὶ ἐκείνων.*

[38] 4. 49. 1: *Κορινθίων πόλιν.*

[39] Strabo (452) suggests that Gorgos was the founder, but Nic. Dam. (frg. 57, 7) says it was Pylades.

[40] Hdt. 3. 48–53; Graham, *Colony and Mother City,* 129.

believe that Anactorium was a lesser naval state than the others, the degree of disparity remains surprising. When Thucydides lists the states who supplied ships to each side at the beginning of the Peloponnesian War, Leucas and Ambracia are named, but Anactorium is missing. In 435 the Corinthians were compelled to capture the city, and Thucydides explains the need to do so, in the passage we have already cited, by pointing out that the city was the common property of Corinth and Corcyra. Even as late as 425 there was a powerful anti-Corinthian party in Anactorium which helped the Athenians and Ambracians take the city by treachery. It is not too daring a guess that the traitors may have been the remaining Corcyreans.[41] The pattern at Anactorium is much the same as in the other cities we have discussed. There was some dispute between Corinthians and Corcyreans over the control of the city, and in Anactorium, as in all the others except Epidamnus, the Corinthians seem to have had the upper hand.

The picture that emerges from a study of the individual states where conflict arose between Corinth and Corcyra is something like this: Corinth had established colonies like Syracuse and Corcyra under the Bacchiads. These were altogether independent states, and Corcyra, in fact, soon became hostile. Perhaps the quarrel first arose from conflicting interests in the northwest, perhaps from less rational causes; we simply do not know. With the coming of the Cypselids, Corinth established a sphere of influence in the region by planting a series of colonies on the major sea route. Some of these may have conflicted with the interests of Corcyrean colonies already established or asserted Corinthian predominance in mixed colonies. The fall of the Cypselid dynasty may have given Corcyra a chance to assert her own influence in her neighborhood, perhaps even to dominate mixed colonies. All of this competition could only exacerbate the pre-existing ill will between the states. By the fifth century it looks very much as if Corinth had regained the upper hand. On the eve of the war she seems to have controlled all the disputed colonies with the exception of Epidamnus.

Thus, it might appear that we have discovered a rational, if not

[41] Graham, *Colony and Mother City,* 132–133. The relevant passages in Thucydides are: Sybota, 1. 46. 1; list of ships, 2. 9. 2–3; Corinthian capture of city, 1. 55. 1; treachery, 4. 49. 1.

wholly admirable, reason why Corinth should have been willing to risk an almost certain war with Corcyra by going to the assistance of a political faction alien to its own constitutional and political outlook, in a far-off region where it had no vital economic interests. The answer seems to lie in the struggle for power, for political influence, for imperial control. This is a very Thucydidean answer, so it is surprising to find that it is not the answer he gives. He says instead that the Corinthians accepted the invitation of the Epidamnian democrats

> in part because they thought that the colony was no less theirs than the Corcyreans; at the same time also out of hatred for the Corcyreans, for they paid no attention to the Corinthians even though they were their colonists. In the common festivals they did not give them the customary privileges nor did they begin by having a Corinthian commence the initial sacrifices, as the other colonies did, but treated them contemptuously.

The Corcyreans were a haughty people, proud of their wealth, their naval power, and their imagined descent from the legendary Phaeacians of Homer's epic.[42] All this had puffed them up and made them intolerable to the Corinthians. The irrationality of this motive has set off the hunt for better ones. "Is it really credible that the Corinthians disliked the Corcyreans to such an extent as to fight them for the reasons that Thucydides gives . . . ?" Beaumont asked. "It is surely justifiable to look for something more concrete." [43] His search for the concrete led him to the putative Corinthian mining interests in Illyria, which we have rejected above.

To explain Corinth's action as an imperialistic attempt to extend her power at Corcyrean expense may be more satisfactory, but it is hardly more rational. Our own century has good reason to know that the competition for power and empire, though cloaked by public assertions of rational advantage, is often nothing more than the satisfaction of an irrational urge and yields no tangible gain. We may not wish to go so far as Joseph Schumpeter, who says that " 'objectless' tendencies toward forcible expansion, without definite, utilitarian limits—that is, non-rational and irrational, purely instinctual inclinations toward war and conquest—play a very large role in

[42] 1. 25. 3–4.
[43] *Op. cit.,* 183.

the history of mankind," and believe that imperialism is a kind of cultural atavism.[44] But we can hardly deny that the scramble to divide up the undeveloped areas of the world after 1870 was less than a completely rational activity. It is difficult to discern the economic, strategic, or other practical benefit which Ethiopia, Libya, or Eritrea could have given Italy in return for the money and lives she spent gaining control over them.

The real motive for Italian imperialism is more likely to be found in the psychology of a nation unified late and discontented with her weakness in comparison with her European neighbors. Rather than in economic statistics, it may be found in a speech made by Mussolini to Italian veterans in which he reminded them of the glories of ancient Rome, saying, "Nothing forbids us to believe that what was our destiny yesterday may again become our destiny tomorrow." [45] The true motive for Japanese imperialism may likewise be found in the minds of the Japanese rather than in their account books. They were a proud people embarrassed by the revelation of their backwardness in regard to the West and eager to assert themselves as equal, if not superior. One of their statesmen revealed the sentiments underlying Japanese policy in the following terms:

> As soon as the Meiji Restoration lifted the ban on foreign intercourse, the long-pent-up energy of our race was released, and with fresh outlook and enthusiasm the nation has made swift progress. When you know this historical background, and understand this overflowing vitality of our race, you will see the impossibility of compelling us to stay within the confines of our little island home. We are destined to grow and expand overseas.[46]

These modern analogies are introduced merely to show that even in a world where economic considerations are far more dominant than they were in the world of the Greek city-state, imperial ventures are not always guided by the search for tangible gain. Corinth's willingness to fight for Epidamnus was caused by similar non-rational motives. The sixth century had seen Sparta grow to be the dominant

[44] *Imperialism and Social Classes,* tr. Heinz Norden (New York, 1955), 64.

[45] The speech is quoted by William L. Langer in *Foreign Affairs,* XIV (1935–36), 102–19. My views on imperialism owe much to his article.

[46] Quoted by Langer, *op. cit.*

power in the Peloponnese. Since the Persian Wars, Athens had become her equal. Corinth, with a proud history as a commercial, industrial, artistic, and naval power, had seen her prestige shrink in comparison with the two superpowers who had arisen since the middle of the sixth century. She had learned to cope with Sparta and had reached a *modus vivendi* with Athens. At the same time, she determined to build a sphere of influence in the northwest of Greece to compensate for her diminished prestige elsewhere. This brought her into conflict with Corcyra, which had grown in power and influence while Corinth had declined. Corcyra had remained aloof from the wars that had troubled Greece in the fifth century and seemed to profit by it. At the time of the outbreak of the war she had accumulated one hundred and twenty ships, the second largest navy in Greece. Our investigation indicates that she had even tried to challenge Corinthian hegemony in the northwest. To these injuries the Corcyreans added the insult of public disdain for Corinth at the religious festivals common to them and to the other colonies of Corinth. We may well agree with Thucydides when he judges that this public insult inflamed the deep-seated hatred felt by the Corinthians and best explains their acceptance of the Epidamnian appeal.

Nothing compelled the Corinthians to intervene in Epidamnus when they knew that the intervention could mean war with Corcyra. No interest of theirs was threatened, no diminution of their power or prestige. It was they who took the initiative, who seized on what seemed a favorable opportunity to alter the situation in their own favor. Far from trying to avoid a war with Corcyra, they sought it as a splendid chance to damage that insolent offspring and perhaps crush it once and for all. The result, as we know, was not what the Corinthians had expected, but that is often the consequence of policies that are more emotional than rational.

14. *Corcyra*

The Corinthians had sent their troops to Epidamnus overland by way of Apollonia because they expected trouble from Corcyra, and their expectations were justified. The Corcyreans were prepared to stand aside and let the Epidamnians destroy one another, but they could not allow the Corinthians to establish themselves in a colony belonging to Corcyra. When they learned that garrisons and new settlers had arrived and that the Epidamnians had given the colony over to Corinth, they were annoyed. Their angry response showed their customary arrogance and their failure to appreciate the seriousness of the Corinthian undertaking.

As we have seen, the exiled aristocrats had already been to Corcyra and asked for help in their restoration. Only now, after the Corinthian intervention, did the Corcyreans agree. They sailed to Epidamnus with a considerable fleet and laid down the law: the Epidamnians were to send away the garrison and settlers and to take back the exiled aristocrats.[1] This was not a proposal for discussions or negotiation; it was an ultimatum, delivered in insolent language, whose terms were totally unacceptable. Corinth could not accept them without disgrace, and the Epidamnian democrats could not accept them without the greatest danger to themselves.

It is difficult to speculate on the thinking of the Corcyreans, for we have little evidence, and they seem to have been an erratic people. On this occasion, however, it seems clear that they overestimated their own strength in respect to Corinth, while underestimating the

[1] Thuc. 1. 26. 3.

determination and potential strength of Corinth. In 435, Corcyra had one hundred and twenty warships, while the Corinthians had almost no navy. This disparity in strength lured the Corcyreans into a confidence very close to complacency. The contemptuous tone of their ultimatum suggests that they hardly expected the Corinthians to fight, and if fighting should be necessary, Corcyra expected to win an easy victory.

Epidamnus rejected the demands of Corcyra. The Corcyreans, with forty ships, the Illyrians, and the exiled Epidamnian aristocrats, besieged the city, which was located on a promontory and connected to the mainland by an isthmus. Before sealing off the city, the Corcyreans offered safe conduct to any foreigner or Epidamnian who wished to leave, but no one accepted.[2]

The Corinthians responded with a vigor that showed how badly Corcyra had misjudged their intentions and capacities. Their first action showed that the scope of their undertaking had already broadened. It was no longer merely a matter of assisting the Epidamnian democrats against their enemies, or even of declaring Corinth the metropolis of the old colony. The Corinthians undertook to found an altogether new colony which would be Corinthian, but on a new basis. Anyone who wished to take part would have an equal share in the new colony. Presumably this meant a redistribution of the land; at the very least it would mean the confiscation and distribution of the land of the exiles and perhaps some land would be taken from the barbarians as well.[3] The Corinthians were eager to collect as many settlers as possible and added a provision that anyone who wished to join the colony but was unable to go immediately could reserve a place by the deposit of fifty drachmas. The response of both immediate colonists and depositors was gratifying.

The military preparations were no less thorough and ambitious. The Corinthians themselves provided thirty ships and three thousand hoplites. These could take care of themselves in case of Corcyrean attack, but the large body of colonists needed protection. To this end the Corinthians went round to their friends asking them to supply ships for convoy duty. Megara sent eight, Cephallenia four, Epidaurus five, Hermione one, Troezen two, Leucas ten, and Am-

[2] Thuc. 1. 26. 4–5.

[3] Thuc. 1. 27. 1; Gomme, *Hist. Comm.*, I, 161–162.

bracia eight. The landlubbers of Thebes and Phlius were asked to give money in support of the expedition, while Elis provided unmanned ships as well as money.[4] The scope of Corinth's influence is made very clear by the response to her requests. With the exception of Leucas and Ambracia, these states were not Corinthian colonies or obliged to assist her in war. Although many of them were members of the Peloponnesian League, it was not in that capacity that they were asked for aid or gave it. However we understand the workings of that organization, it is clear that a league meeting would be necessary before Corinth could ask for help. As we have argued above, the league was in fact a Spartan alliance, and only Sparta could call out the forces of the league. There was, of course, no such meeting. Even more interesting, Sparta was not asked to assist. We would hardly expect her to be asked to supply ships or money, but why wasn't she asked for troops, at least a token detachment to indicate support, even a general? Little Troezen and Hermione had been asked to make their tiny contributions, surely more for psychological than military purposes. The presence of a Spartan contingent at Epidamnus could hardly fail to have an intimidating effect on the Corcyreans, yet so far as we know Sparta was not asked for help. We begin to suspect that the Spartans did not favor the Corinthian expedition.

Even without the Spartans, the massive support gathered by the Corinthians did not fail to have its effect on the Corcyreans. By now it had dawned on Corcyra that the fleet in being did not reflect the true power of Corinth, whose wealth and political influence in the Peloponnese could crush a friendless and isolated Corcyra. Frightened out of their previous arrogance, the Corcyreans came to Corinth to undertake serious negotiations. They began by repeating their demand that the Corinthians withdraw their garrisons and colonists from Epidamnus on the grounds that they had no right to be there. If the Corinthians would not agree to that, Corcyra was prepared to submit the matter to the arbitration of any mutually acceptable Peloponnesian states. Failing this, they were willing to put the case before the oracle at Delphi. After this display of reasonableness, they put forward a veiled threat. If the Corinthians proved obdurate, the Corcyreans would be forced to seek friends elsewhere, others

[4] Thuc. 1. 27. 1–2.

beyond those whom they now had. They did not wish to do so, but necessity would compel them.[5] The veil was not hard to penetrate; the reference was to Athens.

We need not question the sincerity of the Corcyrean desire for a peaceful settlement. The Corcyreans knew that they had miscalculated, and they were frightened. They believed themselves legally in the right, as their offer of impartial arbitration shows, but they must have realized that arbitration would probably result in a compromise of some sort, and they were ready to accept one. At the same time, they were not frightened enough to surrender their position in Epidamnus. Unless a suitable compromise were reached, Corcyra would fight, and the Corcyreans were prepared to seek the help of mighty Athens if necessary.

It was clear now that what had begun as a minor incident in a remote corner of the Greek world had developed into a very dangerous situation and a threat to the general peace. We have good evidence that the Spartan government was keenly aware of the danger. Thucydides tells us that when the Corcyreans went to Corinth to parley they were accompanied by ambassadors (πρέσβεις) from Sicyon and Sparta.[6] It has been suggested that these Spartans were not official representatives but private citizens lending their good offices to the Corcyrean cause.[7] But, as Gomme has pointed out, "the Greek for private persons is 'ιδιῶται τινες, not πρέσβεις." Thucydides is very careful to distinguish official ambassadors from private citizens who engage in diplomatic negotiations.[8] The report of Thucydides shows us that the peace party was still in power at Sparta and that it took a serious view of the conflict between Corinth and Corcyra. The Spartans knew that there was a chance that Athens would be involved, which meant that Sparta might also be dragged into the affair. The Spartan ambassadors were sent to lend weight to the Corcyrean request for a peaceful settlement, not necessarily to sup-

[5] Thuc. 1. 27. 1–4.

[6] 1. 28. 1.

[7] W. H. Forbes, *Thucydides Book I* (Oxford, 1895), *ad. loc.*

[8] See 1. 115. 2–3, where the official representatives of Miletus go to Athens to complain against Samos accompanied by ἄνδρες ἰδιῶται, who wanted to overthrow the Samian government, and 2. 67. 1, where Thucydides carefully distinguishes between the envoys (πρέσβεις) from Corinth, Sparta, and Tegea, and Pollis, a citizen of Argos, who is acting ἰδίᾳ.

port Corcyra's claim to Epidamnus. They could not, of course, force the Corinthians to negotiate, but they could at least make their attitude clear.

Under the eyes of the ambassadors from Sicyon and Sparta, the Corinthians could not flatly reject the Corcyrean proposal, but their response shows that they wanted no peaceful settlement. They said that if the Corcyreans withdrew their ships and the barbarians from Epidamnus, they would think about the Corcyrean proposal (βουλεύεσθαι), but so long as the city was under siege it would be improper to negotiate. The Corinthian conditions for negotiation were altogether unacceptable and patently insincere. They asked the Corcyreans to withdraw their forces but said nothing about the garrison and colonists with which Corinth had reinforced Epidamnus. If Corcyra had agreed, Corinth would have been given the opportunity to strengthen its hold on the city and to reinforce it against a siege. In return for this strategic advantage, Corinth offered not to accept arbitration, but merely to think about it.

It would have been madness for the Corcyreans to accept, and they did not. Unlike the Corinthians, however, they showed their sincere desire for a peaceful solution by offering counter-proposals. They agreed to withdraw their forces from Epidamnus if the Corinthians would do the same. If this were not acceptable, they were also prepared to leave both forces where they were, but to make a truce in the fighting until peace negotiations were completed.[9] This left the Corinthians with a very simple choice. If they wanted to avoid war they had merely to select a procedure. Every provision would be made to save the prestige of Corinth, and she could have her choice of arbitrators. Instead they turned a deaf ear to the Corcyrean offers, gathered their ships and allies, and wasted no time in declaring war on Corcyra.[10]

The Corinthian force, consisting of seventy-five ships and two thousand hoplites, sailed north as far as Actium on the Ambracian Gulf, where it was met by a Corcyrean herald who asked it to stop. Once again Corinth refused, and a naval battle ensued. Eighty Corcyrean ships won a total victory, destroying fifteen of the Corinthian vessels. On the very same day Epidamnus capitulated, on condition

[9] Thuc. 1. 28. 1–5.
[10] Thuc. 1. 29. 1.

that the other immigrants should be sold as slaves, but the Corinthians should be imprisoned until some settlement was made.[11] The Corcyreans clearly did not want to anger the Corinthians further and were eager to keep open the possibility of a negotiated peace even now. The same hope and intention was demonstrated by the Corcyreans who had won the naval battle. After setting up a trophy to commemorate their victory, they killed such prisoners as they had taken, but not the Corinthians, who were merely kept in bonds. This caution was in vain, and the Corcyrean hopes were not rewarded. The defeated Corinthians were in no mood for a settlement, but more eager than ever for revenge.

Since there was no prospect of peace, the Corcyreans took advantage of their victory and consequent mastery of the western seas to punish those states who had assisted the Corinthians. They ravaged Leucas, burned the Elean naval base at Cyllene, and harried the Corinthian colonies of the neighborhood. Toward the end of the summer of 435 the Corinthians were compelled to defend their allies and sent an expedition to Actium. Its purpose was to protect Leucas and the other friends of Corinth near by from further attacks. The Corcyreans sent a similar force to Leucimne, where they had set up their trophy of victory and which gives its name to the battle, on the coast opposite the Corinthian camp. For the rest of the summer the two armies looked at each other across the bay but took no action. When winter came each side went home.[12]

Far from chastening the Corinthians, the defeat at Leucimne had only hardened their determination to punish and humiliate Corcyra. For almost two years after the battle they made preparations for revenge. They realized that a large fleet would be needed to defeat Corcyra and began to build ships, but men were needed to row these ships, men experienced in naval tactics. Corinth took advantage of her wealth to hire oarsmen from the Peloponnese and the rest of Greece, even from the Athenian Empire.[13] These preparations thoroughly frightened the Corcyreans, who realized that they alone could not hope to withstand the attack of an aroused Corinth supported by many allies and mercenary oarsmen. Corinth had called

[11] Thuc. 1. 29. 1–5.
[12] Thuc. 1. 30. 1–4.
[13] Thuc. 1. 31. 1; 1. 35. 3.

the bluff of the Corcyreans, who now had no choice but to go to Athens in search of assistance. When the Corinthians heard of what was happening, they too sent ambassadors to Athens to argue against the Corcyrean appeal.

It is difficult for us to imagine the scene that took place in Athens in the summer of 433. If a similar situation arose in the modern world there would be private, if not secret, discussions in which first the ambassadors of one state would make their plea, and then, in another session, their opponents would present their case. The government would decide its course of action and go before the legislative body to seek approval. Only then, when the foreign ambassadors were gone, would there be a debate. Far different was the Athenian procedure. All discussion took place on the Pnyx, where the people of Athens were gathered in their assembly, on a hill from which they could see their market place and the temples on the Acropolis. Each speaker addressed this assembly, and when the speakers had finished, it was the business of their audience to decide what should be done. Presumably the foreign ambassadors withdrew after the speeches, but everything they had said was known directly by each citizen who must vote to decide Athenian policy. Thucydides has reported the speeches of both sides; he was surely present, and we may be sure that he has given us an accurate account of the arguments used.[14]

The Corcyrean ambassadors were faced with a difficult task.

[14] Without getting into the general question of the nature and reliability of Thucydidean speeches, I should like to argue for the general accuracy of his accounts of the speeches in the Athenian assembly during the period when he himself was in Athens. In the famous and disputed passage in which he speaks of his technique in reporting speeches, Thucydides says that he gives the speeches "in a way which, it seems to me, each speaker might most likely express himself to suit the occasion" (ὡς δ' ἄν ἐδόκουν μοι ἕκαστοι περὶ τῶν ἀεὶ παρόντων τὰ δέοντα μάλιστ' εἰπεῖν). This has rightly given rise to much debate, for it is far from ambiguous. But the clause that follows is too often ignored, and it is perfectly clear: "holding as closely as possible to the general sense of what really was said" (ἐχομένῳ ὅτι ἐγγύτατα τῆς ξυμπάσης γνώμης τῶν ἀληθῶς λεχθέντων) (1. 22. 1–2). Unless we believe that Thucydides is a liar, we must concede that he tried to give an accurate report of what was said. Unless we believe he was a fool or had an especially bad memory, we must concede that when he reports speeches at which he was present, he has given us a reasonably accurate account of them.

Hindsight can sometimes be a disadvantage to the historian; because we know that Athens ultimately accepted an alliance with Corcyra and came to her assistance, it is too easy to assume her decision was a foregone conclusion. In fact, as we shall see, there was good reason to expect an Athenian refusal. Corcyra was remote from Athenian interests, especially from the more modest interests Athens had pursued since 445. The presence of the Corinthian ambassadors made it impossible for the Athenians to ignore the fact that a favorable answer to the Corcyrean request would alienate Corinth and probably lead to war. Athens obviously had much to fear from a Corcyrean alliance, and it was up to the Corcyreans to prove that she had more to gain. It was, of course, also necessary to deal with all the arguments that were likely to come up. Thus, the Corcyreans argued that they were in the right in the quarrel over Epidamnus. The colony was theirs and the Corinthians were the aggressors. Most telling of all the moral arguments was the fact that Corinth had refused arbitration.[15] They further demonstrated the legality of an Athenian alliance with Corcyra by pointing out that the Thirty Years' Peace had expressly provided that neutrals, such as Corcyra, could join either alliance with impunity.[16]

Such matters of right and legality are never without some significance, for their persuasiveness, or lack thereof, are to some degree instrumental in affecting foreign policy through public opinion, even in the modern world, where public opinion is rather remote from the places where policy is made. They were all the more important in Athens, where public policy was formulated by the people sitting in view of the temples of the gods. But the men of Athens, like modern men, were more readily moved by fear and interest than by right and legality, and the heart of the Corcyrean appeal is an attempt to demonstrate the practical advantages to Athens of the alliance. After a brief reference to the honor that will accrue to Athens for helping men who are in the right and the debt of gratitude they will incur by accepting Athenian help, the Corcyreans make it clear how valuable that gratitude will be. "We possess a navy that is the greatest except for your own," which will be added to the power of Athens by the alliance. "In the entire course of time

[15] 1. 34. 1–3.
[16] 1. 35. 1.

few have received so many advantages all at once, and few when they come to ask for an alliance offer to those whom they ask as much security and honor as they expect to receive." [17]

The force of the Corcyrean appeal was immeasurably strengthened, moreover, by their assertion that not only would the alliance be useful in the future, it was already necessary. A war between Athens and the Peloponnesians is coming:

> If any one of you thinks it will not happen his judgment is in error, and he does not perceive that the Spartans are eager for war out of fear of you, and that the Corinthians have great influence with them and are your enemies; they are making an attempt on us now with the thought of attacking you in the future, in order that we may not stand together out of common hatred toward them and so that they may not fail to accomplish two things before we do: either to harm us or strengthen themselves.[18]

Since the war is inevitable, it is of the greatest importance that the Athenians should not allow the mighty Corcyrean navy to fall under Corinthian control but should rather try to acquire it for themselves. Corcyra, the ambassadors further pointed out, was conveniently located for the coasting voyage to Sicily and Italy. Whoever controlled it could prevent fleets from coming to the aid of the Peloponnesians or could send a fleet there in safety. There might be Athenians who saw the expediency of an alliance with Corcyra but who feared to make it lest it be a breach of the peace. That fear was dangerous to Athens, for if it led to the refusal of the alliance, confidence in the security provided by a treaty would be unsupported by power. The acquisition of new strength, on the other hand, fortified by a demonstration of confidence, would put fear into the other side. The Athenians should consider that they were deciding the fate of Athens, not merely Corcyra, in a war which was all but upon them. It would be far more dangerous to reject the alliance and allow Corcyra to fall under Corinthian control than to accept it. The Corcyreans summed up their argument:

> There are three fleets worthy of mention in Greece, yours, ours, and the Corinthians'; if the Corinthians get control of us first, you will see two of

[17] 1. 33. 1–2.
[18] 1. 33. 3.

them become one and you will have to fight against the Corcyrean and Peloponnesian fleets at once; if you accept us you will fight against them with our ships in addition to your own.[19]

The Corinthian speech must have been shaped, in part, by the need to reply to the remarks of the Corcyreans. Since the case for their intervention in Epidamnus was weak, they said as little about it as possible. As they had no acceptable moral grounds for their actions, they launched into an attack on the character of the Corcyreans. They called them an insolent and arrogant people whose previous policy of isolation was prompted not by an admirable prudence but by the desire to shield their infamous actions. The burden of the Corinthian case for Corcyrean immorality was the outrageous behavior of Corcyra as a colony towards the Corinthian metropolis. All their other colonies, they claimed, showed them exceptional deference and honor; only Corcyra insulted them. The claim that right was on the side of Corcyra because she alone had been willing to accept arbitration the Corinthians rejected as specious. If the Corcyreans were sincere, they should have asked for arbitration before they laid siege to Epidamnus. Now they sought an alliance only after they were in danger, seeking to embroil Athens in their troubles, without having given previous service to deserve Athenian assistance in their moment of peril.[20]

All this is very weak and unconvincing, and the Corinthian speaker must have been glad to move on to a more satisfactory topic. The Corcyreans had insisted that an alliance with them would not be a violation of the treaty of 445, and technically they were right. But the Corinthians pointed out that if Athens accepted the alliance it would be contravening the spirit of the Thirty Years' Peace.

For although it says in the treaty that any of the unenrolled cities may join whichever side it likes, the clause is not meant for those who join one side with the intention of injuring the other, but for whoever seeks security without depriving another of his services and whoever will not bring war instead of peace, if they are prudent, to those who accept him.[21]

The argument is difficult and somewhat obscure, perhaps even more so in Greek than the English translation can indicate. The

[19] 1. 34–36; the quotation is from 1. 36. 3.

[20] 1. 37–39.

[21] 1. 40. 2.

Corinthians appear to suggest that Athens should not make a treaty with Corcyra because in so doing she would help the Corcyreans deprive Corinth of their services, to which the Corinthians have a right. We have no reason to believe that anyone would have recognized such an obligation, and it is puzzling that the Corinthians could have hoped to impose on the Athenians with such an argument. Their second claim seems more reasonable. They assert that the clause in the treaty permitting neutrals to join either side was never intended to cover cases such as that which Corcyra now presented. No state should accept an alliance with a neutral if the acceptance of such an alliance is likely to cause a war. In this the Corinthians appear to be quite right. Surely no one in 446/5 envisaged a situation in which a signatory would accept into an alliance a neutral state already at war with the other signatory. The strictest interpretation of the letter of the treaty permitted Athens to accept Corcyra, but common sense argued that to do so would almost amount to an act of war against Corinth, and so, by extension, a breach of the Thirty Years' Peace.

The Corinthians left no doubt about their response to a treaty between Athens and Corcyra. Not only would the Athenians become allies of the Corcyreans, but enemies of Corinth, "for if you join them it will be necessary for us to include you in our punishment of them." [22] The Corinthians would be particularly aggrieved to find Athens allied with their enemy, for they could recall services that they had rendered the Athenians over the years. They had lent the Athenians twenty ships with which to fight Aegina before the Persian Wars, and they had opposed Peloponnesian intervention against Athens in the recent Samian War. These actions had taken place "at critical moments when assistance is most valuable and the giver of assistance most deserving of future friendship." [23] The Corinthian action during the Samian War they regarded as the most deserving of gratitude. For Athens to turn its back on that service would not only be dishonorable but dangerous, for the Corinthians had meant to establish a general principle by their restraint. They had argued that each one should be free to discipline his own allies. If the Athenians received Corcyra into an alliance now, they would

[22] 1. 40. 3–4.
[23] 1. 141.

be setting a precedent which would have evil consequences for themselves, for in a future crisis they would find their own allies deserting to the side of Corinth.[24]

In this way the Corinthians tried to show that the rejection of the Corcyrean treaty was not only just but expedient. It remained to counter the most telling argument of the Corcyreans: war was inevitable, and in that war the Athenians must be sure to have the Corcyrean fleet on their side. The Corinthian answer was very simple; they merely denied that the war was inevitable, arguing that the Athenian decision about the alliance would determine whether the war would come. "The imminence of war, with which the Corcyreans frighten you and bid you do wrong is still uncertain," they said, urging the Athenians not to turn the hostility of Corinth from a possibility into a certainty. Instead they should try to remove the suspicion that existed because of the Megarians, "for the most recent favor, which comes at an opportune time, even if it is smaller, can erase greater complaints." [25] The best policy would be to resist the temptation of a great naval alliance, which was as dangerous as it was attractive. Instead, Athens should pay Corinth back in kind for past services and particularly observe the rule established by Corinth, that each side should punish its own allies with impunity. "In doing these things not only will you be doing what is proper but also what is in your own best interest." [26]

The Corinthian speech tells us a great deal about the diplomatic climate in the Greek world in the years between the two Peloponnesian wars, and we learn as much from what the Corinthians did not say as from what they said. It provides the most forceful refutation of the view that Athens was engaged in aggressive imperialism between 445 and 435. If this was the view of the Corinthians, we could not fail to find references to it in their speech. We should expect them to complain about Athenian encroachment in the west at Thurii. We should be certain to hear of Phormio's campaign in

[24] 1. 40. 6.

[25] 1. 42. 2–4. I shall argue later that the decree excluding Megara from the harbors of the Athenian Empire had not yet been proposed, so the reference here is to some other grievance. Such grievances must have been many and continuous in the long history of mutual suspicion between Athens and Megara, which went well back into the sixth century at least.

[26] 1. 43.

Acarnania, if it had really taken place in 437, as is sometimes alleged.[27] The speech we have is far from tactful. It does not flatter and it does not beg. It speaks of past favors and demands a *quid pro quo*. It does not hesitate to mention complaints against Athenian behavior in regard to Megara or to suggest improvement in that behavior. If the Athenians were doing other things to trouble the Corinthians, the Corinthian ambassadors would certainly have mentioned them. In the absence of complaints against aggressive Athenian imperialism, we are justified in concluding that there were none.

The tone and arguments of the Corinthians point in quite a different direction and give us a vital insight into the thinking that led them to undertake the campaign against Corcyra in the face of Spartan disapproval and the threat of an alliance with Athens. The key may be found in their action during the Samian rebellion and the principle they derived from it. We may imagine that the conclusion of the Thirty Years' Peace had left Corinth far from satisfied and her suspicions of Athens unallayed. The Athenians, after all, continued to control Naupactus on the Corinthian Gulf, and it remained to be seen whether they would not try to extend their power westward into the Corinthian preserve. The establishment of Thurii as a Panhellenic colony and the subsequent restraint shown by the Athenians in refusing to interfere in its affairs must have gone a long way toward persuading the Corinthians of their good intentions. The Corinthians responded by arguing for Peloponnesian neutrality during the Samian rebellion. They had received the Athenian diplomatic signal, to employ the current jargon, and replied with one of their own. They believed that they had established a mutually accepted principle: each side could punish its own allies without interference. Put in slightly broader terms, this meant that the Athenians were to refrain from expansion into the Corinthian area of influence in return for similar security in their own.

The Corinthians were surely not mistaken in their understanding that the Athenians had accepted this *modus vivendi*. As we have seen, all Athenian actions between the wars may be understood as measures to make the new arrangement workable. It is surely this mutual understanding that gave the Corinthians the confidence necessary to persevere in their war against Corcyra. When the Spar-

[27] See Appendix G, pp. 384–385.

tans intervened in behalf of arbitration out of fear that Athens would become involved, the Corinthians must have soothed them by assuring them that Athens would not, in respect for the tacit agreement that had been reached. Sparta need not participate, for together with her friends, Corinth could defeat Corcyra and put an end to her insolence. Athens would not interfere just as the Corinthians and Spartans had not interfered at Samos. Peace would be even more secure.

The Corinthian expectation was not altogether mistaken, for Pericles had no taste for western expansion and a great desire to avoid war; he did accept the general principle enunciated by Corinth. Where the Corinthians went tragically wrong was in their assessment of the particular case of Corcyra. To begin with, Corcyra was not an ally nor a subordinate of Corinth, but a neutral. Corinth might regard her as her subject or subordinate because of colonial ties, but no one else, least of all the Corcyreans, had the same view. For this reason Corcyra was in no way comparable to Samos. This might not have been too serious had it not been for the Corcyrean navy. Whatever her desire to keep the peace and to avoid remote entanglements, Athens could not allow the second largest navy in Greece to fall under the control of another potentially great naval power. This was not simply a matter of spheres of influence, of allowing the two great blocs freedom from external interference; it involved a major change in the balance of power. The entire plan for Athenian security depended on the unchallenged control of the sea by Athens. The sustenance of her population depended on imports; her prosperity depended on trade and imperial revenues guaranteed by an overwhelmingly superior navy. Her very defense against any attacker was based on her unquestioned superiority at sea. To allow the creation of a fleet to rival her own by the union of the Corinthian and Corcyrean navies was unthinkable.

It may seem surprising that the Corinthians did not see the danger of their policy as we do and, apparently, as the Spartans and Sicyonians did. If we believe the account of Thucydides, they seem to have expected that the Athenians would really desist from aiding the Corcyreans and might even be persuaded to join with Corinth against Corcyra.[28] It is clear, in any case, that they did not want war

[28] 1. 40. 4.

with Athens and did not expect it. How are we to explain the terrible miscalculation of the Corinthians? They were far from a naive and inexperienced people. Their history shows that they were shrewd diplomats and generally well informed as to the politics and policies of the other states and skillful in diplomatic negotiations, yet they made the most serious of errors in judging that the Athenians would refuse the alliance with Corcyra. There is no way to be sure of the answer, but perhaps a clue may be found in one of those recurring features of human nature that Thucydides did not choose to underscore. The leaders of states often undertake policies that assume an understanding of their consequences. The prudent thing to do is to ascertain carefully whether all the involved parties share a common understanding and also to consider in advance the possible consequences of miscalculation.

The fact is that states rarely behave with such prudence. In the crisis following the Sarajevo assassination of 1914, Germany urged Austria to attack Serbia and to do so quickly. It was her opinion that the war could be "localized," that is, that Russia would not become involved. The Germans argued further that England would not take a hand, although the German ambassador in London sent telegram after telegram to Berlin asserting that England would fight. In this instance there was excellent reason to believe that a major and dangerous general war would result, a war whose dangers were hardly justified by the provocation or opportunities presented by the Serbian crisis. The Germans did not want a general war, yet they persisted in their policy. They were prepared to fight a great war if necessary, but they hoped and expected that it would not come and were both surprised and infuriated when their opponents did not behave according to expectations.[29]

[29] For a very revealing insight into the thoughts and emotions of the German leaders, see the somewhat hysterical marginal notes made by Kaiser Wilhelm II on the report of Russia's decision to mobilize on July 30, 1914. (Max Montgelas and Walter Shücking, eds., *Outbreak of the World War:* German Documents Collected by Karl Kautsky [1924], No. 401, 348–50, translated by Carnegie Endowment for International Peace). My interpretation of the July Crisis of 1914 is based on the second volume of Luigi Albertini's *The Origins of the War of 1914,* translated and edited by I. M. Massey (Oxford, 1953), and the pertinent chapter in A. J. P. Taylor's *The Struggle for the Mastery of Europe* (Oxford, 1954), 520–531.

The Corinthians, we may be allowed to suspect, behaved in a similar fashion. They were determined to crush Corcyra, and they hoped that they could do so without Athenian interference. They had reason to believe that their hope might be ill founded, and we may be sure that the Spartans and Sicyonians pointed the danger out to them. In their anger and optimism they engaged in wishful thinking rather than prudent calculation and forced the Athenians to make a decision they would have liked to avoid.

Thucydides provides us with our only account of the Athenian deliberations, and it is most unsatisfactory. We are told that the Athenians needed two meetings of the assembly to arrive at their decision. After the first they inclined towards the Corinthian view, but on the second day they changed their minds. Even then they refused to make the offensive and defensive alliance (ξυμμαχία) that the Corcyreans requested, but agreed only to a defensive alliance (ἐπιμαχία).[30] From this brief account it is obvious that there must have been a hot debate and a significant difference of opinion. At least two sharply different attitudes must have been presented, and the situation is ideal for a typically Thucydidean pair of speeches, an antilogy to illustrate the situation in Athens most graphically. This is precisely what we will find later on, when Thucydides takes us into the Spartan assembly to hear the debate between Archidamus and Sthenelaidas on the decision for war. Thucydides himself was surely present at the debate in Athens in 433, yet he gives us no account of the speeches; he does not tell us who spoke on either side. We are not even told what position Pericles took. This is the most surprising of all the Thucydidean omissions and must be taken into account by all those who seek to penetrate the secrets of his mind. Such a goal is beyond our present purpose, but it is hard to ignore the possibility that Thucydides has deliberately ignored the factional conflict in Athens out of a conviction that it was irrelevant. In his view the war would have come in any case; the growth of Athenian power made it inevitable. We shall see that it was Pericles who advocated the alliance with Corcyra. The common view held Pericles responsible for bringing on the war. This was precisely the view Thucydides wanted to refute, and his technique was to treat the Athenian decision impersonally, as a consequence of all the Athe-

[30] 1. 44.

nians' deliberations and an inevitable response to the situation.[31] The modern historian, however, may not assume such an interpretation and must try to understand how and why the Athenians came to their decision, and who led the contending parties.

Plutarch tells us in a direct statement what we should have believed in any case, that it was Pericles who "persuaded the people to send aid" to the Corcyreans.[32] We have no reason to doubt the accuracy of his report, for it is fully confirmed by Pericles' actions from 433 to his death. The account of Thucydides proves that he fully supported the policy that finally led to war, while arguing against a policy of aggression. The decision for limited involvement with Corcyra for defensive purposes is fully Periclean, and we may be sure that Pericles argued in behalf of the treaty that was finally adopted. But what was the nature of the opposition which came so close to carrying the day? The two assemblies took place in the summer of 433. In the spring of that year the ten years of the exile of Thucydides, son of Melesias, had come to an end. He must have been in Athens for the debate. It is more than likely that his return gave new life to his scattered and disheartened faction and that he led the opposition to Pericles. Such a position is entirely consistent with his opposition to Athenian imperialism, but that opposition had long been discredited. What gave him the support to challenge Pericles so severely was the general realization that an alliance with Corcyra might ultimately bring war with Sparta. Once again the moderates on whom Pericles relied so heavily must have been attracted by the arguments of his rival. The danger to Athens must have seemed remote and problematical, her economic interests in the quarrel negligible. Why should Athens risk a great war in the interests of Corcyra?

We do not know what arguments Pericles employed to bring a

[31] F. M. Cornford (*Thucydides Mythistoricus* [London, 1907], 43) has suggested that Thucydides does not mention Pericles in the debate on the Corcyrean alliance "because the Athenians had a policy of their own, which Pericles adopted only when his hand was forced. The historian conveys the correct impression, that the policy in question was not originated by the nominal leader of the demos." He appears to have been unaware of Plutarch's direct statement that Pericles persuaded the Athenians to make the alliance (*Per.* 29. 1).

[32] *Per.* 29. 1: ἔπεισε τὸν δῆμον ἀποστεῖλαι βοήθειαν.

majority around to his view, but his rhetorical and political skill must have been taxed to the utmost. Thucydides, speaking in his own voice, tells us why the Athenians finally made the decision they did. The foremost of the reasons is that they were persuaded that a war with the Peloponnesians would come, and they wanted to be sure of the Corcyrean fleet in that event. But he also gives another reason, and some modern scholars have believed it to be primary: "The island [of Corcyra], moreover, seemed to them to be well situated for a coasting voyage to Italy and Sicily." [33] Some scholars have taken this to mean that the prospect of commercial advantage led the Athenians to accept the Corcyrean alliance. They have imagined a "Piraeus Party" of merchants and financiers with unlimited commercial and imperial ambitions who, even in 433, dreamed of adding Sicily and Italy to the Athenian Empire,[34] or a fear on the part of Athens that if Corcyra fell into Corinthian hands, the Athenians would be deprived of a vital source of grain in Italy and Sicily.[35] Their view is that Thucydides did not comprehend or suppressed the economic motives that really caused the war.

There is little point in attacking this position here at any length, for it has won few adherents and is little more than a straw man.[36] Suffice it to say that it was Pericles and not any Piraeus Party who made the vital decisions that led to war, and nobody suggests he was a member of or controlled by that party. Whatever reasons he had for his policy, they were surely not to gain commercial advantages in the west. Similarly, the argument of Grundy that Athens had to defend Corcyra from Corinth to prevent the Corinthians from cutting off an important grain supply is altogether unconvincing. He argues that Athens was not only reluctant to lose a trading interest in Sicily, but also that

Sicily was an all-important resource to her in case she were cut off at some future time from the Pontus; and her connection with that region through the narrow waters of the Hellespont and Bosporus was in the very

[33] 1. 44. 3.

[34] See Cornford, *Thucydides*, 1–51.

[35] G. B. Grundy, *Thucydides and the History of His Age*, 328–329.

[36] For a direct assault that is more effective in its negative accomplishments than in making a case for the Thucydidean interpretation, see G. Dickins, *CQ*, V (1911), 238–248.

nature of things most precarious. The question whether she should turn to the Pontus or to Sicily for her food supply had been, up to 446, a disputed one in Athenian politics. She could face the risk in the Hellespont and Bosporus so long as she had access to Sicily.[37]

There is more than a little doubt that Athens ever contemplated Sicily as an alternative to the Black Sea region as a primary source of grain. More geographic, if not geopolitical, reasons would seem to argue against such a dependency, and as we have seen, the evidence of any serious Athenian interest in western expansion is slender at best. However that may be, it is perfectly clear that such ideas were no part of Periclean policy after 445, and that, after all, is what is at issue. Pericles could face no risk whatever in the Hellespont and Bosporus, and between 440 and 435 he took every possible measure to guarantee the security of the route to the northeast. In 433, Athens had a perfectly abundant and secure source of grain and was not compelled to involve herself in the west on that account.

It is, moreover, far from clear that trade with the west required that Corcyra be in friendly hands. Merchant ships could sail directly across to Sicily from the Corinthian Gulf if necessary, but why should it be necessary? Would the Corinthians bar Athenian merchantmen from Corcyrean ports if they controlled Corcyra? There was certainly no precedent for such action and no reason to expect it. The Corcyreans had not barred Corinthians from their ports during the many years of their hostility, else we should have heard the Corinthians complain of it. Only in case of war need the Athenians fear such economic interference, and at such a time the objection would be strategic rather than commercial. The brief notice of Thucydides cited above does not, in fact, justify any economic interpretation of Athenian actions. It is better seen as a strategic consideration. In case of war, both sides would seek military, naval, and economic help from the Greeks of the west, as in fact they did. Sicily and southern Italy contained a large number of wealthy and powerful Greek states. The state controlling the route to the west would be in a very advantageous position to win their assistance for themselves and to prevent it falling into hostile hands. Thus, the reference to the convenient location is merely one of two strategic reasons for supporting Corcyra, given the assumption that war was inevitable: in the first

[37] Grundy, *Thucydides,* 328–329.

place, Corcyra had a large fleet that must not be allowed to fall under Corinthian control; secondly, Corcyra was strategically located with regard to the western Greeks.

According to Thucydides, then, the main reason why the Athenians agreed to aid Corcyra was because they believed the war with the Peloponnesians to be inevitable and wanted to gain a strategic advantage before it came. It remains for us to ask whether the Athenians held this belief. We have already seen that the affair at Corcyra did involve a vital Athenian interest: it threatened the naval supremacy of Athens. To expect the Athenians to allow the Corcyrean navy to fall into Corinthian hands is to expect more than is possible in human affairs. For Pericles to allow a major unfavorable shift in the balance of power without objection would not be statesmanship but saintliness. It would be a reckless and foolish policy, for whatever the friendly and peaceful intentions of the Corinthian government in 433, there could be no guarantee of its attitude five years, or even one year, later, by which time the balance would have irrevocably shifted.

Still, we may ask whether there was no alternative to accepting the treaty. The Athenians might have suggested an international conference, such as were common among European powers in the nineteenth and early twentieth centuries, where some compromise might have been reached. Perhaps Corinth would have been willing to guarantee the autonomy and continued neutrality of Corcyra and her navy in return for a chance to chastise her and assume the control of Epidamnus. We may well doubt whether such a solution would have been possible, given the anger of the Corinthians and their expectation of Athenian neutrality as a *quid pro quo* for their forbearance during the Samian War. In any case, the idea of such a conference is altogether out of place in fifth-century Greece, where there was no precedent for it and no professional diplomatic corps. Given the situation, there seems to have been no real alternative to an alliance with Corcyra of some kind.

If the Athenians had not made the treaty with Corcyra, it is not certain that the war with the Peloponnesians would have come, but it is fair to say that the Athenians were compelled by reasons of strategy and their own security to make that treaty. Once it was made, the likelihood of war with Corinth became much greater. The belief that war would come helped the Athenians decide to ally themselves with Corcyra and so was a self-fulfilling prophecy, for the alliance drove the states closer to war.[38] Yet even at the moment of decision, the Athenians seem to have hoped to achieve their ends without provoking a war over Corcyra.

A full defensive and offensive alliance with Corcyra while she was at war with Corinth would have violated the peace, so Athens made a defensive alliance only.[39] We know that some Athenians favored a more active policy,[40] so the Athenian policy appears to be a compromise between the war party, who wanted an offensive alliance, and the peace party, who wanted no alliance at all. Meyer suggests that Pericles, who already knew that war was inevitable, favored a full treaty with Corcyra. Under the pressure of the mass of Athenians, who still had the idea that they could choose freely, he was compelled to yield and accept a middle way in the defensive alliance, "which gave nothing away and at least avoided the appearance of a breach of the peace." [41] We may well doubt this suggestion. For one thing, it ignores the fact that at least part of the Athenian people sharply criticized Pericles for the halfheartedness of his policy of aid to the Corcyreans.[42] This shows that the "middle way" adopted by the Athenians was the policy of Pericles himself and not the unperceptive masses. Its execution, still under the leadership of Pericles, was prudent and defensive. The evidence seems to indicate that the cautious policy of defensive alliance was Pericles'. Perhaps his great difficulty in having it adopted by the Athenians may be explained by the likelihood that it fully pleased neither the party led by Thucydides nor the men around Cleon.[43]

[38] A keen insight into the way this worked is provided by Hans-Peter Stahl (*Thukydides, Die Stellung des Menschen im geschichtlichen Prozess* [Munich, 1966], 40), who says: "die den Beschluss bestimmende Überzeugung von der Unverniedbarkeit des Krieges, d.h. die intellektuelle *Vorstellung* vom weiteren Ablauf der einmal begonnenen Kausalkette, *schafft* überhaupt erst die *Voraussetzung* dafür, dass der Geschehensablauf sich in derselben Zielrichtung fortsetzt. . . ."

[39] 1. 44. 1.

[40] Plut. *Per.* 29. 3.

[41] *Forschungen,* II, 325.

[42] Plut. *Per.* 29. 3.

[43] For a similar interpretation of Pericles' policy, see De Sanctis, *Pericle,* 230–231.

The way in which the Athenians chose to fulfill their obligation to Corcyra shows clearly that Pericles had not yet despaired of avoiding a war. On or shortly after the thirteenth day of the first prytany of 433/2, probably in July, he sent a squadron of ten ships to Corcyra under the command of Lacedaemonius, son of Cimon, Diotimus, son of Strombichus, and Proteas, son of Spicles.[44] The choice of generals was very important, for their mission was delicate and the execution of their instructions would require experience, judgment, and cool heads. Diotimus and Proteas obviously met these requirements, for both continued to play an important part in Athenian affairs.[45] But the choice of Lacedaemonius was the shrewdest and most typically Periclean stroke. To be sure, he was an experienced soldier,[46] but it was as the son of Cimon that he was most valuable. By employing Lacedaemonius in this controversial mission, Pericles was cleverly striking a devastating blow against his conservative political opponents. If Thucydides, son of Melesias, was to rebuild his opposition party, he must find his support among old Cimonians who would rally to his apparently Cimonian policy of peace with the Peloponnesians. But here was Lacedaemonius, the son of Cimon, taking the lead in executing the policy of Pericles. It was a graphic assertion that the Cimonian policy and the Periclean were one and the same. As Cimon had carried his spurs up to the Acropolis and supported the policy of Themistocles in the moment of peril to the fatherland before Salamis, so did his son now take the lead in carrying out the policy that the safety of Athens required. The gesture could not have failed to have a destructive effect on the political fortunes of the son of Melesias.

It is true that the opposition took every opportunity to attack

[44] 1. 45. 1; the date is fixed precisely by a decree recording the money paid for the expedition, *IG*, I², 295 = Tod, 55. See Meritt, *Athenian Financial Documents*, 68–71.

[45] Diotimus appears to have been sent to help the Neapolitans, probably during the same generalship and after the Battle of Sybota (see above, pp. 000 and 000). He was also the head of an Athenian delegation to Susa (Strabo 1. 3. 1, p. 47), which may have been the one Aristophanes laughed at in the *Acharnians* (61ff). Proteas was sufficiently important to be re-elected to the strategia for the following year (2. 32. 2 and *IG*, I², 296, 1. 31).

[46] He had been hipparch in about 446 (*IG*, I², 400).

Pericles' motives in appointing Lacedaemonius. He sent Lacedaemonius with only ten ships, they said, to insult him. He was jealous of him, as of all the sons of Cimon, and gave him only a few ships and sent him out "against his will." He knew that the house of Cimon was very friendly to Sparta, and did this so that "if he should accomplish no great or outstanding deed, he might be blamed for his Laconism." [47] These are the charges of an outwitted and outraged faction and are not, of course, to be credited. Yet their suggestion that the assignment was given to Lacedaemonius out of political calculation is quite right.

In addition to embarrassing his opponents, Pericles may have had another reason for selecting the son of Cimon and a friend of Sparta to lead the squadron at Corcyra. The generals were ordered not to fight with the Corinthians unless they sailed against Corcyra itself and were about to land on some part of its territory. If that should happen, the Athenians were to prevent the landing by force. "These orders were given in order not to break the treaty." [48] These were very difficult instructions to carry out. How, in the midst of a naval battle, can a man be absolutely certain of the intentions of the participants? The Corinthians might approach Corcyra as part of a tactical maneuver, with no intention of landing, but this might not be clear until the last moment. By then it might be too late to prevent a landing if that were the true Corinthian intention. An Athenian general might very well have to attack the Corinthian fleet. This could bring on a war with Corinth, which might soon bring in Sparta. If that should happen, it would be best that the crucial decision be made by a man well known to be a friend of the Spartans.

The orders themselves give evidence of a policy that was not halfhearted but shrewdly cautious. The dispatch of ten Athenian ships was less a military maneuver than a diplomatic one. By sending that small squadron, Athens was not declaring war but raising its bid in the diplomatic game. There was still time, the Athenians indicated, to avoid a great war if the Corinthians would refrain from the conquest of Corcyra and the seizure of her fleet. The presence of an Athenian force was proof that Athens was serious in its determination to prevent a shift in the balance of power, but its small size

[47] Plut. *Per.* 29. 2–3.

[48] 1. 45. 3.

showed that the Athenians had no wish to take advantage of the situation to destroy or diminish Corinthian power. At the same time, Pericles seems to have believed that it might be possible for the Athenian ships to stand aside throughout the entire battle and avoid involvement. It was not, after all, clear in advance that Corinth would win a sea battle with Corcyra. The two fleets were well matched, and it was altogether possible that the Corinthians would lose as they had at Leucimne. An even better result from the Athenian point of view was also possible. The two fleets might do great damage to one another, the Corinthians would be unable to take Corcyra, and the battle might end in a stalemate in which the power of both the second and third greatest Greek naval states would be shattered. Thucydides tells us that the Athenians had just such a thought in mind when they made the purely defensive alliance with Corcyra. They hoped "to wear the two sides out as much as possible against each other so that they might find Corinth and the other naval powers weaker in case it should be necessary to go to war with them." [49]

The strategy of Pericles, therefore, had three levels. The first was essentially diplomatic, in which a controlled show of force would avoid a technical breach of the Thirty Years' Peace and might even avoid war altogether. The second was optimistically strategic, in which the Athenians hoped to achieve the destruction of both great naval powers at no cost to themselves. The last was also strategic and, as it turned out, more realistic. When this level was reached, the Athenians would intervene to prevent the capture of Corcyra and its fleet even if that brought war with Corinth.

After the Athenian squadron had arrived at Corcyra, the Corinthians set sail with a fleet of one hundred and fifty ships. Of these, ninety were Corinthian, and the rest came from Elis, Megara, Leucas, Ambracia, and Anactorium.[50] Each contingent was commanded by its own general, so that there can be no question of volunteers who accompanied the expedition as private citizens. They were official representatives of their own states, presumably acting under the terms of an alliance with Corinth, and any action in which they became involved would involve their governments as well. All

[49] 1. 44. 2.
[50] 1. 46. 1.

the allied states except for Megara and Elis were Corinthian colonies. The presence of Megara is evidence of her close cooperation with Corinth since the restoration of the Megarian oligarchy during the First Peloponnesian War. Perhaps Elis was present to avenge the damage the Corcyreans had done to her port after Leucimne.

It is interesting to note, however, that Epidaurus, Hermione, Troezen, and Cephallenia did not join with Corinth as they had in the earlier battle, and Thebes and Phlius seem not to have contributed money. The situation in 433 was very different from what it had been two years earlier. There was now a real chance that a war with Athens might result from this campaign. There is every reason to believe, moreover, that the supporters of peace still ruled at Sparta and strongly disapproved of the Corinthian adventure. It is very likely, as Gomme suggests, that the Spartans applied some pressure on their more susceptible allies to keep them home.[51]

The Corinthians and their allies gathered at Leucas and then sailed northwards, setting up a base at Cheimerium on the mainland across from Corcyra. When the Corcyreans learned what was happening, they established their base on one of the group of islands called Sybota which gave a name to the battle which ensued. The Corcyrean naval force consisted of one hundred and ten of their own ships and ten from Athens. In addition, they placed their infantry, reinforced by one thousand hoplites from Zacynthus, at the Leucimne promontory. Against these the Corinthians could muster an army of barbarians from the mainland, where Corinth had always been influential.[52] When the Corinthians sailed out to offer battle, they placed their own ships on the left wing and found themselves opposite the Athenians, who were on the right wing of the Corcyrean line. The battle tactics employed made the difficult decisions required of the Athenian generals even more uncertain. Instead of

[51] Gomme, *Hist. Comm.*, I, 178.

[52] 1. 47. 1–3. It is difficult to explain the presence of the Zacynthians. B. Schmidt (*Die Insel Zakynthos,* cited by Classen-Steup, I, 148) suggests that the two islands had been friendly in the past, but if such friendship existed it did not reach the point of a military alliance (see Thuc. 1. 31. 2.). Classen is probably right in suggesting that the alliance was as new as the one just made in Athens, and Gomme (*Hist. Comm.*, I, 183) may be right in connecting the Zacynthian action with the island's friendship for Athens (Thuc. 2. 7. 3 and 2. 9. 4).

employing the elegant and skillful maneuvers and ramming tactics that the Athenians had perfected, they fought in the old clumsy way. The ships, their decks loaded with hoplites and archers, came together and clung to one another. Instead of a naval battle, it became a hoplite encounter fought on stationary ships; skill gave way to brute strength. "Everywhere there was uproar and confusion." [53]

When the Athenians saw that the Corcyreans were in difficulty, they came up to assist but avoided fighting, in strict obedience to their instructions. The Corcyreans were successful on the left wing, but they made the mistake of pursuing the enemy with too much zeal. They detached twenty ships from the line to pursue the routed ships and plunder the Corinthian camp. The Corinthians took advantage of the weakness thus created to press the right wing of the Corcyrean line. This compelled the Athenians, who were stationed at the vital spot, to make the fateful decision, and Thucydides describes with great skill the stages by which they reached it.

When the Athenians saw the Corcyreans pressed, they began to help them without reservation. At first they held back from making an actual attack on an enemy ship, but when it became plain that a rout was taking place and that the Corinthians were in hot pursuit, then at last each man took part in the work and fine distinctions were no longer made; the situation had devoloped to the point where the Corinthians and Athenians had necessarily to fight one another.[54]

The number of ships engaged in the battle was so large and the area it covered so great that confusion reigned. Disabled ships littered the sea, and the survivors sometimes killed their own men swimming in the sea, for they could not tell who had won in each quarter of the battle or which ships had been sunk. Finally, after driving the Corcyreans to the shore, the Corinthians cleared the sea, picked up their dead, and regrouped on the mainland. Then they came forward again to finish the job.

The Corcyreans, now reinforced by an Athenian contingent ready to fight, likewise reorganized their forces and prepared to defend their island from invasion. The scene that followed would be too dramatic to believe if it had been told by Herodotus or Plutarch,

[53] 1. 49. 4.
[54] 1. 49. 7.

but since we have it from the most sober and austere of historians, we cannot doubt its historicity. The Corcyreans literally had their backs to the wall, and it is plain that total defeat and annihilation were imminent. The Corinthians had already sounded the signal to attack, when suddenly they began to back water. No doubt the Corcyreans and Athenians were at a loss to understand what was happening, but soon the explanation was plain enough. On the horizon there appeared twenty Athenian triremes that had been sent as reinforcements.

An inscription recording the payment made to the generals leading the relief force tells us that it was sent out twenty-three days after the first ten ships sailed.[55] Thucydides says that these additional ships were sent because the Athenians feared that the original ten would be too few to help the Corcyreans, who were likely to be defeated,[56] but we should like to know what made them alter their first decision. Plutarch provides us with the answer: his political opponents criticized Pericles sharply on the ground that "he had provided little help for the Corcyreans by sending ten ships, but a great pretext for complaint by their enemies." It was for this reason that he later sent the additional twenty ships.[57] Here is evidence that at home as well as on the seas it was increasingly difficult to limit the Athenian involvement, once the original commitment had been made.

The effect of the Athenian reinforcement was decisive. The Corinthians assumed that the twenty were merely the precursors of a great Athenian fleet and began to withdraw. As night was rapidly approaching, both sides broke off the battle and retired to their respective camps. By the dawn of the next day the military situation had changed radically. The Corcyreans, who had been on the verge of annihilation, were now supported by thirty undamaged Athenian ships. This time it was they who sailed out and offered battle to the Corinthians. The Corinthians, who had been within sight of victory the previous afternoon, put out to sea in a defensive formation but refused to take the bait. They now sought to avoid a battle, for not only did they fear the Athenians whom they saw before them, but

[55] *IG*, I^2, 295 = Tod, 55. See also J. Johnson, *AJA*, XXXIII (1929), 398–400 and Meritt, *Athenian Financial Documents*, 68–71.

[56] 1. 50. 5.

[57] *Per.* 29. 3.

they could not be certain that more Athenians might not be on the way. They feared that the previous day's skirmish might be seen by the Athenians as a *casus belli* and an excuse to destroy the Corinthian fleet before it could get home.[58] But even at this late date both sides hoped to avoid an irrevocable conflict.

The Corinthians sent some men to parley with the Athenians. They did not carry a herald's wand, the equivalent of a flag of truce, for to do so would be an admission that a state of war existed between Corinth and Athens, something both sides wished to deny. They reproached the Athenians with doing wrong, breaking the treaty, and beginning a war by preventing the Corinthians from punishing their enemies. "If you intend," they said, "to prevent us from sailing to Corcyra or anywhere else we like, and in this way you break the treaty, first seize us and treat us as enemies." The Corcyreans who heard this speech immediately roared their approval of the suggestion and urged the Athenians to kill them, but they were disappointed. Instead, the Athenians returned a very careful answer in perfect accord with their strict orders and limited objectives:

> We are not beginning a war, O Peloponnesians, nor are we breaking the treaty, but we have come to bring help to our Corcyrean allies. If you want to sail anywhere else we will not hinder you; but if you mean to sail against Corcyra or some part of her territory, we will not permit it, insofar as it is in our power.[59]

It is possible to believe that the Corinthians acted as they did out of fear that the Athenians would destroy their fleet and that they already regarded war with Athens as inevitable. The Athenian generals were still under orders, although the events of the previous day had made them obsolete. They knew, for the newly arrived generals could tell them, that no additional ships were underway and that the arrival of reinforcements did not represent a change in policy. If Pericles knew that Corinthians and Athenians had fought one another, if he had heard the Corinthian heralds announce officially that they regarded the Athenian defense of Corcyra as a breach of the peace and an act of war, he would have known that the war

[58] 1. 52.
[59] 1. 53. 4.

could no longer be avoided. But he was far away in Athens. As a result, the Athenian generals had no choice but to allow the Corinthians to sail away.

Each side set up a trophy claiming victory at the Battle of Sybota, evidence of how indecisive it had been tactically, thanks to the Athenian intervention. From the strategic point of view, however, it was clearly a victory for Corcyra, for it had been the intention of Corinth to destroy the Corcyrean fleet and seize the island, and that they had altogether failed to do. Far from giving up the project, the Corinthians wasted no time in preparing for the next round as they sailed home. They seized Anactorium by treachery and settled it with Corinthian colonists. Of the many Corcyreans they had captured in battle, the Corinthians sold eight hundred as slaves. But two hundred and fifty, leading men in Corcyra, they held in custody and treated well. It was their hope that the captives might return to Corcyra in the future and bring it over to Corinth by treachery also. From all this it became perfectly clear that the Corinthians had no intention of giving up the war with Corcyra, which must unavoidably cause them to fight Athens. As Thucydides says, the Battle of Sybota was "the first ground which the Corinthians had for war with the Athenians, because they had fought on the side of the Corcyreans in a naval battle while still under a treaty with Corinth." [60]

[60] 1. 55. 2.

15. *Megara*

After the news of Sybota and the Corinthian seizure of Anactorium reached Athens, the chances of conflict were greatly increased, and the Athenians were compelled to take steps in case war should come. The policy of Pericles was to make Athens ready for war with Corinth but to avoid any step that might involve Sparta or make Athens guilty of a technical breach of the peace.

Perhaps Athens' most vital resource in a war was money, so Pericles took steps to see that the Athenian treasury would be full if and when war came. We have the stone containing the inscription of two decrees offered on the same day by Callias, the son of Calliades, and passed by the Athenian assembly. Both deal with the reorganization of Athenian public finance. The first provides that since three thousand talents have been paid to Athena on the Acropolis, the debts owed to the other gods should now be repaid. The fund so accumulated should be administered by a new board of treasurers, like those of the treasurers of Athena, and kept likewise on the Acropolis. Any surplus should be used for dockyards and walls. The second decree provides that certain golden statues of Nike and the gateway to the Acropolis, the Propylaea, were to be completed, but after that, no sum exceeding ten thousand drachmas should be spent without a previous special vote of sanction in the assembly.[1] The Athenians were battening down the hatches and preparing for trouble. It is clear that this was merely a prudent precautionary measure and not

[1] I follow the text in *ATL*, II, 46–47 (D1 and D2) where a useful bibliography may also be found.

the product of panic, for major public works still under way were to be completed, but no important new projects would be allowed to drain the reserves without a special vote. At the same time, the reserve funds were collected under a unified jurisdiction and taken up to the safest place in the city, "where they would be safe from invading Peloponnesians and readily available if the state needed to use them." [2]

These decrees were passed in 434/3, at least some months before the Athenian clash with Corinth, even before the Athenians accepted the alliance with Corcyra.[3] It is certainly possible that even before the summer of 433, Pericles "already saw a war coming from the Peloponnese," [4] but such an assumption is not necessary. A prudent statesman, even one who hoped and expected to keep the peace, would want to take such precautions.

After the Battle of Sybota, however, prudence demanded more decisive measures. One of these measures was the expedition of Phormio to Acarnania. Amphilochian Argos was an early Greek settlement in barbarian territory on the east coast of the Ambracian Gulf. At some point in their history the Amphilochian Argives were hard-pressed, called upon their Ambracian neighbors to join them as fellow citizens (ξύνοικοι), and a union resulted.[5] It must have been sometime in 433 or a little earlier that the Ambraciots, colonists of Corinth, took advantage of the presence of a powerful Corinthian military and naval force in the region to expel the original Argives and seize the city for themselves.[6] The Argives, however, turned to their Acarnanian neighbors for protection, and together they did

[2] J. B. Bury, *A History of Greece,* third edition, revised by Russell Meiggs (London, 1952), 396A.

[3] For the date of the decrees, see *ATL,* III, 326ff. and Wade-Gery and Meritt, *Hesperia,* XXVI (1957), 163ff., especially 184–187. I am particularly grateful to Professor Meritt for making it clear to me why the 434/3 date is to be accepted.

[4] The quotation is one of the chronologically vague reports given by Plutarch (*Per.* 8). Meyer (*Forschungen,* II, 324) suggests that the words were spoken some time in 435 and 434, "Bald nach dem Scheitern der Friedensvermittlung, während der Rüstungen der Korinther. . . ."

[5] 2. 68. 2–5.

[6] For a discussion of the date of this event and the expedition of Phormio that resulted, see Appendix G, pp. 384–385.

what the Corcyreans had done, turning to Athens for help. The Athenians responded by sending Phormio with thirty ships. From the Athenian point of view the expedition was a total success. The Athenians and their allies took Argos by storm and reduced the Ambracians to slavery. The Amphilochian Argives and Acarnanians resettled the city. The Acarnanians became firm allies of the Athenians, who had established a base from which they could trouble the Corinthians in their own sphere of influence.[7] All this probably took place in the spring of 432 and was another measure to give Athens the most advantageous position possible when war came.[8]

It was probably about the same time that Diotimus took a fleet to answer the appeal of Naples.[9] We do not know what he accomplished; it could not have been much. Probably the idea was to win allies from southern Italy for the coming war, or, at any rate, to get the lay of the land and remind the Italians of Athenian power and influence, absent from the region for almost fifteen years.

There can be no doubt that a similar Athenian action took place in the year 433/2 after the Athenian expedition had sailed for Corcyra.[10] This was the acceptance of requests made by ambassadors

[7] 2. 68. 6–9.

[8] I adopt the date suggested by Wade-Gery (*Essays,* 253–4 and n. 5 on 253). I am convinced that a date between 445 and 443 is ruled out by the failure of the Corinthians to complain about the enslavement of Corinthian colonists by Athenians. If this had happened since the Thirty Years' Peace, the Corinthians could not have failed to mention it in their speech at Athens. A date in the 450's is possible, but less likely than one in the period suggested here. Wade-Gery's argument is very persuasive: "I am convinced that Phormio made it [the expedition] in the spring of 432, and that the previous seizure of Argos (Thuc. 2. 68. 6) is parallel to the seizure of Anactorion (1. 55. 1), two attempts by Korinth, on the morrow of Sybota, to secure at least the Ambrakiot Gulf" (253, n. 5). The main argument, far from powerful, against such a date is the silence of Thucydides. To quote Wade-Gery again: "Thucydides' narrative of near-western events is *not* continuous after the battle of Sybota; and Phormion had the time for such action before he was sent to Potidaia."

[9] See Appendix G, pp. 384–385.

[10] Dittenberger (*SIG* [4th ed.; 1960], No. 70, 89) points out that since the expedition to Corcyra was sent out in the first prytany of 433/2, when Aiantis held the prytany, and the treaties with Rhegium and Leontini were renewed during the prytany of Acamantis, "Intelligimus igitur, tum demum, cum iam Atheniensium classis Corcyram missa esset, Leontinorum et

from Rhegium and Leontini to renew their old treaties with Athens.[11] The likelihood is that the Sicilians came to Athens after they heard of the Battle of Sybota. They knew that the Athenians would have to abandon their policy of hands off the west and probably hoped to get the advantage over their local enemies by using the immense power and prestige of Athens in their own behalf. The Athenians accepted because there was no longer any need to avoid offending Corinth and because they hoped to win friends in Sicily to help in the coming war.[12]

These measures were relatively insignificant compared with two steps taken by Athens in the months following the Battle of Sybota. The first of these, the extraordinary demands made on Potidaea, we will consider in the next chapter. At about the same time, however, as these demands, the Athenians passed a decree barring the Megarians from the ports of the Athenian Empire and the market of Athens.[13] In spite of the fact that Thucydides did not treat it as an important factor in bringing on the war, and does not even include it among the *aitiai* that preceded it, the majority of ancient opinion regarded it as the main cause of the war. Most modern opinion does not go so far, but it is generally agreed that the Megarian Decree played a very significant role in the events leading to the war. For this reason it is important to try to resolve the many questions surrounding the decree. We are not certain of its precise contents, of whether there was only one decree, of when it was passed, of its purpose, or of why Thucydides treats it as casually as he does.

Thucydides reports only one decree, barring the Megarians from the ports of the empire and the market of Athens. But some scholars have thought his version represents in a single decree measures im-

Reginorum legatos Athenas venisse." The ambassadors, of course, may have come as early as September 433 or as late as July 432, but in any case, their arrival must be placed after Sybota.

[11] *IG*, I [2], 51 and 52 = Tod 57 and 58. For the date of the original treaties, see above, p. 155, n. 3.

[12] *ATL*, III, 320 and n. 84.

[13] The sources for the Megarian Decree are Thuc. 1. 67. 4; 1. 139. 1–2; Aristoph. *Acharnians*, 515ff. with scholia to 527 and 532; Aristoph. *Peace* 603 ff. with scholia to 246, 605 and 609; Andocides 3. 8; Diod. 12. 39. 4; Plut. *Per.* 29ff.; Aristodemus 16 = *FGrH*, IIA, No. 104.

posed in two steps, or at any rate gradually.[14] Their arguments derive from two rather enigmatic pieces of information. The first comes from the *Acharnians* of Aristophanes and is typically difficult to interpret. Dicaepolis is compelled to try to justify the Spartan action in going to war against Athens. He, too, like the angry Acharnians, hates the Spartans. His vines, too, they have cut down:

> But come, for only friends are here, why do we blame the Laconians? Some of our men (I do not say the state, mind you, I do not say the state), some vice-ridden wretches, men of no honor, false men, not even real citizens, kept denouncing Megara's little coats; and if anyone ever saw a cucumber, a hare, a suckling pig, a clove of garlic, or a lump of salt, all were denounced as Megarian and confiscated.[15]

Next he tells of the theft by some drunken Athenians of a Megarian woman and the counter-theft by the Megarians of three prostitutes from the house of Aspasia. Pericles, in his fury,

> Enacted laws which sounded like drinking songs, "That the Megarians must leave our land, our market, our sea and our continent." Then, when the Megarians were slowly starving, they begged the Spartans to get the law of the three harlots withdrawn. We refused, though they asked us often. And from that came the clash of shields.[16]

Aristophanes appears to be describing two stages of Athenian economic action against Megara, the first in which imports from Megara seem to be forbidden, the second in which Aristophanes parodies the fuller embargo described by Thucydides. It would be rash, however, to accept his evidence at face value. If we take it seriously, we must be troubled by his assertion that the state had nothing to do with the earlier denunciations, but only private informers. This would be incompatible with a theory of two official decrees. If we regard his remarks about the state as ironical, we open a Pandora's

[14] Busolt (*GG*, III: 2, 810–811) believes that a ban on the importation of Megarian goods into Attica was enacted some time before the summer of 433, that is, before the treaty with Corcyra. Later, in the winter of 433/2, he believes that the full decree cited above was passed (p. 814). A similar, but not identical, view is held by F. A. Lepper (*JHS*, LXXXII [1962], 25–55, especially 51–55). He suggests that the decree cited by Thucydides may have been a late step in a gradual "cold war" that Athens had been waging against Megara for some years.

[15] 515–522.

[16] 532–539.

box of inscrutable ironies and even of comic inventions. The evidence of Aristophanes can not be used to establish the reality of an earlier and milder decree.

The second item comes from the Corinthian speech at Athens in 433, which we have already examined. One of the points on which the Corinthians insist is that war is not yet inevitable. The Athenians, they say, should not turn a possibility of war into a certainty by joining Corcyra and winning the hostility of Corinth. "Instead, it would be prudent to remove the suspicion that formerly existed on account of the Megarians." [17] Some scholars have taken this to be a reference to an earlier Megarian decree,[18] but this is quite unjustified. The force of the word *proteron* is clearly to show that "whatever the suspicion was, the occasion for it had passed away." [19] The reference of the Corinthians is to the suspicion they had formed of Athenian aggressiveness from the aid Athens had given Megara in the First Peloponnesian War, the chief cause of Corinth's "bitter hatred" for Athens.[20] Their suggestion is that instead of confirming Corinthian suspicions by joining with Corcyra, another enemy of Corinth, they should wipe away the memory of an earlier affront to Corinthian interests, the aid to Megara. The statement, therefore, tells us nothing about any Athenian pressure on Megara before the decree described by Thucydides. Neither Aristophanes nor Thucydides provides sufficient evidence to make us believe that the Athenians took any economic measures against Megara before the passage of the decree barring Megarian commerce from Athens and her empire.[21]

[17] 1. 42. 2. . . . τῆς δὲ ὑπαρχούσης πρότερον διὰ Μεγαρέας ὑποψίας σῶφρον ὑφελεῖν μᾶλλον.

[18] E.g., Classen, 140; Busolt, *GG,* III: 2, 811–812.

[19] Brunt, *AJP,* LXXII (1951), 271, n. 9. Lepper (*JHS,* LXXXII [1962], 54) suggests an alternative interpretation of the passage: "ὑπαρχούσης πρότερον need not mean, as Brunt thought, 'which existed formerly (and is now over)'; it could (though certainly not so easily) mean 'which was in existence earlier (before the start of the Kerkyra affair) and still exists'. . . ." Even Lepper does not insist that this interpretation is preferable to the more obvious one, arguing merely that it cannot be altogether rejected. To me, Brunt's interpretation seems the only one possible.

[20] Thuc. 1. 103. 4.

[21] For similar arguments, with which I concur, see Adcock, *CAH,* V, 476–9.

The date of that decree has been the source of some controversy. Almost all scholars have placed it somewhere between the Battle of Sybota in late 433 and the meeting of the Spartan alliance to hear complaints against Athens in the summer of 432.[22] The complaints of the Megarians to Sparta at the assembly in the summer of 432 is a firm *terminus ante quem,* and the vast majority of scholars has regarded the Battle of Sybota as a satisfactory earlier terminus, but not everyone has been convinced. Steup and Schwartz, on the basis of an erroneous interpretation of the passage in the Corinthian speech discussed above, believed that the decree was already in effect before 433.[23] Brunt, however, who interprets the passage correctly, has put forward a more powerful challenge to the traditional view. In his opinion, we may infer that "the decree was not passed in 433 or 432, but some time earlier, that it was not classed by Thucydides even among the αἰτίαι of the war simply because it was long antecedent to the war and because the long acquiescence of Sparta and her allies in its existence proved that it did not even occasion the war." [24]

His main reason for rejecting the usual date rests on the silence of Thucydides. If the Athenians had chosen the delicate period between 433 and 432 to make such a gesture as the decree implied, he argues, Thucydides could not have ignored it. We have already seen how dangerous it is to base a thesis on the often inexplicable omissions of Thucydides. We must grant, however, that this silence is particularly surprising and calls for explanation. There are many

[22] Nissen (*Historische Zeitschrift,* N.F., XXVII [1889], 409) places it in August or September 432, one or two months before the assembly at Sparta; Busolt (*GG,* III: 2, 814 and n. 4) puts it in the winter of 433/2. On page 811, n. 1, he gives a valuable and thorough summary of opinion up to his time. Bury (*History of Greece,* 394) chooses the autumn of 432; Beloch (*GG* ², II: 1, 293, n. 1) puts it shortly before the Spartan assembly. Meyer (*Forschungen,* II, 307) puts it in the spring of 432, after the beginning of the siege of Potidea. Adcock (*CAH,* V, 477) puts it in the summer of 432, immediately after the departure of the Athenian expedition to besiege Potidea. Glotz and Cohen (*HG,* 618–619) puts it about the same time, as does Bengston, (*GG,* 219). Hammond (*History of Greece,* 320) puts the decree before the affair at Potidea.

[23] Classen, I, 140; Eduard Schwartz, *Das Geschichtswerk des Thukydides,* reprinted from 1929 edition (Hildesheim, 1960), 123, n. 2.

[24] *AJP,* LXXII (1951), 271.

possible explanations for it, one of which we will offer later on. Brunt's answer is by no means the only one possible, and as we shall see, there are serious objections to it. He seeks to bolster it by the analogy of the complaints made by Aegina.

At the meeting of Sparta's allies in the summer of 432, the Aeginetans complained that "they were not autonomous as they should be according to the treaty." [25] The restoration of Aeginetan autonomy became one of the Spartan demands on Athens, along with the demand for the raising of the siege of Potidea and the repeal of the Megarian Decree.[26] Brunt assumes that Aegina had lost her autonomy in 457, that she did not regain it by the peace of 446/5, and still did not have it by 432. "Sparta had thus long given *de facto* recognition to Athens' control of the government of Aegina but that did not prevent her in 432 from demanding the restoration of Aegina's autonomy." By analogy, Sparta might have allowed the Megarian Decree to stand for some time and then suddenly decided to deliver an ultimatum in 432.[27]

The analogy is not a bad one, but we may doubt whether it serves its intended purpose. We have no reason to believe that anyone regarded Aegina as having lost her autonomy in 457. To be sure, she lost her walls and ships and agreed to pay tribute, but this need not mean that she was no longer autonomous. As Brunt himself has pointed out, the term autonomy is far from precise, and we cannot know just what it meant to a particular city at any particular time. The point is that the Thirty Years' Peace seems to have made no change in the status of Aegina, yet it regarded her as autonomous, even though she had been stripped of walls and fleet over a decade earlier and forced to pay tribute. In a polemical addendum to his article Brunt attacks the assumption made by the ATL that the Thirty Years' Peace provided both that Aegina should be autonomous and pay tribute. He suggests that it may merely have called Aegina autonomous and listed her as an ally of Athens, saying nothing about tribute. Each side would then have interpreted the situation differently, the Athenians claiming the right to collect tribute, the Aeginetans paying under protest, the Spartans ignoring the situ-

[25] 1. 67. 2.

[26] 1. 140. 3.

[27] Brunt, *op. cit.,* 272.

ation until 432. This is surely a forced interpretation. It is better to accept the view of ATL that the tribute payments, which began at least as early as 454/3, were never interrupted and never questioned. Thus, if the Aeginetans in 432 claimed that the Athenians were interfering with their autonomy, the likelihood is that the interference was recent. We may well believe that it was one of the series of steps that followed the Battle of Sybota and aimed at preparing Athens and her empire in case a general war should break out.

Unfortunately, Thucydides typically tells us nothing about the nature of the Aeginetan complaint, its source, justification, or even its precise time of origin. The suggestion of the ATL is, of course, not certain, but it is at least plausible. "Possibly Athens installed a garrison; strategic control of Aegina was vital in case of war." [28] Such an action is at least consistent with the Athenian expedition to Potidaea, which is firmly dated to the same year, and with the other security measures we have attempted to date to the period after Sybota. If it is proper to associate the complaints of the Aeginetans with those of the Megarians, and it may well be, then the Aeginetan

[28] The authors of *ATL* also speculate that the fact that Aegina paid only nine of the fourteen talents in the spring of 432 instead of her former thirty may have been the cause of the Athenian action. Brunt is quite right to point out that the gaps in the tribute lists make it less than certain that Aegina was still expected to pay thirty talents after 440/39 or that the low payments must mean that Aegina was in default. H. B. Mattingly (*Historia,* XVI, [1967], 105) has tried to connect the inscription *IG,* I², 18 with Athenian measures taken against Aegina at this time. The inscription appears to record Athenian regulations for Aegina, but it is very fragmentary and cannot be dated on the basis of internal evidence. Orthodox epigraphers place it somewhere between 457 and 445 B.C. Mattingly, in accordance with his general revision of the dates of Athenian inscriptions, thinks a date in the late 430's possible and suggests that the inscription belongs to the year 432, soon after the Megarian Decree: "I would suggest that assurances were given to the Aeginetan envoys about Athenian intentions. The blockade was not directed against Aegina, but was designed solely to damage Megara. Athens was anxious to maintain the Thirty Years' Peace and to deal with Aegina on the basis of the legal agreements between the two cities (συμβολαί). But this depended upon Aegina's refraining from behavior or attitudes prejudicial to Athenian interests. If Aegina were guilty of anything of the sort, Athens would not hesitate to use its fleet against the island" (pp. 4–5). This is an ingenious reconstruction of a puzzling fragment, but the evidence appears too slim to support so much weight. My own view is that the Athenian action, whatever it was, was motivated by strategic considerations, not financial ones.

case appears to strengthen the traditional dating of the Megarian Decree.

It is further true that although no reliable ancient source explicitly dates the decree, all, even Thucydides, speak of it only in close connection with the outbreak of the war. If it had existed for some time, we might expect to learn that fact explicitly from one of the many ancient authors who deal with the decree. The argument from silence can cut both ways. There is one final argument for the traditional date which is very persuasive. When the Megarians complain to Sparta about the Athenian embargo, they have many other complaints (ἕτερα οὐκ ὀλίγα διάφορα), but the only one regarded as a breach of the peace (παρὰ τὰς σπονδάς) is the Megarian Decree. It is hard to deny the force of Adcock's assertion: "If it was regarded as a breach of the Thirty Years' Peace, the Megarians must have challenged it immediately upon its publication, and we may assume that it was passed immediately before the Megarian complaint."[29] The vast majority of scholars over a century of study have fixed on the period between Sybota and the summer of 432 for the issuing of the Megarian Decree. To be sure, arguments should be weighed and not counted, but both weight and numbers lead to an affirmation of the traditional view.

The commercial embargo against Megara, then, was enacted in 433/2. But Plutarch reports yet another Megarian decree, which requires our attention. First he tells of the measure we have already discussed. Then he describes the attempts of the Spartans to get Pericles to rescind the decree. Pericles refused, but according to Plutarch, he was sufficiently concerned to try to justify it. He proposed a decree ordering a herald to go to Megara and to Sparta to make plain that the embargo was imposed because the Megarians had worked sacred land. Anthemocritus was chosen herald and went out with the "reasonable and humane" justification of Athenian policy, but he never completed his task. He was killed, so it seems, through the agency of the Megarians. So much for sweet reasonableness. Now Charinus proposed another decree concerning the Megarians with the following provisions: Athens should be the enemy of Megara without treaty or negotiation; any Megarian found on Athe-

[29] *CAH,* V, 477.

nian soil should be put to death; the generals are to include in their annual oath the promise to invade Megara twice a year; Anthemocritus is to be buried near the Dipylon Gate.[30]

The story looks suspiciously aetiological, as though it were an attempt to explain the semiannual invasions of Megara that the Athenians in fact launched during the early years of the Archidamian War. Yet Plutarch appears to be citing records of real decrees, perhaps the collection of Craterus.[31] We have seen, moreover, that it is a mistake merely to dismiss Plutarch when he tells us something omitted by Thucydides. It is, of course, impossible that the Athenians could have ordered any invasion of Megara, not to speak of two a year, before war had been declared, and this has led some scholars who accept the fact of the decree to place it after the attack on Plataea which opened the war.[32] It is also possible that Plutarch or his source is misguided or confused.[33] A further possibility is that Pericles did formulate an explanatory decree, a herald was sent and murdered, Charinus proposed a harsh decree, though certainly not containing all the provisions reported, but the decree failed of passage. Our investigation shows that there was certainly no Megarian Decree except for the commercial embargo proposed by Pericles before the outbreak of war, and probably none afterwards.

We are now free to consider why Pericles proposed a decree sometime between the fall of 433 and the summer of 432 that barred the Megarians from the market of Athens and the ports of her empire. Among the first to question Thucydides' slight estimation of the importance of the Megarian Decree were the economic determinists.

30 Plut. *Per.* 30.

31 W. R. Connor, *AJP*, LXXXIII (1962), 226.

32 E.g., Busolt, *GG*, III: 2, 814, n. 4; Beloch (*GG* 2, II: 1, 293, n. 1) accepts the same date for the Charinus Decree, but altogether rejects the murder of Anthemocritus as having anything to do with it.

33 L. Holzapfel (*Untersuchungen über die Darstellung der griechischen Geschichte* [Leipzig, 1879], 176–86) argued that the Charinus Decree was spurious, the result of contamination of the real decree by some references in Aristophanes as well as an attempt to explain the semiannual invasions. Connor (*loc. cit.*) has given the argument a new twist by trying to show that Plutarch confused events of the fourth century with the ones we are considering here. His argument is far better supported than Holzapfel's, but as he himself recognizes, it is not conclusive.

Cornford believed that it was an act of economic imperialism on the part of Athens, a step in the western policy that culminated in the Sicilian expedition. Since it is clear that Pericles opposed such a policy, Cornford supposes that he was forced to adopt it because of "thunder on the left" from the Piraeus party headed by someone like Cleon.[34] Among the many flaws in this argument, the most telling is the assumption that Pericles yielded to pressure from the imperialists and was not sincerely in favor of the policy represented by the Megarian Decree. Who can believe that, can believe anything, and the theory has won few adherents in the sixty years since its invention.

Beloch, accepting the evidence of most of the ancients, but not of Thucydides, thought it was a device for bringing on war in order to solve Pericles' domestic political troubles.[35] Few have accepted this interpretation, but there is widespread agreement that when Pericles proposed the decree he already believed a general war to be inevitable and acted either to bring it on, or to give Athens a strategic advantage when it did come.[36] The latter view assumes that Pericles expected economic pressure to force Megara out of the Peloponnesian alliance and under Athenian control. This would make Athens safe from invasion when war came. If that was the purpose of the decree, it failed totally, and as Brunt has shown, there is very little reason to believe that it could have succeeded. In peacetime it would have been very difficult for Athens to enforce the policy in the empire. Even during the war, when the Athenians blockaded Megara and invaded her territory twice annually, when her condition was very serious indeed, Megara did not give in. In spite of her suffering in the Archidamian War, Megara refused to accept the terms of the Peace of Nicias in 421.[37] It looks as if the Athenian policy only stiffened the Megarians' will to fight instead of causing them to yield to the Athenians. We may imagine that Pericles could have antici-

[34] F. M. Cornford, *Thucydides,* 25–38.

[35] *GG* ², II: 1, 292; *Attische Politik,* 21–22.

[36] Among those who adhere to this view in one form or another are Busolt (*GG,* III: 2, 814); Meyer (*Forschungen,* 307 and *GdA,* IV: 2, 15–17); Bury (*History of Greece,* 394); Adcock (*CAH,* V, 186–7); Glotz and Cohen (*HG,* II, 618–19); De Sanctis (*Pericle,* 232–233 and *SdG,* II, 265; *ATL,* III, 320).

[37] Brunt, *op. cit.,* 276–277.

pated that mere economic blockade would not detach the Megarians from the Peloponnesian League.

It has also been suggested, however, that the force of the Megarian Decree was chiefly psychological. With it Pericles "threw down the gauntlet before his enemies; he wanted to show his enemies that Athens had not the slightest fear of them. . . ." [38] Another version is somewhat more forceful, suggesting that it was intended precisely to make the war inevitable, to bring it on.[39] In its most advanced form, this theory suggests that the decree was actually the first act of war: "The decree was not what vulgar tradition came to see in it, a cause of war; it was an operation of war, the first blow at the courage and will of Athens' adversaries." [40] Finally, one ingenious interpretation has combined this view with the strategic one discussed above. In this view, Pericles was prepared to accept either of two possible consequences of his policy. Either Megara would submit, "and the Athenian fleet, based at Pegae, would dominate the Gulf of Corinth and the route to the West, and that would be a victorious peace; or it would resist, and Sparta would this time be forced to abandon its waiting and that would mean war." But it would be war under conditions very favorable to Athens; the Athenians would not have declared it, they were better prepared than their adversaries, and Pericles, who was getting old, was still on hand to lead them. Seen in this way, the decree was an act of defiance.[41]

These arguments are not implausible and are supported by an impressive weight of opinion, but they seem to suffer from a serious flaw. It is true that if Pericles hoped to bring the Megarians over to Athens, he chose a singularly ineffective weapon. It is likewise true that the weapon was not particularly well suited to the task of bringing on the general war. It is perfectly clear that the decree was only one of several factors that influenced the Spartan decision. Nor should we forget that the decision for war was not a foregone conclusion even after the decree was in effect. Archidamus possibly could have persuaded the Spartans to abstain from war. The two purposes suggested for the decree, moreover, are connected. If Peri-

[38] Meyer, *Forschungen,* II, 307.

[39] De Sanctis, *SdG,* II, 265.

[40] Adcock, *CAH*, V, 186.

[41] Glotz and Cohen, *HG,* II, 618–619.

cles expected it to bring on a war with Sparta, he should have been sure to bring Megara over to the Athenian side and thus guarantee the security of Attica. To plan to bring on a war without taking steps to fight it on the most favorable terms is foolishness, and we have no reason to suspect Pericles of that kind of incompetence. If the majority is right and Pericles was already convinced that war with Sparta was inevitable, he should have launched an unexpected attack on Megara. If the surprise assault succeeded, so much the better. Even if it was anticipated, the Athenians could besiege the city and occupy the passes of Geranea, which would seal off Attica from Peloponnesian attack with equal effectiveness. To be sure, that would have been a breach of the treaty, but if Pericles thought the war inevitable, the moral damage Athens would suffer from the technical guilt would be amply compensated by the strategic gain. Whether or not this is a just estimate of the situation, it is at least clear that an attack on Megara was one of the options available to Pericles. It is usual to speak of the Megarian Decree as though it were the most extreme measure possible, but we may now see it as a mean between the two extremes of doing nothing whatever and launching an attack on Megara.

It is instructive to compare Pericles' policy in regard to Megara with his treatment of the Corcyrean affair. On that occasion there were three options: to do nothing and suffer a strategic loss; to make an offensive and defensive alliance and so guarantee war with Corinth; or to choose the middle way and make a defensive alliance only in the hope that Corinth would see reason, refrain from altering the balance of power, and preserve the peace. Pericles characteristically chose the moderate policy because he did not yet consider war with Corinth inevitable. The Battle of Sybota and the Corinthian actions that followed made it clear that war had become very likely, but it was not yet clear that Sparta need be involved. As yet no interest vital to Sparta had been touched. The Spartans had indicated their disapproval of Corinthian policy; they had themselves stayed aloof and seem to have restrained their allies. The peace party seems to have had the situation well under control, and since 446/5, Pericles on the one hand and Archidamus on the other had preserved a satisfactory *modus vivendi* on the basis of live and let live. In the winter of 433/2, Pericles had good reason to hope that if Corinth insisted on provoking a conflict with Athens, it could be localized and Sparta kept out. We may well believe that Pericles' policy in regard to Megara was shaped by his desire to avoid a war with Sparta which he did not yet regard as inevitable.

But if Pericles wanted to avoid war with Sparta, why did he take any action against Megara at all? The official pretext offered by the Athenians was that the Megarians had worked sacred land, had encroached illegally upon border lands unmarked by boundary stones, and harbored fugitive slaves.[42] It is generally regarded, and rightly so, as merely one of those trumped-up justifications so easy for neighboring states to manufacture on demand.[43] Such minor complaints, even if justified, hardly required such a powerful response. It is true that Athenian relations with Megara had not been good since the Megarians had rejoined the Peloponnesians in the former war. It is also possible that it was the Megarians who took a leading role in suggesting that the Peloponnesians help the Samians and Byzantines in their rebellion of 440. Even so, we need to explain why the Athenians acted when they did, and not earlier or later. The answer is to be found in the affair at Corcyra. Megara, as we have seen, took part in the Battle of Leucimne on the side of Corinth. This was no offense against Athens, but in 433, Athens was an ally of Corcyra. Megara, in spite of the evident Spartan refusal to involve the Peloponnesians, and in spite of the failure of other states to make a second appearance at the side of Corinth, nevertheless fought at Sybota.

This Megarian action presented Athens with a problem. It was, of course, a hostile act and could not fail to arouse resentment. Much more important, it was a vote for Corinthian policy and against Spartan policy in the councils of the Peloponnese. It was the plan and hope of the Corinthians to involve the Peloponnesian League in their quarrel with Athens, as they had done in the former war. The

[42] 1. 39. 2.

[43] I have seen only one argument in favor of the reality of these claims (Karl Völkl, *Rheinische Museum,* XCIV [1951], 330–336.). Völkl believes that the Megarians really committed the alleged offenses, prompted by the Corinthians, who hoped to provoke Athens to war in this way. This is not persuasive, but Völkl deserves credit for recognizing that the decree was a moderate rather than extreme measure.

Spartans, on the other hand, were applying pressure on their allies to stay aloof. If the Megarian action went unpunished, the Athenians might reason, other states might join Corinth in the next encounter. This would be bad in itself, but might also make it more difficult for Sparta to stay at peace. There must have been men at Athens who advocated no action at all. There must have been others who urged an immediate attack on Megara. Pericles once again followed the middle course, not because of an abstract liking for moderation, but because of his estimate of the situation. War with Corinth could not be avoided if Corinth held to her policy, but war with Sparta could. The policy to be followed should hurt the Megarians and teach them and other potential enemies how costly such enmity must be. At the same time, however, it must not include a technical breach of the peace or any other situation that would force Sparta to fight. The Megarian Decree seemed an admirable compromise.

Some have argued that the decree was in fact a breach of the peace.[44] In doing so they accept the claim of the Megarians themselves, who complain to the Spartans that the decree is in violation of the treaty of 446/5. An assertion made under such conditions would in itself be more than a little suspicious, but we have even better reasons to doubt its accuracy. In a speech to the Athenians, Pericles flatly denied the Megarian claim, asserting that nothing in the treaty forbade an action like the decree.[45] It is altogether unbelievable that Pericles should not tell the truth on that occasion. His political enemies were present, and nothing could have been more convenient for them than to catch Pericles in a lie about a simple matter of fact.[46] It is, moreover, quite impossible to think that the treaty could have guaranteed free trade to all signatories. We have several treaties from the fifth century, but none contains such a provision. Let us also remember that Athens was doing nothing

[44] Nissen, *Historische Zeitschrift,* N.F., XXVII (1889), 413; Meyer, *Forschungen,* II, 303; Beloch, *GG* ², II: 1, 293.

[45] 1. 144. 2.

[46] As Adcock put it, "Pericles declared that this decree was not a violation of the Thirty Years' Peace, and we may accept his testimony against that of the aggrieved Megarians" (*CAH,* V, 186). To the same effect, see also Völkl, *op. cit.,* 332–333, and H. Nesselhauf, *Hermes,* LXIX (1934), 289.

more than passing a trade regulation effective in her own territory and that of her allies. Pericles ridiculed the demand the Spartans would later make that the Athenians repeal the decree. He agreed to repeal it if the Spartans would also repeal their long-standing law barring foreigners from their territory. His point was that both were internal matters and not subject to negotiation. His analogy was tendentious and far from exact, but it makes clear that any clause preventing each state from controlling its own trade would be absurd in the treaty of 446/5. As Völkl points out, that treaty was neither a Versailles nor a St. Germain.[47]

We may be sure, then, that the Megarian Decree was not a technical breach of the peace. If we have conjectured correctly that the herald Anthemocritus really was sent to Megara and Sparta with a soft answer to justify the Athenian action, we may see in his mission a further attempt by Pericles to reassure the Spartans. The action he regarded as necessary and not subject to retraction, but he seems to have been eager to make it clear that it did not imply a new Athenian policy of aggression. The murder of the herald, allegedly by the Megarians, must have strengthened the hands of the aggressive faction in Athens, who tried to bring on an immediate attack against Megara through some form of the Charinus Decree. If, however, our reconstruction is sound, Pericles opposed the harsh proposal and defeated it, allowing nevertheless a heroic burial for Anthemocritus. He held to his moderate policy of firmness toward Corinth and her allies, and restraint and conciliation toward Sparta.

No doubt Pericles' confidence in his ability to remain on good terms with the Spartans rested on his long experience, his knowledge of the political situation in Sparta, and his personal associations with important Spartans. There was a Spartan called Pericleidas who led a Spartan embassy that came to Athens for help during the famous helot rebellion after the great earthquake.[48] He is very likely the father of Athenaeus, son of Pericleidas, who signed the Peace of Nicias on Sparta's behalf in 421.[49] The significance of the names is not to be ignored any more than is Cimon's decision to name his son

[47] Völkl, *op. cit.,* 333.
[48] Plut. *Cim.* 16. 8; Aristoph. *Lysistrata* 1137ff.
[49] 4. 119.

Lacedaemonius.[50] The names of Pericleidas and his son indicate a friendship with Athens, as do the missions each is asked to perform. It is obvious that the Spartans would only send a man to ask for Athenian help in an emergency who was very much *persona grata*. It is likewise clear that the Spartans who signed the Peace of Nicias were in favor of a policy of peace with Athens. Perhaps it is not too much to suppose that the family of Pericleidas chose that name for him because of some special relationship they may have had with the family of Pericles.

However that may be, we know with certainty that Pericles had very close relations with King Archidamus. Their relationship was the one called *xenia*, guest-friendship, the old Homeric association based on mutual hospitality.[51] Their friendship was so close and so well known as to cause Pericles serious embarrassment when war came. Archidamus led the Spartan invasion of Attica, and Pericles was very much afraid that his friend would bypass his fields while destroying those of other Athenians, "either of his own accord as a favor to Pericles, or at the command of the Spartans in order to create a prejudice against him." [52] As a result, Pericles was forced to make a public statement. He admitted his friendship with Archidamus but denied that it was made to the harm of the state. Then he turned over his private property to the state, asking that "no suspicion should fall on him because of it." [53]

With such associations among influential Spartans, Pericles must have been well informed as to the state of Spartan opinion and may have hoped, with reason, that war could be avoided, for his friends in the peace party had done a fine job of restraining Sparta and her allies since the Epidamnian crisis first threatened the stability of Greece. He chose to employ only economic sanctions against Megara to strengthen the hands of his Spartan friends and to avoid the appearance of Athenian aggression. In spite of the excellence of his information and the caution of his policy, the event shows that Pericles miscalculated. It is true that Pericles was technically correct, and no clause in the treaty was violated by the Megarian Decree. But in

[50] V. Ehrenberg, *PW*, XIX, *s.v.* "Pericleides," 747–748.
[51] Thuc. 2. 13. 1–2; Plut. *Per.* 33. 2.
[52] 2. 13. 1.
[53] 2. 13. 2.

practice it amounted almost to an act of war against a member of the Spartan alliance. No doubt Pericles counted on a friendly Spartan government to put a different interpretation on it, and so it would have, had the friends of Pericles remained in control of the situation. But the issuance of the Megarian Decree gave a powerful weapon to those Spartans who had always opposed the existence of the Athenian Empire and the policy of peaceful coexistence with Athens. The Megarian Decree, unlike any other Athenian action since 446/5, could be made to appear an act of aggression against a Peloponnesian state. It would be of no use to point out that Athens had not invaded the Megarid and was making a carefully limited response to a specific provocation. The fact remained that Pericles, in raising his diplomatic bid in an attempt to localize the coming war with Corinth, frightened many Spartans and drastically changed the political situation in Sparta.

Perhaps the decade of secure control he had exercised in Athens dulled his keen understanding of the vagaries of domestic politics; perhaps he overestimated the political power of his friends; perhaps, as most statesmen do at one time or another, he believed what he wanted to believe. It is not impossible, moreover, that political pressure from aggressive Athenians helped him decide against a policy of doing nothing in regard to Megara. The decision and the responsibility, however, were his, for he resisted their more extreme demands and chose a policy that suited him. If we have judged his intentions rightly, it was a blunder. The Megarian Decree put the Spartan war party into power and by so doing made a general war more likely. Seen in this light, it was a very important factor in bringing on the war, and there is no way to deny that Thucydides has slighted it.

Thucydides' neglect of the importance of the Megarian Decree has troubled all intelligent students of Thucydides and of the causes of the war. The explanations offered have been many and various: the purpose of the decree was economic and Thucydides did not understand economic factors in history; Pericles was responsible for the decree that brought on the disastrous war, so Thucydides suppressed its importance to protect the statesman he most admired; the insignificance of the decree in the Thucydidean account is evidence that Thucydides changed his mind about the causes of the war while writing and never finished the parts he planned to add in order to make his final opinion clear; Thucydides records only official policies, and since the Megarian Decree was a policy of the Piraeus party forced upon an unwilling Pericles, Thucydides does not report it; Thucydides reports only effective policies, and the Megarian policy was not effective. One explanation we have already examined disposes of the problem by suggesting that Thucydides does not treat the Megarian Decree as an important cause of the war because it was put in effect well before the final crisis.[54] Most of these have been amply refuted, while some hardly require refutation. None has won wide acceptance. Probably there will never be general agreement on this question, for it goes to the very root of the Thucydidean problem. It involves the question of how and when he composed his history, what were his methods, his intentions, and his philosophical preconceptions, and a thorough examination of these matters is beyond our present intention and competence. Here it is possible only to make a tentative suggestion arising from a comparison with Thucydides' treatment of the Corcyrean debate at Athens.

On that occasion, as we have seen, Thucydides omits information that he surely had and which we would very much like to have. He speaks of Corinthians, Corcyreans, and Athenians, never of individuals or political groups. In the case of the Athenians, at least, we know from Thucydides' own account and from independent evidence that there was an important division in Athens over what action to take, and the decision almost went the other way. There could be no question of deliberate concealment on the part of Thucydides, for all his readers knew the facts and were well aware of the position taken by Pericles. The treatment of the Megarian Decree is very similar. We would like to know who proposed it, who opposed it, what were

[54] The economic theory is implicit in the work of Cornford and often appears, unacknowledged, elsewhere, especially in popular treatments. The chief proponent of the view that Thucydides shielded Pericles, apart from Beloch, is Eduard Meyer (*Forschungen* II, 307). The notion that Thucydides changed his mind and did not finish his revision is set forth by Schwartz, *op. cit.*, 92–101 and 117–128. Gomme (*Hist. Comm.*, I, 465–467) does not accept Schwartz's theory of a change of mind but believes the work is unfinished. The official policy theory belongs to Cornford (25–38). The effective policy theory is set forth by J. B. Bury in *The Ancient Greek Historians* (paper edition; New York, 1958), 91–101. The early date idea is put forth by P. A. Brunt, *AJP*, LXXII (1951).

the arguments pro and con, when precisely it was passed, and what its purposes were. Thucydides knew all this but chose not to tell. Once again there can be no question of concealment. Everyone knew that Pericles had proposed the decree; Thucydides himself makes it clear that he supported it fiercely. The common opinion was that Pericles was responsible for causing the war precisely because he had proposed the decree and refused to withdraw it. That view was at least as old as the presentation of Aristophanes' *Acharnians* at the Lenaean Dionysia of 425. By 391, Andocides could coolly mention in passing that the Athenians had gone to war in 431 "because of the Megarians." [55]

It is precisely the prevalence of this interpretation, we may suspect, that explains Thucydides treatment of the Megarian Decree. As Meyer has shrewdly pointed out, the Thucydidean account of the causes of the war is a "latent polemic" against the popular interpretation.[56] Thucydides was persuaded that the war was inevitable from the time Athens became an imperial power. He was convinced that forces were at work beyond the control of individuals. The war would eventually have come whatever the internal political conditions in each state and regardless of which leaders supported which policies. Although he believed this was generally true, it was especially important to emphasize it in the case of Athens, for there the vulgar view had taken hold that one man, Pericles, had brought on the war by rigid adherence to a single policy, the affirmation of the Megarian Decree. To his mind that interpretation was altogether wrong. The decree was really a measure in the preliminary maneuverings of a war that was already determined, if not in progress. Thus, his omission of names and an account of internal politics was deliberate: he omitted them because he was profoundly convinced that they were irrelevant. He knew that his readers would not only be aware of the omissions, but they would be surprised and perhaps shocked by them as well. The slight importance he allotted to the decree was a most artistic way of making the point of its insignificance. His intelligent readers would not miss that point.

We, of course, are free to disagree with Thucydides' estimate, especially if we are not fully persuaded of the war's inevitability. In

[55] 3. 8.

[56] *Forschungen*, II, 307.

our view it may appear to be one of several steps Pericles took to prepare Athens for the approaching war with Corinth. The Callias Decrees, the treaties with Rhegium and Leontini, the expedition of Phormio to Acarnania, possibly also the journey of Diotimus to Naples, the demands on Potidea, as we shall see, are all measures that might be taken by an Athenian statesman preparing for war with Corinth but careful to avoid an offense against Sparta or her other Peloponnesian allies. The Megarian Decree is part of the same policy, but it was a mistake, for it could be made to appear as an unprovoked attack against a Peloponnesian ally and so a threat to Sparta's position of leadership in the Peloponnese.

16. *Potidaea*

Certainly the most clear-cut instance of Athenian preparation for a war with Corinth after the Battle of Sybota was the ultimatum the Athenians delivered to Potidaea. The Potidaeans, who lived on the isthmus connecting the peninsula of Pallene with the Chalcidice bordering on Thrace and Macedonia, were in the anomalous position of being tribute-paying allies of Athens, but at the same time loyal colonists of Corinth who received annual magistrates from the mother city. In the winter of 433/2, perhaps in January, the Athenians ordered them to pull down the city walls on the side of Pallene, to give hostages, and to send away the Corinthian magistrates and refuse to receive them in the future.[1] Had the Potidaeans obeyed these orders, the results would have been to estrange the city from Corinth and to put it completely at the mercy of Athens. In the event, Potidaea refused to comply with the Athenian demands and joined in a rebellion that cost Athens heavily in men, money, and time. The Athenian effort to suppress that rebellion also played a significant part in bringing Sparta into the war. We need to know why the Athenians acted as they did and how their action related to their policy in general.

A satisfactory answer to these questions requires some knowledge

[1] 1. 56; for the date, see Busolt, *GG*, III: 2, 793, 799, n. 1; Gomme, *Hist. Comm.*, I, 196–198, 222–224, 421–425, for the chronology of the events from Epidamnus to the Spartan invasion of Attica. In general, I follow Gomme's chronology, which is summarized in a table on pp. 424–425. Alexander (*Potidaea,* 66 and n. 16) argues against Gomme's chronology. His note offers a useful bibliography of the problem.

of the relations between Athens and Potidaea in the years before the crisis. Our only literary source, however, is Thucydides, and he tells us far less than we need to know. In addition we have the evidence of some inscriptions, the tribute lists in particular, but it is fragmentary and difficult to interpret. The one thing the inscriptions make absolutely clear is that there was important information available bearing on the outbreak of the war, and Thucydides either could not or chose not to give it.

Potidaea was one of those Corinthian colonies founded by the sons of Periander toward the end of the seventh century.[2] The Potidaeans fought in the Greek army at Plataea. Since they had revolted from Persia after Salamis, we may well imagine that they were quick to join the Delian League and happy to see Athens take the responsibility of leadership.[3] The likelihood is that at first they provided ships, for they do not appear on the list of tribute-payers until 445/4.[4] We have no reason to doubt that the Potidaeans fulfilled their obligations to both Athens and Corinth right down to the rebellion with neither difficulty nor conflict. Even during the First Peloponnesian War, when hegemon and mother city were in open conflict, there is no evidence that Potidaea was in any way involved.[5]

All we know about Potidaea between the wars is what we learn from the remains of the tribute lists. In 445/4 she paid six talents, and it is possible that she paid the same in the previous year, the beginning of an assessment period. The same figure is preserved on the lists for 444/3, 443/2, 440/39, and 435/4, and it is assumed that Potidaea regularly paid the same amount for each of the missing years. In 434/3 the name of Potidaea appears on the stone, but the amount paid is missing. In the following year, however, the tribute

[2] Nic. Dam. frg. 59 in *FGrH,* IIA, 358; Alexander, *Potidaea,* 16 and n. 21,

[3] Hdt. 8. 126–129; 9. 28; *ATL,* III, 223.

[4] *ATL,* III, 58, 238, 249ff.; Alexander, *Potidaea,* 41–42. The authors of *ATL* also restore Potidaea on the list for 446/5, on the grounds that it was the beginning of an assessment period. They may be right, but it was not uncommon for changes in the assessments to be made in the course of an assessment period.

[5] The authors of *ATL* (III, 321 and n. 88) entertain the possibility that Aeschylus' *Eumenides,* which was performed in 458, alludes to the war and trouble in Potidaea in lines 292–296 and 762–774. This seems to me quite fanciful.

paid by Potidaea was fifteen talents. After that came the rebellion, and the Potidaeans disappear from the tribute lists.[6]

Before we can attempt an interpretation of this evidence, we must compare the experience of Potidaea with what happened to its neighbors. On the peninsula of Pallene, Aphytis had paid only one talent in the 440's but was raised to three by 435/4 and perhaps as early as 438/7. Mende, which had paid only five talents in 440/39, was raised to eight in 438/7 and consistently paid that amount until its rebellion during the war. Scione, which had always paid six talents, was raised to fifteen in 435/4.[7] To be sure, the tribute of other states was not altered. It is also true that the previous tribute record of the states of Pallene had experienced some fluctuation. Aphytis had once paid three talents before the figure had been reduced to one. Mende had paid eight talents in 451, fifteen in 446 and 445, five talents in 443, nine in 442, and five in 439 before the assessment leveled off at eight in 437. It is further possible but not likely that the sharp rise in the tribute of Scione is not a fact but the product of a stonecutter's error.[8] In spite of all this, there seems to be some pattern to the increase of tribute in the four states of Pallene during the 430's.

The significance of that pattern is increased by a similar development at the same time in the region to the north of Pallene called Bottice. There, in 434/3, the tribute of Spartolus was raised from two talents to over three, and money was collected for the first time from small Bottic cities nearby. The result was to double the tribute of Bottice.[9] It is very risky to make firm judgments on the basis of such incomplete evidence as we have, but it seems not too much to say that in the 430's, and particularly in the second part of the decade, the Athenians were increasing their demands on the regions of Pallene and Bottice. The authors of ATL go further and suggest

[6] *ATL,* III, 64–65; 321 and n. 89.

[7] See Gomme, *Hist. Comm.,* I, 211.

[8] Such is the suggestion of *ATL,* III, 64–65, which is regarded by Gomme (*Hist. Comm* , III, 608) as "attractive." I find it hard to believe that such an error in an important and permanent public document could have gone unnoticed and uncorrected. It seems to me to be necessary to explain the record as we have it without the admittedly clever and attractive emendation. Perhaps the *lectio difficilior* should be preferred on stones as well as in manuscripts.

[9] *ATL,* III, 319.

that Athens was exerting its influence and raising its demands on other regions in the neighborhood of Macedon as well, and they may be right, although the evidence is less clear.[10]

It might be tempting to connect all this activity with events in the west, to see it as evidence of the farsighted wisdom of Pericles, who already saw war coming and was making financial preparations for it, but such temptation must be resisted. The first steps appear to have been taken as early as 438, before the Epidamnian trouble and soon after the Corinthians had shown restraint at the Peloponnesian conference concerning Samos. All the rises in tribute were imposed before the Battle of Sybota.[11] The events in the northeast had nothing to do with Epidamnus or Corcyra or any expectation of a general war. To explain them we must look instead to the immediate vicinity and to the history of Athenian relations with Macedon.

We have seen that Athens had some reason to be concerned about the power and growth of Macedon.[12] Some time before the outbreak of the rebellion at Potidaea, the Athenians made an alliance with King Perdiccas II, probably soon after his accession to the throne after the middle of the fifth century.[13] After the revolt of Samos and Byzantium and the troubles in the northeast that followed, the Athenians appear to have decided that stronger measures were needed to contain the power of the Thracian tribes and the Macedonian kingdom. They established colonies at Amphipolis and Brea, and by 436 both were serving the function of Athenian garrisons on the

[10] III, 318–319.

[11] If, with *ATL* and Gomme, we restore the change in Potidaea's tribute to the year 434/3.

[12] See above, p. 182.

[13] Thuc. 1. 57. 2, ξύμμαχος πρότερον καὶ φίλος ὤν, makes it clear that Perdiccas had been an ally of Athens before 433. *IG*, I², 71 partially preserves a treaty between Athens and Perdiccas, which the editors date to 423/2. The same date is maintained in the republication of the text in *SEG*, X, 86. The authors of *ATL* (III, 313 and n. 61), however, date it to the foundation of Amphipolis. They have made an excellent case for an earlier date and for believing that the document we have is the original treaty, not a later "patching up of differences." They have not, however, given any reason for putting the treaty so late as 436. I think it more likely that the Athenians made the alliance soon after the accession of Perdiccas in the hope of containing him in that way. The establishment of colonies at Brea and Amphipolis appears to be a later stage in the development of relations between Athens and Perdiccas.

borders of Macedon. Perdiccas may well have wondered whether this was the action of a friend and ally. It is possible that he began to reconsider the wisdom of his alliance with Athens and to give evidence that he was not to be trusted. However that may be, at some time before 433 the Athenians changed their strategy towards Macedon once again. Breaking off their treaty with Perdiccas, they made one instead with his brother Philip and Derdas, his nephew.[14] It seems as if the Athenians had abandoned a policy of containment and replaced it with an attempt to divide and conquer.

To support Philip and Derdas in their struggle with Perdiccas would cost money. Since the purpose was to protect the Athenian allies in the neighborhood of Macedon, it must have seemed only right to ask the more prosperous states of the area to pay more of the cost of their own protection. It is this, we may believe, which explains the raising of the tribute in Pallene and Bottice. The situation is not altogether dissimilar from the one that existed in England's American colonies after the Seven Years' War. England had fought that war in large measure to protect her colonists from the French and Indians. After succeeding in that endeavor, she thought it right to ask the colonist to pay a greater share of the expense of their protection. The colonists did not see the matter in quite the same way and looked upon the new exactions as improper, unjust, and evidence of tyranny. We should be surprised if the allies of Athens did not look upon the demands of the Athenians in much the same way. However irritated they may have been, the allies took no action. Athens was far closer to them than England to America, and they were fully exposed to action by the mighty Athenian fleet. Amphipolis and Brea, moreover, were nearby and contained Athenian garrisons. The allies might grumble, but they would not act without assistance from some powerful outsider.

Perdiccas, too, however angry he may have been, was in no position to act alone. The power of an undistracted Athens, coupled with

[14] Thucydides (1. 57. 2–3) says merely that the treaty with Philip and Derdas had been made at some time before Perdiccas became hostile to Athens and had, in fact, been the cause of his hostility. ἐπολεμώθη δὲ ὅτι Φιλίππῳ τῷ ἑαυτοῦ ἀδελφῷ καὶ Δέρδᾳ κοινῇ πρὸς αὐτὸν ἐναντιουμένοις οἱ Ἀθηναῖοι ξυμμαχίαν ἐποιήσαντο. I think it likely that the hostility developed soon after the foundation of Amphipolis and that the treaty with Philip and Derdas may have come as early as 435.

the rivalry of his brother and nephew, was too great to encounter. Instead he kept his peace until an opportunity should come. After the Battle of Sybota it became likely that Athens and Corinth would come into conflict, and Perdiccas was quick to take advantage of the chance their dispute offered him. Even before the Athenians had delivered their ultimatum to Potidaea, Perdiccas had done something to arouse their suspicion.[15] The announcement of that ultimatum encouraged him to take overt action. He sent ambassadors to Sparta to try to make the Spartans fight Athens. He tried to bring Corinth over to his side by talking of encouraging a rebellion at Potidaea. He also approached the cities of the Thracian Chalcidice and the Bottiaeans who lived on the north shore of the Thermaic Gulf, urging them to join in a war against Athens. As we shall see, he was successful in bringing on a serious and widespread upheaval, and there can be no doubt that the issuance of the Athenian ultimatum to Potidaea helped him to do so.

Once again we must ask ourselves why the Athenians, led by Pericles, took such an action. Thucydides tells us that after Sybota the Corinthians were openly hostile to Athens and preparing to take vengeance.[16] In their speech at Athens in the summer of 433, the Corinthians had made a not very veiled threat to stir up trouble among the allies of Athens.[17] It was precisely the fear that the Corinthians, and Perdiccas, would persuade Potidaea to revolt that led the Athenians to make their harsh demands. We must understand the delivery of the ultimatum to Potidaea in the context of the other measures Athens took between Sybota and the Congress at Sparta in the summer of 432 and especially in connection with the Megarian Decree, which was probably issued soon after the ultimatum. Both were measures prompted by the new realization that war with Corinth was likely. Both were attempts to prevent Corinth from extending the area of conflict and from gaining allies. Neither was a step which need alarm Sparta, if properly understood. Like the Megarian Decree, the Potidaean ultimatum was not the most extreme action that Athens might have taken. If Athens wanted to be absolutely sure of Potidaea, she should have sent a fleet along with her

[15] 1. 56. 2.
[16] 1. 56. 2; 1. 57. 1.
[17] 1. 40. 6.

ultimatum; at least she might have sent troops from Amphipolis to tear down the wall of the city. Instead the Athenians made their demands known in early winter but took no action to enforce them until the following spring. Even then they only gave additional instructions to the commanders of an expedition already en route to Macedon on a different mission. Subsequent events show that the Athenians expected no difficulty and were unable to cope with the situation when they found Potidaea in rebellion.

Like the Megarian Decree, the Potidaean ultimatum was in part a gesture of defiance to Corinth. It was also a warning to potential troublemakers in the empire, as the decree had been to potential allies of Corinth. Like the Megarian Decree, too, it was a serious miscalculation which helped convert the limited war that Athens expected to fight against Corinth into a general war against the Spartan alliance.

When the Potidaeans received the Athenian demands in the winter of 433/2, they undertook to protect their autonomy by diplomatic means. They sent an embassy to Athens to try to dissuade the Athenians from carrying out their intentions. These negotiations were protracted, probably extending through the entire winter, but they achieved no favorable result for Potidaea. Instead the Athenians saw for the first time that they might expect some resistance to their demands and, in the spring, gave additional orders to the captains of their Macedonian expedition to act against Potidaea as well.[18]

The Potidaeans, however, were far more determined than the Athenians knew, and they had taken steps to anticipate an Athenian refusal. At the same time as they had sent envoys to Athens, they had also sent ambassadors to the Peloponnese. Accompanied by their Corinthian kinsmen, they went to Sparta with the idea of seeking aid from the Spartans in case it should be needed. There they conferred with the ephors and received a surprisingly favorable reply to their request for help.[19] The Spartan magistrates flatly prom-

[18] 1. 57. 1.

[19] Thucydides (1. 58. 1) says that they were received by τὰ τέλη. As Busolt and Swoboda (*GS*, II, 687 and n. 4) points out, τὰ τέλη is not always identical with the board of ephors. At times it may mean the ephors and the assembly and at other times the ephors and the gerousia. It is possible that the gerousia may have been involved in the discussions on this occasion, but

ised to invade Attica if the Athenians attacked Potidaea. These ephors had taken office in the spring of 433, which means that they had been elected well before the Athenian alliance with Corcyra and the Battle of Sybota.[20] There is no reason, therefore, to believe that they were elected as enemies of Athens. The results of the battle and the measures taken by Athens since then, however, had changed their attitude. Taken individually each step might appear understandable and without aggressive intention to a shrewd and experienced Spartan not ill disposed to Athens. To some Spartans not especially friendly to the Athenians, their actions since Sybota, in particular the Megarian Decree and the Potidaean ultimatum, must have seemed the acts of a tyrannous, aggressive, and dangerous state.

The promise the ephors made to invade Attica is firm proof of the existence of a significant war party in Sparta at least as early as the winter of 433/2. But the Spartans failed to keep that promise, and that proves that the war party was still a minority as late as the spring of 432. Right down to the moment when the Spartans voted for war in the summer of 432, there was enough sentiment in Sparta that favored a continued peace to prevent action against Athens, even under the provocation of an Athenian embargo that was doing serious damage to a Peloponnesian ally and of an Athenian attack against a state that the Spartan magistrates had promised to defend. But the actions of Athens were working to undercut that sentiment.

It was probably about the middle of April, 432 that the Athenian expedition against Perdiccas left port. It consisted of thirty ships and one thousand hoplites and was commanded by Archestratus, son of Lycomedes, and four other generals.[21] It is possible that this Archestratus was the same man who collaborated with Pericles and Ephialtes in attacking the Areopagus. If so, we should not find it hard to identify him with the man who moved an amendment to the decree which regulated Athenian relations with Chalcis in 446/5.[22] It

the promises to Potidaea could only be made by the ephors. The fact that they were unable to carry out the promises proves that the assembly was not consulted in these discussions.

[20] For the beginning of the ephors' tenure of office, see Busolt and Swoboda, *GS*, II, 686 and n. 5.

[21] 1. 57. 6.

[22] For the attack on the Areopagus, see *Ath. Pol.* 35. 2; for the Chalcis decree, see *IG*, I², 37 = Tod 42. Busolt (*GG*, III: 2, 795, n. 1) accepts the

would certainly be part of the pattern of Periclean activities in this period of his career to employ an experienced and trusted man to deal with the difficult problem of the northeast. Even so, Pericles seems to have altogether underestimated the troubles Archestratus would encounter when he casually added to his assignment in Macedonia orders "to take hostages from the Potidaeans, take down their wall, and keep watch over the neighboring towns so that they should not revolt." [23]

The Potidaeans wasted no time. Aware of the imminent arrival of the Athenian expedition and armed with the promise of Spartan help, they revolted from Athens. At the same time they made an alliance with the cities of the Chalcidice and the Bottiaeans, who joined in the rebellion. This was precisely the opportunity for which Perdiccas had hoped. He acted immediately, persuading the Chalcidians who lived on the coast and were thus exposed to the attacks of the Athenian fleet, to abandon and destroy their cities. He persuaded them to move inland to Olynthus, which would in this way become a center of strength. In return he gave them some of his own territory for the time when they should be at war with Athens.[24]

When the Athenian expedition reached the coast of Thrace, they found Potidaea already in rebellion, and the generals quickly concluded that their forces were not great enough to accomplish both tasks that they had been given. For the moment they ignored Potidaea and decided to wage war against Perdiccas in concert with Philip and the army of Derdas, who had already begun an invasion of Macedonia from the west.[25] The insufficiency of the Athenian army is ample evidence that Pericles had not anticipated the Potidaean response to his demands, for if he had, he would at once have sent the troops that he was soon compelled to send as reinforcements. If he had, Potidaea might have yielded immediately and spared Athens many lives, great expense, and two years of distraction.

As in the case of the Megarian Decree, Pericles expected the ulti-

---

identification "aller Wahrscheinlichkeit." Gomme (*Hist. Comm.*, I, 208) believes that the name was too common in Athens to permit certain identification.

[23] 1. 57. 6.

[24] 1. 58. 2.

[25] 1. 59. 2; Gomme, *Hist. Comm.*, I, 212.

matum to Potidaea to produce no trouble. He anticipated that the Potidaeans would immediately comply with the wishes of Athens as they had obediently complied with the increase in their tribute by 150 per cent. To be sure, the Potidaeans had sent envoys to remonstrate, but as late as March 432 their obedience could be relied upon, for that was when they paid the assessment of fifteen talents. If they were going to rebel, one would expect them to do so before making the payment. Pericles could not have been aware of the unofficial promise the Spartan ephors had made to the Potidaeans when he calmly added the order to enforce the Potidaean ultimatum to the assignment of Archestratus, without increasing his forces. No doubt he expected that a show of force might be necessary to win a reluctant compliance, but that would be enough. When Archestratus met strong resistance, indeed a full-scale rebellion in the Chalcidice in which Perdiccas was involved, Pericles had no choice but to increase his commitment, an action quite contrary to his original intention. He had expected the Potidaeans to act reasonably, and reason showed their cause to be hopeless; he had not reckoned with the courage, even recklessness, of desperate men who felt they had little to lose.

When the Corinthians learned that Potidaea had revolted and that an Athenian expedition had been sent to the region, they determined to send help. Even at this point, however, they were unwilling to take a formal action in violation of the Thirty Years' Peace. The best they would do was to sponsor and support a private expedition of "volunteers" under the command of the Corinthian general Aristeus, son of Adimantus. He was an old friend of the Potidaeans and highly esteemed by the Corinthians as well. It was chiefly on his account that the Corinthian volunteers went along, and their number was supplemented by Peloponnesians who served for pay provided by Corinth. Together they numbered sixteen hundred hoplites and four hundred light-armed infantry.[26] This extreme care to avoid a formal breach of the peace shows that the Corinthians were well informed of the state of opinion and the political situation at Sparta. They knew that the war party needed every possible propaganda advantage to win the reluctant Spartans over to their view. It was very important to avoid the appearance that Corinth and not Athens

[26] 1. 60.

had violated the peace, and the fiction that Aristeus led a volunteer army was meant to show that Corinth was not officially involved. The army of Aristeus arrived in Thrace on the fortieth day after the outbreak of the revolt at Potidaea, probably towards the end of May.[27]

When the Athenians heard of the rebellion in Potidaea, the Chalcidice, and its vicinity and of the expedition of Aristeus, they quickly realized the seriousness of the situation. They sent an army of two thousand Athenian hoplites with forty ships under Callias, the son of Calliades, another close associate of Pericles. When they arrived, they found that the army of Archestratus had taken Therme and was engaged in a siege of Pydna, in which they joined. But the orders of Callias were clearly different from those of Archestratus. By now Pericles knew that a general rebellion of Athenian allies in the Thraceward region was a possibility and far more dangerous than Perdiccas. Callias was certainly told that the reduction of Potidaea was his first priority. As a result, the Athenians quickly patched up an agreement with Perdiccas and made a new alliance with him.[28] It was an act of expediency and cynicism on both sides. Perdiccas was delighted to see the Athenians abandon the siege of an important Macedonian city and to extricate him, at least temporarily, from the vise in which the concerted attack had placed him. The Athenians were glad to be free of the Macedonian campaign so that they could use all their forces against Potidaea. Both sides regarded the alliance as a temporary arrangement that could be broken when convenient.

From Pydna the three thousand Athenian hoplites, who had been joined by many allies and six hundred Macedonian cavalry, marched without undue haste to Potidaea, while their seventy ships sailed along the coast. At Potidaea, Aristeus had been chosen to command the infantry, and Perdiccas, who had already broken his agreement and abandoned the alliance with Athens, was selected to command the cavalry. We need not trouble ourselves with the details of the

[27] 1. 60. 3; Gomme, *Hist. Comm.*, I, 425. It is not clear from Thucydides' account how the army travelled. Gomme (*Hist. Comm.*, I, 213) thinks by land, while Alexander (*Potidaea*, 67 and n. 22) thinks by sea. Both routes would have presented difficulties.

[28] 1. 61. 1–3.

battle that followed, probably in the middle of June.[29] It is enough to say that, although Aristeus and his Corinthian volunteers routed the troops who opposed them, the Athenians were successful on the other wing, forcing the enemy to take refuge behind the walls of Potidaea and winning the battle.[30] The Athenians held the field and so were able to set up a trophy of victory. The Potidaeans lost almost three hundred men and the Athenians half that number, including their general, Callias.[31]

The Athenians had no choice now but to lay siege to the city, for the successful storming of a walled city is unheard of in the fifth century. It was soon apparent that even now the Athenian forces were insufficient for a complete blockade. It was not until the arrival of Phormio with an additional sixteen hundred hoplites that the circumvallation was completed.[32] Aristeus, who had earlier shown great heroism by breaking through the Athenian lines to join his Corinthians to the Potidaeans in the city, recognized that there was no hope for the relief of the city unless he could win outside support, especially from the Peloponnese. Realizing that there was no need in Potidaea for anything more than a small garrison to defend the walls, he slipped out of the city to do more useful work. He stayed in the Chalcidice stirring up trouble for the Athenians and negotiating with the Peloponnesians in an attempt to bring them into the conflict.[33]

These events show once again how ill prepared Pericles was for what happened at Potidaea. Each stage of the campaign caught him unaware and required him to increase the Athenian commitment. The course of events shows that he did not plan a major campaign in the Chalcidice but merely reacted to the surprising events as they took place. His initial belief that a mere ultimatum would suffice to secure Potidaea and prevent trouble among the allies of the region was wrong. His next idea that a passing show of force would be

[29] Gomme, *Hist. Comm.*, I, 425.

[30] 1. 62.

[31] 1. 63. A tombstone for Athenians who died at Potidaea, now at the British Museum (*IG*, I², 945 = Tod 59), probably commemorates the men who died in this battle, though it may belong to those who died in the siege that followed. See Gomme, *Hist. Comm.*, I, 220.

[32] 1. 64.

[33] 1. 65.

enough was likewise shown to be mistaken. The despatch of reinforcements under Callias proved insufficient for carrying on a siege, which had not been anticipated, so the additional force under Phormio was sent. By the summer of 432, four thousand and six hundred Athenian hoplites in addition to many allied troops were engaged in the siege of Potidaea. If Pericles expected war with the Spartans to come in the near future, if, indeed, he was already trying to bring it on, his actions at Potidaea were mad. The strategy he employed when war finally came was one of attrition. He hoped to fight a strictly defensive war, avoiding adventures and expensive campaigns which would drain his financial reserves, and avoiding the exposure of his army to combat as much as possible. The siege of Potidaea took a large army far from home and kept it engaged for over two years and cost two thousand talents.[34]

As initially conceived, the Potidaean ultimatum was nothing to alarm the Spartans, but the situation that had developed by the summer of 432 was something quite different. Once again Corinthians and Athenians had come to blows, but this could be overlooked, for on this occasion Corinth was not officially involved. On the other hand, the Athenians had been provoked into taking ponderous military and naval action against a number of small states who asked only to be given their freedom and autonomy. Joined together with the Megarian Decree, the Potidaean ultimatum might be seen to cast a different light on the Athenian action in regard to Corcyra. That might now be made to appear as an unwarranted and arrogant interference by the Athenians in a quarrel that need not involve them. Joined together, these incidents could be used by the enemies of Athens to paint a picture of a state that had become arrogant, aggressive, and a threat to the liberty of all Greeks as well as the security of Sparta. Perhaps the main cost of the affair at Potidaea was neither military nor financial, but psychological. It may have enabled the war party at Sparta to gain enough support to win control of Spartan policy.

[34] 2. 70. 1–3.

17. Sparta

The Athenian siege of Potidaea further angered the Corinthians and intensified their haste to bring Sparta into a war against the Athenians. Corinthian citizens were in the besieged city, and at any moment it might surrender, exposing the loyal colony of Corinth to Athenian vengeance. The Corinthians hurried to their Peloponnesian allies, urging them to go to Sparta. Among those who sent delegates were the Aeginetans, who did so secretly out of fear of Athens. They immediately joined the Corinthians in persuading the others who had come that Athens had broken the treaty.[1] It is worth emphasizing that even at this point it was left to the Corinthians to force the Spartans to act. Only Sparta could call a meeting of her allies, but she had not done so. The Corinthians, therefore, on their own, invited aggrieved allies to Sparta to exert pressure on the Spartans.

This tactic was successful, and in July of 432 the ephors invited their allies as well as anyone else who had a complaint against Athens to a meeting of the Spartan assembly.[2] This was not a meet-

[1] 1. 67. 1–3.

[2] This interpretation is based on the reading provided by the best manuscripts, *ABEFM:* οἱ δὲ Λακεδαιμόνιοι, προσπαρακαλέσαντες τῶν ξυμμάχων καὶ εἴ τίς τι ἄλλο ἔφη ἠδικῆσθαι ὑπὸ Ἀθηναίων, ξύλλογον σφῶν αὐτῶν ποιήσαντες τὸν εἰωθότα λέγειν ἐκέλευον. Classen-Steup changes ἄλλο to ἄλλος, following the suggestion of Reiske, among others. Hude accepts this emendation and, with *CG,* reads τε after ξυμμάχων. Jones simply accepts the reading of *CG.* Gomme's note (*Hist. Comm.,* I, 226) is not as helpful as it might be, for it appears to suggest that the reading of *ABEFM* does not imply an invitation to two

ing of the Peloponnesian League, and that fact is significant. It was a meeting of the Spartans to which foreigners were invited for the purpose of giving testimony and information. It is clear that the citizens of Sparta were not of a mind to go to war, and the ephors called the meeting to change their views. For this purpose all complainants would be helpful, whether or not they were allies. Aegina, in fact, was not an ally, but her complaints would help the cause of the ephors and the war party.[3] In the same way, all complaints, whether or not they could be called violations of the Thirty Years' Peace, would help to fan the flames of Spartan resentment.

Among those who spoke, the Megarians made the loudest complaints, chiefly because of the Megarian Decree. The last to speak were the Corinthians, after they had shrewdly allowed the others to excite the Spartans. As the audience was composed of Spartans, the main purpose of the Corinthian speaker was to persuade the Spartan peace party and the Spartans who wavered between war and peace to break with Athens.[4] The war party, of course, was already convinced; what was needed was an indictment of the policy of peaceful coexistence that Sparta had followed since 445 which would show that it had harmed Sparta and would harm her still more if it were not immediately abandoned. Even more, it was necessary to frighten Sparta into action, for fear seemed to be the only way to move her. The Corinthian speech tried to accomplish both purposes in the face of a serious difficulty. The Spartans did not trust the Corinthians or their motives.

---

groups, i.e., allies of Sparta and others. But it is clear that all the suggested readings imply just that. The Spartans did invite others besides allies, and if our reading is correct, they invited complaints of all kinds, not only breaches of the treaty.

[3] For arguments that Aegina was not a member of the Spartan alliance, see Gomme, *Hist. Comm.*, I, 225–226 and D. MacDowell, *JHS*, LXXX (1960), 118–121. Cf. D. M. Leahy, *CP* XLIX (1954), 232–243.

[4] We have less reason to be confident of Thucydides' accuracy in reporting this speech than in his accounts of the speeches delivered in Athens, which he himself heard. Still, he could well have gotten the main facts from the Athenian envoys who were present and heard all the speeches (1. 72. 1; Gomme, *Hist. Comm.*, I, 233). It seems reasonable, therefore, to assume that the Corinthian speech that Thucydides gives us is relatively close to the one actually delivered.

The Corinthians complain with some asperity that although they had given the Spartans repeated warning of Athens' evil intentions, Sparta had paid no attention, for the Spartans believed that the Corinthians spoke on behalf of their own private interests.[5] In this the Spartans were quite right, for as we have seen, the Athenians had taken no action that directly interfered with Spartan interests. Even the Megarian Decree and the affair at Potidaea, which were at least doubtful cases, had arisen as a result of Corinth's own quarrel with Athens. The Spartans knew quite well that it had long been the Corinthian habit to use the Spartan alliance for purely Corinthian purposes. It was this knowledge that the Corinthians must counteract to succeed.

Suspicion of Corinthian motives, they argued, is the cause for Spartan inaction, and that suspicion is both unjustified and dangerous. It is unjustified because Athenian arrogance and aggression are now patent. The Athenians have already enslaved some states, presumably a reference to Aegina. They have long been preparing for war and are now on the point of enslaving still other states, among them allies of Sparta. This last reference, of course, is to Megara. This suspicion and consequent delay have already cost the Peloponnesians dearly. Corcyra, which could have supplied a large fleet, is in Athenian hands; Potidaea, which would provide a valuable base in Thrace, is under siege.[6]

For all this the Corinthians blamed Sparta, but it was perfectly clear that their barbs were aimed solely at the peace party which had dominated Spartan politics and formulated the policy under attack. They subjected the whole history of that policy to a brief but scathing review. Sparta had allowed Athens to fortify her city after the Persian Wars and then to build the long walls that made their city invulnerable. By this passive policy Sparta shared in the blame for the enslavement of Greece, for she had the power to prevent it but did not, although she had the proud reputation of being the liberator of Greece. Now the Athenian power had already doubled itself (the reference must be to the acquisition of the Corcyrean fleet), and Sparta was still inert. In the same way the Spartans had allowed the Persians to reach the Peloponnese before they had

[5] 1. 69. 1–2.
[6] 1. 68. 3–4.

offered serious opposition, and it was only because of the Persians' own mistakes that they had been beaten. In the same way, the Corinthians point out, the previous success of the Peloponnesians against Athens had been caused by Athenian mistakes. The reference here must be to the Egyptian campaign and possibly to the campaign in Boeotia. In short, the Corinthians argued that the Greeks enjoyed their freedom not because of the Spartan policy of caution but in spite of it.[7]

It next behooved the Corinthians to emphasize that the traditional Spartan policy was especially ill suited to stop Athenian aggression. To begin with, the Athenians were far closer than the Persians. They were, moreover, particularly dangerous and deceptive opponents who moved against their neighbors little by little. This remark, apparently made in passing, was particularly important to the Corinthian case. The Athenians had in fact done nothing expressly contrary to the treaty, nothing directly against Sparta, and nothing in itself very menacing. The Corinthians tried to turn these very facts to their advantage by suggesting that in the very indefiniteness of the Athenian actions lay their greatest danger. Indeed, the greatest part of the Corinthian argument rested not on what Athens had already done, not on the moral, legal, or strategic significance of the actions the Athenians had already taken, but rather on an interpretation of the Athenian character that indicated Athens' future actions.

This interpretation is presented in the most striking way possible by contrasting the Athenian character with that of the Spartans. Since the rhetoric is no less important than the matter of this argument, the invidious comparison deserves quotation.

> You have never considered what sort of men you are going to fight and how totally different they are from you. They are revolutionary and quick to formulate plans and put them into action, while you preserve what you have, invent nothing new, and when you act do not even complete what is necessary. Again, they are daring beyond their power, run risks beyond wisdom, and are hopeful amidst dangers, while it is your way to do less than your power permits, to distrust your surest judgments, and to think that you will be destroyed by any dangers. Besides,

[7] 1. 69.

they are unhesitating while you delay, they are always abroad while you stay at home, for they think that by their absence from home they may gain something while you believe that by going out for something you will lose what you already have. When they have conquered their enemies they pursue them as far as possible and if beaten they yield as little ground as they can. In addition to that they use their bodies in the service of the city as though they belonged to someone else, at the same time as they keep their judgment solely their own so as to use it for the city. And when they have thought of a plan and failed to carry it through to full success, they think they have been deprived of their own property; when they have acquired what they aimed at, they think it only a small thing compared with what they will acquire in the future. If it happens that an attempt fails, they form a new hope to compensate for the loss. For with them alone it is the same thing to hope and to have, when once they have invented a scheme, because of the swiftness with which they carry out what they have planned. And in this way they wear out their entire lives with labor and dangers, and they enjoy what they have the least of all men because they are always engaged in acquisition and because they think their only holiday is to do what is their duty and also because they consider tranquil peace a greater disaster than painful activity. As a result, one would be correct in saying that it is their nature neither to enjoy peace themselves nor to allow it to other men.[8]

Some scholars interpret this speech in a rather broad sense, as a contrast between the quietism of oligarchy and the revolutionary activism of democracy,[9] but its point is much more intensely immediate. The message it carries is that Athens is and has been a dangerously aggressive and revolutionary state that must be stopped before its power becomes overwhelming. Its character is such as to make traditional Spartan policy obsolete and even dangerous. The policy of cautious, watchful waiting, the Corinthians argued, was not praiseworthy prudence. It was, instead, evidence of a suicidal incapacity to lead the struggle for freedom against a foe of the restless, innovative, and aggressive character of the Athenians.

It is immediately evident that the Corinthian portrait of both Spartans and Athenians is enormously exaggerated. A people so sluggish and unimaginative as the Spartans depicted by the Corinthian speech could hardly have won mastery over the Peloponnese, leader-

[8] 1. 70.

[9] John H. Finley, Jr., *Thucydides,* 122–123.

ship of the Greeks in the successful resistance to Persia, and victory in the First Peloponnesian War. Even if we make allowances for the intensity of Corinthian feelings and the heat of the moment, we must admit that such a caricature could hardly have hoped to win the sympathy of the Spartans. But it was not intended to be a picture of the whole Spartan people; instead it was an indictment of the leaders of the peace party and their policy. We have seen that not all Spartans had favored the policy of quietism that Sparta had adopted after the disgrace of Pausanias. The Corinthian speech was intended in part to show that the aggressive dissenters had been right and the pacific victors wrong. The inflammatory rhetoric was well designed to encourage criticism of the peace party and support for its enemies.

The depiction of Athenian actions and character is even more remote from the facts. Athens had made no significant territorial acquisitions since the 450's. Her policy in regard to Sparta and her allies had, since 445, been a model of restraint. In suppressing revolution and defection in their empire, the Athenians had done no more than the Spartans had in consolidating their hold over the Peloponnese in the decade or so after the Persian War. Only within the last year had the Athenians taken actions that could even remotely fit the characterization of the Corinthians, and it was clear that those actions had been brought on by Corinth's quarrel with Corcyra, precisely the kind of private quarrel that made Spartans suspicious of Corinthian motives. It was important for the Corinthians to shift the emphasis away from these recent actions, for they might be regarded as a momentary aberration brought on by a specific conflict that could be resolved by prudence, patience, and restraint. Instead, they must be depicted as the continuation of a well-established policy that arose inevitably from the institutions and character of the Athenian people. That character must be shown to make peaceful coexistence impossible, even if the present crisis could be passed. Prejudice, suspicion, and fear, all are employed to overshadow the facts of recent history and to drive the Spartans toward war.

The Corinthians concluded their appeal, turning away from generalities, with specific demands capped by an open threat. The Spartans must keep their promise to the Potidaeans by quickly invading Attica. If they do not, the Corinthians, and perhaps others, will renounce the Spartan alliance and seek allies elsewhere.[10] No doubt some Spartans took this threat seriously, and at least one modern scholar of great shrewdness has done the same. Eduard Meyer believes that Corinth's threat to seek allies elsewhere, probably in Argos, was "a knife at the breast" of Sparta. He compares the situation with the one after the Peace of Nicias. On that occasion Sparta completely disregarded Corinthian interests with the result that Corinth organized a separate alliance that threatened to destroy Sparta's control of the Peloponnese.[11] In fact, the situations are not at all comparable. In 421, Argos, just then freed of her treaty with Sparta, was eager to take advantage of Sparta's problems to regain lost territories which had been long disputed. Sparta, moreover, was worn out by ten years of unsuccessful warfare, her strength was impaired, and her prestige at very low ebb. Other important allies of Sparta, such as Megara, Thebes, Elis, and Mantinea, were thoroughly dissatisfied with Spartan hegemony. It is important to point out, moreover, that even with such a splendid opportunity to form a separate alliance of the discontented powers, Corinth never joined the new coalition that she helped to create. She used it instead as a threat with which to compel Sparta to resume a war that Corinth wanted but Sparta did not.[12]

In the summer of 432 the situation was quite different. Argos was bound to Sparta by treaty and, more important, by her impotence in the face of a Spartan army whose power and prestige were unchallenged. There was no threat of defections from Spartan hegemony elsewhere. Besides Corinth only Aegina, which was impotent and under Athenian control, and Megara, a negligible power unaided by Sparta, were dissatisfied with Spartan policy. The fact is that Corinth's threat of defection was completely empty. If the Corinthians could not drive the Spartans to fight, they had nowhere else to go. They must either fight Athens alone, which would be suicidal, or accept the situation, which would be irritating, embarrassing, perhaps even infuriating, but which would not damage any of Corinth's vital interests. The damage would be largely psychological; Corinth

[10] 1. 71. 4–7.

[11] *Forschungen,* II, 315–316.

[12] See my article, *AJP,* LXXXI (1960), 291–310.

would have to accept the fact that, unlike Sparta and Athens, she was a power of the second rank. She refused to accept this, and that refusal drove the Corinthians to bring on a disastrous war.

Even the Spartan peace party could not know that the Corinthian threat was vain with the confidence that we know it, although they surely suspected it. But before its leaders could defend their policy against the Corinthian attack, another speech intervened. It was made by an Athenian, part of an embassy that Thucydides tells us "happened to have been present beforehand on other business." The ambassadors were present at the Spartan assembly, and when they heard the other speeches they decided to make a speech of their own. It is often supposed that no such embassy was present and that the speech was invented by Thucydides out of whole cloth, "as a device for introducing as early as possible a telling apology for the Athenian empire." [13] There are very persuasive artistic arguments against this view,[14] but the best argument is very simple. When Thucydides tells us that there was an Athenian embassy in Sparta, that it attended the assembly, and that its spokesman rose to speak, he is making flat statements of facts. To doubt them is to doubt that Pericles delivered a funeral oration, that a battle took place at Mantinea, or that Melos was destroyed. We have a duty to question Thucydides' interpretations, but if we are to deny his simplest statements of fact, we must give up any hope of dealing with the history he purports to describe. On the principle that it is proper to accept the facts presented by Thucydides unless they are contradicted by better evidence, we are compelled to believe in the reality of the Athenian

[13] Forbes, quoted by Gomme, *Hist. Comm.*, I, 233. Mme de Romilly (*Thucydides and Athenian Imperialism,* 243) finds it "difficult to believe that the Athenians actually spoke." She finds that their speech is not related to the debate as a whole, treating "the problems of imperialism in the abstract: it takes account neither of the speakers who have criticized Athens nor of the aim which the Athenian speakers in such an assembly might be expected to pursue; it neglects the politicians present in Sparta in order to speak directly to the future readers of Thucydides' History." With all this I disagree totally. As we shall see below, we have every reason to believe in the historicity of the Athenian speech. The speech fits very well into the actual situation if its purposes and the Athenian policy are properly understood. For a very confident denial of the historicity of the speech, see E. Schwartz, *Thukydides,* 105.

[14] Gomme, *Hist. Comm.*, I, 252–253.

speech at Sparta, if not in the perfect accuracy of the Thucydidean version.[15]

It is, moreover, altogether natural and reasonable that the Athenians should have been in Sparta and acted as they did. Pericles must have heard of the Corinthian machinations in Sparta and of the Spartan invitation to those who thought themselves wronged by Athens. If he learned of these things from no one else, he must have done so from his friends in Sparta who had an interest in thwarting the Corinthians and the Spartan war party. The fact that he sent no official spokesman to present the Athenian side of things is no accident. It was his position that Athens had taken no action to put her in conflict with Sparta; thus, it would not be appropriate to defend the Athenian actions to the Spartans. This point is made emphatically both by the Athenian spokesman and by Thucydides himself.[16] On the other hand, it would be very useful to have firsthand information of what took place in the Spartan assembly with all the nuances. At the same time, it was very possible that the occasion might arise where a statement of the attitude and policy of Athens might prevent the Spartans from taking reckless actions that they might regret. We may imagine that the Athenian ambassadors, like the generals at Sybota, were chosen for their wisdom, asked to use their judgment as to whether and when to act, and given very explicit instructions as to what they should say if the occasion arose.

The embassy, whose official cover story we never learn, arrived in advance of the assembly, and when the opportunity arose, they intervened. The content of their speech has given modern scholars no little trouble. It does not seem to provide a direct defense against the Corinthian attack, which, as we have seen, was in any case something more subtle and complicated than merely an attack on the Athenians. It is ignored by the speech that Archidamus makes a little later on. Thucydides does not tell us the name of the Athenian ambassadors or of their spokesman, although he surely knew them. But the most difficult problem of all has been to decide on the purpose of the speech, for it has seemed to many to be deliberately

[15] Something very like this view is presented by Busolt (*GG*, III: 2, 833). For an excellent statement on why we should believe in the reality of the Athenian speech, see F. E. Adcock, *Thucydides and his History*, 31–32.

[16] 1. 73. 1; 1. 72. 1.

provocative and calculated to bring on the war, yet Thucydides clearly believed the contrary to be true.[17] Most of the problems disappear, however, if we regard the speech that Thucydides reports as a reasonably accurate account of the general tenor of what was said and examine that speech in the light of its political context.

The Athenians at the very outset try to make clear what their purpose is and what it is not. They have not come to argue against the allies of Sparta, nor do they want to answer the specific charges alleged against Athens by the several cities. That would be altogether inappropriate, for the Athenians do not recognize the Spartans as their judges. Their intentions, rather, are threefold: to prevent the Spartans from yielding to the arguments of their allies and thereby too quickly making a bad decision about very important matters; to show that Athens has come into possession of its empire fairly; and to demonstrate that their city was far from contemptible in its power.[18] They began by pointing out at some length the extraordinary services Athens had performed in defense of the Greeks, not least among whom were the Spartans themselves, during the Persian War. This was hardly a tactful recitation and could not be expected to soften the Spartan attitude towards Athenian actions, but the Athenian spokesman himself makes it clear that he did not intend it to do so. "We will recount these facts," he says, "not as a plea but as an evidence and a demonstration of what sort of city you will encounter if you make the wrong decision." [19]

In any case, the recital of Athens' deeds in the Persian War is a necessary preliminary to the account of how Athens acquired her empire. That account, of course, makes no attempt to answer the specific complaints made by Sparta's allies about Corcyra, Megara, Aegina, and Potidaea. In a deeper sense, however, it does answer the charge implicit in the entire Corinthian attack that the Athenian Empire is an arrogant, tyrannous, and aggressive power which

[17] 1. 72. 1. The problems of the speech are discussed most intelligently and modestly by Gomme (*Hist. Comm.*, I, 252–254). It is also treated interestingly by Mme de Romilly (33–34 and 242–272), but the value of her discussion is severely damaged by her assumption that the speech is a thoroughgoing invention of Thucydides, intended by him as a general consideration of Athenian imperialism.

[18] 1. 73. 1.

[19] 1. 73. 3.

Athens has acquired by a continuous application of force and guile. In the process it carries out the promise that the speaker has made to show that the Athenians have acquired their empire justly. He asserts that the Athenians have not gained their empire by force, but that the allies accepted their leadership voluntarily after the Spartans had refused to accept the hegemony of the Greek war against the Persians. They were compelled to extend the boundaries of their empire at first from fear, then for the sake of honor, and finally, he frankly admits, out of self-interest. With remarkable candor he goes on to admit that in the process of gaining and ruling their empire the Athenians incurred the hatred of many of their allies. Some of them had already revolted and been made subject as a result. By that time Sparta had become hostile to Athens, and it was no longer safe to relax Athenian control for fear that her subjects would secede and join the Spartan alliance.

It is hard to believe that the Athenian speaker was quite so candid. His altogether objective account of the growth of the Athenian Empire is a splendid summary of Thucydides' account in chapters 89 to 118 of his first book, and we may well imagine that Thucydides, who was not present to hear the speech, may have put more than a little of his own thought and language into it. In spite of that, there was probably quite a bit of frankness, even bluntness, in the original speech where it would serve the speaker's purpose. His remarks were addressed to a hostile audience; any attempt to put a better face on Athenian actions than they deserved would be immediately detected and earn nothing but contempt. It was, on the other hand, not the Athenian purpose to pretend that the Athenian actions were virtuous, but rather that they were justified and even necessary. The Athenian spokesman thought that the necessities that had compelled his city's actions should be readily comprehensible to another hegemonal power. The Spartans, he pointed out, dictate the form of constitution that their Peloponnesian allies employ in accordance with the interests of Sparta. If they had maintained their hegemony in the war against Persia, they would have found it necessary to take similar measures too, would have become equally unpopular, and would have faced the same choice: to rule strongly or surrender leadership. All this was quite understandable, for it was always the rule of human nature for the strong to rule over the weak.[20]

In this last statement it is easy to see an anticipation of the argument the Athenians use in the Melian Dialogue, but the two situations are quite different. On the later occasion, the Athenians justified an atrocity they were about to commit to a lesser state. At the assembly in Sparta the Athenian spokesman addresses his observation to a powerful state on the verge of launching a great war against Athens. The argument asserts that, given the power that the two great super-powers have achieved, it is idle to talk of liberty or autonomy. The simple fact is that all the other states must accept the leadership of the hegemonal states whether in the open or covertly. The Athenian argues that Athens accepted the leadership of her allies because "we thought we were worthy, and you thought so too, until now, having calculated your interests, you employ the argument of justice." [21] The fact is, argues the Athenian, that anyone in a position of leadership, no matter how just and moderate his hegemony, will soon become unpopular.

Indeed, the Athenians complain that their very moderation and their attempts to treat their allies as equals has made their rule harder to bear. "It seems that men who are victims of injustice are more resentful than those who are the victims of violence, for the former seem to be deprived by an equal while the latter are coerced by someone stronger." [22] This is illustrated by the fact that the Athenian allies were more acquiescent under Persian rule than they are under Athenian leadership. And now the Athenian drove home the point of this lesson. If the Spartans destroy the Athenian Empire, the result will not be the restoration of independence to all the subjects of Athens. Instead, Sparta will succeed to the hegemony, and that will be neither pleasant nor suitable for the Spartans. Sparta will soon lose the good will it now enjoys as a result of Athenian unpopularity. The management of an overseas empire, moreover, is incompatible with Spartan mores and institutions. The debacle of Pausanias has already demonstrated that fact. "The customs you employ at home are not reconcilable with those of the other Greeks,

[20] 1. 75. 1; 76. 2.
[21] 1. 76. 2.
[22] 1. 76. 4.

and whenever any one of you goes abroad he acts in such a way as to conform neither to these nor to those of the other Greeks." [23]

Thus, the account the Athenians have given of their acquisition of empire and the nature of their rule is not a general discussion of imperialism thrust into the debate by Thucydides, nor is it an attempt to defend or palliate Athenian actions. It is instead part of a very intelligent and practical argument, the point of which is to make Sparta think twice before plunging into a war that will not only be dangerous but will be likely to bring results very different from what the Spartans anticipate. The argument is not only very pointed in its application to the immediate decision on foreign policy, but it also is subtly directed to the continuing split in internal Spartan politics. One of the main reasons for Spartan conservatism had always been the realization of some of its leaders that involvement in adventures outside the Peloponnese threatened the cherished stability of the Spartan constitution and the preservation of the Spartan way of life. The adventures of Cleomenes, Pausanias, and Leotychidas had all led to danger, corruption, and disgrace. As we shall see, the Spartan war party and those they persuaded imagined that the war would be quick and probably settled by a single great battle. Afterwards, they thought, Greece would be free and Sparta could retire to the Peloponnese with renewed prestige, honor, and power. No doubt there were some who saw things more clearly and were glad to try to replace Athens as the head of a great empire and unafraid of the great wealth that would come with hegemony. But they were surely in a minority and not eager to have their ambitions broadcast to the conservative majority.

In his peroration the Athenian emphasized the gravity of the Spartan decision. He urged the Spartans to be slow in making such a momentous choice. He spoke with particular emphasis of the incalculability of war and the role of mere change in a war of long duration, as this one was likely to be. Finally, he asked the Spartans not to break the treaty in violation of their oaths, but instead to accept arbitration on all disputed points as provided by the treaty. If the Spartans refuse, however, "calling on the gods by whom we have sworn as witnesses, we shall try to take vengeance on

[23] 1. 77. 6.

those who have started the war where you have led the way." [24]

It should be clear from this summary and analysis that we have no reason to believe that the Athenians intended their speech to provoke a war. Thucydides tells us just the opposite: the Athenians wanted to persuade the Spartans not to decide hastily. "At the same time they wanted to make clear the great power of their city, to offer a reminder to the older men of what they already knew and to the younger men of the things of which they were ignorant, thinking that because of their arguments the Spartans would incline to peace instead of war." [25] It is true that on this occasion Thucydides is not merely stating a fact but offering his understanding of an intention. Yet he had every opportunity to ask the Athenian ambassadors what their intention was and he surely did so. If he reports it incorrectly he is not guilty of an error of interpretation but of a total and deliberate deception. We have no reason to suspect him of such falsification. It is perfectly true that the Athenian line may be characterized as hard, perhaps even as unyielding, in spite of the offer of arbitration that concludes the speech. But this does not mean that it could not have been intended to persuade the Spartans to keep the peace. In any such confrontation, there are two basic tacks that may be taken. The line of sweet reasonableness tries to minimize differences, to yield wherever possible, to palliate actions that have caused friction. Such a line was taken by the western powers against Hitler in the 1930's, and its enemies gave it the pejorative epithet "appeasement." Sometimes such a procedure is justified and brings peace; sometimes it does not. The other basic approach tries not to appease but to deter. It assumes that the other side has more to lose than to gain by fighting a war and tries to demonstrate that fact to the adversary. It is careful to be and to appear unyielding with the intention of depriving the adversary of false illusions of a cheap and easy victory and of bringing home to him the determination of his foe and the costliness of a war. Such a policy was followed by the United States after the Second World War *vis à vis* Russia. It is a dangerous policy and may in some cases bring on the very war it tries to avoid. Up to now, at least, it has not done so; peace has been preserved for over two decades and the tension between the adver-

[24] 1. 68. 5.
[25] 1. 72. 1.

saries seems somewhat less than it was at the beginning of the confrontation.

The point is that the toughness of the Periclean line says nothing about its intentions. We have every reason to believe that Pericles wanted peace, still thought it possible in July, 432 and sent his ambassadors to Sparta in the hopes of preventing a Spartan declaration for war. The Athenian speech already made clear the terms he insisted upon and to which he would hold without deviation to the end. He would not defend Athens to Sparta, because Sparta was not involved and was certainly not a proper judge of Athenian actions. Athens would not yield to threats but would fight if forced to do so. On the other hand, the Athenians were prepared to submit all disputes to impartial arbitration.

If the speech had achieved its desired result, it would have had a sobering effect on the Spartans and inclined them to the conservative position of the peace party. But the ephors, the allies, and the cumulative effect of Athens' recent actions had done their work too well. After the Athenian speech the Spartans asked all strangers to withdraw and discussed their decision among themselves. The majority clearly believed that the Athenians were in the wrong and that Sparta should go to war immediately. At that moment Archidamus rose to speak. The venerable king, a personal friend of Pericles and the leader of the peace party, "a man with a reputation for wisdom and prudence," [26] made a final attempt to stem the tide moving his city toward a war that he knew would be dreadful.

Although a large part of his speech is devoted to the task of answering the Corinthian charges and defending the conservative peace policy that he supported throughout his career, Archidamus did not ignore the Athenian speech, as some have thought. In fact, the first part of his address is a subtle expansion and documentation of the points made by the Athenians: Athens is an unusual and powerful state which will prove a dangerous enemy; the war will be long and its outcome incalculable; the Spartans should not rush into such a serious and fateful decision. Athens is unlike the other Greek states of the Peloponnese and its environs. The Athenians have ships, experienced sailors, horses, weapons, money, a very large population, and many allies who pay tribute. In all these respects

[26] 1. 79. 2.

Sparta is inferior.[27] What kind of a war can the Spartans hope to fight against such a foe?

It is clear that the average Spartan who favored war looked to the past for a model of what the next war would be like, as men have never ceased to do. They expected that the Athenians would never allow the Spartans to destroy their crops, but would come out to their frontier to defend their fields in the traditional way. Either they would surrender before fighting as they had in 446, or they would be defeated in a single battle. The Spartans would never have undertaken a war that they truly believed would be long and costly. One of Archidamus' major aims was to emphasize the point made by the Athenians. He admitted that the Spartans had the military superiority easily to invade and lay waste the fields of Attica. "But they have plenty of other territory which they rule, and they will get what they need by sea." [28]

If the Spartans answered by encouraging revolt among the Athenian allies, they would need a navy to support the rebels, and where would they get it? Unless the Spartans could gain control of the seas or cut off the financial resources of Athens, they could not win such a war as they must fight. It would be vain for the Spartans to hope that "the war will quickly come to an end if we ravage their land." [29] Nor should they expect the Athenians to be so foolish as to "enslave themselves to their land" or to give way to panic when the war should come. In prophetic words Archidamus told the Spartans, "I fear, rather, that we shall pass this war on to our children." [30]

It was also necessary for the aged king to defend his policy against the Corinthian attack, and since that attack came in such general terms, the defense amounted to an apologia for the entire way of life in which Archidamus believed. At the same time it contained sharp refutations of many points made by the Corinthians. The slowness and caution with which the Corinthians reproach us, he said, is no cause for shame. That caution has served Sparta well in the past; because of it "we have always lived in a city that was both free and

[27] 1. 80.
[28] 1. 81. 2.
[29] 1. 81. 6.
[30] *Idem.*

of the best reputation."[31] Just as the Corinthians contrasted the Spartan character with that of the Athenians to make their point, Archidamus compared the Spartan character with the Corinthians' to make his. Although he never mentions the Corinthians by name, his target is perfectly clear. What the Corinthians call sluggishness (τὸ βραδύ) may be more correctly designated prudent self-control (σωφροσύνη ἔμφρων). Because we have it we do not become arrogant when successful nor unduly yielding when things go wrong. Because of this quality we can neither be flattered nor goaded into imprudent decisions. We have become good at war and government because we are a well-ordered people (διὰ τὸ εὔκοσμον). The same qualities the Corinthians criticize make us brave fighters and disciplined, law-abiding citizens.

Then Archidamus turned the attack against the Corinthians. "We are not so clever at useless things that we can disparage the enemy's preparations in a fine speech but not carry it through in action."[32] This was a jarring and not unduly subtle reference to the naval and military reversals Corinth had suffered at Athenian hands, first at Corcyra and then at Potidaea. No doubt Corinth had encouraged her allies with confident words on those occasions too, but had fought without success on both occasions. "We think that the plans of our neighbors are very much like our own and that what will happen by chance is beyond determination by reason."[33] The Spartans go to war on the assumption that their opponents are not fools, counting not on mistakes they hope the enemy will make, but on their own preparations. In a single sentence Archidamus rejects the entire line of argument put forward by the Corinthians based on the special character they attribute to the Athenians. "We must not believe that man differs from man very much but that he is best who is disciplined in the hardest school."[34] The Athenians are men such as we are, is his implication; do not try to paint them as supermen and drive us to war out of irrational and unjustified fear.

Although Archidamus was opposed to a rash decision for war, he did not advocate a supine policy of allowing Athens to do whatever

[31] 1. 84. 1.
[32] 1. 84. 3.
[33] *Idem.*
[34] 1. 84. 4.

she liked. In the first place, that had never been the policy of the Spartan peace party. Besides, the mood of the Spartan assembly made such a policy politically impossible. Instead, Archidamus offered a policy that was a practical and realistic alternative. First the Spartans should send ambassadors to Athens to make official complaints without making clear the intentions of Sparta. At the same time the Spartans should prepare for the kind of war they must face if negotiation failed. They should seek help in ships and money from barbarians as well as Greeks, while building their own resources at home. If the Athenians yielded to the Spartan complaints, there would be no need of a war. If the Athenians returned unsatisfactory replies, there would be plenty of time to fight, when the Spartans were properly prepared *in two or three years*. The very period of preparation, combined with continued Spartan firmness, might serve to make war unnecessary. The Spartans should not be eager to ravage the land of Attica. "Do not think of their land as anything but a hostage for us, and the better it is cultivated the better hostage it will be." [35] The best course for Sparta is to leave the land untouched as long as possible so that when the Athenians think of possible concessions, they will know that they have something very important and tangible to lose. To destroy it first would enrage the Athenians, make them desperate, and deprive Sparta of a useful hostage.

Again and again Archidamus urged the Spartans not to be dragged into a war in which no proper Spartan interests were involved by allies with selfish motives. "Complaints on the part of cities or individuals can be resolved, but when a whole alliance begins a war whose outcome no one can foresee, for the sake of individual interests, it is hard to emerge with honor." [36] We must not, he said, be carried away prematurely by the words of our allies, who, in any case, will not carry the main burden of the war, but we must prepare properly. Let us maintain our traditional ways, which have served us so well, that cautious deliberation, which we can use not because we are weak, but precisely because we are strong. Archidamus concludes with his very specific proposals: send envoys to Athens to discuss Potidaea and the other complaints of the allies; this must be done

[35] 1. 82. 4.
[36] 1. 82. 6.

because the Athenians have offered arbitration, and it is against our laws (οὐ νόμιμον) to make an immediate attack against someone offering arbitration. At the same time we are negotiating, let us prepare for war. "If you do this you will be making the best decision for yourselves and the one that will most frighten your enemies." [37]

The proposals of Archidamus were altogether in accord with the views expressed by the Athenian ambassadors in the Spartan assembly. If adopted they would have avoided a hasty decision for war, opened a period of negotiation, and submitted all disputes to arbitration on their individual merits. As we shall see, this would have suited Pericles perfectly. It did not, however, suit the Corinthians and their aggrieved allies. If Potidaea could be saved at all, the attempt must be made immediately; every day that passed brought its capitulation closer. More important still, an impartial arbitration of each case would not help the Corinthians. By now they did not want the settlement of grievances; they wanted revenge on Athens to restore their prestige; they wanted a free hand against Corcyra; it is probably not too much to say that at this point they wanted nothing less than the destruction of the Athenian Empire. The war party in Sparta was of a similar mind. It was not the troubles of Corinth, Megara, Aegina, or Potidaea that concerned them, but what appeared to them the arrogant and dangerous power of Athens. About this there could be no negotiation or compromise; Athens must be humbled.

When the ephor Sthenelaidas rose to answer Archidamus he must have felt confident that most Spartans had not been persuaded by the old king, for he made little effort to counter his arguments. His brief and blunt speech, as Gomme says, "is excellently in character" [38] and deserves quotation.

> I don't understand the lengthy arguments of the Athenians. They praise themselves highly, but they don't deny that they are doing wrong to our allies and to the Peloponnesus. If they behaved well against the Persians and are now behaving badly towards us, they deserve a double punishment because they have become bad after having been good. But we are the same now as we were then, and, if we are wise, we will not look on while they wrong our allies, nor will we delay in seeking

[37] 1. 85. 2.
[38] *Hist. Comm.*, I, 251.

vengeance; for our allies are already suffering. Others may have much money, ships, and horses, but we have good allies whom we must not betray to the Athenians. Nor should we submit to judgments by courts or words, for we have not been injured by words. Instead we must take swift vengeance with all our forces. And let no one tell us that we must take time to consider when we have been wronged; rather let those who contemplate doing a wrong reflect for a long time. So vote for war, Spartans, in a manner worthy of Sparta. Do not allow the Athenians to grow stronger and do not betray your allies, but let us, with the help of the gods, march out against the wrongdoers.[39]

After he had finished his speech, Sthenelaidas, as ephor, put the question to a vote. The usual Spartan procedure was to vote by voice, but on this occasion Sthenelaidas claimed he could not tell which shout was louder and asked for a division, putting the question as follows: "Let whoever thinks that the Athenians have broken the treaty and are doing wrong go to that spot [to which he pointed], and whoever thinks not let him go to the other side." It is perfectly clear that Sthenelaidas was in no real doubt about the outcome of the vote; he wanted to make the size of the majority dramatically evident in case of a later shift in Spartan opinion.[40] The division revealed that a large majority (πολλῷ πλείους) agreed with Sthenelaidas and decided that the treaty had been broken.[41] It is important to recognize that this was not a declaration of war, and much time would pass before any hostile action was taken, but the Spartan decision meant it would be very difficult, if indeed possible, to avoid a general war.

Why did the Spartans decide as they did? For Thucydides their decision was predetermined. "The Spartans voted that the treaty had been broken and that they must go to war not so much because they had been persuaded by the arguments of their allies, but because they were afraid that the Athenians might become more powerful,

[39] 1. 87.

[40] This view is shared by Gomme (*Hist. Comm.*, I, 252). Classen (I, 240) and Busolt (*GG*, III: 2, 838) believe that the ephor really could not tell which vote was greater on the first ballot. The tone of the ephor's speech, the final vote, and the entire narrative of Thucydides seem to me to make this interpretation impossible.

[41] 1. 87. 3–4, 6.

seeing that the greater part of Greece was already in their hands." [42] This amounts to a repetition of the judgment he has already made on "the truest cause of the war." [43] On this occasion it is supported by a long excursus (1. 89–118) giving the history of the growth of the Athenian Empire, which proves that for Thucydides the cause of the Peloponnesian War must be sought long before the trouble at Epidamnus. At the end of that excursus he makes it clear that the decision for war was merely the last step in a continuous process that began immediately after the Persian War.

> All these actions that the Greeks performed against each other and against the barbarian took place in the period of about fifty years between the retreat of Xerxes and the beginning of this war. In this time the Athenians established and reinforced their empire, and themselves attained great power. Although the Spartans perceived this, they made only a small attempt to prevent it and remained quiet for the greater part of the time. For even before this they had never been quick to go to war unless they were compelled, and in this period they were hindered, to a degree, by wars at home. This quiet lasted until the power of the Athenians began to manifest itself and to lay hold on their allies. Then the situation became unendurable and the Spartans decided they must try with all their resolution to destroy that power if they could and to launch this war.[44]

To us, however, the inevitability of the Spartan decision is not so clear. As we have seen, and as even Thucydides admits, the Athenians thought it could still be averted when they spoke to the assembled Spartans. Archidamus did not treat the decision for war as a *fait accompli* and tried to avert it. If we trace the history of Spartan policy since the Epidamnian crisis, moreover, we find no reason to be confident that the Spartans would be eager for war in July, 432. From the beginning they had worked for a peaceful settlement of the dispute between Corinth and Corcyra. During the ensuing struggle they remained at least neutral and probably exerted their influence to prevent their other allies from becoming involved.[45] They

[42] 1. 88. *φοβούμενοι τοὺς Ἀθηναίους μὴ ἐπὶ μεῖζον δυνηθῶσιν, ὁρῶντες αὐτοῖς τὰ πολλὰ τῆς Ἑλλάδος ὑποχείρια ἤδη ὄντα.*

[43] 1. 23. 6.

[44] 1. 118.

[45] See above, pp. 225–226 and 246.

were probably troubled by the growth in Athenian power that accompanied the successful defense of Corcyra, and it is likely that a majority of the ephors who took office shortly after Sybota, among whom was Sthenelaidas, were or became members of the war party.[46] The Megarian Decree, which probably came soon after the ultimatum to Potidaea, may explain why the ephors were moved to promise an invasion of Attica to the Potidaeans. In any case, the combination of the decree and the ultimatum in the winter of 433/2 were enough to produce a warlike majority in the ephorate. But what we must not forget is that even then the feeling for peace among the Spartans in general was so great that the ephors could not keep their promise to Potidaea. Even after Potidaea was under siege, it was left to the Corinthians to call the aggrieved allies to Sparta to make their complaints. Only then did the ephors feel able to call an assembly of the Spartans to give an official ear to the charges against Athens.

It is impossible to avoid the conclusion that if it had not been for Corinth the Spartans would probably have taken no action whatever.[47] Throughout the course of Spartan history the forces favoring peace had almost always been in the majority. Even in this crisis the war party was unable to maintain firm control for very long. As we shall see, they were unable to bring Sparta to action for more than a year after the assembly we have described, and even then, the first act of war was left to an ally. Although Archidamus had been defeated on this occasion, he remained a figure of great political and military importance who clearly influenced Spartan policy long after he was outvoted in the assembly of July, 432. Up to the very outbreak of the war, the peace party remained powerful, and even during the Archidamian War, they were strong enough to compel their countrymen to seek peace on several occasions. Thucydides, of

[46] Busolt (*GG,* III: 2, 835–836) is confident that at least a majority of the ephors belonged to the war party. But we must remember that although they took office in the autumn, after Sybota, they had been elected in the spring, before Athens had even made an alliance with Corcyra. We have no reason to think that the Spartans, who had heretofore maintained a consistently peaceful policy, elected a majority of war hawks without any apparent reason. It is more likely that the events of the summer converted some of them to a hostile attitude.

[47] See the similar conclusion of Busolt (*GG,* III: 2, 840–841).

course, is quite right in emphasizing the role played by the old fear and suspicion of Athens in bringing about the Spartan decision, but that fear had been insufficient to dislodge the peace party until the Battle of Sybota, at the earliest, or to cause Sparta to act even after that battle. What turned the tide was the performance of the Corinthians, aided by the recent actions of Athens.

The Corinthian contribution to the Spartan change of policy can be divided into three parts. First, they organized and contributed to an effective propaganda campaign waged by the aggrieved friends and allies of Sparta, which gave the warlike ephors a chance to put their case in the most favorable circumstances. Next, they employed a very effective weapon in their threat of secession from the Spartan alliance, which seemed to promise the dissolution of that alliance. We may think that the threat was only a bluff, but most Spartans were unwilling to call it. Probably the most effective device employed by the Corinthians, however, was the picture they painted for their Spartan audience of the Athenians. By tying together the early history of the Athenian Empire with Athens' recent actions in response to the Corcyrean affair, they were able to depict the Athenians as a permanently restless, aggressive, and dangerous people who must be stopped before it was too late. Reasonableness, caution, delay, and negotiation would only be thought weakness by such people. The only thing to do was to stop them before their power, already grown too great, should become even greater and all Greece was enslaved.

Cooler consideration might have shown that this picture was not altogether consistent with historical fact. Since 445 the policy of Athens had been consistently unaggressive; Corinth, even more than Sparta, had recognized that fact by its recommendations in regard to the Samian rebellion. The peace party might argue that the recent actions of Athens were not part of a general policy of aggression but were merely an isolated response to a particular situation brought about by Corinth against the advice of Sparta. Given some time for the incident to pass, the Athenians would very likely return to their policy of preserving their empire, avoiding involvements on the Greek mainland and the west, and seeking accommodation with the Peloponnesians on terms of equality and mutual respect. This view of things, in fact, seems to be what was behind

Archidamus' policy of slow preparation for war coupled with negotiation.

Cooler heads did not prevail, and for this the rhetoric of the allies, and especially the Corinthians, was largely responsible. We must admit, however, that the Corinthians could not have succeeded without the unintended help of Pericles. His policy after Sybota was meant to prepare Athens for a conflict with Corinth while avoiding a clash with Sparta, but it did not have that result. The financial measures he took even before Sybota were, of course, very reasonable and not inflammatory.[48] The expeditions of Phormio to Acarnania and Diotimus to Italy, as well as the renewal of the treaties with Rhegium and Leontini, were all easily explicable measures aimed at a possible war with Corinth, but need not alarm Sparta unless she were already determined to defend the Corinthians. The Megarian Decree, however, was something else again. Here the Athenians were not moving against Corinth directly but against an ally of Sparta strategically located at the gateway to the Peloponnese. Archidamus and his friends might be aware that it was not intended as an aggressive act by Pericles and that Athens had no intention of seizing Megara. They might know that the trade embargo, far from being an extreme act of aggression, was really a compromise measure to limit the scope of a possible war with Corinth by warning off potential allies. To the ordinary Spartan, however, it looked like an arrogant, aggressive, and unnecessary action.

We do not know just what Athens did at Aegina or what action, if any, provoked it. Apparently, however, its necessity was not clear to the Spartans. The ultimatum that Athens casually delivered to Potidaea could only contribute to the image the Spartan war party wanted to fix on the Athenians. So far as we know it was altogether unprovoked. The Athenians were quite right in thinking that Potidaea was the one place most vulnerable to Corinthian agitation and so a likely trouble spot, but at the time the ultimatum was delivered, the Potidaeans had done nothing to justify the harsh demands made upon them. To the Spartans the affair at Potidaea must have seemed

[48] S. B. Smith (*HSCP*, LI [1940], 283–288) suggests that it was growing *financial* power of the Athenians that drove Sparta to war. This highly original interpretation of Thucydides has, so far as I know, rightly won no support.

another instance of arrogant Athenian aggression against an innocent bystander. Such impressions were not enough to produce any action on the part of the Spartans until the Corinthian speech put all the pieces together.

In such circumstances the tone and character of the Athenian reply seem ill chosen. A firm, unyielding line backed by a show of strength is a fine tactic of diplomacy against an adversary who is convinced of its employer's basically unaggressive intentions. Such was Sparta's attitude when it was controlled by Archidamus and the peace party. It is far less useful, indeed it is very dangerous, when used towards a state that has come to fear that its user is too powerful, aggressive, and ambitious. These were the fears of the war party, and it seems likely that the hard line of Pericles helped convince uncommitted Spartans and some who had favored peace to support the war.

Pericles appears to have believed that his careful policy of limited response to the Corinthian challenge would be understood by Sparta, and the record of the previous fifteen years gave him good reason to believe it. What he did not recognize was that his policy could contribute to a change in the internal situation of Sparta and bring to power men who could not or would not understand him. Once again we may speculate that his long period of power at Athens had made him insufficiently aware of how different the political situation at Sparta was from that at Athens. When Pericles spoke, he spoke confidently for Athens and her empire. When Archidamus spoke, he could not be sure that he controlled Sparta, much less the Peloponnesian League. Given the instability of Spartan politics in the summer of 432, Pericles seems to have made a fateful miscalculation.

The decision in the Spartan assembly was that the treaty had been broken; it was not a vote for war. At the same time, the decision was binding only on the Spartans, for their allies had not formally considered the question. Thus, the Corinthians, even though they had carried the day, did not get the quick action they wanted. Instead the ephors called for an assembly of the allies to deliberate on the matter and to vote for war if that were their decision.[49] Meanwhile, they sent to the oracle at Delphi to ask the god if they should go to war. Thucydides reports the reply with uncharacteristic

[49] 1. 87. 4–5.

hesitation. "The god answered them, so it is said, that if they fought with full vigor they would achieve victory, and he said that he himself would give his aid whether he was called upon or not." [50] Thucydides did not know the actual response of the oracle, and his hesitation is likely caused by the suspicion, probably correct, that he has the version of the war party.[51] Still, their report must have been correct in essence if not in detail. After Athens' defeat at Coronea and her abandonment of central Greece, she had lost influence at Delphi. She had already gained the enmity of the priests by her support of the Phocians.[52] The ephors, of course, knew all this and were confident of a favorable answer when they put the question. It was another step in their difficult campaign to drive the Spartans to war.

The congress of Sparta's allies convened in August of 432.[53] It is worth pointing out that even though Sparta had already made its position clear and Corinth and Megara were openly and enthusiastically in favor of the Spartan decision, a unanimous vote of agreement by the allies was not a foregone conclusion. It is most likely that not all the allies attended the congress.[54] It is possible that they stayed home because they lacked sympathy with the Spartan decision. Far more telling is the action of the Corinthians. Before the meeting they had gone to each city in private, urging each ally to vote for war, "fearing that Potidaea would be taken before they could act." [55] From the language of Thucydides [56] it is impossible to be certain whether this electioneering took place in Sparta before the meeting convened or whether the Corinthians had gone from city to city even before the delegates had arrived at Sparta. The desperation of the Corinthians makes the latter possibility seem more likely.

[50] 1. 118. 3.

[51] Gomme, *Hist. Comm.*, I, 413.

[52] 1. 112. 5; Gomme, *Hist. Comm.*, I, 413.

[53] Gomme, (*Hist. Comm.*, I, 425) puts it early in the month. Busolt (*GG*, III: 2, 841–842) puts it a bit later, i.e., late August to early September.

[54] Thucydides (1. 125. 2) tells us that the final vote was taken by *ὅσοι παρῆσαν*, which clearly implies that some allies were absent. Gomme, *Hist. Comm.*, I, 414.

[55] 1. 119.

[56] *καὶ οἱ Κορίνθιοι δεηθέντες μὲν καὶ κατὰ πόλεις πρότερον ἑκάστων ἰδίᾳ ὥστε ψηφίσασθαι τὸν πόλεμον, δεδιότες περὶ τῇ Ποτειδαίᾳ μὴ προδιαφθαρῇ. . . .*

When the congress began, the several allies repeated the complaints they had made in July before the Spartan apella. Once again the Corinthians spoke last and most vigorously.

The first and most obvious task of the Corinthians was to convince those allies who were reluctant to fight Athens that they should vote for and support the war. These reluctant allies must have included most of the cities of Arcadia: Tegea, Mantinea, Phlius, Clitor, and many others.[57] These cities must have wondered what such a war had to do with them. As inland cities they had no quarrel with Athens, its navy, or its empire. They were physically remote from most of the quarrels and not much interested in commercial embargoes like the Megarian Decree. To them the Corinthians addressed their first remarks. The inland cities should realize that if they did not help their coastal allies, they would be unable to use them freely as *entrepôts* where they could dispose of their own surpluses and obtain imports. They should pay careful attention to the debate as something that touched them closely, for if they ignore the appeals of the coastal states, "the danger may one day reach them, and they are deliberating about their own fate no less than ours." [58]

It was not only the inland states, however, who needed convincing. Sicyon, for instance, unless it had changed its policy, was not eager for war, for the Sicyonians had tried to avert a conflagration as early as 435. It is likewise probable that Epidaurus, Hermione, Troezen, and Cephallenia, all of whom abstained from aiding Corinth at Sybota, although they were present at Leucimne,[59] were not yet persuaded. As coastal towns, they recognized the enormous power of the Athenian navy and empire and the damage it could do them. It may have been precisely because of that power that they were reluctant to enter into a war with Athens over issues that did not concern them directly. They seem to have suspected that the Corinthian policy was not rational, that it did not aim at the redress of particular grievances but at a holy war to destroy the Athenian Empire. In any case, the Corinthians found it necessary to assure them that their war aims were reasonable and limited. "As for us, we are now stirring up war because we have been injured and have sufficient complaints.

[57] See Gomme, *Hist. Comm.,* I, 415.

[58] 1. 120. 2.

[59] See above, pp. 223–224 and 245–246.

When we have warded off the Athenians, we will put an end to it when the opportunity offers itself." [60]

The most important task for the Corinthians was to convince the allies that they could win a war against Athens. The speech of Archidamus had not convinced the Spartans, but its practical and hardheaded discussion of the difficulties of fighting the Athenians had been given at least a month to make an impression, and the peace party, we may well imagine, had not failed to inform the allies of the arguments the King had put forward. The Corinthians offered the following reasons for optimism: the Peloponnesians were superior in numbers and military experience; they depended on allies, not undependable mercenaries; they could overcome the naval superiority of the Athenians not only from their own resources but by borrowing money from the treasuries at Delphi and Olympia, both of which would be available to the Peloponnesians. It was the naval power of Athens that was most difficult to combat, so the Corinthians had to spend some time in explaining it away. They argued that since the Athenian navy was made of paid foreigners instead of Athenians, it would be easy to hire them away for money. The Athenians, unlike the Peloponnesians, were subject to defection, being dependent on foreigners. One defeat at sea should be enough to destroy the Athenian navy, and thus Athens. Even if Athens should hold out, the Peloponnesians would have time to acquire the necessary naval skills, and since they were naturally more courageous than Athenians, this would guarantee a Peloponnesian victory. The money necessary to bring all this about would come from voluntary contributions by the Peloponnesian allies.[61]

The Corinthians mentioned still other techniques whereby the Athenians, regarded as so formidable by Archidamus, might be attacked. The Peloponnesians might assist the allies of Athens to revolt and thereby deprive the Athenians of the money and sailors that made them strong. If the Athenians chose not to fight a land battle, the Peloponnesians, in addition to ravaging Attica, could establish a permanent fort in Attica and so make continued depreda-

[60] 1. 121. 1.
[61] 1. 121. 2–5.

tions. Besides these measures, other, unforeseen opportunities would surely present themselves.[62]

This Corinthian forecast of devices to be used in the war to come, most particularly the reference to the establishment of a permanent fort in Attica, has often been taken as evidence that this speech was composed by Thucydides, and quite late, for the fort at Decelea was established in 413.[63] There is little reason to believe it. On the one hand, many of the Corinthian predictions were wrong: one battle did not end the war; the Peloponnesian navy did not prove the equal of the Athenians after a little practice; the war was not a short one. On the other hand, there is every reason to think that the speech looks backward and not forward. The revolts of Samos and Byzantium, if not the many earlier rebellions, were fresh in the minds of all. It was natural to think that similar rebellions would take place if Athens were distracted by a Peloponnesian war. The idea of establishing a permanent fort in hostile territory hardly requires oracular vision, and there is good evidence that the thought occurred to many well before 413 and even before the Peloponnesian War.[64] The intention of the speech was to encourage the allies to vote for war, and optimistic predictions based on past experience were the obvious rhetorical weapons.

The Corinthians argue further that the war is absolutely necessary and the alternative unthinkable. Athens, they argue, is so powerful that she can defeat all the Greek states one by one; the only chance is to unite in a war against her; the alternative is slavery. To submit to the Athenians would be to permit the establishment of a tyranny.[65] That unhappy result can be avoided, for Apollo has promised his help and all the rest of Greece apart from the Spartan alliance will gladly join in the struggle out of fear or interest. The approval of Apollo, moreover, proves that the war is just and will not be a violation of the treaty, but rather a defense of a treaty already violated.[66]

[62] 1. 122. 1.

[63] Grundy, *Thucydides,* I, 320–321; see also the discussion of Gomme, *Hist. Comm.,* I, 418–419.

[64] Gomme, *Hist. Comm.,* I, 418.

[65] 1. 122.

[66] 1. 123.

This is, of course, a fine piece of sophistry, though we need not imagine that the wily Corinthians learned it from the sophists. Their peroration employed a splendid array of arguments to achieve their goal; it reminds the modern reader of countless similar arguments that have since been used by the advocates of war. This is a particularly favorable moment to go to war. This war is not in our own interest only, but in the common interest. We must hurry to save the Potidaeans, for they are Dorians besieged by Ionians: the racial argument so often invoked. Now that we have met to consider action, we cannot afford not to take any, for that would be a fatal sign of weakness. War is, in any case, inevitable. The war, moreover, will bring a more lasting peace, "for peace is more secure after a war." [67] The speech concludes with an appropriate statement of the noble purposes of the proposed war. "Recognizing that the state which has established itself as a tyrant in Greece threatens all alike, that it already dominates some of us and is planning the domination of the others, let us march out and subdue it, make a secure future for ourselves, and liberate those who are now enslaved." [68]

After the Corinthian speech the vote was taken by "all the allies who were present," which implies, as we have seen, that not all were present. Of these a majority (τὸ πλῆθος) voted for war. Thucydides does not report the size of the majority, but since he does not indicate that it was overwhelming, as he does on the occasion of the Spartan vote earlier,[69] perhaps we may believe that it was far from unanimous. It may be that the division in the alliance reflected the division within Sparta. Not everyone was convinced that the war must come; not everyone believed that it was a just war; not everyone thought it would be easy and successful; not everyone thought it was necessary. To be sure, the alliance had voted for war, and orders were issued to make the appropriate preparations without delay, which would seem to have closed the matter. But, as Thucydides points out, it still was nearly a year before the Spartans invaded Attica and openly began the war.[70]

This delay is noteworthy. Thucydides' own explanation is not

[67] 1. 124. 2.

[68] 1. 124. 3.

[69] 1. 87. 3. πολλῷ πλείους.

[70] 1. 125. 2.

altogether satisfactory; indeed it is hardly an explanation. He says that they spent the year "putting in order the things they needed" (καθισταμένοις ὧν 'έδει).[71] As Busolt has observed, the preparations for an invasion of Attica such as was envisioned by Sthenelaidas and the war party would have taken only a few weeks.[72] These compelling considerations make it clear that we need to explain the delay of the Spartans. The answer must be that in spite of the vote in favor of war, the allies and the Spartans themselves were not totally converted to the views of Corinth and the Spartan war party. The arguments of Archidamus must have had their effect after the rhetoric of the Corinthians and the fiery, single-minded patriotism of Sthenelaidas were more carefully assessed. No doubt the Spartans and their allies were persuaded that Athens was a threat and must be stopped, but they now seemed to believe that it was necessary to go somewhat slowly, to make greater preparations than usual, perhaps even to try to achieve their ends without war. It was probably at this time that they sent envoys to Persia and to their friends in Italy and Sicily to ask for help in the coming war.[73] At the same time they began to send a series of embassies to the Athenians, ostensibly at least to avoid the war with Athens.

[71] 1. 125. 2.
[72] *GG*, III: 2, 844. See Appendix K.
[73] Diod. 12. 41. 1.

18. *Athens*

Between August of 432 and the Theban attack on Plataea that began the war in March of 431, the Spartans sent no less than three embassies to Athens claiming to offer means of avoiding the war. Such offers would in any case be very suspect, coming as they did from a state and an alliance that had already agreed on a war against Athens. That suspicion is not diminished for us by the way in which Thucydides reports the purpose of the missions: the Spartans sent them "so that they might have the best possible pretext for war if the Athenians did not accept them." [1] He does not say what the Spartans would have done had the Athenians accepted their demands. The implication is very clear that he thought there was no chance that the Athenians would accept, and many modern scholars have taken the view that the Spartan negotiations were consistently and altogether insincere, merely attempts to gain a favorable moral position in the war to come.[2] Not everyone, however, has been convinced, and the negotiations deserve our careful attention.[3]

The first Spartan embassy demanded that the Athenians "drive out the curse of the goddess." [4] This was a reference to the conspiracy

[1] 1. 126. 1.

[2] E.g., Grote, V, 21; Adcock, *CAH,* V, 188–189; Glotz and Cohen, *HG,* II, 622.

[3] Among those who have thought that the Spartan embassies may have sincerely aimed at preserving peace are Beloch (*GG* ², II: 1, 296–297); Meyer (*GdA,* IV: 2, 19–20); Busolt (*GG,* III: 2, 845–848), and DeSanctis (*SdG,* II, 265–266).

[4] 1. 126. 2–3.

of Cylon, which had taken place two centuries earlier. On that occasion the unsuccessful conspirators had taken refuge at the altar of the Furies. Members of the Alcmaeonid family, maternal ancestors of Pericles, had violated the divine sanctuary and killed the refugees, thus incurring a curse on themselves and their descendants. This "curse of the Alcmaeonidae" had been put to political use by the Spartan king Cleomenes at the end of the sixth century, and the Spartan war party obviously saw an opportunity to use it again.[5]

This first embassy was probably sent out soon after the Congress of August 432 while the war spirit was relatively high and the war party in control of policy. There is no reason to question the cynical motives that Thucydides attributes to this mission. The Spartans pretended that they wanted to avenge the honor of the gods, but in fact they were aiming at Pericles, for they knew that he would be the greatest barrier to their success. They believed that if Pericles were banished it would be easier to win concessions from Athens, but they had no real hope of achieving his exile. What they hoped was that he would be discredited and blamed for the troubles of Athens, "for, as the most powerful man of his time and the leader of his state, he opposed the Spartans in everything and did not allow the Athenians to yield but kept driving them towards war."[6]

Although we may accept Thucydides' interpretation of the Spartan demand as an attempt to influence the internal political situation of Athens, his account does not make very clear what precisely the Spartans hoped to achieve. They believed Pericles' banishment would make Athenian concessions more likely, but they did not expect him to be exiled. Apparently, then, they wanted him to remain in Athens and in power, but to be troubled and weakened by suspicions. Troubled or not, he would continue to oppose concessions and the war would come. Thus, it would appear that the Spartan war party put forth their demands not in order to help stop the war but to undermine Athens' political unity.

Although the motives of the Spartans are not described as clearly as we should like, Thucydides does present us with some important facts that are quite plain. By the time of the first embassy, Pericles was altogether in favor of a hard policy toward Sparta, which by

[5] 1. 126. 3–12; Hdt. 5. 70–72; Plut. *Solon* 12.

[6] 1. 126. 3.

now could legitimately be described as "driving the Athenians to war." We have seen that as early as July he had opposed making concessions to the Spartans except under arbitration, as prescribed by the treaty. At that time he still believed that a show of firmness coupled with a willingness to arbitrate particular disputes could avert a conflict. In the interim, however, the Spartans and their allies had voted for war. Pericles could hardly be blamed for taking these two solemn and official votes seriously and for believing that further negotiations that offered no concessions on Sparta's part and that did not offer to submit disputes to arbitration were merely tactical maneuvers in a psychological war. By the autumn of 432, Pericles had become altogether unyielding.

A second fact that emerges from Thucydides' account of the first Spartan mission is that there was enough political opposition in Athens for the Spartans to think it worth while to try to exploit it. It is, of course, in this period that many scholars have tried to date the attacks on Pericles and his friends that we have dated over six years earlier.[7] That Pericles had survived those attacks does not mean that his political troubles were at an end. Thucydides, son of Melesias, was back in Athens and probably at the head of at least a remnant of his faction. Cleon was still on the scene, constantly gaining in political experience, and a rival to Pericles, however unequal, for influence with the masses. Opposition had been very effective and almost decisive during the debate on the Corcyrean alliance in 433. All the prejudices that the average Athenian felt towards their aloof and unusually intellectual leader must have come to the fore in these dangerous and difficult times, and his political enemies might be expected to reap whatever advantage they could. The trials of Phidias, Anaxagoras, and Aspasia had all involved impiety, and it can be no accident that the Spartans revived an old charge that also dealt with a breach of religious practice. We may be sure that both the aristocratic friends of the son of Melesias and the democratic supporters of Cleon made much of the air of impiety surrounding Pericles. Almost certainly, both sides attacked him personally on other grounds. No doubt they accused him of arrogance, and it is

[7] See above, Chapter 12, pp. 193–202.

probable that the old story of his resemblance to the tyrant Peisistratus was revived at this time.[8]

The third fact that we learn from Thucydides, however, is that these attacks were unavailing; Pericles remained "the most powerful man and the leader of his state." Plutarch supports this judgment, saying that the Spartan demand produced the opposite results of what was intended. "Instead of suspicion and slander, Pericles achieved a still greater confidence and honor among the citizens as a man who was most hated and feared by the enemy." [9] It is important to emphasize that all the evidence testifies to Pericles' unshaken position of power when he was making the crucial decisions on the eve of the war. This is not to say that he was free of all political pressure and could do precisely what he wished. We have seen already and shall see again that he needed to consider carefully the internal effects of his foreign policy at all times. Nonetheless, the policy of Athens was the one put forward by Pericles, and he formulated it chiefly because he thought it the right one and not because his hand was forced by domestic politics.

To the first Spartan demands, Pericles, who was not a neophyte in the art of political propaganda, returned a similar demand. The Spartans had insisted on the banishment of the curse of the Alcmaeonidae, so the Athenians bade the Spartans expel the curse of Taenarus and doubled the bid by insisting that they drive out the curse of Athena of the Brazen House as well. The Spartans had once put to death some helots who had taken sanctuary at the temple of Poseidon at Taenarus, and it was the common belief that this sacrilege had caused the great earthquake at Sparta.[10] This seemed closely parallel to the curse attached to the Alcmaeonidae and was a very convenient means with which to embarrass the Spartans. The curse of the Brazen House refers to another sacrilegious breach of sanctuary. King Pausanias, the notorious victor at Plataea, who tyrannized over the Greek allies, committed treason with the Persians, and plotted with the helots, had been shut up in the temple of Athena and allowed to starve to death. This was clearly a viola-

[8] Plut. *Per.* 7. 1 and 31. 1.
[9] Plut. *Per.* 33. 1.
[10] 1. 128. 1.

tion and was so recognized by the priests at Delphi, who insisted on a complicated and expensive act of atonement.[11]

The reference to this second sacrilege might seem a bit strained and unnecessary, but it had a very definite value as propaganda. In fixing attention on the scandals surrounding Pausanias, Pericles reminded the Greek cities how objectionable Spartan hegemony had been when it was unchecked by Athenian power. Members of the Spartan alliance who were not directly involved in the quarrels with Athens, Athenian allies who might be contemplating rebellion, and neutral states like Argos might all regard the coming war as something other than a simple struggle for freedom against tyranny when compelled to think of the Spartan record in the years after the Persian War. At the same time, the reference to Pausanias may have had an effect on the internal politics of Sparta. The aggressive policy of Pausanias and Leotychidas had brought Sparta unpopularity, treason in the highest places, loss of respect, and rebellion within the Peloponnese. The forerunners of Archidamus had opposed that aggressive policy and could claim to have restored Sparta to a position of power, respect, and leadership by eschewing extra-Peloponnesian adventures. The policy supported by Sthenelaidas would involve actions outside the Peloponnese and seemed likely to produce a long war in far-off places. Pericles could not have been unaware that his response to the Spartan demand was likely to help the peace party in Sparta and hurt its enemies. It seems clear that he emerged the victor from the first diplomatic skirmish.

After their initial rebuff, the Spartans continued to send ambassadors to Athens to make demands whose acceptance, it was implied, would avert the war.[12] They told the Athenians to withdraw from Potidaea and restore autonomy to Aegina. "And especially they proclaimed publicly in the clearest of language that there would be no war if they withdrew the Megarian Decree." [13] Once again we need to determine the purpose of the Spartans. It is hard to believe that

[11] 1. 128. 1–1. 135. 1.

[12] 1. 139. 1. Thucydides says that the Spartans made their demands *ὕστερον δὲ φοιτῶντες παρὰ 'Αθηναίους. φοιτῶντες* indicates a repeated action. See Classen's note (I, 358). There is no way of fixing the time between the embassies.

[13] 1. 139. 1. *καὶ μάλιστά γε πάντων καὶ ἐνδηλότατα προύλεγον τὸ περὶ Μεγαρέων ψήφισμα καθελοῦσι μὴ ἄν γίγνεσθαι πόλεμον.*

these repeated visits, which we may consider together as a second embassy, were altogether insincere. Even if we concede that the first two demands were exorbitant and not seriously intended,[14] we can hardly believe that of the last demand, and it was on this last demand that the Spartans put the greatest emphasis. As we shall see, the whole debate in Athens centered on the Megarian Decree, which shows that there was at least some chance that it might be repealed. If it had been withdrawn, the Spartan war party would have found it difficult to bring on a war for some time.[15] The evidence indicates that the Spartans made their demands in the hope that at least the last one would be accepted and the war averted.

It is clear that a change had taken place in the very unstable political situation at Sparta since the rejection of the first embassy. The cool confidence of Athenian diplomacy could not fail to affect the feelings of the Spartans and their allies. The farsighted caution of Archidamus must have gained ground at the expense of the impetuous zeal of his opponents. The second Spartan embassy bears the unmistakable signs of a compromise and gives evidence of the return to a position of influence by Archidamus. We have no reason to doubt Plutarch's report that Archidamus tried to settle the complaints of the allies peacefully and to soften their anger against Athens.[16] The period of his activity must be the time between the first and third Spartan embassies, for both of those are patently not designed to bring peace. The second embassy shows that neither Archidamus nor his opponents were in full control. If Archidamus held unquestioned control, he would have submitted the quarrels to arbitration; at the very least he would have been willing to discuss each grievance separately. If the war party were in full control, we might expect no further negotiations after the dismissal of the first embassy; in any case, we should not have so simple and attractive an offer as the one that was finally made: peace in exchange for the cancellation of the Megarian Decree. The likelihood is that Archidamus was strong enough to insist on continued negotiations, the war party demanded

[14] Such is the implication of Glotz and Cohen, *HG,* II, 623.

[15] Even Eduard Meyer, who believes that the war was already inevitable, thinks there was a chance that Athens might have repealed the decree, since it brought her no material benefit and was unpopular (*GdA,* IV: 1, 20–21).

[16] *Per.* 29. 5.

Athenian concessions on all points, and Archidamus was able to get a concession that made the rescinding of the Megarian Decree the only *sine qua non* for peace.[17]

It is notable that this last offer amounted to the betrayal of Corinthian interests, and this has led to doubts of its sincerity. Remarking on Thucydides' report that the Spartans announced there would be no war if the decree were repealed, Adcock says, "This can hardly be the whole truth, for Sparta was bound at least to satisfy Corinth, and the simple repeal of the Megarian Decree would hardly do that." [18] But the assumption that Sparta would not readily abandon Corinthian interests in favor of its own is hardly self-evident. That is precisely what Archidamus intended to do, and his speech, which we have already examined, shows it. He made it plain that no Spartan interests that he could see were involved in the several quarrels with Athens. He hinted darkly that the Corinthians were using the Spartans and their allies for private purposes and selfish Corinthian ends, a hint the Corinthians found it necessary to refute. That is, moreover, precisely what the Spartan peace party did in 421 with the Peace of Nicias. That peace served Spartan interests only, leaving not merely Corinth, but Thebes, Elis, and Megara as well, so dissatisfied that they refused to sign the treaty.[19]

It is altogether likely that Archidamus and his party were prepared to call the Corinthian bluff and reach an accommodation with Athens. Megara was a member of the Spartan alliance, and it was under economic attack. The Spartans must interpret that as a violation of the spirit if not the letter of the Thirty Years' Peace, which provided that each side should not interfere in the territory of the other. Sparta could not allow Athenian interference with the livelihood of Megara any more than the Athenians could permit the Corinthians to stir up and support rebellion at Potidaea. The lifting of the Megarian Decree was therefore an absolute necessity for a peaceful solution. The other conflicts, however, did not touch on Sparta and could be abandoned. If the Corinthians were dissatisfied and threatened secession, Archidamus was prepared to let them try.

[17] This interpretation is very close to the analysis of Busolt, *GG*, III: 2.

[18] *CAH*, V, 189.

[19] 5. 17. 2.

Perhaps the time had come to show the Corinthians who was hegemon in the Spartan alliance.

If the Athenians had accepted the Spartan offer of a compromise, war could have been averted, but they did not. Pericles was determined to stand fast and to yield on no point. It is clear, however, that the sincere effort at compromise that the second Spartan embassy offered caused him a good deal of embarrassment in a way that the crude propaganda of the first embassy had not. The Spartan proposal made it appear that Athens was going to war over the Megarian Decree, originally a mere tactical diplomatic maneuver and certainly not worth fighting for in itself. The clamor from the Athenian peace party to accept the proposal must have been very great, and even the more docile supporters of Pericles must have stopped to think. Thus, Pericles could not simply reject the Spartan demand; he had to justify his policy in a rather unusual manner. Thucydides says that the Athenians charged the Megarians with encroaching on sacred land, with border violations, and with harboring runaway slaves.[20] These charges, Plutarch tells us, were embodied in a decree sent by herald to Megara as well as to Sparta to present a defense of the Athenian action. "This decree was proposed by Pericles and contained a reasonable and humane justification of his policy." [21]

Plutarch records an anecdote that further indicates the embarrassment Pericles felt. When the Spartan ambassadors made their proposals, Pericles tried to defend his refusal by pointing to some law that he claimed prevented him from taking down the tablet on which the Megarian Decree was engraved. The Spartans replied: "Then don't take it down, turn the tablet around, for there is no law against that." [22] Whatever the truth of the story, we may at least believe that it arose from the knowledge that Pericles had to look hard for devices with which to defend his actions: *se non é vero é ben trovato*. In spite of his embarrassment and political difficulties, Pericles did not lose his control of Athens and was able to persist in his policy of firmness.

At last the Spartans sent a third and final embassy. The ambassadors did not repeat their earlier offers but made instead the following

[20] 1. 139. 2.
[21] *Per.* 30. 3.
[22] *Per.* 30. 1.

Laconic statement: "The Spartans want peace, and there will be peace if you give the Greeks their autonomy." [23] The curtness of the tone, the failure to deal with specific issues, and the enormity of the demand make it clear that this ultimatum was intended not to continue negotiations but to end them; it was aimed not at the Athenians but at their allies and at Greek public opinion in general.[24] It is plain that Pericles' refusal of the proposals made by the second Spartan embassy had once again altered the delicate balance of Spartan politics. The hard line at Athens had in turn hardened opinion in Sparta. It was now easier to believe that compromise was impossible, that Athens was bent on a course of aggression, and that war was inevitable. The influence of Archidamus was severely reduced, and the war party was in firmer control than it had ever been.

So secure did the war party feel that they included at least one member of the peace party in the embassy that delivered the ultimatum. In a rare moment of specificity, Thucydides tells us the name of the Spartan ambassadors: Ramphias, Melesippus, and Agesander. Melesippus was very close to Archidamus. When the Spartans were already on the march to invade Attica, Archidamus sent Melesippus on a final vain embassy to the Athenians in the hope of avoiding war at the last moment.[25] It is possible that Ramphias too was inclined towards peace.[26] No doubt these men were selected by the war party as ambassadors to demonstrate the new unity of purpose in Sparta. We cannot know whether they accepted the assignment against their own inclinations out of patriotism, or if they had themselves been converted by Athenian intransigence. The former seems more likely.

There was no more room for negotiation. The Athenians must now decide whether to yield or fight. An assembly was called to debate the most momentous of issues, war and peace. The calling of such an

[23] 1. 139. 3.

[24] Busolt, *GG,* III: 2, 848. The proof that any conceivable opinion on a subject in classical antiquity has been held by somebody is given by the fact that some scholars doubt that this last Spartan demand was really an ultimatum. Adcock (*CAH,* V, 189) and Nesselhauf (*Hermes,* LIX [1934], 293) are of that opinion. The statement of Adcock is briefly but adequately refuted by Gomme (*Hist. Comm.,* I, 451).

[25] 2. 12.

[26] 5. 13. 2; Busolt *GG,* III: 2, 849 and n. 1.

assembly was, of course, inevitable, but it seems likely that the enemies of Pericles organized the discussion in a way not to his liking. Since he was determined to make no concessions, he would certainly have preferred to limit the debate to whether or not to accept the Spartan ultimatum. Instead, it was decided "to give an answer after having considered everything once and for all." [27] As a result of this decision, it was possible for his opponents to raise once again the subject of the Megarian Decree, the one thing Pericles did not want discussed. Many speakers rose on each side of the question. We may suppose that among those who argued that "war was necessary" [28] was Cleon, and that one of those who urged that "the decree should not be an impediment to peace but should be withdrawn" [29] was Thucydides, son of Melesias, but Thucydides reports none of these speeches. The only speech he gives us is the lengthy defense of his policy offered by Pericles. To those who suggest that Pericles was not in full control of the political situation in Athens, it is worth pointing out Thucydides' assessment of his position at the moment of decision: he was "at that time the first man among the Athenians and the most powerful in speech and action." [30]

The speech of Pericles, like the speeches of the Corcyreans and Corinthians in the Athenian assembly of 433, was surely heard by Thucydides himself. It was a memorable speech on a vital subject at a crucial moment, and we may well imagine that Thucydides and other Athenians would remember it especially well. Unless we are to disregard Thucydides' claim to report the speeches he heard as accurately as possible, we must treat his account as reasonably accurate.

The address of Pericles to the Athenians falls naturally into two parts, the first a defense of the policy that will lead to war and the second dealing with the prospects of victory and the strategy to be followed when the war should come. It is quite clear that Pericles did not expect to see his advice and policy rejected by the people of Athens. The section of his speech in which he defends his policy is

[27] 1. 139. 3. *ἐδόκει ἅπαξ περὶ ἁπάντων βουλευσαμένους ἀποκρίνασθαι.*

[28] 1. 139. 4. *ὡς χρὴ πολεμεῖν.*

[29] *Idem.* *ὡς μὴ ἐμπόδιον εἶναι τὸ ψήφισμα εἰρήνης ἀλλὰ καθελεῖν.*

[30] 1. 139. 4. *ἀνὴρ κατ' ἐκεῖνον τὸν χρόνον πρῶτος Ἀθηναίων, λέγειν τε καὶ πράσσειν δυνατώτατος.*

far less than half as long as the part that lays out his hopes and strategy for war. The tone, moreover, is austere and unbending, hardly one likely to sway an undecided electorate. The opening words clearly establish the mood: "I am of the same opinion as always, O men of Athens, that we should not yield to the Spartans." [31] This is followed not by a plea but by a warning. Knowing that during the course of a war men are likely to change their minds with the turn of events, he demands that those who now support his views and vote for war should abide by that common decision in the hard times to come or else make no claim to good judgment if the war should be successful. One is reminded of a similarly lofty speech attributed to Pericles on an earlier occasion. When criticized by his enemies for spending too much on his building program, he had replied by offering to pay the cost himself if the dedication would honor not the Athenians but Pericles.[32] In both cases he had no doubt about the outcome of the debate, and in each instance he was right.

Next he turned to the defense of his policy. "Even before this," he said, "it was clear that the Spartans were plotting against us, and now it is plainer than ever." [33] The promise of the Spartan ephors to invade Attica on behalf of Potidaea fully justified the first statement; by now it must have been widely known. The Spartan ultimatum supported the second one, for it meant the destruction of the Athenian Empire if accepted. This interpretation of the Spartan demand has been challenged by Nesselhauf. He makes a distinction between an Athenian league in which the autonomy of the members was duly observed, although they paid tribute to Athens, and one in which the Athenians interfered with local autonomy. The former is a league and the latter an *arché*. The former was quite conformable to Greek law and usage, the latter a violation of the unwritten laws of the Hellenes. The former was acceptable to the Spartans, the latter quite unacceptable.[34] This is a distinction without a real difference. The fine legalities observed by Nesselhauf are mythical. Autonomy was a very vague concept for the Greeks, as it remains for

[31] 1. 140. 1.
[32] Plut. *Per.* 14. 1.
[33] 1. 140. 2.
[34] Nesselhauf, *Hermes,* LIX (1934), 291–292.

us. Strictly interpreted, it could hardly permit the payment of tribute; loosely interpreted, it could permit the inclusion of everything the Athenians had ever done. The realities of power and politics, not legal misunderstandings, were behind the actions of both sides. We may be sure that Pericles and the Athenians were correct in thinking that the Spartan ultimatum demanded the abandonment of their empire.

The most important point of Pericles' defense rested on what might seem to be a legality, but which is something far more basic. The Spartans have consistently refused to submit to arbitration. The treaty specifically stipulated that each side should retain what it had while differences were submitted to arbitration, but the Spartans have "never themselves asked for arbitration and do not accept it now that we offer it." [35] Instead they hope to win their point by force. "They want to resolve their complaints by war instead of by discussion, and now they are here, no longer requesting but already demanding." [36] They have ordered the Athenians to abandon the siege of Potidaea, give Aegina her autonomy, and withdraw the Megarian Decree; finally they have sent this last embassy, which publicly demands that the Athenians give autonomy to all the Greeks. "Only a flat and clear refusal of these demands will make it plain to them that they must treat you as equals." [37]

These remarks offer the best clue to the thinking behind Pericles' policy of firmness. He was not unwilling to give way on any of the Spartan grievances. If the Spartans had accepted his offer of arbitration, he would surely have abided by the decision. What he could not accept was the precedent of Spartan interference in the Athenian Empire at Potidaea and Aegina, or with Athenian commercial and imperial policy as represented by the Megarian Decree. To accept such interference under the threat of force would have returned to the situation in the Greek world after the Persian War: Athenian hegemony in the Aegean would depend on the sufferance of Sparta and would be at the mercy of the fluctuations of Spartan politics. The peace to which Pericles had agreed in 446/5 guaran-

[35] 1. 140. 2.

[36] *Idem.*

[37] 1. 140. 5. *ἀπισχυρισάμενοι δὲ σαφὲς ἄν καταστήσαιτε αὐτοῖς ἀπὸ τοῦ ἴσου ὑμῖν μᾶλλον προσφέρεσθαι.*

teed the Athenians equality with the Spartans as hegemonal powers in discrete spheres. It rested on the principle of mutual noninterference and provided carefully for relations with neutral states and for the arbitration of differences. If the Athenians had given way to the threat of war now they would have abandoned their claim to equality and opened themselves to future blackmail whenever it should be convenient for the Spartans.

Pericles understood this very well, as he made clear in refusing to withdraw the Megarian Decree.

> Let none of you think that you are going to war over a trifle if we do not rescind the Megarian Decree, whose withdrawal they hold out especially as a way of avoiding war, and do not reproach yourselves with second thoughts that you have gone to war for a small thing. For this "trifle" contains the affirmation and the test of your resolution. If you yield to them you will immediately be required to make another concession which will be greater, since you will have made the first concession out of fear.[38]

The Spartan peace party, of course, understood the attitude of Pericles very well and had some sympathy for it. They had negotiated the treaty on which Pericles rested his case and had done so in good faith. Since then both sides had done their utmost to abide by its terms, and with great success. If they had retained power, they would, as we have suggested, have accepted arbitration and allowed the crisis to pass. But the war party was now in power, and they were not interested in arbitration. If we have interpreted their purposes correctly, Pericles was quite right in his assessment of what an Athenian policy of appeasement would mean. Men like Sthenelaidas were not interested in the particular grievances of Megara, Potidaea, or Aegina. They were jealous of Athenian power, feared it, and wanted to destroy it. Men like them had supported the aggressive policies of Cleomenes in the sixth century and of Pausanias and Leotychidas after the Persian Wars. They had promised to invade Attica in behalf of the Thasians in the 460's and had expelled the army of Cimon in 461. They had fought vigorously and joyfully in the First Peloponnesian War and joined in the attacks on King Pleistoanax and his advisor Cleandridas, who had made a peace possible. They had forced a meeting of the Peloponnesian alliance

[38] 1. 140. 5.

to discuss aid to the Samians in their rebellion against Athens, and most recently they had promised to invade Attica on behalf of the Potidaeans. In 432 they enjoyed one of their rare moments of power, which coincided with an opportunity to launch a major war that would bring down the Athenian Empire and restore the unique and unchallenged hegemony of Sparta which they had always cherished. For these reasons they rejected all thought of arbitration. Their failure to mention the Megarian Decree in the ultimatum was neither accident nor oversight.

Although the Spartan ultimatum made no mention of the Megarian Decree, it clearly dominated the debate in the Athenian assembly and is treated as a central issue by Pericles. This raises difficulties that have long troubled historians. Nesselhauf has put the problem very well. Pericles speaks of the Megarian Decree as a trifle, but when he says that the Athenians should expect greater demands immediately after yielding on this small matter, why doesn't he point out that the Spartans already have made much greater demands by insisting that the Athenians restore autonomy to all the Greeks? [39] How can the Megarian Decree be the center of discussion when the final demand seems to have made such discussion pointless? [40] Busolt assumes that the members of the peace party who delivered the ultimatum must have given the Athenians to understand that even then the Spartans would be satisfied, if only the Athenians would rescind the Megarian Decree.[41]

Megara was the most vulnerable point in Pericles' policy. It was the one action that exposed Athens to the charge of violating the Thirty Years' Peace; it brought Athens no profit and probably cost something in the loss of commerce and taxes from Megara. Most important, it had been made the *sine qua non* for peace by the Spartans. No matter that the Spartans had stiffened their demands since the Athenians had rejected the earlier ones. The peace party could always argue that a show of reasonableness, however belated, would

[39] *Op. cit.*, 286.

[40] G. Pasquali (*Studi Italiani di filologia classica,* V [1927], 299 ff.) found the problem so troubling that he was led to suggest that the report of the last embassy is a later insertion that Thucydides added when he heard about it from the Spartans. The absurdity of that suggestion is clearly demonstrated by Nesselhauf (*op. cit.*, 287).

[41] *GG*, III: 2, 849.

finally bring the Spartans round. Thus, it was altogether natural that the advocates of appeasement, concession, and peace in Athens should fix on the Megarian Decree as the focus of their attack on Periclean policy. Few would agree that the Athenians should give way on all the earlier demands, to yield at Potidaea and Aegina as well as Megara. Almost none would be willing to accept the final demand of Sparta, which they correctly interpreted as a demand to give up their empire. Many, however, might be persuaded that a concession at Megara would avoid war, and that Megara was a mere trifle not worth the trouble. For these reasons the opposition talked only of the Megarian Decree, and Pericles had no choice but to give it a prominent place in his defense.

For Pericles, as we have seen, there was no further room for concession or negotiation. The issue had been drawn, as he saw it, by the Spartans. The choice was between a war that would preserve the Athenian Empire and leave its hegemon, Athens, equal to Sparta and free of the fear of Spartan interference and domination, or a series of concessions that would ultimately dismantle the empire and subordinate the Athenians to Sparta. Pericles closed the first part of his speech with a powerful statement of his view.

> Make your decision right now either to yield before any harm is done, or, as I, at least, think best, if we go to war, make up your minds not to yield on any pretext, whether great or small and not to live in fear for what we possess. For when a claim is imposed upon neighbors by equals not by the process of law but by force, the result is just as much slavery whether the claim be very large or very small.[42]

It was necessary for Pericles to convince the Athenians that they should go to war, but he needed also to persuade them that they could win such a war. He therefore offered a discussion of Athenian prospects that amounts to a rebuttal of the speech the Corinthians made to the allied congress at Sparta. This has led some to question whether the speech was composed not by Pericles but by Thucydides, but there is no good reason to do so. The contents of the Corinthian speech would soon have been made known in Athens. No doubt the advocates of peace had used the points made by the Corinthians to dampen the enthusiasm of the Athenian war party.

[42] 1. 141. 1.

It was, therefore, not only natural but necessary for Pericles to answer the Corinthian arguments.

He begins with an analysis of the weaknesses of the Peloponnesians. For the most part they are farmers who have no accumulated wealth. Their attachment to the land and their poverty restrict them to very short campaigns, and they have no experience in long or overseas wars. Such people cannot fight the kind of war that will be necessary, for they cannot be long away from their crops; they must quickly diminish whatever resources they have, since they have no external source of support. Special war taxes will not be a satisfactory substitute for an accumulated war fund. The admitted bravery and military excellence of the Peloponnesians will hardly make up for their economic deficiencies. Though they may be careless of their lives, they are necessarily cautious of their limited property and so in no position to sustain a long war.

In a single battle, to be sure, the Peloponnesians are a match for all the other Greeks, but the Athenian strategy will be to refuse to engage in such a battle. It is not only their economic weakness that will tell against the Peloponnesians in a long war; their organization is equally inadequate. They are without a regular political assembly and so are prevented from making decisions and putting them into effect quickly. Each state has an equal vote and pursues its separate interests. "Some want the greatest possible vengeance against a particular enemy, while others want the least possible damage to their property." [43] Even when they come together to make plans, they spend little time thinking of the common interest but pursue their own goals. But their greatest difficulty will be in the shortage of money, for they will be slow in providing it while "the opportunities of war do not wait." [44]

It will be no easy thing for the enemy to establish a fort in Athenian territory, but even if they do, the Athenians can retaliate in kind by erecting forts in their territory and making raids on them with the Athenian fleet. The Athenians have far more experience in fighting land battles and making raids than the Peloponnesians do in naval warfare. Nor will that situation be changed in the course of the war. It is quite absurd for the Corinthians to say that the Peloponnesians

[43] 1. 141. 7.
[44] 1. 142. 1.

can quickly learn to be sailors. The Athenians have been practicing since the Persian Wars and are not yet perfect; how can their enemies expect to reach a high level of skill in such a short time? To begin with, they are landlubbers, and the Athenians will not give them a chance to practice, for wherever they set out to sea, an Athenian fleet will be lying in wait to pounce on them. As a result they will remain inactive, such skill as they have will deteriorate, and they will be afraid to fight. The art of naval warfare is no mere pastime; it requires continuous practice and serious attention.[45] The expectation that they can use the wealth of Olympia and Delphi to hire away the mercenary sailors is a vain hope.[46]

The Athenians, Pericles asserted, were in a far better position to conduct a war of the kind that would be necessary. They were free from the evils of poverty and divided counsel which would bedevil the enemy. The great advantage held by Athens was control of the sea. It meant that the Athenians could afford to allow their lands to be devastated, relying for sustenance and income on the empire, while retaliatory devastation of the Peloponnese would be unendurable to the enemy. This fact must dictate Athenian strategy: since Athens would be invulnerable if it were an island, the Athenians must abandon their lands, retreat behind the city walls, and act as if their city really were an island. On no account should they allow anger or impatience to lure them into an open battle. Not only were they inferior in numbers to the enemy, but a victory in battle would be of little use. The Peloponnesians would only return with another army, but if the Athenians should lose, all would be finished. The allies would take advantage of the Athenian defeat to rebel and so deprive Athens of her sustenance. The main danger to Athens would be the impetuousness of her citizens, who might be persuaded to fight a fruitless battle by the sight of their wasted fields and burning houses. "If I thought I could persuade you," said Pericles, "I would tell you to go out yourselves and lay them waste and show the Spartans that you will not give way to them for the sake of these things." [47] This impetuousness offered yet another danger; the Athenians might try to extend the area of warfare and to increase their

[45] 1. 142. 2–9.
[46] 1. 143. 1–2.
[47] 1. 143. 5.

empire by means of the war. This would be disastrous, and Pericles warned the Athenians not to add to the necessary perils of war "dangers of their own choosing. For I am more afraid of our own mistakes than of the schemes of our enemies." [48]

At last, Pericles set out the answers he proposed to return to the Spartan ultimatum and to the specific demand they had made earlier in respect to the Megarian Decree. The Athenians would withdraw the decree if the Spartans would repeal the law that expelled aliens from their territory, in so far as Athens and her allies were concerned. Here Pericles carefuly pointed out that nothing in the treaty forbade either law. The Athenians, moreover, would grant autonomy to their allies if they were independent when the Thirty Years' Peace was made and only if the Spartans equally granted autonomy to their own allies in a way which conformed to the views of each state, not to those of Sparta. Finally, Pericles repeated his offer to submit to arbitration as provided by the treaty. "We will not begin the war, but we will defend ourselves against those who do. These are the answers which are just and proper for this city to make." [49]

Pericles concluded his speech with a peroration intended to fill his fellow citizens with pride in the glory of their city and its previous achievements and a determination to be equal to them. His main points, however, were that the war was inevitable, and that "the more willingly we accept it, the less eager will our enemies be to attack us." [50]

The latter part of Pericles' speech gives us a clear idea of the strategy he planned and no less clearly reveals the nature of his war aims. Pericles intended to fight a limited, strictly defensive war. The Athenians were to abandon the countryside and rely on their empire and navy. They were to keep the seas clear of the enemy and refuse to enter into a decisive land battle. By means of unopposed landings from the fleet and, perhaps, the establishment of fortified places in the Peleponnese, they would devastate the enemy's land, retaliate for raids on Attica, annoy, irritate, and wear down the foe. On no account should the Athenians abandon their strictly defensive purpose and try to take advantage of opportunities to extend their empire. It

[48] 1. 144. 1.
[49] 1. 144. 2.
[50] 1. 144. 3.

would be a war of attrition and would not be short. After a while the enemy would be compelled to see the hopelessness of his situation and feel the economic pinch of waging a fruitless war. The natural divisions within the loose organization of the Spartan alliance would assert themselves in costly quarrels. Soon it would be apparent that the Peloponnesians could not win, and a peace would be negotiated. Thoroughly discredited, the Spartan war party would turn over control of affairs to the reasonable men who had kept the peace since 446/5. Athens could then look forward to an era of peace even more firmly based than the one coming to an end.

Those who think that the speech represents the thought of Thucydides and not of Pericles believe that since it anticipates later events, it must have been written later. It speaks of fortified places in the Peloponnese, and we know that the Athenians established a fort at Pylos in 425. It mentions the split in the Spartan alliance, and we know that that alliance suffered serious defections in 421. It warns the Athenians against extending their empire in the midst of the war, and we are reminded of the Sicilian expedition. These references, however, do not require astonishing foresight. The reference to forts is an inevitable rebuttal to the point made by the Corinthians, and the others do not require political genius to foresee. The fact is that the speech and the strategy it presents are based largely on experience and look backward rather than forward. The organizational weakness of the Spartan alliance had been demonstrated many times, and the Athenians had themselves benefited from it when the Corinthians had prevented Cleomenes from invading Attica at the end of the sixth century. The incapacity of the Peloponnesians at sea had been proved on several occasions. The brief Spartan leadership of the war to free the Aegean and Hellespont of the Persians had been a fiasco; the Athenians had won all the major naval battles in the First Peloponnesian War; just recently the Corinthians had shown that their navy and its tactics were obsolete and vulnerable in the battles near Corcyra. The First Peloponnesian War, moreover, had shown that the Peloponnesians fought only short campaigns, did not sustain a continuous war effort, and readily made peace after a short period of war.

The strategy outlined by Pericles emerged directly from the Athenian experience in the First Peloponnesian War. The Athenians had made three mistakes, and each was terribly costly. They had embarked on the Egyptian campaign in the midst of the war against Sparta. The consequent defeat cost men and money, shook Athenian confidence, and brought on a rash of defections and rebellions in the empire. The attempt to conquer central Greece had likewise been a disaster. It required major land battles to defend the conquered territory, the last one of which ended in a rout of the Athenians and the abandonment of their gains. It also produced a crisis in the empire which compelled the Athenians to sue for peace. Finally, the determination of the Athenians to protect their fields turned those fields into a hostage for the enemy and compelled the Athenians to come to terms. The strategy of Pericles was simply to avoid all these errors in the next war.

Strategy is never merely a matter of military plans, as tactics may sometimes be; it is always based on political realities and has political consequences. It is very unusual for political leaders to launch a war or even to allow their states to be drawn into a war unless they have good hopes of winning. Rightly or wrongly, they rely on their strategic plan to bring about a happy outcome to their diplomatic activities. Sometimes the very strategy they fix upon may help determine the political and diplomatic decisions they make. It is now generally agreed that the fact that Germany had only one strategy in 1914, the Schlieffen Plan, which required that Germany take the initiative in a war with both France and Russia, helped bring on World War I, for it forced the Germans to react quickly, indeed too quickly, to the possibility of a war. The same plan required the Germans to invade Belgium in order to knock France from the war quickly, but this made it certain that England would join the war against Germany, a diplomatic and military misfortune of a very high order. At the same time, military and strategic considerations persuaded the German generals that the likelihood of success in a great war was greater in 1914 than it would be a few years later. Although we know that there was no German plot to bring on a major European war in August 1914, the German strategy and military considerations that provided the expectation of success in case of war helped bring on the war.[51]

[51] I have accepted the interpretation of A. J. P. Taylor, *The Struggle for the Mastery of Europe 1848–1914* (Oxford, 1954), 520–531.

The strategic ideas of the Spartan war party undoubtedly made it easier for them to pursue policies that led to war. Had they believed, as Archidamus did, that the war would be long, difficult, costly, and of doubtful outcome, they might have taken a different attitude. As it was, they had a simple plan that they were convinced would bring a swift and sure victory, so they unhesitatingly drove their people and allies toward war. How does it stand in the case of the Periclean strategy? At first glance, at least, his strategy appears to have been realistic, farsighted, and hardly conducive to a warlike policy. To be sure, it has come under severe attack. It has been from Germany chiefly that the most severe criticism has come.[52] In general, Pericles has been blamed for being too pusillanimous, for fighting a defensive war that wore down his material superiority and eroded the fighting spirit of his people. He should have seized the passes leading to Megara, it is alleged, and so saved Attica from devastation. He should have built forts in Attica to harass the Spartans when they made their invasions. He should have been more aggressive immediately in using his sea power. The capture of Cythera, the seizure and fortification of Pylos should not have been delayed until years after Pericles' death. But Pericles has not been without defenders; in fact, it is safe to say that most scholars believe that the strategy was sound and would have worked had Pericles remained alive to see that it was followed.[53]

Our interest, of course, is whether or not Pericles' choice of strategy influenced the coming of the war. Let us admit at once that it did; at a certain point it helped convince Pericles that concessions to the Spartans would not only be useless, but in the light of his strat-

[52] The harshest attacks have come from J. von Pflugk-Hartung (*Perikles als Feldherr* [Stuttgart, 1884]) and K. J. Beloch (*Die Attische Politik,* 22–24 and *GG* ², II: 1, 300 and n. 1).

[53] The foremost defense of the Periclean strategy is Hans Delbrück, *Die Strategie des Perikles* (Berlin, 1890) and *Geschichte der Kriegskunst,* I, *Das Altertum* (Berlin, 1920) reprinted 1964, 123–133. Among those who generally share his views are Eduard Meyer (*GdA,* IV: 2, 22–25), De Sanctis (*Pericle,* 254–255), and Adcock (*CAH,* V, 190). An intelligent evaluation from the purely military point of view may be found in B. W. Henderson, *The Great War between Athens and Sparta* (London, 1927), 47–68. Henderson accepts the policy in its main outlines but thinks it could have been carried on more vigorously.

egy, they might be disastrous. Delbrück has shrewdly seen that the essence of the Periclean plan was political. To be sure, the Athenians calculated that Pericles had won nine victories as general, but it is chiefly because of the way he formulated and carried out his plan of warfare that Pericles deserves a place "among the greatest generals in world history." [54] It is not merely the plan which is so great; it was rather the decisiveness of his action in doing what clearly must be done immediately and yielding all of Attica instead of taking half measures. His greatness lies rather in his ability to put such a measure through a democratic assembly by the force of his personality and to see that it was carried out. "The fulfillment of this decision is an act of generalship that may be placed on a level with any victory." [55]

Pericles knew that only he could make the Athenians adopt and hold to the one strategy that he believed could bring victory. In his absence he might expect the more aggressive groups to gain control and to insist on a military confrontation, which he believed would be a grave mistake. Even if they adopted his strategy at first, there was no one he could trust to avoid the errors the Athenians were likely to make. On the one hand, they were certain to become tired of their besieged condition and be tempted to offer battle. On the other hand, if they were doing well, they might attempt to increase their empire by diversionary expeditions as they had done in the past. Pericles was the only man who could manage his strategy; that was his strength and his strategy's weakness. Knowing how difficult the war he foresaw would be, Pericles tried to avoid it as long as he could. After the Spartan vote for war in 432, however, he became persuaded that war would come. His strategy now dictated that it should come as soon as possible. He was already in his seventh decade, and although his political position was solid, he could not be certain he would live very much longer. To delay the outbreak of war for an uncertain peace would be very costly, possibly fatal for Athens. For these reasons, Pericles refused to appease the Spartans during the final period of negotiation.

We may speculate further that there were other aspects of his strategy that helped make Pericles intransigent in the final months. All wars depend on the morale of the population that supports them,

[54] *Geschichte der Kriegskunst* I. 125.
[55] *Ibid.* 126.

but this is particularly true for the defensive side in a war of attrition. The balance between arousing sufficient determination to prevent defeatism and exercising sufficient restraint to avoid rash decisions is very hard to maintain. Pericles might rely on his political power and enormous personal authority to exercise the necessary restraint, but his task would be to inspire enough determination. The blunt, aggressive tone taken by the Spartans in the first, and especially in the third, of their embassies provided him with the necessary weapon. From the Athenian point of view these words showed the Spartans to be the aggressors determined to destroy the power, the empire, and the freedom of the Athenians. By refusing arbitration they put themselves in the wrong both legally and morally, a belief the Spartans themselves came to share.[56] After the Spartan ultimatum the Athenians had plenty of reason to hate their enemies enough to sustain a war.

The second embassy, which was conciliatory in tone, embarrassed Pericles seriously. It evoked the forces in Athens that favored peace and friendship with Sparta and also those who at least believed it would be better to try for an accommodation before embarking on a course for war. The harshness of the Spartan ultimatum made the task of Pericles easier; it relieved him of the necessity of defending his policy at length and in detail. It was now enough to allow the Athenians to think of the haughty words of the Spartans in order to inflame them with the martial spirit. Another time the Spartans might not be so accommodating. They might offer apparent concessions without yielding on the essential question, the equality and independence of the Athenian Empire. Negotiations might stretch out for years. Each year the Athenian will to fight would grow weaker and Pericles older. Meanwhile the enormous advantage in money and ships accumulated with such difficulty by Pericles would be reduced as the plan of Archidamus was carried out by the Spartans. It must have been clear to Pericles that if Athens must fight—and it now appeared to him that she must—her chances of victory would be better sooner rather than later. In these ways the Periclean strategy helped decide Athens against concessions and in favor of a war which must result from her determination not to yield.

It is possible that Pericles would have been slower to go to war

[56] 7. 18. 3.

had he been gifted with as much foresight as he is credited with by Thucydides. It is certainly too much to expect that Pericles should have foreseen the great plague that struck Athens, destroying a significant fraction of its population and weakening its will to continue the war. Yet it should have been evident that the prolonged crowding of the people into a city far too small to hold them would produce grave difficulties. Perhaps the fierce discontent that led the Athenians to depose Pericles from the generalship and to fine him,[57] which even led them to send envoys to seek peace at Sparta contrary to his will,[58] would not have been so keen without the plague, but it would surely have developed in time.

Pericles had made a point of the fact that the Spartans had never fought a war of the kind Pericles planned to impose on them. What he had not emphasized, if indeed he realized it himself, is that the Athenians were equally inexperienced in such a war. They had never had to withstand a siege, to see their fields ravaged over a period of time while they looked on. The longer the war dragged on, the surer it was that they would either yield or, more probably, depart from the purely defensive strategy.

It seems likely that Pericles really did not count on a very long war. He imagined that after one or two useless invasions the Spartans and their allies would become discouraged. The Athenians would refuse to fight, and the Spartans would be at a loss. The blockade of the Peloponnese and naval raids would take their toll on the economy and patience of the enemy. Soon the war party would be discredited and lose power. The Spartans, Corinthians, and Megarians would have learned their lesson and allow Athens to go its way peacefully in the future. What he did not anticipate is what few statesmen anticipate at the outset of a major war, that the enemy is likely to be no less determined than they are, that often frustration leads not to capitulation but to an intensification of efforts to win. Pericles did not expect that the Spartans would be embittered by their failure to bring the Athenians to battle. He must have been surprised when the Spartans flatly rejected an Athenian offer of peace that had been made over his objections. Had he lived he would have had no choice but to intensify the war effort and raise the level of Athenian military

[57] 2. 65; Plut. *Per.* 35; Diod. 12. 45.
[58] 2. 59.

action. Had he known all this in advance, he might have been more careful in his response to the Corinthian provocations and less rigid in his attitude towards Sparta.

The speech of Pericles was altogether successful. The Athenians supported his policy and adopted his very language in the answers to the Spartan ambassadors. Thucydides presents the essence of their reply: "They would do nothing under dictation, but they were prepared to resolve the complaints by arbitration according to the treaty on the basis of reciprocal equality." [59] The Spartans took the answer home with them and no further embassies came.

It would be interesting to know how long a period passed between the return of the last Spartan embassy and the outbreak of the war at the beginning of the spring of 431, but Thucydides gives us no clue. It is important to notice that even after the Athenian reply, no state of war existed; intercourse between the two sides continued without interruption.[60] We may imagine, therefore, that some months passed before hostilities began. It is noteworthy that when they did, the Spartans were not responsible. Early in March the Thebans, "foreseeing that war would come, wanted to get hold of Plataea, which had always been at odds with them, even in peacetime, before the war was openly begun." [61] Gomme has asked an interesting question: "Was this attack made perhaps in part from a desire to force the issue, to prevent Sparta from sending more embassies?" [62] It is very tempting to answer in the affirmative. Every day that passed was a day in which the Spartan peace party might regain control of a majority of the ephorate and prolong negotiations with the Athenians. The Thebans must have wondered why Pericles did not take the obvious steps that strategy seemed to dictate. They surely expected him to try to seize Megara, or at least besiege it and control the Geranea range to guard his southern frontier and to garrison Plataea to defend his border on the north. They could not believe that he would make no effort to defend Attica. No doubt they too looked back to the previous war and expected the Athenians to try to conquer central Greece once again. This time they wanted

[59] 1. 145. 1.
[60] 1. 146.
[61] 2. 2. 3.
[62] 1. 450.

to control Plataea, which guarded the road to Thebes from Athens, before the war got under way.

Their action was a clear breach of the treaty and the first act of the war.[63] Only now did both sides make final preparations for war, sending embassies to seek aid from Persia and other barbarian states, and asking help from their allies. It was not until May that the Spartans gathered their allies at the Isthmus of Corinth and launched an invasion of Attica. Even at the last moment, when they were already on the march, Archidamus, who commanded the Peloponnesian force, made a final attempt to avoid battle. He sent Melesippus to Athens in the hope that the Athenians might yield at the last moment when they saw the Spartan army really on the march. Once again we may imagine that Archidamus was looking back to the former war, when the Spartans had only needed to ravage a bit of the Thriasian plain to bring Athens to her senses. Then, however, the empire had been in revolt, the Athenian treasury was depleted, and Pericles was eager for peace. This time the empire was under firm control, the coffers were full, Athens was safe behind her walls, and Pericles was determined not to yield.

Melesippus was not allowed to enter the city, much less speak to the assembly, for Pericles himself had passed a law that forbade the reception of Spartan embassies while an army was in the field. The terse words of Thucydides have the ring of an accurate report of the Athenian state of mind.

> They sent him away without listening to him and ordered him to be outside their boundaries on the same day. In the future the Spartans must withdraw to their own territory if they wanted to send an embassy. And they sent an escort with Melesippus so that he might approach no one. And when he arrived at the frontier and was about to depart, he went off speaking these words: "This day will be the beginning of great evils for the Greeks." [64]

When he returned and reported that the Athenians had refused to make concessions, Archidamus could delay no longer. He gave the order to march out into Athenian territory. The Spartans had embarked on a war that, as Archidamus had predicted, they would leave to their sons.

[63] 2. 7. 1.
[64] 2. 12. 1–4.

Part Five

Conclusions

19. The Causes of the War

It was Thucydides who invented the distinction between the underlying, remote causes of war and the immediate causes. In his history of the Peloponnesian War he considered the immediate causes, which in fact went back almost five years before the actual commencement of hostilities, to be far less important than the more remote cause that arose from the growth of the Athenian Empire almost fifty years before the start of the war. Thucydides' view that the war was the inevitable consequence of the growth of that empire, its insatiable demand for expansion, and the fear it must inspire in the Spartans has won widespread acceptance.[1] Our investigation has led to conclude that his judgment is mistaken. We have argued that Athenian power did not grow between 445 and 435, that the impe-

[1] An excellent and compact analysis and summary of the Thucydidean view is provided by Jacqueline de Romilly in her introduction to her edition and translation of Book I of Thucydides in the Budé series (Paris, 1958), xliii-xvl. Among those who share the Thucydidean view, more or less, are Busolt, (*GG*, III: 1, 438; III: 2, 758 and 761); Eduard Meyer (*Forschungen*, II, 296–326) (his view, however, is somewhat ambiguous); Beloch (*GG* [2], II: 1, 297 and *Attische Politik*, 22); Glotz and Cohen, (*HG*, II, 604–607); and De Sanctis (*SdG*, II, 257–258). A typical statement of the received opinion is that of Hermann Bengston (*GG*, 217): "Mit vollem Recht sieht der bedenkende Historiker die tieferen Gründe, die in erstmals von den äusseren Anlässen scheidet, in dem historischen Faktum des athenisch-spartanischen Dualismus sowie in dem Gegensatz der von den beiden führenden griechischen Staaten vertretenen innenpolitischen Grundsätze. Die moderne Forschung ist in überwiegenden Mehrzahl dem Thukydides gefolgt. . . ."

rial appetite of Athens was not insatiable and gave good evidence of being satisfied, that the Spartans as a state seem not to have been unduly afraid of the Athenians, at least until the crisis had developed very far, that there was good reason to think that the two great powers and their allies could live side by side in peace indefinitely, and thus that it was not the underlying causes but the immediate crisis that produced the war.

It is true, of course, that the war could not have taken place in the absence of certain pre-existing conditions. If there had been no history of Athenian expansion and no sentiment in Sparta hostile to Athens, Corinth could never have driven the two powers into conflict. But tensions and suspicions exist in most diplomatic relationships; it remains to be proven that there is something in a particular historical situation which must permit those tensions and suspicions to bring on a war. It is far from clear, for instance, that the First World War was inevitable, but it can at least be argued with more than a little plausibility that some major change in the European situation must result from the disintegration of the power of Austria-Hungary, and that disintegration was not only inevitable, but already under way. The instability caused by that change in the European balance of power was unavoidable, and given the mutual suspicion and distrust of the major powers, there was a very good chance that war would result. The situation in Greece between the two Peloponnesian wars, however, was in no way parallel. There was no inherent instability; on the contrary, the settlement of 446/5, which was carefully adhered to by both sides, promised a greater stability than had been possible before. One may believe that the growing power of Athens and Sparta's fear of it made the First Peloponnesian War inevitable, but hardly the second.

Some scholars who have not been convinced by the Thucydidean formulation of the causes of the war have nonetheless been dissatisfied with an explanation arising from the events immediately preceding the war. They have discovered its origins not in the decisions and actions taken by statesmen in the period 435–431 but in forces, sometimes impersonal, that are greater than the men who are their instruments. Some have imagined that the cause of the war was naked Athenian aggression, which deliberately brought on the war to achieve greater conquests. In their view, Pericles carried out this policy, but it was the policy of the Athenians as a people.[2] That judgment is contradicted by all the evidence we have and supported by none.

Others have rested their thesis of the inevitability of the war on such shadowy concepts as the conflict between Dorian and Ionian and between democracy and oligarchy.[3] Although it is true that there were Dorians and Ionians, democrats and oligarchs, on either side, it is fair to say that the Athenian side was made up chiefly of Ionians and democrats, while the better part of the Spartan force was composed of Dorians and oligarchs. Yet there is not one whit of evidence for the view that these divisions contributed to the outbreak of war. Dorian, oligarchic Corinth had not hesitated to support Ionian, democratic Athens against Sparta in 506 and against Aegina in the 490's. Democratic, Ionian Athens had been willing to help Dorian, oligarchic Sparta in her war against the Messenians. Once decisions had been made on other grounds, similarities and differences of race and constitution could make relations between states easier or more difficult, but they were never an important factor in determining policy.

Economic causes in several forms, as we have seen, have been proposed as the real source of the conflict. Cornford's notion that there was a party of merchants from the Peiraeus who hoped to make great economic gains by seizing control of the route to the west via Megara, Acarnania, and Corcyra and forced Pericles to drive Athens to war is altogether fanciful. In the first place, it is plain that the Athenians had no intention of seizing Megara at the beginning of the war. It is further clear that Athens' interest in Corcyra was strategic and not economic. Finally, although there were aggressively imperialistic Athenians who hoped to gain economically from the extension of empire, not all of them merchants from the Peiraeus, the simple fact is that they did not make Athenian policy. That policy was made by Pericles, who had fought them successfully in the past and was not swayed by them in the years of the final crisis.[4]

[2] *E.g.*, Nissen, *Historische Zeitschrift,* N.F., XXVII (1889); Cornford, *Thucydides,* 1–51.

[3] These reasons, among others which are somewhat better, are put forth by Glotz and Cohen (*HG,* II, 604–607).

[4] See above, pp. 238–242.

Grundy's version of the economic causes of the war is no more acceptable. His conviction that the states of the Peloponnese were dependent on imported grain and went to war because Athenian domination of Corcyra threatened to cut them off from the granary of Italy and Sicily is wholly without support. The best refutation of his theory is that the Peloponnesians went through the long war, blockaded much of the time by the Athenian fleet, without starving. None of our sources mention widespread hunger in the Peloponnese, and they could not fail to do so if it had been there. Even poor Megara, whose starving farmers Aristophanes put on the stage with such comic effect, survived and even resisted an Athenian invasion and an internal revolution rather than yield. Grundy's view that the Athenians became involved at Corcyra likewise because of the search for western grain we have already dismissed.[5] Nor is his suggestion that the Athenians must continue to expand in order to prevent unemployment at home at all persuasive. We have reason to think that at the time of the crisis Athens had disposed of its excess population and was even hard-pressed to fill up the quota of settlers for her colonies.[6]

None of these economic explanations have won much support, but another one continues to have champions. It is that the rivalry between Corinth and Athens for the western trade was, if not the only cause of the war, at least a major factor in bringing it on.[7] We have already seen that Corinth's involvement in the affairs of Epidamnus and her subsequent conflict with Corcyra were not caused by economic considerations. Her involvement with Athens arose out of the Corcyrean affair; there is no reason to believe it would have happened otherwise. The Corinthians at first did not try to bring on a war but merely attempted to persuade Athens to allow the humiliation of the Corcyreans. Pride and considerations of power, not economics, brought on the conflict between Athens and Corinth. It is perfectly true that Athenian trade in the western areas formerly

[5] See above, pp. 239–240.

[6] For Grundy's views, see *Thucydides and the History of his Age,* I, 315–332.

[7] As excellent a scholar as Hermann Bengtson places great emphasis on the trade, seeing fit to put his version of the outbreak of the war in the following words: "Entzündet hat sich die Flamme des grossen Krieges an dem Zwist der Handelsmächte Athen und Korinth." (*GG,* 218).

dominated by Corinth had grown enormously. But the better part of that growth had taken place by the end of the sixth century and had not prevented Corinth from being very friendly to Athens. Thucydides tells us clearly just when and why the Corinthians first became hostile. It was in 459 when the Athenians helped the Megarians in their war against Corinth. The hatred Corinth thereafter felt toward Athens had little if anything to do with economics. If economic rivalry, moreover, is to explain the Corinthian hatred of Athens, we are at a loss to understand Corinth's decision to restrain the Spartan alliance from aiding the Samians in their rebellion from Athens. Surely the commercial rivalry with Athens, if there was one, did not significantly increase in intensity between 440 and 432, yet on the former occasion Corinth was outstandingly pacific and on the latter she was altogether bellicose. We are finally forced to conclude that economic rivalries did not make the Peloponnesian War inevitable and that economic considerations played no significant role in bringing on the war. Thucydides was altogether correct in fixing his attention on politics and power.

We have been presented lately with an up-dated version of the Thucydidean thesis that the war was the inevitable outcome of the division of the Greek world into two power blocs.[8] In its new guise, the Thucyididean view is fortified with the weapons of modern social science. The condition that troubled the Greek world and brought on the war is discovered to be "bipolarity." Typically, such words are borrowed from the physical sciences to lend an air of novelty, clarity, and authority to a shopworn, vague, or erroneous idea. In our context, bipolarity is used to describe a condition in which "exclusive control of international politics was concentrated in two powers solely responsible for preserving the peace or making war." [9] (The word bipolarity, incidentally, does not seem to have any advantage over the word polarity, another word borrowed from the physical sciences for use in other contexts.) That seems to be a fair statement of the way in which Thucydides saw the Greek world on the eve of the war, although it is hardly correct to assert that a consciousness of the "limitations which that power constellation has steadily imposed

[8] Peter J. Fliess, *Thucydides and the Politics of Bipolarity* (Baton Rouge, 1966).

[9] *Ibid.*, 14.

on the freedom of action of states" [10] has been neglected. It has in fact been understood and given great weight by most scholars who have accepted the interpretation of Thucydides. It is true, of course, that they did not realize they were talking about bipolarity.

In any case, the argument runs something like this: The creation of the Athenian Empire after the Persian War and Sparta's refusal to "contain" its expansion produced a bipolar world. As the years passed, "the bipolar mold hardened." Thus, when the Corcyrean crisis came along, "there seemed to be no formula available that could lead out of the bipolar impasse." Political forces became too strong for the political leaders, and the war became a necessity. To be sure, this was not a metaphysical necessity, and in many situations the possibility of choice exists, but "events must be judged differently in a bipolar context." In such a context each side is in terror that the other will gain a monopoly of power and use it to enslave its rival. At some time in the growth of Athens, Sparta might have taken steps to check its rise, "but once the threshold of bipolarity was reached, events had passed the point at which peace could have been preserved indefinitely through settlements." [11]

It is true that this particular formulation is not worth dissecting in detail, for it is the consequence of scattered piratical raids on the scholarly literature, ignores the evidence of the inscriptions, fails to consider the influence of internal politics, and makes only a cursory analysis of the final crisis. Yet it is valuable in putting into sharp relief the assumptions that underlie the view of Thucydides and dominate many modern interpretations of the causes of the war. The major assumptions are that the causes of the war must be sought chiefly, if not only, in Athens and Sparta, and that there was no way to avoid a final reckoning between these two great powers. But the Greek world of the years between the Persian War and the Peloponnesian War was not bipolar. By 435, Athens had come to dominate her allies to the degree that they were eliminated as independent factors in foreign affairs, but Sparta had not. Thebes and especially Corinth were free agents. To combat Athens with any hope of success, it is true, they must bring Sparta over to their cause. On the other hand—and this is decisive—Sparta could not prevent them

[10] *Idem.*
[11] *Ibid.*, 66–72.

from engaging in their own policies. This independent exercise of foreign policy was sometimes conducive to peace and sometimes to war; it was not, in any case, predictable. Its possibility is a serious argument against the inevitability of the war.

The unpersuasiveness of all theories of inevitability is best demonstrated by a resumé of the events that led to the war. At each step it is clear that the decisions were not preordained, although, of course, the options narrowed as time went on. Our analysis of the years between the wars shows that the theory that peace between Athens and Sparta could not last must be imposed on the facts from the outside; it does not arise from the evidence. The internal quarrel at Epidamnus had no relation to the outside world and need not have affected the international situation in any way. Corinth's decision to intervene was in no way the necessary consequence of previous conditions. Corinthian control of Epidamnus was not necessary for Corinth's economic well-being, her security, even her prestige. Corinth decided that the affair at Epidamnus would provide a splendid opportunity for revenge on its traditional enemies, the Corcyreans. The Corinthians could have chosen to refuse the Epidamnian appeal; had they done so there would have been no crisis and no war. To be sure, they knew in advance that intervention would probably mean war with Corcyra, and they did not flinch from the prospect, for they were confident that they could defeat Corcyra with the help of their Peloponnesian allies.

When some of their friends tried to dissuade them from their course out of fear that Corcyra would obtain the help of Athens and so bring on a larger war, the Corinthians ignored their counsel. They did not do so because they wanted a war with Athens, but because they expected that Athens would not fight. They were led to this belief by their interpretation of the informal detente between the Peloponnesians and the Athenians. Their interpretation was not correct, because Corcyra and its navy presented special problems not easily and obviously dealt with by the unspoken understanding that each side would be permitted freedom of action in its own sphere of influence. Sparta and Sicyon, at least, understood the danger, and the Corinthians should have too. They proceeded with their dangerous policy because they miscalculated the Athenian response. Their miscalculation arose not from a traditional hatred of Athens caused by a commercial rivalry, but rather from a combination of irrational hatred for the Corcyreans and wishful thinking, which led them to expect from Athens the response that they wanted. Had reason prevailed, the Corinthians would have accepted the Corcyrean offer of arbitration, which would have left them in a better position than when they first became involved at Epidamnus. The crisis would have ended before it ever involved either Athens or Sparta, and the war would have been averted.

By the time Athens became involved in 433, her freedom of action was somewhat limited. Corcyra was at war with Corinth. If Athens remained aloof, the Corinthians might win and attach the Corcyrean fleet to the Spartan alliance and challenge the unquestioned naval supremacy that was the basis of Athenian security. Once it became clear that Corinth would not retreat, the Athenians had no choice but to meet the challenge. It is clear, however, that the Athenians did not seek a confrontation with Corinth for commercial, imperial, or any other reasons; the conflict was forced on them. They first tried to limit their commitment in the hope that Corcyra would win with its own forces.

When the Battle of Sybota blocked this resolution, they did what they could to localize the conflict and avoid involving Sparta. The preparations they made for a likely conflict with Corinth were calculated to avoid giving the Corinthians a valid pretext for demanding Spartan assistance. Two of these measures, the ultimatum of Potidaea and the Megarian Decree, were errors in judgment by Pericles. In the case of Potidaea, he reacted too vigorously to the threat that Corinthian machinations might produce rebellion in the empire and gave the impression of Athenian tyranny and aggressiveness. In the case of Megara, again his reaction was greater than the situation required. He intended to punish Megara for helping the Corinthians in the Battle of Sybota and to issue a warning to them and to any other friends of Corinth to stay out of the affair and prevent its spread. The action was probably unnecessary, for Sparta seemed to be exercising a restraining hand on most of her allies; yet the decree had a very serious effect on the internal politics of Sparta. It appeared to be an attack on an ally of Sparta launched without sufficient provocation, and it reinforced the impression of Athens as a tyrant and an aggressor. Pericles misjudged the stability of the political situation at Sparta and unintentionally gave the war party a goad with which it could drive Sparta and its allies to war. If his judgment had been better and, perhaps, if the Athenian irritation with the Megarians had been less, he might have taken a gentler tone, avoided provocative actions, and allowed the friends of Athens and peace to keep their control of Spartan policy. If he had, there might not have been a majority of warlike ephors to promise help to Potidaea and to cooperate with the Corinthians in stirring up the war. Had the Athenians shown more restraint, there is a possibility that even after the Battle of Sybota a general war could have been prevented.

All this is not to say that there were no existing forces or conditions that helped bring on the war. The perfectly ordinary civil war in a remote and unimportant town on the fringes of the civilized world could hardly have led to a great war *ex nihilo*. Certainly there needed to be a solid core of suspicion and mutual distrust in Athens and Sparta. Another crucial factor originating long before the outbreak of the crisis was the deep and emotional hatred between Corinth and Corcyra. Still another was the organizational weakness of the Spartan alliance, which permitted a power of the second magnitude to drag the hegemonal power into a dangerous war for its own interests. Connected with that was the constitutional weakness of the Spartan executive, which divided the real responsibility for the formulation and conduct of foreign policy and permitted unpredictable shifts back and forth between policies in a rather short space of time. Such weaknesses made it difficult to restrain outbursts of passion and to follow a sober, cautious policy in times of crisis. After the death of Pericles, the Athenian constitution would show a similar weakness, but so long as he was alive Athens was free of this problem.

It is also true that the machinery of diplomacy was too rudimentary to preserve peace in time of crisis. The Thirty Years' Peace was open to varying interpretations, as are all diplomatic agreements, but it provided only one, rather clumsy, means for settling disagreements. It authorized the submission of all disputes to arbitration, but it made no provision for consultation before minor differences reached the level of disputes needing arbitration. By the time arbitration is required, disputants are often so hostile that they refuse to use it.

When disputes reach the level of arbitration, they have become public issues and aroused powerful emotions not easily controlled.

All these may be considered as remote or underlying causes of the war. They may be seen as contributing to the situation that made war possible, but all of them together did not make war necessary. For that, a complicated chain of circumstances and decisions was needed. If any of its links had not been present, the war would not have come.

It is customary to apply the metaphor of the powder keg or tinderbox to international situations that are deemed the inevitable forerunners of war. The usual way of putting it is that the conflicting interests and passions of the contending parties provided the inflammatory material, and the final crisis was only a spark that had sooner or later to fall and cause the inevitable conflagration or explosion.[12] If we were to apply this metaphor to the outbreak of the Second Peloponnesian War, we should put it this way: The growth of the Athenian Empire and Sparta's jealousy and fear of it provided the inflammable material that ignited into the First Peloponnesian War. The Thirty Years' Peace poured water on that flame and extinguished it. What was left of the flammable material was continually cooled and dampened by the mutual restraint of Athens and Sparta in the decade 445–435. To start the war, the spark of the Epidamnian trouble needed to land on one of the rare bits of flammable stuff that had not been thoroughly drenched. Thereafter it needed to be continually and vigorously fanned by the Corinthians, soon assisted by the Megarians, Potidaeans, Aeginetans, and the Spartan war party. Even then the spark might have been extinguished had not the Athenians provided some additional fuel at the crucial moment.

No one planned the Peloponnesian War, and no state wanted it, yet each of the three great states bears part of the blame for bringing it on. The Corinthians did not want war with Athens but a free hand against Corcyra. They were willing to risk such a war, however, because they hoped Athens would not really bring it on, because they counted on their proven ability to gain the help of Sparta in case of war, and because they were determined to have their way. Theirs is the greatest guilt, for they had the freest choice

[12] Meyer (*Forschungen,* II, 312), for instance, employs the spark metaphor in connection with the coming of the Peloponnesian War.

and sufficient warning of the consequences of their actions, yet they would not be deterred from their purpose.

The Spartans too deserve a share of the blame. They allowed their war party to frighten them with unfounded alarms of Athenian aggression and the Corinthians to blackmail them with empty threats of secession. They ignored the advice of Archidamus, which would have allowed them to avoid the war without any loss of power, honor, or influence. They rejected the opportunity to arbitrate specific disputes as specified in the treaty and were captured by the romantic vision of destroying the Athenian Empire, liberating Greece, and restoring Sparta to unchallenged primacy. They were quite right to go into the war burdened by a guilty conscience.

The Athenians, however, were not without guilt. To be sure, their security required that they accept the Corcyrean alliance and prepare for further conflict with Corinth. They need not, however, have behaved with such arrogance and harshness toward Potidaea and Megara. This frightened their rivals and lent plausibility to the charges of the Corinthians. In one sense, although probably not in the way they intended, the enemies of Pericles were right in fixing on the Megarian Decree as the cause of the war and on Pericles as its instigator. If he had not issued it, the Corinthians might not have been able to persuade the Spartans of the evil intentions of Athens and so to drive them to war. There is even some possibility that if he had been willing to rescind it at the request of the second Spartan embassy, the peace party might have returned to power and the war have been avoided. By that time, however, Pericles' war strategy dominated his thinking. It demanded a policy of firmness, and the Spartan offer was rejected. The political situation at Sparta made arbitration impossible; the intransigence of Pericles prevented any other solution.

All the statesmen involved suffered from what might be called "a failure of imagination." [13] Each allowed war to come and even helped bring it on because he thought he could gain something at a reasonable cost. Each evolved a strategy largely based on past wars and expected the next war to follow his own plan. None seems to have

[13] The term is used by Laurence Lafore in *The Long Fuse: An Interpretation of the Origins of World War I* (New York, 1965) to explain the outbreak of the First World War. It seems to me to be appropriate here as well.

considered the consequences of miscalculation. None had prepared a reserve plan to fall back on in case his original estimation should prove wrong. All expected a short war; none was ready even for the ten years of the Archidamian War, much less the full twenty-seven years that it took to bring the conflict to a conclusion. They all failed to foresee the evil consequences that such a war would have for everyone, victors and vanquished alike, that it would bring economic ruin, class warfare, brutality, erosion of moral standards, and a permanent instability that left Greece vulnerable to foreign conquest. Had they done so they would scarcely have risked a war for the relatively minor disputes that brought it on. Had they done so, we should admit at once, they would have been far better men than most statemen who have faced similar decisions in the millennia since then. The Peloponnesian War was not caused by impersonal forces, unless anger, fear, undue optimism, stubbornness, jealousy, bad judgment, and lack of foresight are impersonal forces. It was caused by men who made bad decisions in difficult circumstances. Neither the circumstances nor the decisions were inevitable.

20. Thucydides and the Inevitability of the War

Our investigations have led us to conclusions that differ from those of Thucydides and the majority of modern scholars. That is a sobering thought, for perhaps it is only arrogance and a peculiar perversity that have led to such conclusions. A glance at the history of the question, however, may acquit us of these charges, for over the years Thucydides' account of the causes of the war has been found unsatisfactory even by those who accept his explanation.

One of the keenest analyses of the problem was made by Eduard Meyer,[1] who finally decided that Thucydides was correct. But his shrewd understanding of the actual events often led him to contradict parts of the Thucydidean interpretation and to explain others away. His final conclusion, moreover, seems to contradict some of his earlier judgments. On the crucial question of the Megarian Decree, for instance, Meyer agrees with Thucydides that the decree itself was not the cause of the war, but he admits that his interpretation of the decree and the causes of the war is not altogether correct. It is clear to him, moreover, "that Thucydides does not give the Megarian Decree sufficient motivation, or rather, he does not give it any motivation at all." [2] He concedes the possibility that the Corinthians might have chosen to accept the Athenian interference at Corcyra, but considers the Athenian intervention at Potidaea the

[1] *Forschungen,* II, 296–326.
[2] *Ibid.,* 302–303.

act that made war inevitable.[3] It is interesting to note that he does not even consider the possibility that Corinth might have chosen not to involve herself in the affair at Epidamnus. Yet his appreciation of the events of the Pentecontaetia is very similar to the one we have given above. He denies that Athenian power grew between 446 and 433 and considers Thucydides' attempt to offer the events of the Pentecontaetia as Sparta's motive for war to be unsuccessful. "On the contrary, his own account shows that it was the Corinthians who brought on the war and that it was quite difficult for them to push through the decision for war in Sparta." [4] He further believes that the decisive causes of the war lay not in the opposition between Athens and Sparta but between Athens and Corinth, where "vital interests collided." [5]

Meyer believed that the mutual acceptance of the Peloponnesian League and the Athenian Empire that had prevailed since 446/5 might have lasted, "but only on one condition: that no displacement of the equal power of both groups took place." [6] The Corcyrean affair destroyed the equilibrium and brought on the war, but Thucydides and Pericles were both right in thinking that war was already inevitable. Athens had to defend Corcyra to defend the empire, and Pericles knew that the alliance would provoke Sparta into war. Thereafter he allowed no concessions, as Thucydides says, and drove Athens into war. "An unprejudiced judgment could not deny that his attitude, which alone appreciated the Athenian power position and the suitable circumstances, was in fact the only one possible and statesmanly. Every other procedure would have brought more serious consequences to Athens and still not have avoided the war." Meyer concluded his argument as follows:

So basically we have returned after long detours to Thucydides' interpretation. If we put in place of Sparta's jealousy and her fear of the growing power of Athens the thesis that the Peloponnesians, and at their head, the Spartans, could not fail to consider the power position of Athens as a serious handicap which they must seek to get rid of as soon as a promising opportunity presented itself then, his interpretation and his

[3] 305–306.
[4] 314.
[5] 315.
[6] 323.

presentation remain perfectly right. And above all: the Corcyrean business was not the cause of the the war but the occasion that made it inevitable.[7]

Meyer's essay remains a very valuable contribution, but it reaches a very surprising conclusion: his analysis of the evidence contradicts his final interpretation. In order to accept the Thucydidean explanation, he is forced in the end to change its formulation. Having shown that Athenian power was not growing between 446/5 and 433, that the events of the Pentecontaetia did not make the war inevitable, that the real causes of the war lay between Athens and Corinth, he concludes by arguing that the power of Athens forced the Peloponnesians to seek a reason to attack. The obvious conclusion is that Athenian power grew only after the alliance with Corcyra, but Meyer does not draw it. If the affair at Corcyra or, as Meyer says also, the affair at Potidaea, made war inevitable, it cannot have been inevitable before. Thus, it would appear Corcyra and the other quarrels were not mere pretexts but the real causes of the war, and Thucydides is mistaken. But Meyer did not follow his arguments to their logical conclusion. He was persuaded by the conclusions of Thucydides and could not or would not see the contradictions between Thucydides' facts and his interpretation. Instead, he employed his great erudition and ingenuity to patch up the cracks.

Meyer's method of historical exegesis is only one of the many attempts to solve the problem of Thucydides' treatment of the causes of the war. A very radical solution was proposed by Eduard Schwartz.[8] He noticed that Thucydides' account of the events leading to the war seemed to lead to an interpretation quite different from the one presented by Thucydides as his own. The former seemed to suggest that the Corinthians were really the cause of the war, while the latter said that the truest cause was Sparta's fear of Athens. Schwartz concluded that Thucydides had written two versions, an earlier one which saw Corinth as the instigator of the war and a later one, written after the war had run its full course, which showed that the war was the inevitable result of Athenian power and Spartan fear. The latter view also vindicated Pericles against the

[7] 326.
[8] *Thukydides.*

general conviction that he had needlessly brought on the war and was responsible for the Athenian disaster. Schwartz' work began anew the old attempt to divide the history of Thucydides into early and late passages and to explain difficulties in the interpretation of the meaning of Thucydides with reference to these chronological levels.

Once the issue was joined, other scholars entered the fray with different systems of distinguishing early passages from late. Soon it became evident that different systems yielded different results, and no two scholars agreed exactly on which passages were early and which were late. A typical example of the hopeless subjectivity of the undertaking has often been noticed.[9] A single reference to the Aeginetans (7. 57–58) is used by one scholar to date all of Books VI and VII, by another for only Chapters 57 and 58 of Book VII, and for a third it dates only the part of the sentence where the Aeginetans are mentioned. At this point, very few passages are generally agreed to be early, and they do not give us much help in interpreting Thucydides. This is, of course, not the place to discuss the problem of composition. We have only raised it to show how it originated in large part from the unsatisfactory state of Book I and Thucydides' account of the origins of the war.

The same difficulty gave rise to Nissen's wild assertion that Thucydides deliberately concealed evidence of Athenian imperialism to shield Pericles.[10] Such suggestions would be neither necessary nor possible had the Thucydidean explanation been more satisfactory. The same thing can be said of Cornford's fanciful theory "that the merchants in the Athenian harbor city carried on a secret conspiracy to force the war, a secret so well kept that Thucydides never discovered it and that is why he missed the key fact in the whole story." [11] He makes it altogether clear that he was led to investigation by his dissatisfaction with Thucydides' version of the causes of the war.

[9] See Romilly, *Thucydides and Athenian Imperialism,* 7 and H. D. Westlake, *CQ,* N.S., V (1955), 53, n. 8.

[10] *Historische Zeitschrift,* NF. XXVII (1889). See also its refutation by Meyer, *Forschungen,* II, 296–326 *passim.*

[11] I quote the satirical but accurate summary of M. I. Finley, *The New York Review of Books,* vol. 8, No. 5, March 23, 1967, 26.

Plainly he thought that his account . . . of the disputes and negotiations on the eve of the outbreak ought to satisfy posterity. He has told us all the ascertained truth which seemed to him relevant. But somehow we are not satisfied. We do not feel, after reading the First Book, that Thucydides has told us all that we want to know, or all that he knew and, if he had considered it relevant, might have told. So attempts have again and again been made to go behind his story. We are still troubled by the question which he thought no one would ever have to ask.[12]

It was Cornford's belief, in fact, that Thucydides was not very much interested in causes, and that opinion has won support in very respectable quarters.[13] Momigliano has exposed the weakness of the Thucydidean account with his customary shrewdness. Modern historians praise Thucydides because he drew the distinction between superficial and profound causes:

Nothing else has contributed so much to Thucydides' reputation as the most scientific of the ancient historians—as the man whom any university would be proud to have as a Privatdozent. But surely there is a misunderstanding here. If there is something that Thucydides does not succeed in doing, it is to explain the remote origins of the conflict between Sparta and Athens. The whole of the diplomatic and social history of the thirty years before the Peloponnesian war is perhaps irretrievably lost for us just because Thucydides was not interested in it. There are so many things we do not know because Thucydides did not care to study them.

The remote causes of a war are as much plain facts as the immediate causes. If the facts are not produced, if we are left with a vague feeling of mystery, then we can be certain that we have been misled. Thucydides is vague about the *ἀληθεστάτη πρόφασις*. He is far superior to Herodotus in explaining the actual conduct of the war with which he is concerned, but he is much less convincing than Herodotus in discovering the remote origins of the war.[14]

The unsatisfactory quality of Thucydides' explanation leads Momigliano to the conclusion that Thucydides, like most Greeks, "came to accept war as a natural fact like birth and death about which noth-

[12] Cornford, *Thucydides,* 3.

[13] E.g., Arnaldo Momigliano in *Studies in Historiography,* (London, 1961), 112–126 and M. I. Finley, in *Generalization in the Writing of History,* Louis Gottschalk, ed. (Chicago, 1963), 27.

[14] *Studies in Historiography,* 117–118.

ing could be done. They were interested in causes of *wars,* not in causes of *war* as such. Yes, the golden age had been free from wars, but then that was the golden age. In ordinary life you could postpone *a* war, but you could not avoid *war.*" [15] This is not the place to discuss the accuracy of Momigliano's generalization about all the Greeks.[16] It is enough here merely to disagree with its applicability to the historian of the Peloponnesian War.

It should be plain that the causes of the war were vitally important to Thucydides. Whatever he may have thought about the nature of war in general, he was determined to set his audience right on the causes of this particular war. Public opinion in Athens was convinced that Pericles had started the war by insisting on the Megarian Decree. Meyer does not go too far in saying that Thucydides' "whole first book, the presentation of the origins of the war, is wholly an uninterrupted polemic against the popular opinion." [17] Yet the shortcomings of the Thucydidean account have led scholars to take more recondite views.

The problems of the Thucydidean interpretation have even led to a debate over the words Thucydides uses to express the idea of cause and the very meaning of his major statement about the causes of the war. It was, of course, inevitable that Cornford's representation of Thucydides as an unscientific historian who had no sense of cause should produce a reaction. Some scholars responded by asserting that far from having no understanding of cause, he had a very scientific and subtle notion of it, deriving from contemporary usage in Greek science, particularly medicine.[18] Subsequent studies have shown that this reaction went too far, that Thucydides does not use

[15] *Ibid.,* 120.

[16] It might, however, be useful to cite Gordon M. Kirkwood's intelligent refutation of Cornford's view: "When Cornford said that 'there is in Thucydidean Greek no word which even approaches the meaning and association of the English "cause" with its correlative, "effect,"' he must have altogether overlooked the historical use of αἴτιον." Further on he denies that Thucydides did not understand causes but only pretext and grievance, by referring to his analysis of the Trojan War, where he is clearly aware of objective causes (*AJP,* LXXIII [1952], 58–59).

[17] *Forschungen,* II, 297.

[18] E. Schwartz, *Thukydides,* 250; C. N. Cochrane, *Thucydides and the Science of History* (Oxford, 1929), 17.

words for cause in a special, scientific way. When he speaks of προφάσεις, and especially of ἡ ἀληθεστάτη πρόφασις, he uses it in a way that accords fully with general Greek usage.[19] Thucydides' main statement on the causes of the war runs as follows:

διότι δ' ἔλυσαν, τὰς αἰτίας προύγραψα πρῶτον καὶ τὰς διαφοράς τοῦ μή τινα ζητῆσαί ποτε ἐξ ὅτου τοσοῦτος πόλεμος τοῖς Ἕλλησι κατέστη. τὴν μὲν γὰρ ἀληθεστάτην πρόφασιν, ἀφανεστάτην δὲ λόγῳ, τοὺς Ἀθηναίους μεγάλους γιγνομένους καὶ φόβον παρέχοντας τοῖς Λακεδαιμονίοις ἀναγκάσαι ἐς τὸ πολεμεῖν. αἱ δ' ἐς τό φάνερον λεγόμεναι αἰτίαι αἵ δ' ἑκατέρων, ἀφ' ὧν λύσαντες τὰς σπονδὰς ἐς τὸν πόλεμον κατέστησαν.[20]

The obvious interpretation and the one most commonly adopted is that the view given is that of the historian himself. This view is best illustrated by quoting a standard English translation that incorporates it.

The reasons why they broke it [the peace] and the grounds of their quarrel I have first set forth, that no one may ever have to inquire for what cause the Hellenes became involved in so great a war. The truest explanation, although it has been the least often advanced, I believe to have been the growth of Athens to greatness, which brought fear to the Lacedaemonians and forced them to war. But the reasons publicly alleged on either side which led them to break the truce and involved them in the war were as follows.[21]

Kirkwood and Pearson on similar but different grounds believe that Thucydides is not giving his own view of the causes of the war,

[19] Kirkwood, *op. cit.*, and Lionel Pearson, *TAPA*, LXXXIII (1952), 205–223.

[20] 1. 23. 5–6.

[21] Translated by C. F. Smith in the Loeb Classical Library. A similar understanding may be found in the translation of Mme de Romilly in the Budé edition and that of Antonio Maddalena, *Thucydidis Historiarum Liber Primus* (Florence, 1961), III, 98. The English translation of Richard Crawley, based on the same understanding, is very free, but in my opinion closer to the real sense of the passage than any other. It deserves quotation: "The real cause I consider to be the one which was formerly most kept out of sight. The growth of the power of Athens, and the alarm which this inspired in Lacedaemon, made war inevitable. Still it is well to give the grounds alleged by either side, which led to the dissolution of the treaty and the breaking out of the war."

but rather the motive of the Spartans.[22] Sealey has shown that this view is mistaken and that the usual opinion is correct: "At 1. 23. 6 Thucydides states the true cause of the war, as he conceives it." [23] But that is not the end of the affair. Though Sealey believes that we have Thucydides' own opinion, he does not share in the consensus of what that opinion is. He translates the crucial sentence as follows: "The truest cause, though least spoken of, was, in my opinion, that the Athenians, who were growing powerful and arousing alarm among the Lacedaemonians, compelled them to make war." [24] When this interpretation is expanded, it suggests that it is not the growth of power or the Spartan fear that is emphasized; it is rather the leading role of the Athenians. "The growth of Athenian power is thus relevant to Thucydides' conception of the cause of the war; but to say that it, or with it the fears of the Spartans, was in his opinion the cause of the war is to overlook the nuances of his statement." [25] It is not unlikely that Sealey was led to this interpretation by his own conviction that Athens really was responsible for the war. "In the years 433–432 the Athenians were spoiling for a fight." [26] Our own analysis has led us to different conclusions, but in any case, Sealey has himself seen problems with the theory. He finds the theory of "the truest cause" not satisfactory, "for even if he [Thucydides] is right in saying that the Athenians compelled the Spartans to fight, he has not answered the further question, why did the Athenians want war?" [27] We might be tempted to suggest that Thucydides did not answer the further question because he did not hold to the earlier premise, for Sealey's translation and interpretation of 1. 23. 6 are not likely to win wide support.[28]

Sealey thinks the answer is that Thucydides had not fully thought out the consequences of his theory. He finds, moreover, an alternate theory of causation that exists side by side with the "truest cause" in the work of Thucydides. This rises out of the account of the inci-

[22] Kirkwood, *AJP*, LXXIII (1952), 47 and 51; Pearson, *op. cit.*, 219–221.

[23] Raphael Sealey, *CQ*, N.S., VII (1957), 9.

[24] *Idem.*

[25] *Ibid.* 10.

[26] *Idem.*

[27] *Ibid.* 11.

[28] It is noted and rejected by A. Andrewes, *CQ*, N.S., IX (1959), 225, n. 1.

dents that led up to the war, the quarrel over Corcyra, the Megarian Decree, the affair at Potidaea, etc. This theory tries to explain the war as the consequence of a series of grievances, much in the manner of Herodotus. It was an earlier theory and the "truest cause," a later and, presumably, unfinished one. And so we are back to explaining the problems of Book I by the suggestion that it is incomplete and contains ideas formulated at different times. The important point here, however, is that the whole problem is brought about by the unsatisfactory relationship between the facts as Thucydides presents them and his explanation of their meaning.

A final example will suffice. An interesting analysis of the coming of the Peloponnesian War is that of F. E. Adcock in the *Cambridge Ancient History*.[29] He is shrewd enough to reject the theory of inevitability and bold enough to deny the truth of Thucydides' "truest cause," saying, "It seems to explain more truly why the war began again in 413 and ended as it did than why it began at all in 431."[30] He explains the difficulty away, however, by resorting to the theory of early and late strata of Thucydidean thought. The early stratum gives us an account "which is true to fact and true to the Greeks and Greek wars of that time."[31] The later stratum, written after the defeat of Athens, looked at the events from a distorted perspective. Mme de Romilly, however, has shown that whatever the state of the history as a whole, Book I at least is a unit. There may be some late additions, but the essential ideas, of which the "truest cause" is the most pervasive, were present in Thucydides' thinking and in the composition of the book from the beginning.[32] There is no way to minimize his responsibility for the only explicit causal theory in the work.

Adcock, furthermore, is led by his own conviction that the war was not inevitable to attribute the same view to Thucydides.[33] In this opinion he appears to be alone.[34] He is surely mistaken. In

[29] 5. 165–192.

[30] 5. 190.

[31] 191.

[32] *Thucydides and Athenian Imperialism,* 16–36.

[33] *CAH,* V, 182; *Thucydides and his History,* 7.

[34] I have been unable to find a single scholar who denies that Thucydides believed the war to be inevitable. Many make no reference to the subject, but the following flatly assert that Thucydides believed in the inevitability

1. 23. 6, Thucydides clearly distinguishes the "truest cause" from the events of the period after 435. In 1. 88 he concludes his account of the quarrels and complaints by saying that the Spartans voted to go to war "not so much because they had been persuaded by the arguments of their allies as because they were afraid that the Athenians might become more powerful, seeing that the greater part of Greece was already in their hands." This assertion is then supported by a long excursus whose purpose is to show just how Athenian power had grown and caused fear for the Spartans.[35] Since the immediate causes are dismissed as incidental, since the growth of Athenian power that goes back to the Persian War is offered as the "truest cause," and since no way of preventing the growth of that power or the fear it engendered is presented, we can only conclude that Thucydides meant us to think that the war was inevitable once the Athenian Empire was permitted to come into existence.

We are compelled, then, to conclude that the general opinion is right in thinking that Thucydides believed the war to be inevitable and that the growth in Athenian power and the fear it produced in Sparta was the true cause of the war. Our own analysis of the facts, both those presented by Thucydides and those reported elsewhere, has led us to believe that he is wrong on both counts. We may seek comfort in the words of F. E. Adcock, who justified his disagreement with Thucydides by saying, "We remain entitled, indeed obliged, to make the best judgment we can on the facts known to us about the historical reasons for the outbreak of the war. That is not a matter to be settled by authority, even the authority of Thucydides." [36]

Two questions remain. They deal with the mind and the methods of the historian rather than with historical events, and a full answer to them would require a detailed historiographical study, which is impossible here. Yet they arise unavoidably from our investigation and deserve at least to be recognized, if not fully answered. If Thu-

---

of the war: Eduard Meyer, *Forschungen,* II, 308–310; J. B. Bury, *The Ancient Greek Historians,* paperback republication (New York, 1958), 94; Werner Jaeger, *Paedeia,* Gilbert Highet, tr. (Oxford, 1954), I, 393; P. A. Brunt, *AJP,* LXXII (1951), 270; Jacqueline de Romilly, *Thucydide I* (Paris, 1958), xliii and *Thucydides and Athenian Imperialism,* 21.

[35] See P. K. Walker, *CQ,* N.S., VII (1957), 27–38.

[36] *JHS,* LXXI (1951), 4.

cydides is wrong about the causes of the war and its inevitability, we must ask how he has been able to convince most of his readers that he is right. We should further like to know how and why he himself came to his conclusions. The first question is rather easier to answer. The devices Thucydides uses in his account of the causes of the war are the same ones he employs throughout his work to make his interpretation clear and persuasive: judgments made in his own voice (such as his statement of the "truest cause" in 1. 23. 6), the selection, omission, and arrangement of evidence, and the speeches. These have always been recognized and form the greatest part of his method.

A fourth device, however, has been given prominence by recent studies: the attribution to people of motives, purposes, and ideas that, at the very least, Thucydides does not support with evidence, and in some cases, he could hardly have known anything about. The clearest example of this device is to be found in Thucydides' treatment of Cleon. We need not concern ourselves with whether or not that treatment is fair or the picture it paints of Cleon accurate;[37] we want merely to know, for instance, how Thucydides goes about convincing us that Cleon is an incapable general who wins battles by luck and loses them out of incompetence. One of those ways is perfectly illuminated by Woodhead in a passage so illustrative that it deserves quotation. The subject is the Battle of Amphipolis, where the Spartan Brasidas defeated Cleon. Both generals died in the battle. The Thucydidean account makes it perfectly clear that the battle was decided by the shrewdness of Brasidas, who took advantage of the foolishness of Cleon, who appears "incompetent, uncertain, self-confident, cowardly, by turns."[38] But a careful analysis of the text reveals interesting things.

> By contrast with the obscurity of the battle narrative, the historian seems remarkably well acquainted with what was *in the minds* of both commanders. Brasidas' plan could presumably have been expounded to him soon afterwards, perhaps by Clearidas himself. But what of Cleon, also dead on the battlefield? What was Thucydides' source of information here? A few prisoners eager to blame their misfortune on their dead

[37] Although A. G. Woodhead's article in *Mnemosyne* (Series 4, XIII [1960], 289–317) should put an end to the controversy.

[38] *Ibid.*, 306.

general? Disgruntled hoplites casting back in their memories nineteen or more years later? . . . Further we may note Thucydides' use of words: "Cleon was compelled . . . he became aware, and was unwilling that they be exasperated. . . ." And later, "He did not expect . . . he had acquired confidence in his own wisdom . . . he thought he could withdraw. . . ." but afterwards, seeing Amphipolis apparently deserted, "he thought he ought to have brought up siege engines." It is, to say the least, remarkable that Thucydides should *know* all this.[39]

This attribution of motives, purposes, and ideas, so difficult to authenticate, is one of Thucydides' most effective means of persuading the reader of the inevitability of the war. After the speeches of the Corcyreans and Corinthians in the assembly at Athens in 433, Thucydides tells that the Athenians voted to make a defensive alliance with Corcyra, "for it seemed to them that a war with the Peloponnesians would come in any case." [40] But almost half of the Athenians did not think the war inevitable, for they had voted against the alliance and had almost commanded a majority against it. It is also worth contemplating how Thucydides knew what was in the minds of the narrow majority of Athenians who supported the alliance. Again, immediately after completing his account of the growth of Athenian power after the Persian War, Thucydides reiterates a version of his view of the causes of the war:

> In this time the Athenians established and reinforced their empire and themselves attained great power. Although the Spartans perceived this, they made only a small attempt to prevent it and remained quiet for the greater part of the time. For even before this they had never been quick to go to war unless they were compelled, and in this period they were hindered, to a degree, by wars at home. This quiet lasted until the power of the Athenians began to manifest itself and to lay hold of their allies. Then the situation became unendurable, and the Spartans decided they must try with all their resolution to destroy that power if they could and to launch this war.[41]

Here the explanation of the causes of the war rests on an interpretation of the feelings, motives, and inclinations of the Spartans over a period of half a century. The resolution of the Spartans to

[39] *Ibid.*, 308.
[40] 1. 44. 2. ἐδόκει γὰρ ὁ πρὸς Πελοποννησίους πόλεμος καὶ ὣς ἔσεσθαι αυτοῖς.
[41] 1. 118. 2.

destroy the power of Athens is made to seem the culmination of an emotion that had grown gradually and could not forever be contained, not a temporary aberration, an outburst of anger and fear resulting from a particular event or chain of events. Once again it would be interesting to know how Thucydides obtained his information on the inner workings of the Spartan psyche. When these passages are put together with two others in the speeches, it is difficult to escape the feeling of inevitability. The Corcyreans say the war is inevitable in 433.[42] Pericles says the same thing in the debate that put an end to negotiations.[43] It is not easy to avoid concluding, as Mme de Romilly does, that "all the different actors in the drama know from the beginning that the war is going to take place." [44] How can the reader believe otherwise?

The same impression is strongly fortified by the arrangement of materials in the first book. After a section on ancient history to demonstrate the relative insignificance of previous wars and the magnitude of the one under discussion, Thucydides gives us his fullest statement of the truest cause of the war. This is followed by an account of the publicly alleged causes, an account already rendered insignificant by the last sentence in the statement of the truest cause. That account makes only the briefest mention of the one event most widely believed to be significant, the Megarian Decree, and the brevity of this treatment, as Mme de Romilly points out, is quite deliberate. "By never mentioning the Megarian decree except among the other incidents, by speaking of its importance in the debate only after the Peloponnesian vote and among so many demands and pretexts, finally, by raising the question of this importance just before the speech of Pericles which denies and refutes it, Thucydides makes us clearly understand that this importance was illusory." [45] The narrative of Thucydides also manages to tell us of the debate on the Corcyrean alliance at Athens, that it required two sessions of the assembly to make a decision, and yet does not tell us what position Pericles took in the debate. We know, of course, that he favored the alliance, but we do not learn that fact from Thucydides.

[42] 1. 33. 2.
[43] 1. 144. 3.
[44] *Thucydides and Athenian Imperialism,* 21.
[45] *Thucydide,* I, xlii.

This omission points up some others equally strange. We know from Thucydides himself that after the Athenians heard the Corcyreans and Corinthians, they had a debate of their own. Not less than two opinions were put forward with enough vigor and persuasiveness to force a second assembly. If not Pericles, then one of his party must have made an effective speech in behalf of the alliance with Corcyra. Yet, although Thucydides gives the speeches of the Corinthians and Corcyreans in full, he presents no Athenian speeches, in spite of the splendid opportunity the occasion afforded for another of the antilogies Thucydides is so fond of. Why does he omit the Athenian speeches? He was surely there to hear them and had every reason to remember what he heard. On a similar occasion at Sparta he presents speeches on both sides of the question and gives us the names of the speakers, Archidamus and Sthenelaidas. Nor does he on other occasions hesitate to indicate political differences within Athens by means of contradictory speeches. The argument over Mytilene is reported in full and highlighted by the speeches of Cleon and Diodotus. The debate over the Sicilian expedition is documented with several contradictory speeches by Nicias and Alcibiades. But we are not given the speeches in the crucial debate that concluded with Athens' first step in the direction of war.

The other striking omission occurs in the final debate at Athens which resulted in the rejection of the Spartan ultimatum and which amounted to a decision for war. On that occasion, Thucydides tells us, there was a great debate indeed. Many rose to speak, much was said for and against the war, a great deal of argument surrounded the Megarian Decree, yet Thucydides reports only the speech of Pericles. It would be instructive to know what arguments his opponents used, and this occasion too is perfect for a typically Thucydidean antilogy, but we are given only the speech of Pericles. We have rejected the notion that Book I is incomplete, and it is impossible to believe that these striking omissions are accidental. The choice and arrangement of evidence and speeches are deliberate. Its purpose is to emphasize what is truly significant (ἡ ἀληθεστάτη πρόφασις) and to diminish the importance of what is really trivial.

If Thucydides had given us a pair of Athenian speeches from the debate on the Corcyrean alliance, one of them most likely by Pericles, he would be emphasizing the fact that two decisions were possible, that the Athenians could readily have chosen not to accept the alliance and almost did, and that vulgar opinion had some reason to believe that Pericles had an important responsibility for bringing on the war. Had he given us speeches that opposed Pericles' refusal to withdraw the Megarian Decree in 432, he would have had to give greater support to the contention that the decree could have been rescinded. In so doing, he could not avoid giving even greater emphasis than he does to Pericles' decisive role in the Athenian determination not to yield. The impression given would be very different from the one that leaps out at us at the first glance we give to the history as we, in fact, have it. It would be, according to Thucydides, a very false impression.

After the narrative of the publicly alleged causes, with the significant omissions we have noticed, comes a restatement of the "truest cause," followed immediately by the description of Athens' rise to power, which is meant to give it support. The omissions in the account of the Pentecontaetia are notorious and too numerous to list here.[46] The point is that there is no way to explain all these omissions and still hold to the belief that the excursus is intended to supply an accurate, objective history of the period. No one has supplied a perfectly acceptable explanation of how Thucydides made his selection of facts for this period, but Walker's suggestion cannot be far from the truth: "The passage 89–118, as an account of the Athenian growth which alarmed Sparta, is at the same time an account of ἡ ἀληθεστάτη πρόφασις: it is, from its introduction and conclusion, no more and no less than an account of the growth of Athenian power written to explain Spartan alarm and a particular Spartan decision: it is parenthetic to the main substance of Bk. I as introduced in 23, i.e. the formal cause or πρόφασις of the war." [47] The excursus is followed by another statement of the "truest cause." Then comes an incredibly brief and sketchy account of negotiations between Athens which went on for months, capped by a long, unopposed speech by Pericles which assumes and flatly states that the Spartans have long been plotting against Athens and that the war is inevitable. A study of the selection and arrangement of materials in Book I should make

[46] Gomme (*Hist. Comm.*, I, 365–369) lists sixteen; it is possible that there are even more.

[47] *Op. cit.* 31.

it clear that a theory that suggests that it is incomplete is untenable. On the contrary, it is a masterpiece of rhetoric, carefully planned and executed, which makes its point with brilliance and subtlety. We need not wonder that it has convinced most of its readers.

Finally we come to the question of why Thucydides chose the interpretation that he presents to us. Why does he offer an explanation for the coming of the war which is not clearly supported by the evidence he supplies? Part of the answer must lie in his polemical intentions. Popular opinion believed that the war was caused by Pericles and the Megarian Decree. That opinion was altogether simple-minded and wrong. Although the decree and Pericles were more important than Thucydides indicates, he was surely right to seek a more satisfactory explanation. It would be a mistake to believe, however, that Thucydides offers his interpretation merely to defend Pericles against the popular charges. Thucydides was an ardent admirer of Pericles and regarded him as the greatest statesman of his time.[48] At the end of the war that had brought Athens so much grief and a crushing defeat, we may be sure that the reputation of Pericles had suffered great damage. Thucydides could not have been unmoved by the desire to restore that reputation, and his history must have contributed much to that end. Instead of believing that Pericles had driven his country into an unnecessary and disastrous war over a trifle, the reader of Thucydides is persuaded that Pericles was a wise and far-seeing statesman who knew that war was inevitable, evolved a sound strategy for winning it, and was thwarted only by such unforeseeable events as the plague and his own death, and by the foolishness of his successors, who would not carry out his strategy. Both versions are exaggerated, although we may be sure that Thucydides is far closer to the truth than Aristophanes and Ephorus. Thucydides would have been very pleased that his defense of Pericles has totally driven the opposition from the field.

Yet the desire to defend Pericles is not enough to explain the Thucydidean interpretation. The play of great impersonal forces is not confined merely to the coming of the war, but plays a leading part in the entire history. The purpose of the work is made very clear quite early. It is intended for those "who wish to see clearly the

[48] See especially Romilly, *Thucydide,* II, xvi–xxix.

things that have happened and those things that, in accordance with human nature, will happen in the same or a similar way again in the future." His work is not intended only for the present, but as a "possession forever."[49] Assuming the essential stability of human nature in the political realm,[50] he tried to establish what amount almost to laws of political behavior. Mme de Romilly's study of the place of imperialism in the work of Thucydides has shown that it is possible to derive from the history such fundamental laws.[51] Nevertheless, he recognized the role of outstanding individuals who possessed wisdom and could affect the course of events. No doubt his book was intended for their use, and its purpose was to provide them with the principles of human political behavior that would enable them to make good judgments in the future. Thucydides wanted to describe and analyze the impersonal forces that operate in human society. A future Themistocles or a Pericles would have the wisdom to use the laws or principles that emerge from that analysis to guide his political actions.[52]

If we keep this purpose in mind, we may arrive at a better understanding of why Thucydides interpreted the coming of the war as he did. Thucydides stood on the edge of philosophy. He was sufficiently a historian to feel compelled to establish the particulars, to present the data as accurately as he could, but he was no less, and perhaps more, concerned to convey the general truths that he had discovered. His passion for truth, his careful distinction between remote and immediate causes, his refusal to explain human events by celestial intervention have all led modern scholars to see him as very much like a modern historian. The fact is that in many ways he is far less modern than Herodotus. The canons of modern historical scholarship demand the presentation of a fair sample of the evidence.

[49] 1. 22. 4.

[50] It is important to emphasize, as Momigliano has done in *Studies in Historiography,* 127–142 and 211–220, that Thucydides limited himself strictly to political history. His statement about the stability of human nature should be understood to apply to that limited context. In that area his confidence does not seem to be misplaced.

[51] *Thucydides and Athenian Imperialism,* 311–343.

[52] For a somewhat fuller statement of my view of Thucydides' purposes, see my chapter on Thucydides in *The Great Dialogue, A History of Greek Political Thought* (New York, 1965), 96–112.

Evidence must be presented on both sides of an argument, and the interpretation must emerge from a demonstration that one thesis is better founded than another. Where there is conflicting evidence, the sources must be cited and reasons given for preferring one over the other. Relevant material known to the historian must be reported even though it contributes to a thesis that he believes mistaken. It should be perfectly plain that Herodotus complies with these demands far more than does Thucydides, who, in fact, violates every one of them at some time or another. Herodotus loves the phenomena in themselves; he is chiefly concerned with composing an interesting and honest narrative. He also wants to suggest some general truths, but that purpose is secondary. Thucydides has a different purpose. The phenomena and the narrative are not ends in themselves, but means whereby the historian can illustrate general truths.

This is not to say that Thucydides means to deceive. Quite the opposite is true. He is determined that the reader will not be deceived, so he selects his material in such a way as to emphasize and clarify the truth. We must remember that his immediate audience knew much more than we do about the events that led to the Peloponnesian War. When Thucydides treated the Megarian Decree with such contempt, they were fully aware of all the evidence on the other side, and Thucydides knew it. His peculiar emphasis was not an attempt at deception but at interpretation. We should also remember that the great majority of the evidence that permits us to reject the Thucydidean interpretation is provided by Thucydides. The purpose of Thucydides was to set before us the truth as he saw it, but his truth need not be ours. If we are to use his history with profit, as we can and must, we must distinguish between the evidence he presents and the interpretation he puts on it. Only then can we use it as a "possession forever."

Appendixes

A. The Willingness of the Members of the Delian League to Accept Athenian Leadership

(Page 39)

In the fourth century the same opinion was held not only by Isocrates (*De Pace* 30, *Paneg.* 72, *Panath.* 67), who might have been prejudiced in favor of Athens, but also by the Spartans, who, according to Xenophon (*Hell.* 6. 5. 34), admitted that the Athenians had been chosen for naval leadership by the allies with the approval of the Spartans. Aristotle (*Ath. Pol.* 23. 2) has seemed to some scholars to argue against Spartan approval by saying that the Athenians took over the hegemony ἀκόντων τῶν Λακεδαιμονίων, and they have tried to emend the text to remove the difficulty. Gomme (*Hist. Comm.*, I, 272) is probably right in arguing against emendation and interpreting the phrase, "Sparta being unwilling to keep the leadership." It is clear in any case that the official Spartan position was one of at least tacit approval. If Aristotle's text is sound and to be interpreted in the more obvious way, then Aristotle may be taking the opinion of the recently defeated war party to be the true attitude of the Spartans.

Meyer (*Historia,* XII [1963], 405 ff.) has seized upon the statement of Herodotus πρόφασιν τὴν Παυσανίεω ὕβριν προϊσχόμενος [οἱ Ἀθηναίοι] ἀπείλοντο τὴν ἡγεμονίην τοὺς Λακεδαιμονίους (8. 5), as the cornerstone of his theory that the formation of the Delian League was the culmination of an Athenian plan dating back at least to 481. His arguments are not convincing, but there is no reason to deny that by 478 the Athenians were more than willing to assume the leadership. Herodotus emphasizes their willingness, while Thucydides lays great stress on the initiative of the allies. Both may be right. As Sealey says: "This difference of judgment and other such oddities doubtless reflect contemporary controversies." He goes on to say that "the student who tries to reconstruct fifth-century history from fifth-century sources is in the position of a foreigner who visits a country and listens to citizens talking politics; at best a tenth of what he hears will be true." This last statement seems to me altogether too pessimistic. Thucydides and Herodotus were not merely two citizens discussing politics; they were learned men who had taken some pains to discover the facts. Their interpretations are not to be too readily discarded.

B. *The Historicity of Diodorus' Account of the Spartan Assembly in 475*

(Page 51)

Many modern scholars simply omit this story, presumably for the same reasons that Busolt denies its historicity (*GG*, III: 1, 71, n. 1). For him, "Die ganze Beratung ist augenscheinlich nur ein Erzeugnis der Phantasie des Ephoros." Grote (*A History of Greece* [4th ed.; London, 1872] IV, 348, n. 1) accepts the conference and considers the role played by an influential Spartan named Hetoemaridas "probable enough," but like Busolt, he considers the speech merely an Isocratean commonplace invented by Ephorus. With what I hope is the higher naiveté of this century, I believe in the conference, the decisive presence of Hetoemaridas, the general tenor of his remarks, and even in the accurate recollection of his words by the Spartan source of Ephorus. There is no doubt that Ephorus knew many true things that neither Herodotus nor Thucydides reports. In this period, which falls outside the main interest of both historians, the argument from silence is worthless. It is bad method to ignore the report of an ancient author that is not contradicted by another source, internally impossible, or self-contradictory. Thus, there is no reason to doubt the conference. It is impossible to imagine why Ephorus or his source should invent Hetoemaridas and attribute a leading role to him, for we know nothing else about him. So we should not doubt him or his important intervention in the discussion.

A. Andrewes (*ASI*, 4–5) accepts the historicity of the meeting and the role of Hetoemaridas without question. The speeches, of course, like all speeches reported by ancient historians, are more suspicious and probably are not completely accurate reports of what the speakers said. Nonetheless, in this case I think Ephorus is reporting the general idea of the discussion correctly and even passes on some of the more striking phrases used by the speakers. The young men of the war party urged in favor of their unwillingness to give up rule of the sea an ancient oracle in which the god had warned them against a "lame" hegemony (μὴ χωλὴν ἔχωσι τὴν ἡγεμονίαν). To abandon one of the two foundations of their leadership, they argued, would leave Sparta lame indeed. I believe this rare burst of eloquence became famous among the Spartans and was often repeated. Little more than a decade later, Cimon, the greatest philolaconian in Athens, who had named one of his sons Lacedaemonius, who admired Sparta and its way of life, and who had very close relations with Sparta, was called upon to argue in behalf of sending an Athenian expedition to help Sparta. He responded with unaccustomed eloquence, exhorting the Athenians "not to leave Hellas lame nor see their city deprived of its yokefellow" (μὴ τὴν Ἑλλάδα χωλὴν μήτε τὴν πόλιν ἑτερόζυγα περιιδεῖν γεγενημένην) (Plut. *Cim.* 16. 8). It appears that he put to good use in a different context a metaphor that he had heard from his Spartan friends. For an excellent discussion of the value of Ephorus-Diodorus as a source, see Mary Morse Fuqua, *A Study of Character Portrayal in the History of Thucydides,* unpublished doctoral dissertation Cornell University, Ithaca, N.Y., 1965, 10–18.

C. *Chronology of Events between* ca. 470-453
(Page 70)

The chronology of this period has been the subject of much disagreement. The important questions are these: When did the great earthquake at Sparta take place? When did the Messenians rebel and when was their rebellion put down? When did the Athenians begin their Egyptian campaign and when did it end? How are these events in foreign affairs related chronologically to such domestic events as the attack on the Areopagus and the ostracism of Cimon?

My answers are essentially the ones that may be derived by putting together the chronological reconstructions of Gomme, *Hist. Comm.*, I, 389–413, the *ATL*, III, 158–180, and Hignett, 337–341. I believe that the earthquake came in 464, that the helot rebellion took place at the same time, and that it came to an end in 461/60. (See p. 79, n. 5.) W. Scharf (*Historia*, III [1954/5], 153–162) and N. G. L. Hammond (*Historia*, IV, [1955], 371–381) believe that the rebellion of the Messenians began in 469/8. Reece (*JHS*, LXXXII [1962], 111–120) thinks it ended in 455. I think the Egyptian uprising occurred in the winter of 461/60, that the Athenians became involved in the spring of 460, and that the great disaster occurred in the summer of 454. J. Barns (*Historia*, II [1953–4], 163–176) and W. Scharf (*Historia*, III [1954–5], 308–325) argue for dating the Egyptian campaign from 462 or 461 to 456. W. Wallace (*TAPA*, LXVII [1936], 252–260) places it from 459 to 453. On the domestic scene, I believe that Ephialtes' attacks on the Areopagites began in 463 and continued until the final victory of the democrats. All this time I believe that he and Pericles were speaking in favor of their democratic program and against the extraordinary powers of the Areopagus. In 462 the Spartans asked for Athenian help, and Cimon persuaded the Athenians to send him at the head of four thousand hoplites. In his absence the democrats carried the reform of the Areopagus. On his return he tried to restore the old order but failed. In the spring of 461 he was ostracized. Not until the next year did the Athenians begin their involvement in Egypt.

D. Reconstruction of the Athenian Tribute Lists

(Page 114)

The attack on the *ATL* version began soon after the publication of the first volume in 1939. Gomme challenged it in a note in *CR*, LIV (1940), 65–67 as did S. Dow in *AJA*, XLV (1941), 642. Dow took up the cudgels (an apt image, considering the tone that the attack has sometimes taken) for 447/6 as the missing year in *CP*, XXXVII (1942), 371–384 and XXXVIII (1943), 20–27, a position that Silvio Accame had already set forth before the first volume of

ATL had appeared (*Riv. di fil.*, XVI (1938), 412–413. Merritt disposed of that suggestion, to my mind decisively, with his article in *CP*, XXXVIII (1943), 223–239. He had already retreated from his original position to the extent of saying that the missing list need not mean that no tribute was collected in that year (*The Greek Political Experience, Studies in Honor of William Kelly Prentice* [Princeton, 1941], 53). In the 1943 article he defended the premise that the missing year was 449/8, but did not insist that no tribute was collected. By 1944 he still had his doubts (B. H. Hill and B. D. Meritt, *Hesperia*, XIII [1944], 9), but by the time of the publication of Volume III in 1950, the authors of *ATL* were again unanimous that no tribute had been recorded for 449/8 because none had been demanded or collected. In 1954, D. M. Lewis, assisted by W. G. Forrest (*BSA*, XLIX [1954], 25–29), studied the Lapis Primus on which the first fifteen years after 454/3 are preserved and questioned the readings that the *ATL* authors had interpreted as a prescript for list 9. This provoked a reply from Malcolm F. McGregor (*Phoenix*, XVI [1962], 267–275), who conceded that the reading of a prescript from the questioned letters was not certain, though he still believed it to be correct. In any case, he continued to insist that there is a missing list, chiefly because no fragments from it have been found.

Recently W. K. Pritchett has launched an attack on the *ATL* (*Historia*, XIII [1964], 129–134), which argues on technical epigraphical grounds that "there may have been space for fifteen complete lists." He is answered vigorously by B. D. Meritt (*Hesperia*, XXXV [1966], 134–140) and M. F. McGregor (*Greek, Roman and Byzantine Studies*, VIII [1967], 102–112). Even if Pritchett is right, it still remains to prove that that space was used for the "missing" list, and for that I know of no evidence. The sophistication of the debate has come to the point where Pritchett has employed a "Professor of Geology and an expert crystallographer, to examine the stone with a hand lens." He himself spent three days building up a thin coating of latex to obtain the best possible impression of the debatable letters. Teams of scholars have been sent to examine the stone and the readings in question, and yet there is no agreement. Into this epigraphic battleground the civilian dare not venture.

E. The Papyrus Decree

(Page 116)

The reconstruction, translation, and dating of the decree are those of Wade-Gery and Meritt (*Hesperia,* XXVI [1957], 163–197). See also *ATL,* II, 61, III, 89, and 281. The Greek text is restored on p. 164 of the *Hesperia* article. The decree reads as follows:

Περικλέους γνώμη[ν] εἰς [τὰ Παναθήναια ἀνενεγκεῖν τῆι Ἀθήναι] τὰ ἐν δημοσί[ωι] ἀποκείμενα τάλαν[τα ἅπερ συνηγμένα παρὰ τῶν πόλεων ἦν πε]ντακισχείλια κατὰ τὴν Ἀριστεί[δου τάξιν καὶ ἄλλα τρισχείλια ἀναφέρ]ειν εἰς τὴν πόλιν μετ' ἐκεῖνο γινο[μένων τῶν ἔργων θαλάσσης δ' ὅπως ἂν κρατ[ῶσι, τὴν βουλὴν τῶν παλαιῶν τριὴ[ρων ἐπιμελεῖσθαι ὥστε ὑγιεῖς παραδι]δόναι, καινὰς δ' ἐπιναυπηγεῖν ἑκάσ[του ἐνιαυτοῦ πρὸς ταῖς ὑπαρχούσαις δ]έκα.

It is important to understand that many crucial restorations are far from certain. Gomme (*Historia,* III [1954–5], 337), who had not seen the restoration cited here, but the earlier one given in *ATL* II, 61, had serious doubts about parts of it. The latest version, nevertheless, seems to be very persuasive. Wade-Gery and Meritt have this to say about their restoration of the commentator's version of the decree of Pericles: "We do not hold that we have recovered word for word the language which he used in making his summary, but we do claim that the structure of this section begins now to be clear and that we may take our stand on the preserved portions of the papyrus with confidence in our interpretation, no matter what the precise restorations may be" (p. 188). This seems to me a fair estimate of the situation.

F. The Foundation of Thurii

(Page 157)

For a discussion of the commercial advantages offered by the site, see Busolt, *GG,* III: 1, 527 and n. 4. Ehrenberg (*AJP,* LXIX

(1948), 152 and n. 15) believes that "Athens—so much was clear from the very beginning of the whole action—was to lead the new colony." This assertion rests on the numismatic evidence. The oldest coin type of Sybaris seems to be that of a bull with its head turned backwards, with the same type, incuse on the reverse. Later an amphora appears on the reverse. The next type shows a bull on one side and Poseidon on the other. Another coin, judged by Head. (*Historia Numorum*, [London, 1911], 84–85) to belong to Sybaris at the same period, has a bird on one side and Poseidon on the other. The next period discerned by the numismatists finds coins with a bull with its head reverted on one side and Athena on the other. The last type of coin bearing the legend of Sybaris shows Athena on one side, and on the other the traditional Sybarite bull has changed his pose. Instead of turning his head back to bite his flank, he now merely lowers it. "It seems almost a symbol that the bull no longer looked back." Finally, as Ehrenberg points out, the coins of the newly founded Thurii retain Athena and the forward-looking bull. It is the head of Athena on the coins of "the third Sybaris," i.e., the Sybaris, which for Ehrenberg is the best proof of the leadership of Athens. This hardly appears to me to be a persuasive argument. The use of coin types to explain political events must be employed with great caution. As we shall see further on, the Thurian settlement did not work out well for the Sybarites. They were soon driven out and proceeded to found a fourth Sybaris, yet Thurii retained the type of the Sybarite bull on its coins. Yet if we use Ehrenberg's reasoning, the Thurians should have removed it, as an unwelcome evidence of Sybarite origins. Ehrenberg's explanation of this phenomenon seems to me to explain nothing: "The bull certainly maintained a Sybarite tradition, probably just because there was now a new, if unimportant, 'fourth' Sybaris, the foundation of the expelled Sybarites. The Thurians naturally did their best to keep it down, and retained the bull coins which were a popular currency" (153).

The appearance of the Athena on the coins also seems not to prove much. Corinthian coins also carried a head of Athena. Does that mean that their first appearance is evidence of Athenian influence? Athena was worshipped in her several aspects in many cities. Head (p. 87) suggested that the Athena on the coins was Athena Skyletria, a sea goddess worshipped in many towns of south Italy.

The changed posture of the bull, of course, can be interpreted in countless ways. The fact that the same coin types were preserved at Thurii proves very little, as we have seen. Suppose we make the opposite assumption from that of Ehrenberg, i.e., that the types were not associated with Athens, but had been adopted at some time by the Sybarites for quite different reasons. We can then interpret their retention, and particularly the retention of the bull, as an attempt by the newly founded Panhellenic colony to flatter the older inhabitants and retain their allegiance. All this is very fanciful, but no more so than the alternative suggestion. Finally, the fatal weakness of the numismatic evidence is that we cannot date the coins in any other way than by historical conjecture of the sort we have been engaged in, which is to say that the coins cannot be used as independent evidence of anything.

G. *Athenian Actions in the West between the Wars*

(Page 162)

One possible instance suggested by Wade-Gery and not treated above is the alliance negotiated with Acarnania by Phormio (Thuc. 2. 68. 8). Thucydides reports it in connection with the events of the summer of 430, but he merely indicates that the alliance of Phormio was concluded at some time in the past, without being specific. Busolt (*CG*, III: 2, 736, n. 6) suggested that the date could not have been before the Samian War, or Corinth would not have been friendly to Athens in 440. It could not have been after the beginning of the Corinthian dispute with Corcyra, or Thucydides would have mentioned it in connection with that affair, and so Busolt places the alliance about 437. He is followed by Adcock (*CAH*, V, 474–475), Glotz and Cohen (*HG*, II, 614) and Cloché (*AC*, XIV [1945], 116). But these limits are far from firmly established and, in fact, they will not withstand examination. The early terminus is not valid if we imagine that the expedition of Phormio occurred during the First Peloponnesian War. By 440 the policy of Athens had changed, and Corinth knew it. There is thus no reason to deny the possibility of a date in the 450's. This is precisely the position taken by Gomme

(*Hist. Comm.*, II, 416), who places the expedition "perhaps in the early 50's, at least as early as the Athenian campaign at Delphi in c. 448." Beloch held much the same view, saying that the treaty was concluded, "wohl schon vor dem dreissigjahrigen Frieden" (*GG*, II: 1, 299, n. 2). The later terminus is based on an *argumentum e silentio,* and no argument is less persuasive when we are dealing with Thucydides, whose omissions are enigmatic to say the least. Wade-Gery (*Essays,* 253–254) places the expedition after 433, although it would be in accord with his theory of Athenian pressure on the west to have it earlier. He believes that "the Akarnanian Treaty is subsequent to the battle of Sybota," more specifically in the spring of 432 (pp. 253–254). In a posthumous article (*JHS*, LXXII [1952], 62ff.), R. L. Beaumont supports the view of Wade-Gery with what seem to me decisive arguments which place the expedition after 433. See also *ATL,* III, 320 and n. 84.

Another instance of Athenian activity in the west is inferred from a fragment of Timaeus reported by the scholiast to Lycophron, *Alexandra,* 732 (*FGrH,* IIIB, 556, no. 98). When this is combined with a comment of Tzetzes to line 733 and a remark by Strabo (5. 4. 247), it is clear at least that at some time the Athenian general Diotimus was called to assist the Neapolitans with a fleet, although we have no reason to believe what is sometimes alleged, that the Athenians strengthened Naples with colonists. (The allegation is made by Beloch, *GG*², II: 1, 202; cf. *FGrH,* IIIB, Kommentar 581.) The problem is to decide when and under what circumstances the event took place. The most common opinion since the time of Nissen (*Historische Zeitschrift,* N.F., XXVII [1889], 400ff.) places it at the time of the generalship of Diotimus in 433/2. This date has been accepted by W. Judeich (*PW,* V [1905], *s.v.* "Diotimus 1," 1147) A. E. Raubitschek, (*TAPA,* LXXV [1944], 10, n. 4), and Bengtson (*GG,* 205, n. 1). Busolt (*GG,* III: 1, 538, n. 5) believes that it happened before the war in the 430's. Eduard Meyer (*Forschungen,* II, 321–322), arguing against some of the wilder aspects of Nissen's theories, was led also to question his date for the expedition of Diotimus to Naples. He thought it possible that the event might have happened in an earlier strategia of Diotimus, although we have no record of it and Meyer offers no argument in its behalf. Meyer also suggests the possibility that the expedition was a response to a Sabellian invasion of Campania during which Capua and Cymae were also attacked. Diodorus, to be sure, dates the attack on Capua to 438, but Livy puts it in 423. De Sanctis (*Riv. di. Fil.*, N.S., XIII [1935], 71ff. and *Pericle,* 118) believes that the expedition of Diotimus and the Alliance of Athens with Naples took place in the 450's in close connection with the alliances with Rhegium and Leontini. My opinion is that we may be certain only of an expedition to help Naples and nothing else. I am inclined to accept the majority opinion and place it in 433/2, in the only known generalship of Diotimus, but this is not certain. What is important here is to note that there is absolutely no reason to believe that it took place between the wars.

H. Athenian Treatment of Byzantium

(Page 177)

Thucydides (1. 117. 3) is our only source for the Byzantine capitulation. Gomme (*Hist. Comm.*, I, 357) points out that the cost of the Athenian campaign at Byzantium was only a tenth that of Samos. He also refutes the assertion made by Miltner ("Perikles," 773) that the settlement deprived Byzantium of Bysbicus and Callipolis, two small places on the Asian shore of the Propontis. Like Amorgus, they do not appear on the tribute lists until 434/3. Édouard Will (*Bulletin de la Faculté des Lettres de Strassbourg* [1946–7], 145–146) had read the brief report more carefully than most scholars and come up with a novel interpretation. Thucydides says, ξυνέβησαν δὲ καὶ Βυζάντιοι ὥσπερ καὶ πρότερον ὑπήκοοι εἶναι. The translation of C. Forster Smith in the Loeb edition ("The Byzantines too came to terms, agreeing to be subjects as before") and that of Jacqueline de Romilly in the Budé version ("Byzance traita, elle aussi: elle redevint sujette comme auparavant") are typical. Will has seen that ξυνέβησαν means that the Byzantines agreed to the conditions under which they returned to the empire. In this he is surely right, for if Thucydides had meant to say merely that it came to pass that the Byzantines were restored to their previous condition, he would have used the impersonal ξυνέβη. Thus he takes the sentence to mean that "Byzance ne se rend qu'a condition de retrouver sa place dans la confédération." For him this means that Byzantium was in a position to set the conditions of her return. The relatively gentle treatment the Byzantines received from Athens came from their crucial position astride the Bosporus. "Pericles pouvait en effet sans trop de risques faire un exemple à Samos, mais il lui fallait traiter Byzance avec bienveillance, pour s'assurer sa fidélité." This seems to me to distort the meaning of the Greek no less than to misread the political realities. To be sure, *ξυνέβησαν* implies the setting and accepting of conditions, but there is nothing in the sentence to tell us who set the conditions and who accepted them. It is surely more likely that Athens laid down the terms. She had an overwhelming superiority of force and had just put down a far more serious rebellion. If Byzantium were dictating the agreement, we should expect her to ask for a reduction in tribute instead of what seems to be a minor but not insignificant rise. I should translate the sentence in question, "The Byzantines agreed to be subjects on the same terms as before," and I understand those terms to have been offered not by Byzantium but by Athens. We have seen that, in fact, Samos was not made a horrible example but was treated with restraint. Will is right to stress the moderation of Pericles' handling of Byzantium, but it was the result not of fear but of policy.

I. The Date of Pericles' Pontic Expedition

(Page 181)

The date of Pericles' Pontic expedition is the subject of some disagreement. Most scholars place it shortly after the reduction of Samos, as I have. For references, see *ATL,* III, 114, n. 2. The main textual support for this dating is provided by Aristophanes in the *Acharnians,* 601, where Lamachus, named by Plutarch as the commander of the thirteen ships that Pericles sent to Sinope, is compared to "youngsters" (*νεανίαι*). From this it is usual to conclude that he could not yet be fifty in 425 when the play was produced, and was, in fact, much younger. By this reasoning, he would have been too young to conduct any campaign much before 440. The authors of *ATL* (III, 114–117) point out the difficulties in getting any hard facts from Aristophanes and suggest a good bit of comic exaggeration. They do whatever is possible to allow for an older Lamachus, but finally I am persuaded that the majority is right is placing the expedition in the 430's on the basis of the chronological indications we have. The authors of *ATL* would like to place the Pontic expedition about 450. I believe their main reason for doing so is that they wish it to take place before the Peace of Callias, for they consider it to be a breach of the terms of that peace, and so impossible after 449. It is easy enough to place the expedition in the 430's by denying the existence of a Peace of Callias, but I think it possible to place the expedition at that time without giving up a belief in the peace. One of the terms of the Peace of Callias which the ancients report to us forbade the Persians to sail within the Chelidonian Islands, or Phaselis, and the Cyanean Rocks. (For the ancient references, see James H. Oliver, *Historia,* VI [1957], 254–255 and Raphael Sealey, *Historia,* III [1954–5], 325–333, both of whom offer explanations of the variations tradition.) Some scholars have believed these rocks to have been located only twenty-five miles from the islands, so the restricted zone was not very large. See Wade-Gery, *Athenian Studies Presented to William Scott Ferguson* (*HSCP*, Suppl., I, 1940, 121–156, especially p. 135), who speaks of it as a "demilitarized zone," and Sealey (*op. cit.*, 330), who rejects Wade-Gery's interpretation. I believe that Oliver has shown that the Cyanean Rocks in question are identical with the Blue Rocks near the Thracian Bosporus. Thus, it is clear that if Pericles sailed to the Black Sea in the 430's, he was certainly breaking the terms of the treaty, if there was one. Since Oliver believes in the Peace of Callias, he supports the authors of *ATL* in dating the Pontic expedition to 450. The only strong reason for this date, it appears, is the belief that Pericles would have been unwilling to break the treaty in the way that he did, but I do not share that belief. In the Samian affair Pissuthnes had clearly broken the peace, both in letter and in spirit. So far as we know, he was not punished nor disavowed by the Great King in Susa. Nothing could be more dangerous than to leave such a violation unavenged. Failure to act could lead the Persians to believe that Athens had become a paper tiger since the death of Cimon and encourage them to further encroachments. The more remote allies, on the other hand, must be shown that Athens was willing and more than able to resist any

Persian attempt at troublemaking. In this context a Pontic expedition about 437 makes very good sense as a retaliation against Persia and a warning against a repetition of the Persian indiscretion at Samos. Pericles did not find it necessary to repeat the warning, for the Persians committed no further violations until the Athenians were embroiled in the Peloponnesian War, and even then only after Athens had suffered severe reversals. If all this is true, the Peace of Callias was not the only real treaty that persisted, even though it suffered some violations on each side. The evidence for Sinope comes from Plutarch *Per.* 20; for Nymphaeum, see *ATL,* I, 527–528. For the relations with Spartocus at the Cimmerian Bosporus, see Busolt, *GG,* III: 1, 586–7 and notes 1 and 2 on 587; for Amisus, see Busolt, *GG,* III: 1, 586 and n. 3; for Astacus, see Busolt, *GG,* III: 1, 586, n. 4. Diodorus places the foundation of Astacus in 435/4, but I think it possible that he is mistaken and that its foundation was part of the Periclean expedition. Amisus was founded under the leadership of a certain Athenocles, and its name changed to Piraeus.

J. The Site and Date of Brea

(Page 183)

The authors of *ATL* (III, 286ff.) place Brea to the east of the Chalcidice in Bisaltia, near Argilos, and believe it to have been founded in 446. I accept the arguments of A. G. Woodhead (*CQ,* N.S., II [1952], 57–62), which also convinced J. A. Alexander (*AJP,* LXXXIII [1962], 265–287 and *Potidaea, Its History and Remains* [Athens, Georgia, 1963], 45, 65, 68, 108, and 114). H. B. Mattingly (*CQ,* N.S., XVI [1966], 172–192) agrees with Woodhead that the date of foundation is after 446. He admits that, according to the generally accepted epigraphical criteria, it should not be put after about 438. Since he rejects those criteria, he is consistent in placing the foundation of Brea in 426/5 and attributing it to Cleon's aggressive imperialism. He is inclined to accept Woodhead's location of the site. Charles Edson (*CP,* L [1955], 169–190) rejects Woodhead's emendation of the text of Thucydides from Βέροιαν to Βρέαν and thus casts some doubt on his location of Brea. A. J. Graham

(*Colony and Mother City in Ancient Greece* [Manchester, 1964], 34, n. 3) believes that the date of its foundation is restricted either to 445/4 or 440/38, but that it is not possible to choose between these two periods. I hope that the strategic considerations I have discussed above may lend support to Woodhead's date.

Professor Meritt has informed me that Woodhead has now abandoned the views I have accepted. Meritt has reiterated the judgment of the *ATL* in an article called "The Choregic Dedication of Teagros" (*Greek, Roman and Byzantine Studies,* VIII [1967], 45–52, especially 49–50). There he again points out the significance of Plutarch's statement that Pericles sent "a thousand settlers to establish a joint colony with Bisaltae" (*Per.* 11. 5). He is convinced that this must be a reference to the establishment of Brea and helps to explain a drop in the tribute of Argilus in 446. Several arguments seem to me to count against the identification of Brea with Plutarch's colony. The first, most obvious, but least important, is that Plutarch does not call it by name. The second is that the reference to the colony among the Bisaltae occurs in one of those omnibus passages where he gathers together a number of colonies Pericles established, including even Thurii. There is no reason to believe that the list is exhaustive. If we take Plutarch's language seriously, moreover, another objection arises. He says that in addition to the settlers Pericles sent to the Chersonese, Naxos, and Andros, he also sent a thousand to Thrace Βισάλταις συνοικήσοντας. This may, of course, be only a loose usage, but συνοικήσοντας seems to suggest the formation of a joint colony, which Brea certainly was not. None of this is decisive, but it justifies resistance to the identification of Brea with Plutarch's Bisaltian colony. The identification remains possible and should not be ignored. My argument for the Periclean policy would not be impaired by such an identification and a shifting of Brea from west to east of the Chalcidice, but I continue to prefer the western location.

The date of the colony is a more important question and no more open to certain decision. Epigraphy does not settle the matter. The date offered by the *ATL* makes sense. In the present state of the evidence, the reader can only judge for himself which theory is more attractive.

K. The Date of the Battle of Poteadia

(Page 316)

This difficulty does not arise for those who believe in a different chronology, which puts the Battle of Potidaea in September of 432 and the congress at Sparta in November of that year. We need not go into the complicated details of the chronological controversy here. It is enough to quote the argument made by Gomme against the later dates and in favor of his dates adopted here.

From Aug. 1 to about May 20, the date of the invasion of Attica is from 9½ to 10 lunar months, about the least we might expect "not a year, but less" to mean. Moreover, a date for the Conference early in August also explains why the Corinthians urge haste, and why the delay of the Peloponnesians is ascribed to their unpreparedness, not to the imminent approach or the early arrival of winter, as would be the case if the battle of Poteidaia had been fought after mid-September and the Conference therefore not held before November. Indeed, if the decision of the Peloponnesians to go to war was made so late in the year, there was no delay (except that of some days next year after the army left the Isthmus); for in that case the invasion took place at the earliest feasible time after the decision . . . , at the season of the year which was to become normal for the annual event. If the decision was made early in August, there was opportunity for invasion in September and October but the Peloponnesians were not ready. Hence the Corinthian plea for haste, and hence the complaint of delay. Moreover, if the Conference is dated to the beginning of November, barely seven lunar months passed before the invasion about May 20; no candid person would say that such an interval would be called "not a year, but less" (A. W. Gomme, *CR*, LV [1941], 65–66).

Gomme offers a bibliography of the chronological debate up to the time of his article on p. 59. He repeats the gist of his arguments in his *Commentary* (I, 420–424).

Bibliography

Accame, Silvio, "L'alleanza di Atene con Leontini e Regio," *Riv. di fil.*, N.S., XIII (1935), 73–74.

Accame, Silvio, "Note storiche su epigrafi attiche del V secolo," *Riv. di fil.*, N.S., XXX (1952), 111–136.

Adcock, F. E., "The Breakdown of the Thirty Years Peace, 445–431 B.C.," *CAH*, V (1940), 165–192.

Adcock, F. E., "Thucydides in Book I," *JHS*, LXXI (1951), 1–12.

Adcock, F. E., *Thucydides and his History*, Cambridge, 1963.

Albertini, Luigi, *The Origins of the War of 1914*, 3 vols., translated and edited by I. M. Massey, Oxford, 1953.

Alexander, J. A., "Thucydides and the Expedition of Callias against Potidaea, 432 B.C.," *AJP*, LXXXIII (1962), 265–287.

Alexander, J. A., *Potidaea, Its History and Remains*, Athens, Georgia, 1963.

Andrewes, A., "Sparta and Arcadia," *Phoenix*, VI (1952), 1–5.

Andrewes, A., "Thucydides on the Causes of War," *CQ*, N.S., IX (1959), 223–239.

Andrewes, A., "Thucydides and the Persians," *Historia*, X (1961), 1–18.

Andrewes, A., "The Government of Classical Sparta," in *ASI*, Oxford, 1966, 1–20.

Badian, E., ed., *Ancient Societies and Institutions, Studies Presented to Victor Ehrenberg on his 75th birthday*, Oxford, 1966.

Barns, J., "Cimon and the First Athenian Expedition to Cyprus," *Historia*, II (1953–54), 163–176.

Barron, J. P., "Milesian Politics and Athenian Propaganda c. 460–440 B.C.," *JHS*, LXXXII (1962), 1–6.

Barron, J. P., "Religious Propaganda of the Delian League," *JHS*, LXXXIV (1964), 35–48.

Bauer, W., "Epigraphisches aus dem Athener National Museum," *Klio*, XV (1918), 188–195.

Beaumont, R. L., "Greek Influence in the Adriatic Sea Before the Fourth Century B.C.," *JHS*, LVI (1936), 159–204.

Beaumont, R. L., "Corinth, Ambracia, Apollonia," *JHS,* LXXII (1952), 62–73.

Beloch, K. J., *Die Attische Politik seit Perikles,* Leipzig, 1884.

Beloch, K. J., *Griechische Geschichte,* 2nd ed., Strassburg, Berlin, and Leipzig, 1912–1927.

Bender, G. F., *Der Begriff des Staatsmannes bei Thukydides,* Diss. Erlangen, 1937; Würzburg, 1938.

Bengtson, Hermann, *Griechische Geschichte,* 2nd ed., Munich, 1960.

Bengtson, Hermann, *Die Staatsverträge der griechisch-römischen Welt von 700 bis 338 v. Chr.,* II, Munich and Berlin, 1962.

Bétant, E. -A., *Lexicon Thucydideum,* Hildesheim, 1961 (reprint).

Boeckh, August, *Die Staatshaushaltung der Athener,* 3rd ed., Max Frankel, ed., Berlin, 1886.

Bradeen, D. W., "The Popularity of the Athenian Empire," *Historia,* IX (1960), 257–269.

Brauer, H., *Die Kriegsschuldfrage in der geschichtliche Überlieferung des Peloponnesischen Krieges,* Emsdetten, 1933.

Brunt, P. A., "The Megarian Decree," *AJP,* LXXII (1951), 269–282.

Brunt, P. A., "The Hellenic League Against Persia," *Historia,* (1953/1954), 135–163.

Bury, J. B., *History of Greece,* 3rd ed., rev. by Russell Meiggs, London, 1952.

Bury, J. B., Cook, S. A., Adcock, F. E., *The Cambridge Ancient History,* I-VI, Cambridge, 1923–1927.

Busolt, Georg, *Die Lakedaimonier und Ihre Bundesgenossen,* Leipzig, 1878.

Busolt, Georg, *Griechische Geschichte,* 3 vols., Gotha, 1893–1904.

Busolt, Georg, and Heinrich Swoboda, *Griechische Staatskunde* in Müller's *Handbuch der Altertumswissenschaft,* 2 vols., Munich, 1920–26.

Calder, W. M., "The Corcyrean-Corinthian Speeches in Thucydides I," *CJ,* L (1955), 179ff.

Carcopino, Jérôme, *L'Ostracisme athénien,* 2nd ed., Paris, 1935.

Cary, M., "The Sources of Silver for the Greek World," *Mélanges Glotz,* Paris, 1932, 133–142.

Chambers, Mortimer, "Thucydides and Pericles," *HSCP,* LXII (1957), 79ff.

Chambers, Mortimer, "Four Hundred and Sixty Talents," *CP,* LIII (1958), 26–32.

Chambers, Mortimer, "Studies on Thucydides, 1957–1962," *CW,* LVII (1963–64), 6–14.

Cloché, P., "La politique extérieure d'Athènes de 462 à 454 avant J.-C.," *L'Antiquité Classique,* XI (1942), 25–39 and 213–233.

Cloché, Paul, "Périclès et la politique extérieure d'Athènes entre la paix de 446–445 et les préludes de la guerre du péloponnèse," *L'Antiquité Classique,* XIV (1945), 93–128.

Cloché, Paul, *Thèbes de Béotie,* Namur, Louvain, and Paris, no date.

Connor, W. R., "Charinus' Megarian Decree," *AJP,* LXXXIII (1962), 225–246.

Cornford, F. M., *Thucydides Mythistoricus,* London, 1907, reprinted 1965.

Davies, O., *Roman Mines in Europe,* Oxford, 1935.

Day, James, and Mortimer Chambers, *Aristotle's History of Athenian Democracy,* Berkeley and Los Angeles, 1962.

Delbrück, Hans, *Die Strategie des Perikles,* Berlin, 1890.

Delbrück, Hans, *Geschichte der Kriegskunst,* Vol. I, *Das Altertum,* Berlin, 1920, reprinted 1964.

De Sanctis, G., *Atthis,* 2nd ed., Rome, 1904.

De Sanctis, G., "La prima spedizione ateniese nell'Occidente," *Riv. di fil.,* N.S., XIII (1935), 71–72.

De Sanctis, *Pericle,* Milan and Messina, 1944.

De Sanctis, Gaetano, *Storia dei Greci,* Florence, 1963.

Dickins, Guy, "The True Cause of the Peloponnesian War," *CQ,* V (1911), 238–248.

Dickins, Guy, "The Growth of Spartan Policy," *JHS,* XXXII (1912), 1–42.

Dienelt, Karl, *Die Friedenspolitik des Perikles,* Vienna and Wiesbaden, 1958.

Dittenberger, W., *Sylloge Inscriptionum Graecarum,* 4 vols., 4th ed., Leipzig, 1915; reprinted Hildesheim, 1960.

Dow, S., "Studies in the Athenian Tribute Lists," *CP,* XXXVII (1942), 371–384 and 38 (1943), 20–27.

Earp, A. J., "Athens and Miletus *ca.* 450 B.C.," *Phoenix,* VIII (1954), 142–147.

Edson, Charles, "Strepsa (Thucydides 1. 61. 4)," *CP,* L (1955), 169–190.

Ehrenberg, Victor, "Sparta (Geschichte)," *PW,* III A, 1929, 1373–1453.

Ehrenberg, Victor, "Polypragmosyne: A Study in Greek Politics," *JHS,* LXVII (1947), 46–67.

Ehrenberg, Victor, "The Foundation of Thurii," *AJP,* LXIX (1948), 149–170.

Ehrenberg, Victor, *The People of Aristophanes,* Oxford, 1951.

Ehrenberg, Victor, *Sophocles and Pericles,* Oxford, 1954.
Ehrenberg, Victor, *The Greek State,* Oxford, 1960.
Essen, M. H. N. von, *Index Thucydideus,* Berlin, 1887.
Ferguson, W. S., *The Treasurers of Athena,* Cambridge, Mass., 1932.
Finley, J. H., "Euripides and Thucydides," *HSCP,* XLIX (1938), 23ff.
Finley, J. H., "The Unity of Thucydides' History," *HSCP,* Suppl., I, 1940, 255ff.
Finley, J. H., *Thucydides,* Cambridge, Mass., 1942.
Finley, M. I., "Generalizations in Ancient History," in *Generalization in the Writing of History,* Louis Gottschalk, ed., Chicago, 1963, 19–35.
Finley, M. I., "Classical Greece," in *Trade and Politics in the Ancient World,* Second International Congress of Economic History at Aix-en-Province in 1962, Paris, 1965, I, 11–35.
Finley, M. I., "The Classical Cold War," *New York Review of Books,* VIII: 5, March 23, 1967, 26.
Fliess, P. J., "War Guilt in the History of Thucydides," *Traditio,* XVI (1960), 1ff.
Fliess, P. J., *Thucydides and the Politics of Bipolarity,* Baton Rouge, 1966.
Forbes, W. H., *Thucydides Book I,* Oxford, 1895.
Forrest, W. G., "Themistokles and Argos," *CQ,* N.S., X (1960), 221–241.
French, A., *The Growth of the Athenian Economy,* London, 1964.
Frisch, Hartvig, *The Constitution of the Athenians,* Copenhagen, 1942.
Frost, F. J., "Pericles and Dracontides," *JHS,* LXXXIV (1964), 69–72.
Frost, F. J., "Pericles, Thucydides, son of Melesias, and Athenian Politics Before the War," *Historia,* XIII (1964), 385–399.
Fuqua, Mary M., *A Study of Character Portrayal in the History of Thucydides,* unpublished dissertation, Cornell University, Ithaca, New York, 1965.
Glotz, Gustave, and Robert Cohen, *Histoire Grecque,* II, Paris, 1929.
Gomme, A. W., *Essays in Greek History and Literature,* Oxford, 1937.
Gomme, A. W., "The Old Oligarch," *HSCP,* Suppl., I, 1940, 211–245.
Gomme, A. W., "Two Notes on the Athenian Tribute Lists," *CR,* LIV (1940), 65–69.
Gomme, A. W., "I.G. I.[2] 296 and the Dates of τὰ ποτειδεατικά," *CR,* LV (1941), 59–66.
Gomme, A. W., *A Historical Commentary on Thucydides,* I-III, Oxford, 1950–1956.
Gomme, A. W., "Thucydides ii 13.3: An Answer to Professor Meritt," *Historia,* III (1954/1955), 333–338.

Graham, A. J., *Colony and Mother City in Ancient Greece,* Manchester, 1964.

Greenidge, A. H. J., *A Handbook of Greek Constitutional History,* London, 1902.

Grote, G., *A History of Greece,* 4th ed., London, 1872.

Grundy, G. B., "The Policy of Sparta," *JHS,* XXXII (1912), 261–269.

Grundy, G. B., *Thucydides and the History of his Age,* 2nd ed., Oxford, 1948.

Gschnitzer, Fritz, *Abhängige Orte in Griechischen Altertum,* Munich, 1958.

Hammond, N. G. L., "Studies in Greek Chronology of the Sixth and Fifth Centuries B.C.," *Historia,* IV (1955), 371–411.

Hammond, N. G. L., *A History of Greece to* 322 B.C., Oxford, 1959.

Hampl, Franz, "Poleis Ohne Territorium," *Klio,* XXXII (1939), 1–60.

Hasebroek, J., *Griechische Wirtschafts und Gesellschaftsgeschichte,* Tübingen, 1931.

Head, B. V., *Historia Numorum,* London, 1911, reprinted 1963.

Henderson, B. W., *The Great War Between Athens and Sparta,* London, 1927.

Highby, L. I., *The Erythrae Decree. Contributions to the early history of the Delian league and the Peloponnesian confederacy, Klio,* Beiheft XXXVI, N.F., 23 (1936).

Hignett, C., *A History of the Athenian Constitution,* Oxford, 1952.

Hill, B. H., and B. D. Meritt, "An Early Athenian Decree Concerning Tribute," *Hesperia,* XIII (1944), 1–15.

Hill, G. F., *Sources for Greek History Between the Persian and Peloponnesian Wars,* new edition by Russell Meiggs and A. Andrewes, Oxford, 1951.

Hiller von Gaertringen, F., *Inscriptiones Graecae,* I, *editio minor, Inscriptiones Atticae Euclidis anno anteriores,* Berlin, 1924.

Holzapfel, L., *Untersuchungen über die Darstellung der griechischen Geschichte,* Leipzig, 1879.

Hude, C., *Scholia in Thucydidem,* Leipzig, 1927.

Huxley, G. L., *Early Sparta,* Cambridge, Mass., 1962.

Jacoby, F., *Die Fragmente der griechischen Historiker,* I–II, Berlin, 1923–1930; III, Leyden, 1940.

Jaeger, W., *Paideia,* tr. Gilbert Highet, I, Oxford, 1954.

Judeich, W., "Diotimus (1)," *PW,* V (1905), 1147.

Kagan, D., "Corinthian Diplomacy after the Peace of Nicias," *AJP,* LXXXI (1960), 291–310.

Kagan, D., "The Origin and Purposes of Ostracism," *Hesperia,* XXX (1961), 393–401.

Kagan, D., "Argive Politics and Policy after the Peace of Nicias," *Classical Philology,* LVII (1962), 209–218.

Kagan, D., "The Enfranchisement of Aliens by Cleisthenes," *Historia,* XII (1963), 41–46.

Kagan, D., *The Great Dialogue: A History of Greek Political Thought from Homer to Polybius,* New York, 1965.

Kahrstedt, U., *Griechisches Staatsrecht,* I, Sparta und seine Symmachie, Göttingen, 1922.

Kienast, D., "Der Innenpolitische Kampf in Athens von der Rückkehr des Thukydides bis zu Perikles' Tod," *Gymnasium,* LX (1953), 210–229.

8—Extract—10 Fairfield

Kirkwood, G. M., "Thucydides' Word for Cause," *AJP,* LXXIII (1952), 37–61.

Klaffenbach, G., "Das Jahr der Kapitulation von Ithome," *Historia,* I (1950), 231–235.

Kolbe, W., *Thukydides im Lichte der Urkunden,* Stuttgart, 1930.

Kolbe, W., "Diodorus Wert für die Geschichte der Pentekontaetie," *Hermes,* LXXII (1937), 241–269.

Kraft, K., "Bemerkungen zu den Perserkriegen," *Hermes,* XCII (1964), 158–171.

Langer, W. L., "A Critique of Imperialism," *Foreign Affairs,* XIV (1935–36), 102–119.

Larsen, J. A. O., "Sparta and the Ionian Revolt: A Study of Spartan Foreign Policy and the Genesis of the Peloponnesian League," *CP,* XXVII (1932), 136–150.

Larsen, J. A. O., "The Constitution of the Peloponnesian League," *CP,* XXVIII (1933), 256–276, and XXVII (1934), 1–19.

Larsen, J. A. O., "The Constitution and Original Purposes of the Delian League," *HSCP,* LI (1940), 175–213.

Larsen, J. A. O., *Representative Government in Greek and Roman History,* Berkeley and Los Angeles, 1955.

Leahy, D. M., "Aegina and the Peloponnesian League," *CP,* XLIX (1954), 232–243.

Legon, Ronald P., *Demos and Stasis: Studies in the Factional Politics of Classical Greece,* unpublished doctoral dissertation, Cornell University, Ithaca, New York, 1966.

Lenardon, R. J., "The Archonship of Themistocles," *Historia,* V (1956), 401–419.

Lenardon, R. J., "The Chronology of Themistocles' Ostracism and Exile," *Historia,* VIII (1959), 23–48.

Lendle, O., "Philochorus über den Prozess des Phidias," *Hermes,* LXXXIII (1955), 284–303.

Lepper, F. A., "Some Rubrics in the Athenian Quota-Lists," *JHS,* LXXXII (1962), 25–55.

Lewis, D. M., "Ithome Again," *Historia,* II (1954), 413–418.

Lewis, D. M., "Notes on Attic Inscriptions," *BSA,* XLIX (1954), 17–50.

Lewis, D. M., "Cleisthenes and Attica," *Historia,* XII (1963), 22–40.

Mac Dowell, "Aegina and the Delian League," *JHS,* LXXX (1960), 118–121.

Martin, V., *La vie internationale dans la grèce des cités,* Paris, 1940.

Mattingly, H. B., "The Athenian Coinage Decree," *Historia,* X (1961), 148–188.

Mattingly, H. B., "Athens and Euboea," *JHS,* LXXXI (1961), 124–132.

Mattingly, H. B., "The Methone Decrees," *CQ,* N.S., XI (1961), 154–163.

Mattingly, H. B., "The Peace of Kallias," *Historia,* XV (1965), 273–281.

Mattingly, H. B., "Periclean Imperialism," *ASI,* 193–224.

Mattingly, H. B., "Athenian Imperialism and the Foundation of Brea," *CQ,* N.S., XVI (1966), 172–192.

Mattingly, H. B., "Athens and Aegina," *Historia,* XVI (1967), 1–5.

May, J. M. F., *The Coinage of Damastion and the Lesser Coinages of the Illyro-Paeonian Region,* London, 1939.

McGregor, M. F., "The Politics of the Historian Thucydides," *Phoenix,* X (1956), 93–102.

McGregor, M. F., "The Ninth Prescript of the Attic Quota-Lists," *Phoenix,* XVI (1962), 267–275.

Meiggs, Russell, "The Growth of Athenian Imperialism," *JHS,* LXIII (1943), 21–34.

Meiggs, Russell, "The Crisis of Athenian Imperialism," *HSCP,* LXVII (1963), 1–36.

Meiggs, Russell, "The Dating of Fifth-Century Attic Inscriptions," *JHS,* LXXXVI (1966), 86–98.

Meritt, B. D., "Tribute Assessments in the Athenian Empire from 454 to 440 B.C.," *AJA,* XXIV (1925), 247–273.

Meritt, B. D., "The Reassessment of Tribute in 438–7," *AJA,* XXIX (1925), 292–298.

Meritt, B. D., *Athenian Financial Documents,* Ann Arbor, 1932.

Meritt, B. D., "Athens and Delian League," in *The Greek Political Ex-*

perience, Studies in Honor of William Kelly Prentice, Princeton, 1941, 50–60.

Meritt, B. D., "The Early Athenian Tribute Lists," *CP,* XXXVIII (1943), 223–239.

Meritt, B. D., "Attic Inscriptions of the Fifth Century," *Hesperia,* XIV (1945), 61–133.

Meritt, B. D. and Wade-Gery, H. T., "The Dating of Documents to the Mid-Fifth Century," *JHS,* LXXXII (1962), 67–74 and LXXXIII (1963), 100–117.

Meritt, B. D., Wade-Gery, H. T., and McGregor, M. F., *The Athenian Tribute Lists,* 4 vols.: I, Cambridge, Mass., 1939, II–IV, Princeton, 1949–1953.

Meyer, Eduard, *Forschungen zur alten Geschichte,* II, Halle, 1899.

Meyer, E., *Geschichte des Altertums,* 5th ed., reprinted in 1954 and 1956, Basel.

Meyer, H. D., "Vorgeschichte und Gründung des delisch-attischen Seebundes," *Historia,* XII (1963), 405–446.

Meyer, H. D., "Thukydides Melesiou und die oligarchische Opposition gegen Perikles," *Historia,* XVI (1967), 141–154.

Michell, H., *The Economics of Ancient Greece,* Cambridge, 1957.

Milne, J. G., "The Monetary Reforms of Solon: A Correction," *JHS,* LXIII (1938), 96–97.

Miltner, Franz, "Perikles," *PW,* XIX (1938), 748–790.

Momigliano, A., "La composizione della storia di Tucidide," *Memoria della Reale Accademia delle Scienze ditorino,* II: 67 (1930), 1–48.

Momigliano, Arnaldo, *Studies in Historiography,* London, 1966.

Montgelas, Max, and Schücking, Walther, *Outbreak of the World War: German Documents Collected by Karl Kautsky,* translated by the Carnegie Endowment for International Peace, New York, 1924.

Nesselhauf, H., *Untersuchungen zur Geschichte der delisch-attischen Symmachie, Klio,* Beiheft, XXX (1933).

Nesselhauf, H., "Die diplomatischen Verhandlungen vor dem peloponnesischen Kriege," *Hermes,* LXIX (1934), 286–299.

Nissen, H., "Der Ausbruch des peloponnesischen Krieges," *Historische Zeitschrift,* N.F. XXVII (1889), 385ff.

Oliver, J. H., *The Athenian Expounders of the Sacred and Ancestral Law,* Baltimore, 1950.

Oliver, J. H., "The Peace of Callias and the Pontic Expedition of Pericles," *Historia,* VI (1957), 254–255.

Oliver, J. H., "Reforms of Cleisthenes," *Historia,* IX (1960), 503–507.

O'Neill, J. G., *Ancient Corinth,* Baltimore, 1930.

Pasquali, G., "L'ultimatum spartano ad Atene nell' inverno 431–0," *Studi Italiani di filologia classica,* V (1927), 299ff.
Pearson, Lionel, "Prophasis and Aitia," *TAPA,* LXXXIII (1952), 205–223.
Pflugk-Hartung, J. von, *Perikles als Feldherr,* Stuttgart, 1884.
Pritchett, W. K., "Review of ATL, Vols. 2 and 3," *CP,* XLVII (1952), 261–263.
Pritchett, W. K., "Dotted Letters in Greek Epigraphy," *AJA,* LIX (1955), 55–61.
Pritchett, W. K., "The Height of the Lapis Primus," *Historia,* XIII (1964), 129–134.
Raubitschek, A. E., "Kimons Zurückberufung," *Historia,* III (1954/1955), 379–380.
Raubitschek, A. E., "The Covenant of Plataea," *TAPA,* XCI (1960), 178–183.
Raubitschek, A. E., "Theopompus on Thucydides the Son of Melesias," *Phoenix,* XIV (1960), 81–95.
Raubitschek, A. E., "The Peace Policy of Pericles," *AJA,* LXX (1966), 37–42.
Reece, D. W., "The Date of the Fall of Ithome," *JHS,* LXXXII (1962), 111–120.
Robinson, E. S. G., "The Athenian Currency Decree and the Coinage of the Allies," *Hesperia,* Suppl., VIII (1949), 324–340.
Romilly, Jacqueline de, *Thucydides and Athenian Imperialism,* tr. Philip Thody, Oxford, 1963.
Sandys, J. E., *Aristotle's Constitution of Athens,* 2nd ed., London, 1912.
Schaefer, H., *Staatsform und Politik. Untersuchungen zur griechischen Geschichte der VI. und V. Jht.,* Leipzig, 1932.
Scharf, J., "Die erste ägyptische Expedition der Athener. Ein Beitrag zur Geschichte der Pentecontaetie," *Historia,* III (1954/1955), 308–325.
Scharf, W., "Noch einmal Ithome," *Historia,* III (1954/1955), 153–162.
Schmidt, Bernhard, *Korkyraeische Studien,* Leipzig, 1890.
Schober, F., "Thebai (Boiotien)," *PW,* V (1934), 1452–1459.
Schumpeter, J., *Imperialism and Social Classes,* tr. Heinz Norden, New York, 1955.
Schwartz, E., *Das Geschichtswerk des Thukydides,* Hildesheim, 1960, reprinted from edition of 1929.
Schweigert, E., "Epigraphical Notes," *Hesperia,* VIII (1939), 170–176.
Sealey, R., "The Peace of Callias Once More," *Historia,* III (1954/1955), 325–333.

Sealey, R., "The Entry of Pericles into History," *Hermes,* LXXXIV (1956), 234–247.

Sealey, R., "The Great Earthquake in Lacedaemon," *Historia,* VI (1957), 368–371.

Sealey, R., "Thucydides, Herodotus and the Causes of War," *CQ,* N.S., VII (1957), 1–11.

Sealey, R., "Athens and the Archidamian War," *PACA,* I (1958), 61–87.

Sealey, Raphael, "The Origins of the Delian League," in *ASI,* 233–256.

Smith, R. E. " Ἀληθεστάτη πρόφασις," *Greece and Rome,* XI (1941–42), 23.

Smith, R. E., "The Opposition to Agesilaus' Foreign Policy 394–371 B.C.," *Historia,* II (1953/1954), 274–288.

Smith, S. B., "The Economic Motive in Thucydides," *HSCP,* LI (1940), 267–309.

Stahl, H. -P., *Thukydides* Die Stellung des Menschen im geschichtlichen Prozess, *Zetemata* Monographien zur klassischen Altertumswissenschaft, Heft 40, Munich, 1966.

Ste. Croix, G. E. M. de, "The Character of the Athenian Empire," *Historia,* III (1954/55), 1–41.

Ste. Croix, G. E. M. de, "Notes on Jurisdiction in the Athenian Empire," *CQ,* N.S., XI (1961), 95–112 and 268–280.

Stockton, David, "The Peace of Callias," *Historia,* VIII (1959), 61–79.

Sutherland, C. H. V., "Corn and Coin: A Note on Greek Commercial Monopolies," *AJP,* LXIV (1943), 129–147.

Taylor, A. J. P., *The Struggle for the Mastery of Europe,* Oxford, 1954.

Thucydide, La Guerre du Péloponnèse, Texte établit et traduit par J. de Romilly, Livres I² et II (Budé), Paris, 1958, 1962.

Thucydides, text and translation by Charles Forster Smith, I–IV (Loeb), London and Cambridge, Mass., 1919–1923.

Thucydidis Historiae iterum rec. brevique adn. crit. instr. H. S. Jones; app. crit. corr. et aux, J. E. Powell, Oxford, 1942.

Thucydidis Historiae post Carolum Hude edidit Otto Luschnat, Vol. I, Libri I–II, editio altera correctior (Teubner), Leipzig, 1960.

Thucydidis Historiarum Liber Primus, testo critico e commento con traduzione e indici, Antonio Maddalena, 3 vols., Florence, 1952.

Thukydides, J. Classen, bearbeitet von J. Steup mit einem nachwort und bibliograpischen nachträgen van Rudolf Stark; 5 Auflage, I, II, Berlin, 1909, 1914; Nachdruck, Berlin, 1963.

Tod, M. N., *Greek Historical Inscriptions,* 2nd ed., Vol. I, Oxford, 1946.

Völkl, Karl, "Das megarische Psephisma," *Rheinische Museum,* XCIV (1951), 330–336.

Wade-Gery, H. T., "The Financial Decrees of Callias," *JHS,* LI (1931), 57–85.

Wade-Gery, H. T., "Strategoi in the Samian War," *CP,* XXVI (1931), 309–313.

Wade-Gery, H. T., "Thucydides the son of Melesias," *Essays,* 239–270 = *JHS,* 1932.

Wade-Gery, H. T., "The Peace of Kallias," *HSCP,* Suppl., I (1940), 126ff.

Wade-Gery, H. T., and B. D. Meritt, "Athenian Resources in 449 and 431 B.C.," *Hesperia,* XXVI (1957), 163–197.

Wade-Gery, H. T., *Essays in Greek History,* Oxford, 1958.

Walker, E. M., "The Confederacy of Delos," "Athens and the Greek Powers, 462–445 B.C.," and "The Periclean Democracy," *CAH,* V (1940), 33–67, 68–97, and 98–112.

Walker, P. K., " 'The Pentecontaetia' in Thucydides, Book I," *CQ,* N.S., VII (1957), 27–38.

Wallace, W., "The Egyptian Expedition and the Chronology of the Decade 460–450 B.C.," *TAPA,* LXVII (1936), 252–260.

Wassermann, F. M., "Thucydidean Scholarship, 1942–1956," *CW,* L (1956–57), 65–70, 89–101.

Wentker, H., *Sizilien und Athen,* Heidelberg, 1956.

West, A. B., "The Tribute Lists and the Non-Tributary Members of the Delian League," *American Historical Review,* XXXV (1930), 267–275.

Westlake, H. D., "Thucydides and the Pentecontaetia," *CQ,* N.S., V (1955), 53–67.

Westlake, H. D., "Thucydides and the Fall of Amphipolis," *Hermes,* XC (1962), 276–287.

Wiliamowitz-Möllendorff, U. von, *Aristoteles und Athen,* Berlin, 1893.

Will, Édouard, "Note sur la défection de Byzance en 440–439 av. J.-C.," *Bulletin de la Faculté des Lettres de Strassbourg,* 1946–1947, 145–146.

Will, Édouard, "Sur l'évolution des rapports entre colonies et métropoles à partir du VIe s.," *La Nouvelle Clio,* VI (1954), 413–460.

Will, Édouard, *Korinthiaka,* Paris, 1955.

Woodhead, A. G., "The Site of Brea: Thucydides I. 61. 4," *CQ,* (1952), 57–62.

Woodhead, A. G., "Thucydides' Portrait of Cleon," *Mnemosyne Series* 4, XIII (1960), 289–317.

Wüst, F. R., "Amphiktyonie, Eidgenossenschaft, Symmachie," *Historia,* III (1954–5), 129–153.

Zahn, R., *Die erste Periklesrede (Thuk. I 140–44),* Diss, Kiel, 1932, Leipzig, 1934.

General Index

(Selected references to Athens and Sparta are listed.)

Index of Ancient Authors and Inscriptions

Index of Modern Authors